FEMININE FASCISM

FEMININE FASCISM

Women in Britain's Fascist Movement

Julie V. Gottlieb

I.B. TAURIS

LONDON · NEW YORK

Published in 2003 by I.B.Tauris & Co Ltd
6 Salem Road, London W2 4BU
175 Fifth Avenue, New York NY 10010
www.ibtauris.com

In the United States of America and in Canada distributed by
Palgrave Macmillan, a division of St Martin's Press
175 Fifth Avenue, New York NY 10010

First published in 2000 by I.B.Tauris & Co Ltd

ISBN 1 86064 918 1
ISBN 978 1 86064 918 9

A full CIP record for this book is available from the British Library
A full CIP record for this book is available from the Library of Congress

Library of Congress catalog card: available

Contents

To Erika and Paul Gottlieb
and
Professor Peter Clarke

Acknowledgements

While I alone am accountable for the views expressed in this book, I am grateful to many people for their help and enthusiasm at various stages in my research on women and fascism in inter-war Britain. Many thanks to Brian Farrell, in whose McGill seminar my interest in aspects of British Fascism was born and cultivated. During the course of my research in Britain, I have benefited from guidance from and discussion with Eugenio Biagini, Jonathan Parry, Chris Andrew, Deborah Thom, Maria Tippett, Claire Eustance, Julia Bush, Thomas Linehan, Martin Durham, Patrick Higgins, Peter Pugh, Joanne Reilly, James Vernon, Tony Kushner and Richard Griffiths. Brian Simpson was very generous to invite me to peruse the documents he collected for his own book on Defence Regulation 18B and kind enough to read an early draft of my own exploration of the female experience of 18B. I would also like to express my appreciation to the staff at the University Library in Cambridge, the Churchill Archive, the Museum of Labour History, the Vera Brittain Collection at McMaster University, the Public Records Office (Kew), the Essex County Council Archive, and Lawrence Aspden at the Special Collections and Archive at the University of Sheffield Library.

I am grateful to Diana Lady Mosley, Louise Irvine, Robert Row and Eugenia Wright, for recounting to me in our correspondence their recollections and the wealth of their individual experiences in the BUF; John Warburton and Jeffrey Wallder for sharing with me their vast knowledge about BUF members and for sending me many interesting items kept in the archive of the Friends of O.M.; Francis Beckett for his insight into his parents' involvement in the BUF; and Nicholas Mosley, the Baron Ravensdale, for his hospitality and openness when I interviewed him in 1996.

In Cambridge, I was fortunate to be able to discuss aspects of this project with many friends and colleagues in the lively settings of the British History Discussion Group, the seminars for British Political History and Social History, and at Corpus Christi College. Hours of animated discussion and commiseration over the trials, tribulations and excitement of the creative process were spent with Meera Raval, Despina Spanou, Richard Noakes, Sigrid Daniel, Ingrid James, Natalie Higgins, Damien Browne, Andrew Horrall, Adrian

Gregory, Max Jones, David Craig, James Thompson, Jennifer Macleod and Kristin Zimmerman, and as many hours in trans-Atlantic calls to Chiheb Drissi.

As this book emerged from a doctoral dissertation into its present book form, John Naylor, Susan Kingsley Kent, Patrick Deane, Phyllis Lassner, Thomas Laqueur, Carla Hesse, Warren Wagar, Eric Jennings, Matthew Hendley, Barbara Todd, Susan Pennybacker, Richard Rempel, Anne Clendenning, Wesley Wark, Jennifer Mori, Franca Iacovetta, Janet Miron, Nazy Sakhavarz, John Hellman, William Cormack, Peter Gottlieb, and especially Eugenio Biagini, Martin Pugh, Richard Thurlow, and my editor at I.B. Tauris, Lester Crook, have each provided me with invaluable advice and thought-provoking comments. My thanks are also due to the Social Sciences and Humanities Research Council of Canada for awarding me a post-doctoral fellowship which gave me the opportunity to put the finishing touches to the book, and to my colleagues at the University of Manchester for their support and encouragement during the last months.

I have saved the most important acknowledgements to last. I wish foremost to thank my doctoral supervisor Professor Peter Clarke for seeing the script through its many drafts, and for his excellent advice and deeply-appreciated mentoring, and my parents, Erika and Paul, for indulging me in my earliest requests to be told 'true stories' rather than fables, as well as for their support, editorial expertise and inspiration. This book is dedicated to them.

Introduction

Feminine Fascism: Women in Britain's Fascist Movement, 1923–45

Images of the British Union of Fascists (BUF) tend to evoke popular memories of a marginal movement, making a strong appeal to ex-servicemen, and drawing support from disgruntled and anti-Semitic elements in London's East End, with columns of male Blackshirts marching in step to vainglorious calls for a 'Greater Britain.' The general impression of the BUF as a para-military organization motivated by the masculine and macho ethos has always been reinforced by inevitable sideward glances to the models of Fascist Italy and Nazi Germany. It follows that one would expect that the British Union of Fascists would have faithfully replicated the existing fascist regimes in Europe, and that Britain's fascist movement would have been ideologically male-chauvinist and structurally exclusive of female participation. However, Britain's first inter-war fascist movement was launched by a woman in 1923, Miss Rotha Lintorn Orman, and during the 1930s, 25 per cent of Sir Oswald Mosley's supporters were women, all of whom had joined the movement without coercion. Admittedly, British fascism advocated the resurgence of 'the masculine principle' in British politics. In his 1932 manifesto of the movement, *The Greater Britain*, Mosley prescribed that the 'part of women in our future organization will be important, but different from that of men: *we want men who are men and women who are women*;'[1] and in 1936 A.K. Chesterton went as far as bidding that 'let us smash the matriarchal principle and return to the grand object of manhood.'[2] Yet the paradox in the case of the BUF was that women were given a forum in which to express feminine concerns alongside these reactionary and anti-feminist assertions.

This study explores both women's visibility in Britain's fascist organizations, and their audibility in the fascist discourse. Measured at the ethically-neutral level of party membership, British fascists were successful in enlisting women for their cause and differed little from the democratic parties in their able mobilization and organization of women's support. As the BUF was fully aware, however, propaganda is never impartial, and women were considered the best equipped to drive home a message with the utmost emotional charge. It was emphasized that women orators 'should always remember that on the platform the intellectual argument should give second place to the emotional appeal, but the knowledge must be there as a firm basis on which rise our highest spiritual convictions.'[3] Our reaction to British fascism's gender ideology, therefore, can be neither emotionally numb, nor ethically detached.

In line with the immense attention paid to the histories of women during the 1980s and 1990s, the history of British fascism has also received ample attention, with a proliferation of scholarly studies emerging during this same period. Although British fascism never grasped the reigns of power, and was, therefore, distinct from European variants of fascism in a number of important ways, the field of historiography on British fascism is vast. It may be true to say that historical interest in the movement even surpasses the attention conferred on the Blackshirts during the 1930s. Notably, there are more studies concerning the BUF than there are on the Liberal Party during the same period. The continued interest in British fascism probably owes a great deal to the direction of post-war politics. In the face of European integration, and some pressure to integrate British studies into European history more generally (particularly in North America), the case study of British fascism presents opportunities to highlight both Britain's distinctiveness and thus isolation from the course of European politics between the wars, as well as punctuate some points in common between political cultures and intellectual heritages. The attention that British fascism has received in past decades can also be attributed to the coincidence of new quantitative methodologies in the social sciences, and the willingness of former members of Britain's fascist movement to come forward and give testimony. In old age, many former members of the BUF have been eager to document their memories by answering questionnaires and agreeing to interviews with historians, or coming together with their former comrades to commemorate their fascist days both informally and through the meetings of the 'Friends of O.M..'[4]

Why is there such a fascination with British fascism? What marks British fascism apart from Continental movements and regimes?

These are related questions. On the one hand, British fascism has captured the imagination, and is undeniably 'sexy.' The heightened enthusiasm called forth by fascist regalia, spiritual yearning, cinematic sensationalism, and charismatic leadership each function in lock-step with the exploitation of the Leader's sex appeal and the representation of women as active cheer leaders. Fascism's aesthetically provocative imagery and seething violence provide a sharp contrast to competing images of Britain in the 1930s as the 'Bleak Age' of Depression and austerity. In the political sphere, this was a period characterized by rather colourless politicians' failure to create any diversion on the road to a second world war and to feed, either with hope or with bread, the columns of desperate men and women in dole queues. Although most historians are justifiably troubled by British fascism's racism, chauvinistic nationalism, and criminality – and these aspects of the British fascist phenomenon are given their due prominence in the historiography – it is nonetheless the case that the British Union of Fascists represents a flamboyant antithesis to stasis and paralysis, and invites speculation of what might have happened had Britain failed to resist the type of authoritarian government so prevalent on the Continent during the inter-war years.

In a similar vein, the appearance of gangs of militant British fascist women provide a striking contrast to the prevalent notions of women's history during the inter-war period as a return to ideals of female domesticity and the retreat of feminism from a former position of prominence in public consciousness in the form of the Edwardian suffrage movement and through the advancement of women's emancipation through civilian and military service during the First World War. Also inviting counterfactual speculation, is the question of what would have happened to British womanhood and British feminism had a fascist government ever come to power and had democratic practices and standards of representation been abandoned. Speculation in this direction is particularly relevant today in view of the expanding interest among historians in the topic of women and the extreme Right, and with the complicated relationship between gender and fascism.

Two seemingly incompatible themes loom large in determining the boundaries of modern history: the pervasive memory of the totalitarian grip of fascism and the atomizing study of gender. It is no wonder then that there is a growing fascination among historians with the lives and thoughts of fascist women. The earliest post-war studies of women and fascism were inspired by the opening of the doors of perception onto the vast vista of disregarded minorities of the past. After retrieving the lives and experiences of those women who did credit to post-war emanations of the women's movement, and those who could be claimed as the pioneers of second-wave feminism, women's history then turned some attention to those women who collaborated with and added longevity to the reign of patriarchal power. Unlocking this Pandora's box inevitably suggested that the lives and drives of the 'evil' women of history had also to be exhumed and investigated.

The initial instinct was to see women under fascism as wilfully misguided, assigned to the status of a minority as an 'out-group' (akin to Jews), and sexually marginalized by fascism's homo-erotic overtures. The frontier-women of the Women's Liberation Movement emphasized the Nazi reaction against the modernizing doctrine of feminism and the denigration of female power, and much lamented the ways in which Nazism crushed the German feminist movement which had made such great strides during the short life of the Weimar Republic. Betty Friedan heard in the oppressive American feminine mystique an echo of '"Kinder, Küche, Kirche," – the slogan by which the Nazis decreed that women must once again be confined to their biological role.'[5] In 1970, Kate Millett argued that, in the case of Nazi Germany, 'every aspect of Nazi sexual regulation including its tinge of neo-paganism, was of a character which might well be described as a state-sponsored and legally enforced counter-revolution.'[6] Seeing through the notorious Nazi celebration of motherhood, Millett contended that 'the actual purpose of Nazi ideology was not, as stated, to return women to the home, but to take women out of professions and put them in low-paid occupations.'[7]

The self-avowed revolutionary-left feminists also took it for granted that the underlying paradigm of fascism was patriarchy, and judged that women had been 'fooled' into granting their consent to the fascist state. In her Structuralist analysis of female sexuality in Italian Fascist ideology, Maria Antoinetta Macciocchi argued that 'the sex struggle is denied, like the class struggle, since fascism takes as its point of departure the subordination of one sex to another, in so far as women voluntarily accept the "royal attributes" of femininity and maternity.'[8] The work of Renate Bridenthal, Atina Grossmann and Marion Kaplan had as its premise the authors' perception of Nazi tendencies in the New Right of the Reagan presidency and the government's assault on women's choice.[9] In the Women's Liberation discourse on women and fascism, the weddedness to the patriarchal model endowed the woman supporter of fascism

4

with the status of a victim, and her subordination to male control diminished her culpability and agency.

With a very definite political agenda of their own, some revolutionary Marxists have been led by their primary loyalty to the Marxist mantra not only to criticize contemporary priorities in women's liberation as evidence of class betrayals, but also to discern the sanction offered to Hitler by German feminist organizations, particularly the Bund Deutscher Frauenvereine (Federation of German Women's Associations). Thus the Spartacist League appraised the relationship between fascism and feminism as an effortless collusion between two capitalist creeds: 'For today's petty-bourgeois feminists, mired in the myth of the "sisterhood" of all women, the accommodation of their "fortress of feminism" to Hitler must remain forever a source of confusion and mystery. But for us revolutionary Marxists, it is only one more striking confirmation of our position that women's liberation is above all a question of class struggle.'[10] The attitudes exemplified by Marxists in the 1980s can be traced back to the inter-war period, when the fixation on Marxist paradigms of class-struggle stunted the development of an anti-fascist ideological revolt specific to the treatment of the female sex in Italy and Germany.[11]

Forms of analytical dissent from the hegemonic model of patriarchy have come from different directions. Some women historians have tried to present a balanced and comparative view of women under fascism by relying on perspectives of national and temporal relativity. Jill Stephenson has shown how 'in the international context, it appears that, on the whole, women in Germany in the late 1930s were neither better nor worse off than women in other countries in terms of status and opportunities, even in the Third Reich.'[12] Stephenson has also made the point that despite Nazism's conspicuous anti-feminist reaction, there was a distinct continuity in women's policy throughout the inter-war period in Germany. In demonstrating the singularity of the Italian Fascist state, Victoria DeGrazia has reminded us how 'the rallying of phalanxes of black-shirted women, the laws against miscegenation, the persecution of non-Aryans, and the publication of draconian statutes to drive women from the workforce were all measures taken after 1935, as the Italian military machine geared up for war and the example of Nazi sexual and racial politics became well known to fascist leaders.'[13] More recently, Gisela Bock has challenged most previous assumptions about the Nazi state's underlying patriarchal structure and the pervasiveness of the policy pronatalism by demonstrating that through its programmes of sterilization and racist massacre, 'National Socialism by no means wanted children at any cost and never propagated the slogan "kinder, küche, kirche." '[14]

As women's studies have granted ever greater agency to the women of the past, the fascist woman has been by necessity reinterpreted as a pro-active culprit, a *femme fatale*, and an accomplice to terror and genocide. This re-evaluation has effectively derailed the train of thought in women's historiography of woman as victim. Recognizing the existence of choice and free will among Hitler's women supporters, Claudia Koonz has asserted that 'next to the dominant motif of male brutality, Gertrud Scholtz-Klink [Nazi Women's Leader] and millions of followers created the social side of tyranny.'[15] This was an acknowledgement that women could be more than manipulated victim figures by becoming full participants equal to men in engineering mass destruction.

As Koonz's has observed, 'the women among Hitler's followers have fallen through the historian's sieve, unclaimed by feminists and unnoticed by men.'[16] To claim these women for history is not to applaud their defiance, nor does historical notice impute justice to their reaction. Indeed, to allow them to pass through time unobserved presents the danger that by the time liberal feminism itself becomes an historical relic, future historians may look back on the fascists and see in their spiritual enthusiasm a legitimate form of dissent. With the distance of time and the fading of the popular memory, we are in danger of allowing these women to go ahead unscrutinized, only to be rediscovered by another generation who do not recall the outcome of fascism's malignant hatreds.

Writing the history of women and fascism in Britain is particularly urgent. On the one hand, if the record is not set straight now, very soon British fascist women could be seen in the same burning light as those women condemned as witches many centuries ago, punished because they dared provoke authority, hunted and tortured by the patriarchal state because they ventured to offer a deviant version of female power. Were British fascist women not heretical democrats, akin to the 'witch' who preserved the practices of paganism against the omnipotent tide of Christianity? It can be predicted how internment under Defence Regulation 18B – attended by alarmism at behind-the-scenes contact with daemons (Nazis), and the hysteria, accusations and denunciations characteristic of the 'Fifth Columnist' scare of 1940 – could be reassessed from the vantage point of a 'losers'' history as a witch-hunt. The revision of 18B has already begun, and from the point of view of the legal miscarriages of justice, A.W. Brian Simpson has presented the British internees as casualties of a 'gross invasion of civil liberty.'

On the other hand, a study of fascist women should not turn into a witch-hunt through the past: for it to do so would be to over-estimate the impact of BUF women, lose sight of the context of their political hereticism, and distort their ideological motivations for joining the movement. In no way were BUF women victims, and it will never be suggested that they were coerced into lending their support to a man's creed. Choice, free will and personal rebelliousness characterized their donations of support to Mosley. As Louise Irvine, Women's District Leader in Birmingham, explained: 'the mere fact of becoming a member was a striking blow for independent thinking. Subconsciously when I joined I may have felt I was making a stand for independence of thinking – even doing something daring and out-of-step.'[17] It was also without undue pressure that women gave their consent to the BUF's doctrine, including its anti-Semitism, and contributed their share by developing a compatible and complementary ideology of *feminine fascism*.

The divergent strands in the post-war historiography of women and fascism were each present in an infant stage during the inter-war period. British socialists, feminists, conservatives, liberals, civil libertarians and some non-partisan critics reacted both to the treatment of women under fascism and to the images of woman constructed by the BUF. Reassuringly, the feminist anti-fascist reaction took on many forms, expressed in both political organization and through the arts and literature. Whether in the form of a nightmarish dystopian vision of women as mere breeding animals in the futuristic land of Hitlerdom in Katherine Burdekin's *Swastika Night* (1937), a realistic vision of the fate of a sensitive and talented female medical student during the first years of Hitler's regime in Phyllis Bottome's *The Mortal Storm* (1938), or in the political writings of Virginia Woolf, Vera Brittain, Winifred Holtby, Margaret Storm Jameson, Sylvia Pankhurst, Naomi Mitchson, among others, British feminist writers were in full agreement that their agenda would be ill served by fascism.

Indeed, the prominence of women activists and intellectuals in Britain's anti-fascist front challenges the prevalent impression that in the period after female enfranchisement a monolithic feminist movement retreated in deference to promised gender co-operation within the Labour, the Conservative and the Liberal parties, and abandoned narrower feminist demands in the face of the escalating threat of a second world war.[18] It can be argued that feminist momentum was maintained when female activists grouped around the anti-fascist cause. Rather than abandoning their demands for women's rights, women in the centre and on the left were far-sighted enough to understand that only by defending democratic government would it be possible to pursue gender-specific demands for political and economic parity. During the 1930s, successful feminism was the child of the marriage between democratic government and regard for human as well as women's rights.

Before we can understand the contemporary anti-fascist explications and apprehensions, however, we must examine closely what they were reacting against. From 1932 through to 1940, BUF women and men designed an array of blue-prints for a fascist future, complete with prescriptions for the ideal woman, the fascist family, sexual normality, the Corporate State, and the specialization of women's work. These were accompanied by proscriptions against sexual abnormality, the narrow political agenda of feminist organizations, democratic effeminacy, and motherly emotional yearnings to protect those outside the 'British race.'

This book traces the main developments in the history of women and fascism in Britain during the inter-war period. In order to make sense of some of the material and record the outcome of women's fascist activities, the final chapter goes beyond the inter-war period and deals with the internment of fascist women from 1940 to 1945. The first chapter examines the relationship between women and fascism during the 1920s by focussing on the early manifestations of British fascism, and the feminization of the British Fascisti under the leadership of Miss Rotha Lintorn-Orman. Chapter 2 traces the history of women in Mosley's British Union of Fascists, from the formation of the Women's Section to the launch of the Women's Peace Campaign, and probes issues related to the sexual division of labour within the movement, membership and demographic patterns, and the roles and activities of women members. Chapter 3 defines, what I have termed, the ideology of feminine fascism, and explores how women's political demands were integrated into a masculine creed. Arguing that women's political activism and the place of woman in fascist policy cannot be properly understood in isolation from male constructs of gender and masculinity, this chapter also explores the psychology and pathology of fascist sexuality, the new Fascist Man, and the implications of the model of the youth-worshipping gang of fascist men for the position of women, mothers and wives. Chapter 4 investigates the legacy of three former suffragettes to British fascism – Norah Elam,

8

Mary Richardson and Mary Allen, and points to some correspondence between British feminism and fascism. The fifth chapter ponders the relationship between Mosley's biography, reputation for philandering, and ominous sex appeal, and the mobilization of female fanaticism in his British Union of Fascists. Chapter 6 traces the evolution of the Defence regulations as they affected BU members during the Second World War, with a central focus on the experiences of British fascist women interned under DR 18B(1A). Finally, the *Who's Who* section provides a prosopography of women and fascism in Britain, and by identifying both the more prominent and the more obscure participants in Britain's fascist movement, seeks to give personality, character and individuality to those women who might otherwise remain faceless statistics or undefined toy soldiers in Blackshirt columns. By tapping a variety of primary sources – oral testimonies, my own correspondence with former members, conducting interviews, using archives in Cambridge, Sheffield, Manchester, Chelmsford, London, and Hamilton, Ontario, and thoroughly examining the public records held at Kew – this study seeks to place in context British fascist women's agency in propagating an anti-democratic, male-centrist, and racist creed.

Notes

1   Oswald Mosley, *The Greater Britain* (London, 1932), p.41.
2   A.K. Chesterton, 'Return to Manhood: Regiment of Old Women Routed,' *Action*, No. 21, 9 July, 1936.
3   'Women as Orators,' *Action*, No. 151, 14 January 1939.
4   See 'The Commemoration Dinner: Women Blackshirts Remembered,' *Comrade*, No. 32, January 1992.
5   Betty Friedan, *The Feminine Mystique* (New York, 1963), p.32.
6   Kate Millett, *Sexual Politics* (London, 1970), p.167.
7   Kate Millett, *Sexual Politics*, p.162.
8   Maria-Antoinetta Macciocchi, 'Female Sexuality in Fascist Ideology,' *Feminist Review*, 1 (1979), 67–82.
9   eds. Renate Bridenthal *et al.*, *When Biology Became Destiny: Women in Weimar and Nazi Germany* (New York, 1984), p.xi.
10   'From Weimar to Hitler: Feminism and Fascism,' *Women and Revolution*, (Spring 1981), 2–7.
11   The intellectual evolution and transmutations of Ellen Wilkinson's contribution to the anti-fascist reaction is a prime example of this. While she was originally alive to the quashing of the women's movement in Germany, her

understanding of the role of fascism became increasing one of the last gasp of capitalism. 'The question is whether the mass drive towards Socialism can be organized before the coming crisis deepens to such and extent that the workers themselves can be stampeded by some British brand of fascism into ranging themselves behind the reaction, and helping to destroy the organization they themselves have built in the sacrifices of the past. This is the real choice before us; for Britain cannot remain isolated from the great economic forces that are sweeping the world.' Ellen Wilkinson and Edward Conze, *Why Fascism* (London, 1934), p.317. Similarly, the content of CPGB women speeches, when claiming to offer a woman's perspective on fascism, concentrated on the more general threat to the working class. At a communist counter demonstration in May 1937 Vera Reed (CP Limehouse Branch) 'said she looked at Fascism from the woman's point of view. Should MOSLEY and his policy triumph here, bloodshed would follow, therefore, the full strength of working-class opposition should be brought to bear and Fascism crushed before it could achieve power.' HO144/21247/23.

12   Jill Stephenson, *Women in Nazi Society* (London, 1975), p.3.

13   Victoria DeGrazia, *How Fascism Ruled Women* (Berkeley, 1992), p.8.

14   Gisela Bock, 'Equality and Difference in National Socialist Racism,' in ed. Joan Wallach Scott, *Feminism and History* (Oxford, 1996), p.278.

15   Claudia Koonz, *Mothers in the Fatherland* (London, 1987), p.xxxiii.

16   Claudia Koonz, *Mothers in the Fatherland*, p.3.

17   Letter from Louise Irvine to the author, 8 May, 1996.

18   Deidre Beddoe has titled her study of British women during the 1930s, *Back to Home and Duty* (1989), for the overwhelming trend towards upholding domestic ideals and rejecting the heritage of feminist militancy. In *Making Peace* (1993) Susan Kingsley Kent has observed that the entire post-war period was characterized by a mood of pacification of sex war, and that Feminists were as active as any in advocating an armistice with the opposite sex. Martin Pugh has argued convincingly that although the British women's movement survived the loss of its formal structure after 1918, and feminist reformism weathered an anti-feminist backlash, a significant dilemma emerged: 'In the aftermath of victory the forces of reform were easily dissipated unless some alternate means could be found to rally support and thus maintain momentum.' Martin Pugh, *Women and the Women's Movement in Britain 1918–1959* (London, 1992), p.43. In *Labour Women* , Pamela Greaves suggests that women's status ceased to be an issue in inter-war labour politics, and that 'the crisis atmosphere of the thirties was an additional factor in discouraging [labour women] from reviving the debate.' Pamela Greaves, *Labour Women*. (Cambridge, 1994), p.181.

Chapter 1

Feminized Fascism: Rotha Lintorn-Orman and the British Fascists, 1923–35

From the outset, British fascism had a very feminine side and was characterized by a high degree of female activism and propaganda directed towards women. Britain's first fascist movement was founded by a woman, Miss Rotha Lintorn-Orman. As the probably apocryphal story goes, the British Fascisti (BF) was conceived while she was digging in her Somerset kitchen garden, and reflecting on the news that the Labour Party had sent a delegation to a Socialist Party conference in Hamburg, Lintorn-Orman awoke to her mission to deliver the nation from the communist menace. She would do so by forming an organization of disinterested patriots – composed of all classes and all Christian denominations – who were prepared to react in defence of King and Country in any emergency. Following her epiphany in the garden, Lintorn-Orman proceeded to plant a series of recruitment articles in the Duke of Northumberland's *Patriot* (1922–50) in May 1923, and a membership soon sprouted. Herself a member of the country gentry, it was thanks to her family's wealth that her seed of an idea could bear fruit. The Founder's mother, Mrs Lintorn-Orman, made over the greater part of her fortune, approximately £50,000, to her daughter to finance the endeavour and paid her a monthly allowance.

Female foundership, and (after 1926) female leadership was almost unique in the history of fascist movements during the inter-war period,[1] and the high level of women's participation in the BF was no doubt facilitated by the revolution in gender roles instigated by the First World War and the achievement of women's emancipation through franchise extension immediately afterwards. While the BF was not an exclusively female organization, the influence of women among the leadership and their direction of the campaigns to deliver Britain from Communism, to rid her of the 'alien menace,' and to protect her children from subversive and blasphemous teachings, demonstrated how women's work was indispensable to the radical Right. However, it was precisely because the BF was popularly identified with the spirited wives of Colonel Blimps and the jingoistic, humourless and eccentric types among politicized women that British fascism was of little real consequence before the formation of Sir Oswald Mosley's British Union of Fascists in 1932.

The BF's equivocal identification with fascism also suggests that the movement was not necessarily the direct predecessor of Mosley's British Union of Fascists, and indicates a discontinuity in the history of British fascism during the 1920s and the 1930s. British fascism's broken road was as much exemplified by the dissimilar styles of leadership and propaganda between the BF and BUF as by their different approach to the role of women and the interpretation of the place of the feminine in fascist ideology. It is ironic, perhaps, that the male-led BUF lent more voices to inter-war feminist discourse, while the female-led BF confronted the issues reserved for women through action and pragmatism rather than by formulating a doctrine of 'fascist feminism.' Lacking the will to define its stand as such, the BF developed a distinctive creed to support female extreme-Right activism that can either be termed feminized fascism or ultra-patriotic feminism.

Precedents and Influences: 'It Seems Unfortunate That a Nationalist Organization Should Have To Go Abroad For its Name and Symbol'[2]

Set beside the history of European fascism, the BF seems a particularly insubstantial and confused expression of fascist ideology and tactics. Gertrude M. Godden, a witness at the birth of Fascism in Italy, believed that 'the influence of Fascismo is an inspiration for which the men and women of all nations made common sacrifice during five years of war – "Our country and not ourselves,"'[3] and such vague understandings also characterized the BF's preliminary identifications with the Italian experiment. As Mussolini's Fascismo became more coherent, the BF's own definition of fascism gained clarity and by the early 1930s the movement championed a Corporate

12

state for Britain. Nonetheless, the BF's interpretation of fascist ceremony and regalia, and the development of their programme were never extricated from the British context and the specific issues which had fuelled the radical Right since the end of the 19th century. One of the BF's self-appointed tasks was to steward Conservative Party meetings, and as a self-described non-political body, members were encouraged to vote Tory at elections.[4] Indeed, the BF took great offence at being labelled a foreign import, and in its bid to represent quintessential Britishness members came to regret having adopted the alien-sounding title. The BF defended itself against allegations that they were following an imported creed: 'Let us accept this cry of "Foreign" for what it is, a red-herring drawn across the trail, a desperate attempt to divert the attention of the people from the soundness of Fascist principles and policy.'[5] Like the BUF after it, the BF was ardent in pointing out that they were co-opting the foreign example for specifically English purposes.

To understand the inspiration for the BF it is as important to consider the influence of Edwardian radical Right organizations, the impact of the female auxiliary services during the war, and the appearance at the same time of other patriotic organizations, as it is to decipher the examples the BF took from Continental fascism. The BF's most enthusiastically claimed precedent was the Scouting movement. R.B.D. Blakeney, BF president from 1924 to 1926, cited fascism as 'the adult growth of ... the Scout Movement. Both uphold the same lofty ideals of brotherhood, service and duty.'[6] In terms of both ideological derivation – Empire Free Trade – and the mobilization of women, Joseph Chamberlain's Tariff Reform League (established in July 1903) offered a precedent for the BF when it formed a Women's Section in 1903, which had forty branches by 1905 as well as a junior Tariff Reform Association.[7] By 1927 the BF, one of whose main slogans was 'Buy British Goods,' noted 'with satisfaction the formation of the League of Empire Housewives. The members of the League wear a distinctive badge, which will intimate to a shopkeeper that the wearers wish to buy only home products or Empire goods.'[8]

Since the Conservative Party's allocations for the female political role so closely resembled that fashioned by the BF in the 1920s, the more obvious precedent for the BF's mobilization of women was the Primrose League.[9] The Primrose League had its own children's section, the Buds, and in the 1920s the Conservative Party had its own anti-Communist and anti-Red Sunday School youth section, the Young Britons.[10] Both rivalled the BF's Fascist Children's Clubs

(FCCs) and tended to render the Clubs redundant. The Primrose League was directed by a 'Grand Council,' bringing into question whether the BF modelled its own Grand Council on that of the League rather than on Mussolini's executive body, which was first established in January 1923. Paradoxically, the League's Grand Council was under male control, leading to a situation where 'the Ladies Grand Council had been the inspiration for the League's breathless rise, and yet women were strictly subordinate to the Grand Council.'[11] A key difference between the BF and Primrose League hierarchy, then, was that the BF's Grand Council was composed of both sexes, ruling over a both-sex organization, and this can go some way in explaining why BF women resisted joining the existing body and sought independence in order to practice their brand of militant rear-guard activism.

The BF's ideal that women should be able to prove their loyalty through unhampered but disciplined action was made possible by the new opportunities opened to women through war work. As an extreme-right expression of an ex-servicemen and women's association, memories of the roles played by women during the war were central to the definition of the movement and to constructing notions of self-worth. Lintorn-Orman praised the women's services during the war for upholding the great tradition of commanding women in British history, and asked: 'Shall British women now do more or less?'[12] The war saw the inauguration of the Women's Army Auxiliary Corps (1917), the Women's Royal Naval Service (1917), and the Women's Royal Air Force (1918). In these services 'women enjoyed a prestigious uniform, military discipline and an official hierarchy corresponding to that of male service.'[13] The Voluntary Aid Detachment of nurses organized by the Red Cross and attached to the Territorial Army, offered new opportunities and freedom to upper and middle-class women. On the home front, women were the main activists in the many patriotic societies, such as the Red Cross Society, the Prince of Wales Fund, and the Soldier's Parcel Fund.

Right-wing women emerged from their war-time experiences with a renewed sense of patriotic endeavour, and during the 1920s the BF was not alone among those organizations which gave vent to women's profound dread of communism. The Loyalty League appeared in October 1922 with the purpose of fighting communism. More closely coinciding with the activities of Lintorn-Orman's women, Dorothy Walthall formed the Victory Corps in 1923 as a successor to the Women's Auxiliary Force. Its objects were to promote patriotism, loyalty and industry, and to administer First Aid in times of strikes

14

and riots. In 1928 former-suffragette 'General,' Flora Drummond, graduated from the Pankhurst's anti-socialist Women's Party (1918) to form her own Women's Guild of Empire with the object of opposing strikes and communism. The ex-suffragette Mary Allen formed the Women's Auxiliary Service in 1923, as the successor to Margaret Damer Dawson's war-time Women's Police Service, and BF women would enlist in Allen's Service during the General Strike. Allen and Lintorn-Orman shared a horror of communism, an infatuation with women in uniform, and the attitude that women's public responsibilities transcended women's right.

Portraits of a Founder: Lintorn-Orman in Myth and Memory

While many women were dedicating themselves to the fight for 'Votes for Women,' the young Rotha Lintorn Orman (1895–1935) joined the Girl Scouts in 1909 and, in her own words, 'had the honour to command the only two troops to be under Royal patronage (First and Second Bournemouth, Princess Louise's own) and in those days the Scouts and Guides carried our own flag, the Union Jack.'[14] Her youthful interests reflected her service background: Lintorn-Orman was the grand-daughter of a Field Marshal, Sir John Lintorn Simmons (1812–1902), and daughter of Major Charles Orman of the Essex Regiment. During the war she served with the Women's Reserve Ambulance and later transferred to the Scottish Women's Hospital Corps with whom she sailed to Serbia in 1916. According to one later report in the fascist press: 'she served in the Drins front as an ambulance driver and was awarded the Croix de Charité (twice) for gallantry and was also recommended for the Order of St Savs, but the papers of recommendation were lost in the fire of Salonika.'[15] In 1917, she was invalided home with malaria, and because she failed to pass any medical board for further service overseas, she joined the British Red Cross Society and was appointed Commandant of the Motor School at Devonshire House where she was in charge of all ambulance drivers. Lintorn-Orman's war experience contributed to her frequent illnesses and her problems with alcohol and drugs, factors which were to serve to discredit her leadership of the BF and place the movement in a precarious position. Male combatants were not alone in returning from the war shell-shocked and paranoid, and the biography of Lintorn-Orman provides a vivid example of a woman's reaction and attempted recuperation from the cataclysm of war.

Lintorn-Orman formed the British Fascisti on 6 May 1923, 'alone and unaided.'[16] The BF claimed that, within a few months, 'she had enrolled over a quarter of a million men and women who, putting country before self, prepared themselves to combat the Red elements which were beginning to get a strangle-hold on the Empire.'[17] During the British Fascisti's early life female foundership did not mean that the organization was to be under female leadership. In June 1925, for instance, Lintorn-Orman held the titles of Founder and President of Women's Units. The presidency was first held by Lord Garvagh (1878–1956), who resigned in 1924, giving the excuse that he lived too far away from London to govern effectively. His successor was Brigadier General Robert Blakeney (1872–1952) who left the BF in 1926 over the conflict of whether the BF should merge with the Organization for the Maintenance of Supplies (OMS), the women on the Grand Council resisting collaboration in order to retain their independent status, the fascist name, and their para-military structure. Following the split at the time of the General Strike, female control over the organization became more manifest, and the first question that must be asked is why female leadership did not materialize earlier.

Again, the development of the BF must be placed in the context of the post-war condition and perceptions of women, particularly that of the unmarried woman. Not only was Lintorn-Orman a single woman, but her preference for women in uniform and the para-military regimentation of the feminine provoked the pejorative description of her as a 'mannish-woman.' At private fascist rallies 'it was rumoured she wore a sword', and she aroused complaints from her own women because she 'made them learn to change tyres.'[18] When the Fascist Children's Club held a Christmas party for 600 children in 1925, Lintorn-Orman played Father Christmas.[19] At the Frivolity Ball organized by the London Dance Committee on 4 April 1930, Lintorn-Orman won one of the prizes for the best costume: she had dressed as a 'grandfather'.[20] Under the post-war conditions of 'our surplus women,' and precisely when the spinster was under severest attack, Lintorn-Orman's spinsterhood and her exploitation of an androgynous appearance rendered her particularly vulnerable to ridicule and mockery.[21]

While he defended the mannish-woman because she could be an advantage to a race that wished to produce virile manhood and dilute effeminacy, Anthony Ludovici wrote in 1923 that 'one of the first facts to be remembered about the spinster ... is that she is an abnormal being – just as the celibate priest is abnormal, and just as

16

the non-reproductive adult animal is abnormal – and therefore that her impulses must inevitably find their adaption in an abnormal manner.'[22] If the spinster was perceived to be a 'morbid influence upon the life of [the] nation,'[23] it followed that the leadership of a redundant woman was not conducive to the propagation of the fascist family in Britain. Stemming from her status as a spinster, and compounded by her personal eccentricities and paranoia, perceptions of Lintorn-Orman were consistently derisive and condescending. They started with negative portrayals by some dissident fellow-fascists, were perpetuated by anti-fascists and the authorities observing the progress of extremists organizations, and are still present in the historiography of the BF, with the result that Lintorn-Orman's 'abnormality' has long been seen to account for the extreme marginality of the organization she founded.

Arnold Leese was an early member of the BF, but left the organization in 1924 because he did not believe that it was a true expression of fascism. He went on to form the virulently anti-Semitic Imperial Fascist League (1928), which, among other things, wished to see 'silly universal suffrage'[24] abolished. The IFL's gender ideology was summed up by one of their stickers which warned: 'Britons! Do not allow JEWS to tamper with White Girls.'[25] Remembering why he defected from the British Fascisti, Leese described how: 'I made a special journey to town to implore them to change their name, as I thought the initials were just asking for it! To my surprise, I failed to gain this obvious reform! After a while, I found that there was no Fascism, as I understood it, in the organization which was merely Conservatism with knobs on.'[26] (Colloquially, B.F. stood for bloody fools). It is not fanciful to assume that Leese's disillusionment with the BF was related to the predominance of women in the organization, particularly when we consider how

> Leese went on to develop a nationalist ideology in which the image of British society [was] that of an austere, conquering elite of Empire-builders, in which women were to play a subsidiary role. He deplored female suffrage and the increasing number of working women, both of which he thought was contravening the laws of nature. According to Leese, the male instinct was to secure the safety of his home and country, the female to care for her children, which naturally narrowed the scope of experience and political judgement ... . "Unmarried men and unmarried women are not living a normal life; it is the married who are normal," Leese observed in 1931.[27]

The influence of the unmarried Lintorn-Orman, who also supported universal suffrage at the age of twenty-five,[28] did not respond to Leese's developing vision of fascist virility and male-supremacist racialism.

In the civil war within British fascist politics in the early 1930s, the feminine character of the BF was a readily accessible target. After a failed attempt at a merger between his own BUF and the BF, Mosley described the BF resisters as 'three old ladies and a couple of office boys,'[29] exemplifying the perceived anomaly of a female-led fascist organization. The BUF's view of the BF was comparable to the general attitude held by the Home Office towards Lintorn-Orman and her 'harmful lunatic' associates.[30] According to a Home Office report, Lintorn-Orman had been a nuisance since November 1923, and H.R. Boyd reported that

> as a result of steps we took then they [the BF] seem to have discontinued their impertinent use of the Royal Crown but are still continuing their activities. I enclose you our file in regard to this body which may amuse you to look at ... Mrs [sic] Lintorn-Orman is one of the leaders of the extreme group of BF which now operates as an independent body of BF.[31]

Although it is apparent that the authorities were relatively ignorant about her – in a 1924 report assuming she was an ex-suffragette, and here presuming that she was a married woman – Lintorn-Orman was only of concern to them in so far as she proved herself to be a public irritant. She had done so by making false allegations to police on 'the existence of ammunition dumps, the dispatch of arms from Russia to this country, and the intentions of Communists to cause damage to property.'[32] She especially aggravated the police by implying in letters sent to other bodies that the BF had special relations with the police. For such impertinence she was interviewed and warned.

Special Branch took particular voyeuristic pleasure in reporting on the influence of quasi-criminal elements in the BF, and how certain members were encouraging Lintorn-Orman in her addictions. In May 1933, the police were called to the home of Mrs Lintorn-Orman in Farnborough at which time the Founder's mother informed them that she had dissociated herself from the BF due to the membership of disreputable persons, and had reduced her daughter's allowance because of the latter's licentious habits. Mrs Lintorn-Orman was 'of the opinion that drunken orgies and undesirable practices take place at her town residence ... which has been loaned to her daughter and that some of the leading members of the BF are living on the latter's allowance.' A friend of Mrs Lintorn-Orman called at New Scotland Yard in October 1933 to make the similar allegation that 'some of the members of the organization were constantly plying Miss Lintorn-Orman with drink and drugs, with a view of extracting money from her.'[33] Certainly the presence of these tragic-comic events in the Founder's personal life permitted the authorities almost completely to ignore the political significance of the BF and the development of fascism for women in Britain.[34]

These contemporary opinions of Lintorn-Orman have been perpetuated by the historiography of British fascism. Inaccuracies concerning Lintorn-Orman's personal history can be accounted for by the fact that earlier studies were preoccupied with the BUF, and the BF was of interest primarily because it was the first movement to call itself fascist, and due to the fact that many of its leading members eventually figured in the story of Mosley's movement.[35] Writing in 1946, Frederic Mullaly misspelled the Founder's name, calling her Miss *Linton*-Orman.[36] Interested in William Joyce's short-term membership in the BF in 1923, Rebecca West described the BF's leader as an 'elderly lady' and observed that Lintorn-Orman's 'creation was patronized by a certain number of retired Army men and a back-bench MP and an obscure peer or two; but the great world mocked at it, and it had as an aim the organization of the amateur resistance to any revolution that might arise. It was a charade representing the word "barricade."'[37] To call a woman in her mid-twenties an elderly lady is obviously inaccurate. However, West was correct in surmising that the political world made a mockery of the BF and the contemporary derision has seeped into the historiography.

As more recent research has begun to look in and around the more influential British Union of Fascists in an attempt to trace the impact of the extreme-right in inter-war politics, Lintorn-Orman's own story has been readjusted. With consideration for the new perspectives and different questions asked by women's history, Griffiths, Thurlow and Storm Farr have been more generous in their portrayals of Lintorn-Orman.[38] Barbara Storm Farr represents a radical departure from the development of the historiography of the BF and of Lintorn-Orman in particular, and her reassessment of the Founder verges on a vindication. Farr sees her as 'a unique expression of an activist right-wing woman who discarded traditional female roles and attempted to build a hierarchical para-military organization among the middle and upper-middle levels of society.'[39] In claiming Lintorn-Orman for women's history, and even for the history of inter-war feminism, Farr prolongs the tradition of the revision of British fascist leaders inaugurated by Robert Skidelsky in his 1975 biography of Sir Oswald Mosley.

Right-wing Women and the Rights of Women: Lintorn Orman's Feminized Fascism

With the development of the revision in mind, we should still be cautious in attributing too much revolutionary fervour and original vision to Miss Lintorn-Orman. While the Founder concerned herself with forging a role for women in a para-military organization, she did not address issues pertaining to women within the parameters of any of the contemporary discourses on feminism. I would argue, therefore, that Farr overstates the case when she brands Lintorn-Orman's gender ideology 'fascist feminism.' The Founder cultivated an ultra-patriotic interpretation of female power, based on her myopic vision of women's duty and service to the nation; there was no room for women's rights in her political conceptions. The real question, of course, is whether there could be a place for any discourse of rights in an anti-alien, anti-Semitic ideology? How can such a discourse be integrated within one which focuses on the denial of citizenship rights to others? Further, while the BF became increasingly centred around the activities of its women members, their appeals were consistently made to both sexes. Indeed, on more than one occasion, the BF press cajoled male members about their inactivity as compared with the women. In December 1927, for instance, Mr Bullen, editor of *The British Lion*, called out: 'Wake up, London men. Are you going to allow the Women's Units to carry on the work of the men in East London ... . It is not Fascism to make the women do the men's work in addition to their own.'[40] That such statements should have been made indicates that traditional female roles were not radically transgressed or subverted.

Lintorn-Orman's own gender ideology was predicated on her militant nationalism and her preference for the regimentation of femininity. To fill the ranks of the Women's Units, she wished to recruit 'women of any age ... for general service, and we make a special appeal to Ex-service women.'[41] Traits of self-reliance and will to perform service were to be harnessed for rear-guard action, and employed in the interests of children's welfare and education. To fill the ranks of the FCCs, the BF made it known that 'women especially should make it their task and duty to prevent the spirit of the Red Menace to influence the future citizens of the Empire.'[42]

Lintorn-Orman desired to ingrain the values of 'women's loyalty' and she admired the spirit which animated the lives of her heroines: Queen Elizabeth, Florence Nightingale, Grace Darling, Nurse Edith Cavell and aviator Amy Johnson.[43]

She deplored the Oxford Union resolution of 1 May 1934, and thought anyone who refused to fight for King and Country 'should be shunned as a pariah among men, the same applies to any woman or girl.'[44] Pacifism was antithetical to British fascism, and the BF was mobilizing for either international warfare, or civil war which would be engineered by the Red element. 'Men will have to fight – women will have to provide the auxiliary services. There will be no men to spare for transport – First Aid for air raids – or Bacteriological warfare. This is the women's duty – and BF Women's Units are organizing on these lines.'[45] Lintorn-Orman's woman had strength on the 'battle field' and in the home.

> She has everything to lose by slackness – and everything to gain by being prepared for an emergency. Women have political power! Let them use it for the country! Women have almost equality with men in business! Let them think of the future welfare to the coming generation by teaching children that British Business is best! Women have superiority in the most essential thing of life – the Home! Let them insist on the purchase of British goods only. Finally, let them all live up as far as possible to the noble and gracious example of our beloved Queen – and devote their service to H.M. the King and the British Empire.[46]

Femininity and female power were intrinsically connected to the perceived good of the nation and the BF's formula of 'country before self and the good of their fellow citizens *before* personal consideration'[47] precluded anything as sectional as women placing the interests of their sex before that of the community. Absent from Lintorn-Orman's categories for women's power were the role of women in the job market and sexual liberation. She herself paid little regard to the value of the female franchise. Her gender ideology was a fascism feminized, the nationalist and selfless content effectively silencing the whispers for women's further emancipation.

Sex and Schism: Women Stand for Independence

Although Lintorn-Orman's gender ideology was rather innocuous, the BF was victim to chronic sex wars. The BF became the British

Fascists Ltd on 7 May 1924. The first schism came in the autumn of 1924 when sixty dissidents split off from the main body to form the National Fascisti. According to the BF press, these 'hot heads' formed 'an almost Gilbertian body ... who guarded their headquarters with wooden swords, whose language on the platform was forceful, but a trifle illogical and who adopted a uniform as closely approaching that of the Italian Fascisti as it can be possible to get.'[48] The next breach in 1926 occurred for the very opposite reason. In April, Blakeney resigned after a confidential discussion with the Home Secretary when he was amenable to the suggestion that the BF should abandon the appellation 'Fascisti' and relinquish military titles in order to be permitted to collaborate with the Organization for the Maintenance of Supply (OMS). The BF Grand Council had passed a resolution on 9 October 1925 to the effect that they would agree to co-operate with the OMS and other like-minded patriotic organizations, but only if they retained their fascist identity.

In the spring of 1926 it was the women on the Grand Council who refused to merge with the OMS, demonstrating their resilience and their commitment to the resolution passed a year earlier. Interviewed by the *Evening News*, Lintorn-Orman described the split and asserted her leadership over the BF:

> It was suggested to us that we should change our name, and that all our members – we have between 150,000 and 200,000 all over the country – would become members of the OMS ... But it was patent that we lose our identity entirely. General Blakeney had the support of four other members of the council for his proposal. As founder of the organization, I took the view of the 300 odd branches and found that 75% of them were against any such change as proposed ... . We feel that we should be under no obligation to, or in control of, any organization which we regard as being of a political character.[49]

It was significant that the women in particular opted for autonomy, and it is likely that they resisted their incorporation into the OMS because of the fact that women were figured as subordinate participants in the OMS.

The OMS was formed in September 1925 and its first President was Lord Hardinge of Penhurst, and Sir William Joynson-Hicks, the Home Secretary, served as a vice-president. While the organization was 'strictly non-party in character' and its aim was to 'register citizens of either sex who are prepared to volunteer assistance for the maintaining of supplies of water, food and fuel, and the efficiency of public services indispensable to the normal life of the community,' women were to be enlisted to serve in Class E, classes A–D being open only to men. The functions of Class E members was 'general unclassified services, including clerical work [and] will include women, who will be enrolled in service in canteens, hospitals, and so on, but in no circumstances will women be employed in places where there is danger of rough handling.'[50] Although women were among the eager recruits for strike breaking, it was not until 1927 that a woman, Dame Helen Gwynne-Vaughan, sat on the council of the OMS. Gwynne-Vaughan, formerly the Chief Controller of the Women's Army Auxiliary Corps (WAAC) during the First World War, became the first woman on the council, 'in the company of generals, admirals, a retired ambassador, and a Knight of the Garter.'[51]

Women members of the British Fascists were not averse to the rough work of street fascism and they were trained to engage in violent confrontation, both defensive and offensive. It is much more likely that the women resisted due to the obvious subordination of women's work, and not because they were in conflict with the political character of the OMS. Indeed, the OMS was charged with being 'the most definite step towards organized fascism yet made in this country.'[52] The OMS accepted the collaboration of the newly constituted British Loyalists, the dissidents from the BF Council, and the diminished BF was left to act independently during the Strike. While this split weakened the BF, it catalysed the evolution of feminized fascism in Britain.

Following the spilt, it was Lintorn-Orman who reassured the membership that the BF was to continue working towards its ends, and that 'Fascism [was] Revived.' And revived just in time, as the General Strike, the event the BF had been preparing for since 1923, broke out within weeks of the schism. The remaining members took great pride in their pro-active work during the Strike, and Captain Smith reported to all Commanders on 25 May 1926 that the members of the BF Women's Section had

> enroled in the Women's Auxiliary Service (Police). Women's Units in London and the different provincial areas rendered signal service to the local authorities in the matters of transport and Commissariat. In one area the Women's First Aid section was requisitioned by the Police, owing to its efficiency. At the GHQ Women's Units took over, and dealt with in the most efficient manner, the Recruiting Department ... Women's Units issued a daily Fascist News Sheet, which was sold in the street with great success.[53]

The success of BF women in countering the 'Reds' on this occasion certainly demonstrated their competence and their self-reliance.

Conflict between the BF and the BUF began soon after Mosley launched his own movement. The BF's antagonism towards the BUF came out in a scornful manner. When Mosley had first formed the New Party, they applauded his political awakening and accepted him as a 'late convert' to fascism.[54] However, when he did own the fascist name, the BF's sense of prior ownership intervened, and by October of 1932 their newspaper emphatically asserted that the BF 'has no connection whatever with Sir Oswald Mosley and his so-called British Union of Fascists ... . Our movement has been established in this country since 1923, and has nearly a million members.'[55] When BF members defected to the BUF or left the movement due to its obvious impotence by 1933, they were deprived of their Order of the Fasces.[56]

By July 1933 hostility between the two organizations was acute. On 20 July a small lorry of BF members made a counter-demonstration in Hyde Park to a Jewish Protest Demonstration which was followed by an attack on the BUF.

> The BF under Miss Lintorn-Orman, have for some time been at loggerheads with the BUF, under Sir Oswald Mosley, and when the lorry mentioned passed other offices of the BUF at 233, Regent St, abusive remarks were again uttered and a number of anti-Semitic pamphlets thrown into the entrance of this address. When the activities of the occupants of this lorry became known considerable resentment was shown by members of the BUF, who thought that they may be blamed for hostility against the Jews.[57]

The BUF was not to be terrorized by this meagre organization which had steadfastly refused to be merged with the Blackshirts, and a number of men decided to take reprisal. Blackshirts raided the BF headquarters at 22 Stanhope Gardens. Fifty to sixty men smashed the ground floor window, entered and upset office furniture and injured four members of the BF, including one woman, Mrs Florence Waters, House Officer, who was struck on the head with a chair and had to be treated in hospital.[58] In March 1934, Adolph Plathen and Wilfred Risden, both of BUF headquarters, went to Norfolk and Suffolk to counter the propaganda tour of A.W.F. Whitmore on behalf of the BF Ltd. Whitmore's tour was embarked upon to 'expose the BUF.'[59]

Surprisingly, while such violent scenes erupted, the British Union of Fascists – in a bid to remain true to its name – persisted with the idea of a merger between the two fascist organizations, and again in

July 1934 negotiations were conducted by the BF's Colonel Wilson to forge an agreement for incorporation.[60] Initially, Lintorn-Orman seemed amenable to a merger on this occasion but, at the last minute, rejected the proposal. She 'was alleged to have been under the influence of drink ... and this is attributed by Colonel Wilson to be the cause for her sudden change of opinion.'[61] By December 1934, Sir Russell Scott, reporting on the fascist movement in the United Kingdom, came to the conclusion that the BF had been virtually eclipsed by the BUF and 'does not appear to be of any further importance.'[62]

The Organization and Activities of Women in the British Fascists

What was the BF's importance before 1934? It is through an examination of the movement's activities that their impact on British fascist politics can best be evaluated. The BF was governed by a Grand Council of nine, consisting of both men and women. Both men's and women's branches were organized under county commanders, which were further subdivided into areas, districts, divisions, and troops. Each unit consisted of seven men or women. Military formation was a tribute to 'the great work achieved by the old volunteers and territorial armies, and the success which attended the brave efforts of the late Lord Roberts, despite obloquy and brainless ridicule.' The BF wished to 'follow in their footsteps, and to get forward with something more than talk towards making preparation to counter the great and deadly menace hanging over us.'[63] The Women's Units had an array of functions. They established a Women's Units First Aid Squad which was to attend meetings in areas where disturbances were expected. The Women's Units organized classes in all subjects, and like BUF women after them, they were trained in ju-jitsu and self-defence. Speakers' classes were offered by 'Mme Anita Sutherland, the well-known singer and one of our earliest members,'[64] and women members were offered First Aid classes commensurate with St John's Ambulance. In addition to the serious work of fascism on the streets, a Fascist Dogs' Club was launched in 1929.

The primary impetus for organization remained action against the Red Menace, and the BF gave form to their hatred by staging counter-demonstrations, running the FCCs, and by making unsubstantiated accusations and circulating their propaganda. Their anti-Communist activities were usually described as preparations for national emergency, and both BF men and women were early on committed to 'meet force with force.' On one occasion in 1927, when in the East End to promote the FCC, Lintorn-Orman was 'attacked by a man with a life preserver, who struck her on the face and caused [a] wound.' Miss Orman explained to the reporter:

"We went down, a party of 15 strong, all women members, to further our campaign for the formation of the Fascist Children's Clubs which are organizing around the country to counteract the propaganda of the Red Sunday School ... . Nearest the platform there were about 200 children, and the Reds behind kept on pushing at the back, so that the children were driven towards us. After a while the children started throwing things at us."[65]

On the same day as this indubitably traumatic attack by the local children, Lintorn-Orman was responsible for writing a letter to the editor of the *Morning Post* in which she charged the communist *Sunday Worker* with making libellous statements against her BF. The *Sunday Worker* had claimed that 'the Fascists are arming for the next General Strike, and they have received stocks of arms, and they now possess not only small arms but artillery and machine guns.'[66] Without artillery, the BF saw its main offensive weapon against the Left as the children's clubs and the show of para-military force in the form of patriotic demonstrations. What they regarded as patriotic counter-demonstrations, the authorities saw as gatherings 'for the purposes of heckling the speakers, and if possible, breaking up the meeting.'[67]

The most important annual event for the BF was Armistice Day and one can see photographs of their women marching to the Cenotaph on the cover of many editions of their newspapers.[68] Holiday camps were also organized for members, and during the summer of 1925 the women campers had a particularly exhilarating experience when 'Reds Raid Women's Camp at Lyndhurst.' 'On the night of August 2, at about 11 p.m., while the women Fascists were sitting round their camp fire singing patriotic songs and entertaining some visitors, they heard what they thought was a rag consisting of the banging of tin cans ... the girls armed themselves with mallets and sticks.'[69] When the 'Reds' tried to raid them again on the following night, the women succeeded in fending them off by keeping watch. The following year, the Women's Units Camp was held under the command of O/C Women's Units and instruction was offered in physical training, ju-jitsu, First Aid, and courses for officers of the Women's Units. Presumably, the events of the previous summer had brought home the need for more vigorous defensive training!

Fascist collective identity was maintained by the regularity of dances, balls, garden parties, and bazaars, and the proceeds from these functions tended to go towards funding the FCCs. In March 1926 the BF held a Grand 'Mi Careme' ball at the Hotel Cecil on the Strand, under the patronage of the Earl and Countess of Glasgow, the Earl and Countess Temple of Stowe, and the Viscount and Viscountess Downe. In the summer of 1928 a Fascist Garden Fête was held at Hampton Court which was inaugurated by the London Special Patrol and Women's Units forming a guard of honour on the arrival of the Founder. In April 1930 the Dance Committee organized a Frivolity Ball, where the 'celebrated actress,' Dorothy Seacombe, presented prizes for the best costumes.

As this glimpse at social activities indicates, the BF was very committed in its adherence to ceremony, and this was even more marked in the organization's development of a distinctively British fascist regalia. The basis of the BF's marketing scheme was the uniform itself which consisted of a dark blue tunic jacket with the lettering 'British Fascist' on the shoulder-straps and a blue beret. Members also wore small round badges with the letter 'F' surrounded by the inscription 'For King and Country.' It was considered 'most desirable that our women members should wear uniform,'[70] and in 1925 Lintorn-Orman made arrangements for members to obtain the official uniform, made to measure, at Messrs. Gamages's in Holborn. The Women's Units were especially proud of their lorry, a half-ton Morris Cowley, jointly owned by the London Special Patrol, the London Women's Units and the FCCs. They used their lorry for a speaker's platform, and during Christmas 1927 'a number of Fascists formed a party of carol singers and the lorry transported them round London.'[71]

In the late 1920s the BF began to award the Order of the Fasces and 42 such awards were presented in 1928: 11 first class, 16 second class and 25 third class. Of these 42, 19 were presented to women, 10 of whom were unmarried. On 6 May 1934, the BF's eleventh (and last) birthday, Lintorn-Orman was presented with a clock bearing the Fascist badge and engraved with the date. At this same event, among those receiving the Order of the Fasces was Troop Leader Mrs Waters 'for loyal service and presence of mind on the evening of 20th July, 1934, on which occasion she helped resist the attack when a party of men wearing blackshirts raided General Headquarters.'[72] This was the incident instigated by the BF's attack on the BUF, and reported by Special Branch.

In addition to the pageantry surrounding female violence, the BF ceremonialized and added the fascist touch to the births, the weddings, and the funerals within the movement. In 1932 they were pleased to receive the enrolment form of Herbert R.J. Lucas, son of Unit-Leader Lucas, of the London Men's Units. With typical fascist infantile jocularity they wrote that 'at present Fascist Lucas is on the non-active list, as his age being just two months, he is still rather too young for either outdoor meetings or street sales. He has started early in the service of his country!'[73] On 28 October 1931 Lucas had married within the movement, taking Miss Doris Harding of the London Special Patrol as his wife. The wedding of Mr W. Hamilton and Miss Eleanor Sizer in 1929, both members of the Holborn Area, was attended by a Guard of Honour commanded by the Founder. The wedding of Miss Barbara MacRae to Captain Henry Laharde Mayne took the bride out of the movement, and it was expressed that 'the London Special Patrol feel the loss of such an officer and are only consoled by the fact that she remains an honorary member and has promised to visit the Patrol whenever she comes South.'[74]

The ceremony surrounding the deaths of Miss W.E. Brigg O/C LSP and Miss E.R. Greenlaw Company Officer, London Women's Units, attests to the fact that the BF could provide a surrogate family for some of Britain's surplus women. Brigg's funeral was conducted with full fascist honours, 'the insignia of the Order, together with badge and shoulder straps were buried with Miss Brigg.'[75] Further, it was attended by a Guard of Honour composed of fifty members of the LSP and the coffin was draped with the fascist flag. Miss Greenlaw's funeral was similarly conducted with full fascist honours, Lintorn-Orman was a pall bearer, and 'the Fascist lorry followed the hearse and was loaded with floral tributes from the late Company Officer's fellow Fascists.'[76] By celebrating each phase of life within a fascist framework, the BF in fact appropriated the functions once carried out by the Church and this substantiated their claim, made in another context, that fascism was akin to a religion.

BF women's most fervently fulfilled task was running the Fascist Children's Clubs, another function which they appropriated from the Church. The FCC was the brain-child of Miss Blake, Area Commander for Edinburgh. As the idea for the Clubs was conceived in June 1925, it is clear that the welfare of children was not one of the BF's initial concerns. Nonetheless, the Clubs became increasingly important, and by the early 1930s they were seen as BF women's main responsibility. The typical programme for a club session was:

I. Roll call and salute the Union Jack. II. Hymn and Lord's Prayer. III. Historical and national subjects – lives of good men and women etc. IV. Games. V Competitions given out for home work. VI. Patriotic songs and items of news. VII. General tidying up. Monitors take special charge of the Union Jack. God Save the King.[77]

Not only was patriotism instilled in the children, but they were instructed in the principles of fascism. Mr Harrison Hill founded the Patriotic Song League in 1926 and presented the following ditty to the children: 'We are all Anti-Red, and We're proud of it,/ All Britons, and singing aloud of it./ If Red, White and Blue isn't good enough for you,/ And if you don't like the Empire – clear out of it.'[78] Their education in racialism was given added encouragement when Lieutenant-Colonel A.H. Lane presented one hundred copies of his book, *The Alien Menace*, to the Fascist Children's Department in 1929.[79]

BF women were the main activists in the FCCs as well as having exclusive control over their London Special Patrol (LSP). The BF Women's Units were not atypical in the hierarchies of radical right organizations, but the presence of a band of militant women patrolling the streets was unique, and the LSP closely resembled Mary Allen's women police.[80] Membership was open to all physically fit women between the ages of 18 to 40, and a height minimum was set at 5 feet 5 inches. The LSP was formed in 1924 by the Founder, and the pioneer members were Miss Colby, Miss N.E. Smith, Miss P. Chaney, Miss Burgess, Miss Brigg and Miss Greenlaw. Noticeably, the Patrols were manned by single women and it was acknowledged that women of all ages and classes joined. By 1926 a second patrol was formed. In 1927 a third patrol unit became necessary, the first and second having reached their quota. In 1928 a London Women's Unit Special Reserve was formed for those who wished to take a more active part but could not join the LSP.

The Patrols seemed to have been popular with BF women and this was as much due to the comradeship they shared as to the fact that there was an air of mystery surrounding their duties. Describing the work of her fellow Patrol women, 'a Patrol girl' reported how the LSP worked at open-air meetings, carried sandwich boards, gave out hand bills, went on route marches, drilled, and debated. In order to arouse the interest of her readers, this anonymous writer described how 'there is another exciting duty we have, which would fill a volume – and in any case I must not mention it here (being in the Patrol I must keep up its name for discipline), but perhaps one day in the dim future, when we are past work a book may be written entitled "Special Duty." For those too curious to wait – I advise them to join!'[81] Regardless of all the BF's attacks on secret societies and the 'hidden hand,' these women would not to reveal the nature of 'Special Duty.'

Membership Figures and Fascist Figures

Another aspect of the BF which has remained somewhat of a mystery is the movement's exact membership. In August 1924 membership was estimated at 100,000, and 'in the beginning, the Women's Units, under the direction of Mrs A.M. Wroughton, of Farnborough, Hampshire, accounted for about 1/6 of the membership.'[82] In 1925 the organization claimed to have 800 branches, each with a membership varying from 200 to 500 persons. Following the split over the issue of collaboration with the OMS, the BF moved its London headquarters from 71 Elm Park Gardens to 297 Fulham Road. In 1928 headquarters moved to 99 Buckingham Place Road, a particularly proud address due to its proximity to the residence of the Monarch. In 1933 the BF moved its headquarters again, to 22 Stanhope Gardens, claiming that such a change was made necessary by the growth of the movement. When in conflict with the BUF in 1933, the BF claimed it had over one million members. Farr has estimated that the BF had 400,000 members in 1933, while the Home Office gauged the BF's strength at between 300 and 400 members for the same year.[83] Without anything approaching reliable estimates of membership, we must be satisfied by trying to determine the types who joined.

In 1926 'Investigator' assumed that the type most attracted to the BF would be persons of military, patriotic, jingoistic character. 'It will appeal also to a rather different kind of person, to the men and women who are bewildered and distressed by the clash of forces going on around them in modern life and who say that "if only we could rid ourselves of these agitators and all get together, like the officers and men did in the trenches" all might yet be well.'[84] 'Investigator' saw the futility of the BF's attempt to make a cross-class appeal, and there can be little doubt that the BF was middle-and upper-middle class in social composition.[85]

Common to the background of many members was military service, experience in running the Empire, and landed status. Many titled women were connected with the BF, including Viscountess Downe,

County Commander for the North Riding; Lady Sydenham who directed the FCCs; the Countess of Eglinton and Wintonshire who was County Commander for Ayrshire; Lady Mowbray, who undertook the temporary command of the Harrogate Area in 1925; the Marquess of Ailesbury, the Baroness Zouche of Haryngworth, and Lady Menzies of Menzies. The fascist ideal of an aristocracy of merit would have assured members of the social elite that the movement did not advocate the abolition of class distinction.[86] Indeed, considering the relative obscurity of the aristocrats the BF enlisted, they could well have thought that dictatorship and the maintenance of hierarchy might check the 'decline and fall' of the British aristocracy.

The other category of female activists was the newly enfranchized women, such as Mrs Hamilton-More Nesbitte, Vice-President of the Scottish Women's Units; Dorothy Waring, author; Miss Wedgewood, O.B.E. of Stone, County Commander for Staffordshire and Cheshire; and D.G. Harnett D/O Ulster Command and editor of *British Fascism* when Lintorn-Orman's illness prevented her from attending headquarters. In the municipal elections in Southampton in 1927, the BF was very pleased that one of the successful candidates was 'Mrs Foster Welsh, JP, a Southampton Fascist, who was recently elected as Sheriff of the Borough, the first woman to hold this position in any Borough in England.'[87] Another member who fits the above profile as well as being a character in her own right was Nesta Webster, the prolific historian of subversive organizations, the occult, and the Hidden Hand.

Webster's object in life, decided upon just prior to the war, was to expose the world conspiracy of the Jews, Freemasons and like schemers.[88] She sat on the BF Grand Council for a few months in 1926 and 1927, and gave lectures for the organization on the 'History of Socialism, Pacifism, Internationalism, and Subversive Movements' at the Chelsea Town Hall amid much publicity. After leaving the BF she opened the Patriots Inquiry Centre in 1927, with offices in Westminster, with the object of disseminating anti-Socialist information.[89] While her pedagogical programme was most concerned with political intrigue in general, Webster expressed particular fears about the effect of subversive elements on women.

> The manner in which the women of this country have been enlisted in the service of the conspiracy can also be traced to illuminized Freemasonry. Just as in the French Revolution the advocates of 'Women's Rights' were persuaded to throw themselves into the movement, so the conspiracy to-day has succeeded

31

in capturing a large portion of the 'Feminist' movement for its purpose of general demoralization.[90]

Her apprehension about the modern woman was mirrored in BF propaganda, and in the movement's difficulty to come to terms with the post-war revolution in gender roles. In certain contexts, this revolution was perceived to be as destructive to civilization as the Bolshevik Revolution of 1917.

Alongside Lintorn-Orman's feminized fascism, the BF expounded a very traditionalist gender ideology in which women were to be protected by their menfolk from the sexually-threatening Red Menace. John Cheshire, DOC Western Command, interpreted militant fascism to be a creed that should appeal to every English man: 'It should be his privilege and duty to prepare himself to defend from contamination of the mob the honour of his wife and daughter, and only men who defend and respect their women are entitled to the love and friendship of life's dearest possession.'[91] In 1926 Philip Lewis wrote how 'the Soviet Government has now ... made divorce so easy that there is no stability in married life. The results are deplorable and show the folly of extremism.'[92] Metaphorically, the BF's protection of female virtue was exemplified by the use of the ultra-patriotic image of Britannia. Britannia unarmed was imagined to be a woman vulnerable to rape and pillage by an over-sexed Red enemy:

> 'What coward would dare attack a protected woman. He would go slyly to work and persuade her to lay her protection aside before he attempted to attack and rob her. Britannia is unprotected to-day, she did not lay her shield aside herself, her traitorous councillors have forced her to do so, and now her lustful enemies are rejoicing, and only waiting for the moment to attack.'[93]

While the BF's approach to women's political activities exhibited some thoroughly modern attitudes, BF propaganda was strikingly anti-modern and uninspiringly traditional.

Minimal Fascism: Measuring up to the Fascist Minimum

In order to conclude this survey of women's activities in Lintorn-Orman's BF, it is necessary to return to one of our first quandaries. Was the BF a fascist movement in name only? Was Lintorn-Orman's feminized fascism a successful marriage of women's power and the new creed introduced by Mussolini, or was it a contrived cohabitation between ultra-patriotic fanaticism and women's post-war political independence? One way in which to assess the extent of the fascist content of the BF's ideology is by testing how their convictions measured up to the 'fascist minimum' prescribed by Ernst Nolte: anti-communism, anti-liberalism, anti-conservatism, leadership principle, party army, and aim of totalitarianism.[94]

Of these six requirements that the BF fulfilled the first cannot be denied. That they established a party army is also clear, even if it was only 'a glorified Boy's Brigade run by women.'[95] The adherence to the leadership principle, however, was thwarted in practice due to the fact that the centre of authority shifted; Lintorn-Orman commanded minimal respect and certainly did not evoke fear in her opponents. Even though they had no candidate for the position, the BF did advocate dictatorship. Nesta Webster was certain that Britain would have to choose between fascism and communism. She explained that

> the stock objection to such an eventuality is always 'Where shall we find a Mussolini?' I would answer 'In the British spirit.' I do not think we will have a one-man dictatorship in England ... but that in the event of the country being thrown into chaos by a revolution we may have the temporary dictatorship of a group which will give a lead to loyal citizens and restore order with a firm hand.[96]

This vision of dictatorship – which was really an oligarchy – was a result of the absence of a viable leader in the BF, and probably a way of making a virtue of necessity. The BF's indecision on the efficacy of dictatorship was also exemplified by their response to the Nazi accession to power in Germany. In February 1933 members called at the German Embassy to offer their congratulations, but it was still mutual interest in fighting International Communism which was given as the reason for their visit.

The BF's anti-liberalism was evident in so far as propagandists belittled a dialogue on rights in favour of one on duty and service. Further, the BF's anti-modernism was obvious, both in their reaction to the modernization of gender roles and their idealization of times gone by.[97] Whether the BF was anti-conservative or not is more enigmatic, since they acted as stewards at Conservative Party meetings, encouraged their members to vote Tory, and replicated the party's position on the Socialist Sunday School and women's political role. By the 1930s, however, the BF became vehement in its reproof of the party system, echoing Mosley's denunciation of old gang politicians. They even went as far as saying that 'our recruits are men and women who, sick of endless betrayals by politicians, turn to a disciplined, revolutionary movement that faces the facts of today instead of living among the political theories of 50 years ago.'[98] The identification with revolution was a late addition as was the turn against tradition. 'Mass patriotism is fascism,' they believed, and 'we British fascists hope to accomplish this metamorphosis by means of the ballot box, but, if our opponents make it necessary, will always be ready to meet force with force.'[99] The BF's anti-democratic diatribes were always balanced by their absolute loyalty to the monarchy and the constitution, although they could sometimes confuse issues by surmising that 'in England we have a monarchy which, though far too constitutional, is the only safeguard against alien interference in our national affairs.'[100] Lacking a candidate for dictatorship, it often seems as though the BF envisioned a return to benevolent despotism in the form of a divine monarch. The BF did not confront the question of totalitarianism, although they began to advocate the Corporate State and consistently opted for law and order.

Since the BF does not pass the test of the fascist minimum with flying colours, the question to be asked is what did define their political mentality? Monarchist, anti-Semitic, anti-alien, and anti-immigration, radically conservative, defenders of Ulster, imperialist, militaristic, anti-pacifist, chauvinistically nationalist, child-centred if not child-minded, the BF cultivated sets of ideals that placed them firmly on the radical Right, but revealed that their understanding of fascism lacked coherence.

The influence of women in the organization, and that of Lintorn-Orman in particular, can account for the failure of the BF to grasp the full significance of fascism and seize a firm position in British fascist politics. Quite simply, what is fascism without a leader, and Lintorn-Orman, due as much to her personal eccentricities and infirmities as to the fact that she was a woman trying to establish a male-centrist and virile creed, was never a viable candidate. It would still be too harsh, however, to discount the consequence of the BF. For many men and women the BF provided a surrogate family, the organization mobilized the will to serve of hundreds of ultra-patriotic men and women, and the BF gave temporary form to the fantasy of a fascism feminized and harnessed for militant female activism in the name of a radical, if not revolutionary, nationalism. If the place of the BF in the history of British fascist politics is indefinite, the important position of the movement in the history of women's fascism is more secure.

Notes to Chapter 1

1 During the 1920s two proto-Nazi, women-led movements emerged in Germany: Guilda Diehl's Newland Movement, which predated the Nazi Party by six years, and the Order of the Red Swastika, founded by Elsbeth Zander in 1926. See Claudia Koonz, 'The Competition for Women's Lebensraum, 1928–34' in ed. Renate Bridenthal et al., *When Biology Became Destiny* (New York, 1984), pp.199–236.

2 T.S. Eliot referring to the BF, quoted in Alastair Hamilton, *The Appeal of Fascism* (London, 1971), p.264.

3 Gertrude M. Godden, *Mussolini: The Birth of the New Democracy* (London, 1923), p.7. It is interesting to note that G.M. Godden was also responsible for sending the Home Office reports on the activities of the Kibbo Kift Kindred and the Federation of British Youth in 1925. She took particular exception to the fact that 'the chairman, Theodore Besterman, of the Guild of the Citizens of Tomorrow, is an oriental effeminate, but handsome youth – very dark – (?) Eastern Jew. Mrs Besterman is a singularly repulsive type – also (?)oriental. The principal speaker, Harold Bing, of the "No More War Movement" was a virile, golden-haired, simple-life type – sunburnt and full of force.' Of the KKK's magazine, *Youth*, she was most offended by the fact that it was 'violently blasphemous and erotic.' HO/45/24966/674112/2.

4 The notorious William Joyce launched his political career in the BF, and it was as one of the movement's stewards in defence of the Jewish Tory candidate Jack Lazarus during the General Election of 1924 that he sustained a razor slash to the face, creating a permanent scar. Cross submits that the BF's 'last big public appearance was when they provided 600 stewards for a Conservative patriotic rally at the Albert Hall addressed by Sir Henry Page-Croft, MP, in the autumn of 1926.' Colin Cross, *The Fascists in Britain* (London, 1961), p.62.

5 *British Lion*, July 1928.

6 R.B.D. Blakeney, 'British Fascism', *The Nineteenth Century and After*, 97 (January 1925), 132–42.

7 Anne Summers, 'The Character of Edwardian Nationalism: Three Popular Leagues,' in eds Paul Kennedy and Anthony Nicholls, *Nationalist and Racialist Movements in Britain and Germany before 1914* (Oxford, 1981), pp.68–87.

8 'The League of Empire Housewives,' *The British Lion*, No. 25 [n.d.]

9 While some overlapping between the BF and Conservative women's organizations is evident, by May 1931 the BF met with the Stratford Branch of the Primrose League in a debate, rather than on terms of collaboration. Mr Mandeville Roe propounded that 'not merely is fascism practicable: it is inevitable, so far as the economic situation goes to-day .... Fascism means democracy in and through industry – a responsible democracy instead of the mere blind mob-vote you have today.' *British Fascism*, No. 11, May 1931.

10 The Young Britons 'were an avowedly non-political movement for pre-adoles-
    cent children set up by the Conservatives in competition with the Socialist Sunday
    Schools.' David Jarvis, 'Mrs Maggs and Betty: The Conservative Appeal to Women
    Voters in the 1920s,' *20th Century British History*, 5, 2 (1994), 129–52.
11 Beatrix Campbell, *The Iron Ladies* (London, 1987), p.57.
12 'Women's Loyalty,' *British Fascism*, No. 4, New Series, June 1934.
13 Martin Pugh, *Women and the Women's Movement in Britain, 1914–1959* (London,
    1992), p.31.
14 R. Lintorn-Orman, 'The B.P. Scouts and Girl Guides,' *British Fascism*, No. 21,
    Summer 1932.
15 *British Fascism*, No. 19, March 1932.
16 *British Fascism*, No. 19, March 1932.
17 *British Fascism*, No. 19, March 1932.
18 Colin Cross, *The Fascists in Britain* (London, 1961), pp.57–8.
19 '600 Children Entertained: Fascist Children's Club Christmas Party,' *The Fascist
    Bulletin*, 23 January 1926.
20 *British Fascism*, No. 1, June 1930.
21 'It has been suggested that new images of the sexually unfulfilled spinster and
    the mannish lesbian were also increasingly common in popular representations.
    Women's magazines in the 20s, for example, cited psychological theories to urge
    women to preserve their femininity and seek marriage, and warned readers
    against following the example of "the woman who tries to be a man; those
    stiff-collared, short-haired, tailor-suited imitation males with which our clubs
    and streets are now abounding."' Alison Oram, 'Repressed and Thwarted, or
    Bearer of the New World? The Spinster in Inter-war Feminist Discourses,'
    Women's History Review, 1, 3 (1992), 413–34.
22 Anthony M. Ludovici, *Woman: A Vindication* (London, 1923), p.229. Ludovici
    was a staunch fellow traveller of the Right, and associated with Captain Ramsay's
    Right Club in the late 1930s. See *Who's Who*.
23 Anthony M. Ludovici, *Woman: A Vindication*, p.231.
24 Barbara Storm Farr, *The Development and Impact of Right Wing Politics in Britain,
    1903–1932* (New York, 1987), p.55.
25 HO45/24967
26 Arnold Spencer Leese, *Out of Step: Events in the Two Lives of an Anti-Jewish Camel
    Doctor* (London, 1951), p.49.
27 Gisela C. Lebzelter, *Political Anti-Semitism in Britain 1918–1939* (Oxford, 1978), p.71.
28 It was BF policy that 'a contributory qualification for the granting of electoral
    privilege shall be the attainment of a standard of civic worth. The age limit is
    to be raised to 25.' *The British Lion*, July 1928.
29 Quoted in Robert Skidelsky, *Oswald Mosley* (London, 1975), p.291.
30 PRO30/69/221
31 HO144/19069/23

32   HO45/25386/37–40

33   HO45/25386/37–40

34   This portrayal of the BF as a para-military organization-cum-drinking society was not reinforced by the organization itself, however. Indeed, the BF press reported on the illness of their Founder in the most sympathetic light, while leaving the causes ambiguous, and emphasized that her debility was the result of her dedication to the cause. Of her first serious illness, *British Fascism* reported that at last she was recovering. 'She was taken ill very early in July, largely as a result of nearly ten years strenuous overwork for the organization. She had a bad heart attack and a serious fall which resulted in concussion, and for some time her life was in danger.' *British Fascism*, No. 22, October 1932.

35   Graduation from the BF to the BUF was indeed a common path for male members. However, I can only identify two prominent women who later joined Mosley: Viscountess Downe and Miss Millicent Bullivant who had been a BF member in West Ham before joining the BUF.

36   Frederic Mullaly, *Fascism Inside England* (London, 1946), p.19. In fact, Mullaly was the first to tell the story of the conception of the British Fascisti in Lintorn Orman's Somerset kitchen garden.

37   Rebecca West, *The Meaning of Treason* (London, 1949), p.59. Cross also inflated estimations of Lintorn-Orman's age, describing her as a 'forthright spinster of thirty-seven with a taste for mannish clothes.' Colin Cross, *The Fascists in Britain*, p.57. This inaccuracy in the reporting of Lintorn-Orman's age is perhaps caused by the confusion between herself and her mother. The Home Office files also call her 'Mrs' on occasion. Her mother was prominent in the BF and did not leave the organization until a very late date. Mrs Lintorn-Orman was awarded the Order of the Faces, First Class, in 1928, and she attended many BF functions, including one at the Lyceum Club which was reported by the *Times* on 25 February 1925. Also in attendance at this meeting were Lady Chadwick, Mrs Bromley and Lady Huntington.

38   Griffiths has attempted to rehabilitate Lintorn-Orman's reputation somewhat by noting the former miscalculations in the claims of her age, and emphasizing the negative connotations of her having been labelled a middle-aged spinster. Richard Griffiths, *Fellow Travellers of the Right* (London, 1980), p.85. Thurlow describes her as a 'spirited young middle-class woman who was concerned about the growing industrial unrest and threat to property posed by the emergence of a socialist Labour party and an a alleged communist menace.' Richard Thurlow, *Fascism in Britain* (Oxford, 1987), p.51. He shows compassion for her substance abuse which contributed to the disrepute of the movement. However, Thurlow does see the relative failure of the BF as symptomatic of the lack of strong leadership and the absence of a leadership cult.

39   Barbara Storm Farr, *The Development and Impact of Right-Wing Politics in Britain 1903–1932*, p.vi.

40 'East London Women's Units,' *The British Lion*, December 1927. Similarly, in 1928 male members were castigated for tardiness in paying their subscriptions: 'If a Fascist fails to pay his subscriptions he is casting an unfair burden on his brother Fascist, or worse still, on a comrade of the Women's Units.' *The British Lion*, No. 25, [n.d.] This attitude certainly demonstrated that the BF had little regard for the contemporary trend of young women insisting on paying their own share.

41 R. Lintorn-Orman, 'Women's Loyalty,' *British Fascism*, No. 4, New Series, June 1934.

42 'Recruits for London Special Patrol,' *British Fascism*, No. 22, October 1932.

43 The presence of Amy Johnson in her pantheon of loyal women was compatible with Lintorn-Orman's stand on British re-armament. 'There is one hope for the Empire. A strong Army, a strong Navy, and most important of all, the strongest Air Force in the world. Britain has always ruled the waves and shall rule the Air.' 'Fascism by the Founder,' *The British Lion*, No. 30, April 1929.

44 R. Lintorn-Orman, 'Women's Loyalty,' *British Fascism*, No. 4, New Series, June 1934.

45 R. Lintorn-Orman, 'Women's Loyalty,' *British Fascism*, No. 4, New Series, June 1934.

46 R. Lintorn-Orman, 'Women's Loyalty,' *British Fascism*, No. 4, New Series, June 1934. It is interesting to note how these appeals to women are almost identical to those made by the Conservative Party in the same period. As Jarvis has shown, 'party propaganda frequently portrayed women as the real locus of power in the household – the source of parental authority, the manager of the domestic budget and the decisive influence on the family's voting habits.' David Jarvis, 'Mrs Maggs and Betty: The Conservative Appeal to Women Voters in the 1920s,' *20th Century British History*, 4, 2 (1994), 129–52.

47 *British Fascism*, No. 19, March 1932.

48 *British Lion*, No. 30, April 1929. These comments were made at the time when the 'Colonel' Barker scandal was front page news, and the BF was anxious to dissociate itself from the National Fascisti of which s/he had been a leading member. See *Who's Who*.

49 Quoted in *Evening News*, 24 April 1926.

50 *Daily Mail*, 25 September 1925.

51 Molly Izzard, *A Heroine in Her Time: A Life of Dame Helen Gwynne-Vaughan, 1879–1967* (London, 1969), p.231.

52 Communist Party and the OMS, *The Times*, 26 September 1925.

53 HO144/19069/34–35

54 'The leader of the New Party has, in short, become a Fascist in theory, if not in name, whether his courage will extend as far as owning the name with pride remains to be seen.' *British Fascism*, No. 18, 1 February 1932.

55 'Important Notice,' *British Fascism*, No. 22, October 1932.

56 The following were deprived of their Order of the Fasces in the summer of

1933: Neil Francis-Hawkins, Mr Hirst, Mrs Fitzroy-Clarke, E.G. Mandeville Roe, Miss I.N.G. Ray, Mrs Swinburne, Mrs Passy, Miss P. Chaney, Mrs R.C. Lucas, Captain E. Smith, Miss Clare, Miss C.N. Kirby, Mr Knight and Miss Pridmore. See *British Fascism*, Special Summer Propaganda Number, 1933.

57 HO144/19069/202

58 HO144/19069/199–200

59 HO144/20140/297–99

60 Wilson was in charge of the BF by this point due to the fact that the organization was deeply in debt and he, 'interested in the question of fascism in this country ... agreed to advance 500 pounds with which pressing debts were liquidated. There is still a considerable amount owing, and the 500 pounds is exhausted. Colonel Wilson, in order to obtain payment of the loan is now compelled either to force BF Ltd. into liquidation or obtain the financial backing from other persons.' HO144/20142/70–71.

61 HO144/20142/70–71

62 HO144/20144/261–74

63 R.B.D. Blakeney, 'British Fascism', *The Nineteenth Century and After*, 97, (January 1925), 132–42.

64 'Speakers' Class,' *The Fascist Bulletin*, 29 August 1925.

65 *Evening News*, 5 May 1927.

66 *Morning Post*, 5 May 1927.

67 HO144/19070/270

68 On 11 November 1927, for example, members of the London Special Patrol and the Women's Units marched to the Cenotaph and attended a memorial service at Westminster Abbey where the entire west transept was reserved for some 600 fascists. 'The reservation of the main part of the Abbey and the presence of the mayor and council of Westminster at the memorial service of the Empire was the greatest honour and compliment that has ever been paid to us in the history of the organization.' 'Memorial Service at Westminster Abbey,' *British Lion*, No. 24, December 1927.

69 'Reds Raid Women's Camp at Lyndhurst,' *The Fascist Bulletin*, No. 8, 15 August 1925.

70 R.L. Lintorn-Orman, 'Women's Units,' *The Fascist Bulletin*, No. 8, 15 August 1925.

71 'The Women's Unit Lorry,' *The British Lion*, No. 27 [n.d.].

72 *British Fascism*, May 1934.

73 *British Fascism*, No. 21, Summer, 1932.

74 *The British Lion*, No. 32, June 1929.

75 *The British Lion*, No. 28, 1929. Members could also purchase photographs of the funeral of the late Miss Brigg for 8d. each, large size 2/6 each.

76 *The British Lion*, No. 29, 1929.

77 'Investigator,' 'The Fascist Movement in Great Britain,' *The Socialist Review*, 1 (February 1926), 22–9.

78 '600 Children Entertained: Fascist Children's Clubs Christmas Party,' *The Fascist Bulletin*, 30 January 1926.

79 In 1931 the BF formed Fascist Cadet Corps for older boys and girls, and by this point they hoped to gain more support from male members: 'Men – Here's your chance! So far, the Women's Units have done nearly all the work for the FCCs. It was their job; they are more suited for it. Now, with the Cadet Corps, the Men's Units can do their full share.' *British Fascism*, No. 14, September 1931.

80 Cross submits that Lintorn-Orman's 'only success was with the women, who patrolled the London streets in uniform on a mixed mission of rescuing prostitutes and heckling communists. The women also held mock political meetings which ended in rough houses as they practised their techniques for ejecting hecklers.' Colin Cross, *The Fascists in Britain*, p.62. It is curious that Cross should say the LSP tried to rescue prostitutes. I have found no evidence for this. It was Mary Allen who made a nuisance of herself in the mid-1920s by embarking on such missions, and it is possible that Cross has confused the two organizations. See HO144/21933/8–9 for complaints by a presumed prostitute who alleged that she was being harassed by Allen.

81 *The British Lion*, No. 32, June 1929.

82 Frederic Mullaly, *Fascism Inside England*, p.19.

83 HO144/21933/54. No membership lists exist. Part of the reason for their absence can be accounted for by the fact that when the BF headquarters in Brighton were raided in July of 1925, 'the raiders carried off a sum of money, the membership registration records, badge and private documents.' *The Times*, 24 July 1925. Further, when prominent members defected to the BUF, they carried off with them BF subscription lists.

84 'Investigator,' 'The Fascist Movement in Great Britain,' *Socialist Review*, 1 (February 1926), 22–9.

85 When the organization tried to put their cross-class ideal into practice, their actions revealed snobbery and ignorance of the working classes. This can be exemplified by the work of the Women's Units in the East End where they held kitchen meetings, attracting those Lintorn-Orman described as 'the poorest kind of women, who were among the very keenest members. This, to my mind, is due to two things – the wearing of the uniforms by all members who can afford to do so, this doing away with class distinction, and the fact that kitchen meetings are held in the poorest parts of the cities.' R.L. Lintorn-Orman, 'Fascist Sunday Schools and Kitchen Meetings,' *Fascist Bulletin*, 13 June 1925. When the Scottish Women's headquarters opened in Edinburgh in 1925, special emphasis was placed on poorer women and a 'Helping Hand Fund' was started for 'our poorer Fascist sisters.' The BF attracted members of the middle classes and some minor aristocrats, and their only contact with women of the lower classes seems to have been in the form of intended philanthropy.

86 The BF reserved special criticism for those titled women who defected to the socialist camp, and during the 1929 General Election they wrote: 'Lady Cynthia Mosley's chief plank in her speeches to women electors in her constituency was the promise that, if they voted Socialist, they would all have pearl necklaces and fur coats like the ones she wore. It would have been somewhat more convincing if "her ladyship" could have proved that she had obtained her own through Socialism!' *The British Lion*, No. 32, June 1929. Lintorn-Orman was no class rebel, and 'it is symptomatic that one of her more constructive ideas as a proposal to cut taxes on gentlefolk, so they could employ more servants and thus ease unemployment.' Roger Eatwell, *Fascism: A History* (London, 1995), p.176.

87 *The British Lion*, 7 January 1927. For details about Lucia Foster Welch's involvement in the BF and the current controversy over the naming of a new student village after her, see Tony Kushner and Ken Lunn, 'Memory, Forgetting and Absence: The Politics of Naming on the English South Coast,' *Patterns of Prejudice*, 30, 2 (1997), 31–50.

88 Webster was born in Hertfordshire, the last of the fourteen children of Robert Lee Cooper Beran, a director of Barclay's Bank and in his youth an intimate friend of Henry (Cardinal) Manning. It was ironic that the daughter of a banker should have dedicated her life to exposing the conspiracy of international finance. She was educated at Brownshill and then Westfield College Hampstead and remained very keen on the utility of higher education for women. She sought her freedom from the constraints of Victorian womanhood and her strict evangelical upbringing through education and travel. Like other BF women, she had little sympathy for the suffragists who were similarly attempting to emancipate themselves from Victorianism. As she recalled, 'the counterblast to this system of repression was the campaign for "Women's Rights", for the Suffrage Movement was just beginning. I took no part in this for I could not see that the vote would prove the panacea for all the disabilities from which women suffered at this period. What they all needed was an object in life.' Nesta Webster, *Spacious Days: An Autobiography* (London, 1949), p.138.

89 *Daily Telegraph*, 19 November 1927.

90 Nesta Webster, *World Revolution: The Plot Against Civilization* (London, 1921), p.322. Webster went on the say: 'Nothing is more extraordinary than the way apparently intelligent women have allowed themselves to be drawn into a plot which they will be the chief victims. Women have obviously far more to lose than men by the destruction or even by the decrease of civilization, whilst the Suffragist has everything to lose by the abolition of the parliamentary system which accords her the right she has so long demanded, but the modern Illuminati, following Weishaupt's precepts by "flattering their vanity," and giving them hints of emancipation, have succeeded in persuading numbers of women to assist in digging their own graves.' p.323.

91 *The British Lion*, No. 28 [n.d.]

92 *The Fascist Bulletin*, No. 37, 27 March 1926.

93 *The British Lion*, No. 25 [n.d.].

94 Stanley Payne, 'The Concept of Fascism,' in ed. Stein Ugelvik Larsen et. al., *Who Were the Fascists: Social Roots of European Fascism* (Bergen, 1980), p.19.

95 Quoted in David Baker, 'The Extreme Right in the 1920s: Fascism in a Cold Climate, or 'Conservatism with Knobs On'?,' in ed. Mike Cronin, *The Failure of British Fascism*, (London, 1996), p.24.

96 Nesta Webster, 'Communism or Fascism,' *The Fascist Bulletin*, 1 May 1926.

97 The BF made some attempt to win the attention of the young generation of women. In 1926 *The Fascist Bulletin* announced an essay competition, the conditions of which were that 'men competitors will submit an essay on: "A man's opinion on the modern young woman," and women competitors will submit an essay on: "A women's opinion on the modern young man."' *The Fascist Bulletin*, 20 March 1926. Interestingly, this flirtatious attempt to awake sexual feeling met with no response, the essays never being published in the paper. Reactions to franchise extension in 1928 were mixed, but the prevalent view was that the Flapper would have to be trained in the arts of citizenship before she merited the vote. Nesta Webster warned that 'those girls will live to curse the day and the men which gave them this dangerous weapon.' *The British Lion*, May 1927. Webster had particular contempt for the new woman and later reflected that if women had greater access to education we would 'have heard less about the escapades of the Bright Young Things, who could not find any other outlet for their animal spirits.' Nesta Webster, *Spacious Days*, p.82.

98 *British Fascism*, Extra Autumn Issue, 1933.

99 *British Fascism*, Extra Autumn Issue, 1933.

100 *British Fascism*, No.22, October 1932.

Chapter 2

Women in the British Union of Fascists:

Organization and Forms of Participation

The British Union of Fascists (BUF) was consistent in claiming that it adhered to the principle of the equality of the sexes, that women would be granted unprecedented political representation in the future Corporate State, and that fascism was the ideal home for the patriotic but independent and active woman. That the BUF's model for organizing women was the Continental Fascist or the Nazi one was denied, and it is in the context of differentiating the treatment of women in his movement from the German example that Oswald Mosley declared that

> we have a higher percentage of women candidates than any other party in this country and they play a part of basic equality. We are pledged to complete sex equality. The German attitude towards women has always been different from the British, and my movement has been largely built up by the *fanaticism* of women; they hold ideals with tremendous passion. Without the women I could not have got a quarter of the way.[1]

While Mosley's statement had an eerie resemblance to Hitler's declaration upon coming to power in 1933 – 'I can only confess that without the endurance and really loving devotion of women to the movement I could have never led the party to victory'[2] – the organization of women in the BUF must be seen as having developed within the British context and with a sideward glance to the successful enlistment of women by the British party system during the inter-war period. By examining the structure of the party hierarchy and the status of the Women's Section, the changing provisions for female leadership with the frequent reorganizations of the movement, and the many roles played by women fascists, it will be seen how female *fanaticism* was rewarded with confidence by the male leadership and how women's activism became indispensable to the movement.

Although BUF propaganda and self-promotion paid ample lip-service to the ideal of the equality of the sexes, the sections were divided by gender, and women were streamed into traditional female tasks from canvassing and spreading the word to being made responsible for keeping branch premises in orderly condition. This state of affairs has led to near consensus in the historiography, and confusion between gender segregation and female subordination to the male leadership. Reflecting on the fact that 'the Women's Section of the party was kept strictly segregated although it worked beside male branches,'[3] D.S. Lewis has surmised that the position of women in the BUF's hierarchy was illustrative of the movement's anti-feminism. With greater appreciation for the ambiguities in the movement's sexual politics, Martin Durham has emphasized that '*despite* the presence of a number of women among its prospective parliamentary candidates and the existence of women organizers at National Headquarters and locally, the movement's leadership was wholly male.'[4] This perspective is one that compares female and male power at face value, rather than delving into the dynamics within the structures provided for women's participation. By giving secondary priority to the impact of female leadership over other women, by paying less than adequate attention to fascist women's approval at occupying their own worlds within the movement, and by not taking into account that in actual personal experience BUF women bypassed rules and regulations by working in collaboration and in partnership with male members, the historiography has tended to perpetuate the spirit behind the BUF leadership's own rigid paradigm of gender compartmentalization.

It is too easy to fall into this tunnel vision by concentrating on men's understanding of the function of women members. For instance, Mosley's recollection of relations with his members focused on male camaraderie and the service of women: 'I joined in free discussion of politics which always prevailed among us, in the sports to which our spare time was often given, in the simple club-room gatherings where we would drink beer together or cups of tea prepared by women Blackshirts.'[5] In contrast, the Women's District Leader in Birmingham, Louise Irvine (née Fisher), remembered how as women members 'you weren't just tea makers, you know.'[6] That in practice the BUF was not as anti-woman as one might imagine does not give legitimacy to the fascist cause. However, stressing anti-feminism, misogyny and the repression of women has too often been used as another nail in the fascist coffin. It is in a sense reassuring to link British fascism's conflict with modernity and absolute negation of the liberal-democratic ethos with a view of women as the acquiescent victims of a male-chauvinist creed; but the successful cohesion of gender demands and the unification of male and female fanaticism in constructing the movement should instead alert us to the universal aspects of fascism.[7]

The Mystery of Membership

In keeping with the fascist movement's organization along revolutionary lines, the BUF never published its own membership figures. To complicate matters further, most branch lists and records were seized by Police during the operation of Defence Regulation 18B starting in May of 1940, and subsequently destroyed. Nonetheless, Special Branch and scholars alike have made many efforts to solve the mystery of membership, attempts which have been consistently thwarted by the hyperbolic statements made by BUF officials, the unreliability of the BUF's organizers in the regions, and the volatile pattern of fascist adherence throughout the 1930s.

At a Home Office meeting in November 1933, attended by the Permanent Under-Secretary, the head of MI5, the Commissioner of the Metropolitan Police and representatives from Special Branch, it was agreed that starting in April 1934 Special Branch and MI5 should begin systematic surveillance of the BUF. The widely varying estimates for general membership contained in the resulting files illustrate the difficulties in reaching conclusions on national totals. In August 1934 Special Branch estimated BUF membership at 50,000; in December 1935 the paying membership of the London Command was stated as 2,750; in March 1936 Special Branch put the active membership at 4,000; in an interview with the *Berliner Lokal-Anzeiger* in November 1936 Mosley was reported as claiming that the BUF had 500 branches and half a million members; in January 1938 the original 100 British Union (BU) prospective parliamentary candidates were recorded as having dwindled to 60; in December 1938 paying subscribers were said to total 6,600, of whom 3,600 were in the London Administration.[8]

Based on his thorough study of the official records, G.C. Webber has outlined the membership patterns of the BUF as a fall from a high point after 1934, a disastrous slump in 1935 and recovery thereafter, culminating in increased support in 1939–40 which attained a level not achieved since 1934.[9] These national figures, however, are given without regard to gender differentials, and it is only by examining specific areas of activity that we can come to some conclusions on the ratio of men to women in the movement. In analysing these specific areas, we see that the proportions of male to female members seem to have remained consistent throughout the period, with the possible exception of an acceleration of women's activism, if not numbers, in 1939–40.[10]

Special Branch observed the anonymous women Blackshirts stewarding meetings and participating in marches and processions (see Tables 2.1 and 2.2). These preliminary figures show that, on average, women represented 27 per cent of those attending fascist gatherings, and 23 per cent of those stewarding meetings. In surveying politicized social functions, Special Branch counted 480 persons attending the London Administration luncheon at the Criterion Restaurant on 1 March 1940. Of the 134 guests identified by name, 50 were women (37 per cent), many of them familiar figures in this history.[11] After the war, former members held a '18B Social and Dance' on 1 December 1945 at the Royal Hotel in London; while it was estimated that 1,150 persons attended, Special Branch only identified 132 by name, including 25 women (19 per cent).[12]

Why was Special Branch attentive to the gender divide? Was it frivolous voyeurism on the part of the authorities to identify the women Blackshirts, or was the motive more pragmatic? On the one hand, the movement's potential for disrupting public order would seem to decrease with the increase of female support, and its para-military character diminish. On the other hand, the organizational strength of the movement would be enhanced by the higher participation of women. Was the success of the Conservative and Labour parties' shift to mass democracy not assured by the effective mobilization of female support and the application of their organizational aptitudes? Whether Special Branch was reflecting on

Table 2.1. **Women stewards at BUF meetings**

Date	Venue	Male	Female (%)	
25 April 1934	Albert Hall	1,500	500	(25%)
24 July 1935	West Ham Town Hall	180	20	(10%)
26 October 1935	Porchester Hall	70	30	(30%)
6 March 1936	Harlesden	12	4	(25%)
16 June 1939	Earl's Court	3,000	1,100	(27%)

Table 2.2. **Proportion of women at BUF meetings**

Date	Venue	Men	Women (%)	
9 September 1934	London	3000	450	(13%)
3 March 1935	London	540	160	(23%)
7 May 1936	Victoria Park	1,120	180	(14%)
7 June 1936	London	1,400	260	(16%)
2 May 1937	London	800	250	(24%)
5 July 1937<	Trafalgar Square	1,900	360	(16%)
4 October 1937	Brixton	2,770	630	(19%)
19 April 1940	London (Women's Peace Meeting)	100	800	(89%)

these universal issues cannot be verified. It is nevertheless worth noting that similar reports on extreme-left activity did not usually identify the gender ratios, and only when tallying up anti-fascist arrests was the gender of interrupters and protesters made apparent.

While most approximations of national membership are given without regard to gender, we are fortunate that a few official estimates of BUF participation run parallel to the movement's own segregated organization by offering a breakdown of male and female membership.[13] Some indications of the composition of branch membership can be gleaned from a sample compiled by the BUF's investigator in January 1935. This showed that the Vauxhall Branch had a book membership of 160 and a paying membership of 40, most of whom were 'young men and women of an average age ... of 19/20, the majority of who are of the illiterate type.' The Seaforth Branch had a book membership of 150, only 20 of whom were active, and 'in addition there is a woman membership of 17, active and paying.' The situation at the Wallasey Branch was that 'internal discord' had led to a serious lapse in activism, and a former membership of 85 men and 35 (29 per cent) women had fallen to 37 and 22 (37 per cent) respectively by 1935.[14]

We have another example of the gender complexion of BUF branches from the membership list Robert Saunders, District Leader for Dorset, compiled for Dorset West, South and North. Precipitating his arrest and internment under DR 18B, when Police searched Saunders' home in 1940 they missed the following list which he had hidden between the pages of an encyclopaedia. In 1939 total BU membership in Dorset was 59 persons, among whom 15 were women (25 per cent).[15]

Special Branch was not alone in monitoring BUF membership and their mobilization of women, and on 12 June 1934 the Labour

Party sent out a 'Questionnaire on Local Fascist Activities' to 900 Secretaries of all Divisional Labour Parties, Industrial Trades Councils and Party Agents. By 27 July replies had been received from 380 organizations. The 'Questionnaire' consisted of eleven questions, including two on women and youth support (see Table 2.3). In their bird's eye-view of local fascism just weeks after Mosley's highly publicized Olympia Rally, Labour Party officials identified the existence of a fascist organizations for women in at least 55 districts. According to these figures, on average, women

Table 2.3. **A bird's eye view of local fascism in 1934: Labour Party estimates of BUF branch membership, and the organization of women and youth: Responses to Question (9) Is there any evidence of local Fascist movements being organized in connection with: (a) women; (b) youth?**

District/Constituency	Membership estimates	9(a) Women	9(b) Youth
Sutton DLQ	*ca.*1000	yes	yes
Bristol	*ca.*500	yes	yes
Bristol (East)	?	yes (+ section)	yes
Bolton	43 men/18 women	yes	yes
Liverpool	750–1000	yes	yes
Loughborough/Leicestershire	<50	at least one woman	yes
South Paddington	3000–4000	yes	yes
S. West St. Pancras	?	?	?
Ealing	*ca.*600	no	no
Stoke	200–300	yes	?
East Grinstead	200	yes (+branch)	yes (+branch)
Horsham	?	yes	yes
Worthing	over 1500	yes	yes
City of Leeds	100–200	yes	yes
Sheffield	350	no	no
Harrogate	?	yes	yes
Dumfries	'considerable'	yes	yes
Crewe	80	'very little'	yes
Bodmin	'considerable'	no	yes
Gateshead	7 men/2 women/5 youth	yes	yes
Durham	?	no	no
Epping	?	no	no
Portsmouth	20 active, 50–100 non-active	yes	yes
Maldon	?	yes	yes
Farnborough	?	no	no
Balham and Tooting	'weak'	no	no
Newcastle (N)	?	yes	yes
Coventry	?	yes (*ca.*12)	?
Wakefield	?	?	?

District/Constituency	Membership estimates	9(a) Women	9(b) Youth
Cambridge	no	no	no
Derby	no	no	no
Exeter	ca.20	no	no
Barnard Castle	ca.12	?	yes
Hackney South	no	?	?
Winchester	no	no	no
West Derby Div. of Liverpool	150 men/ 60 women	yes (+headquarters)	yes
Westminster, Abbey Division	no	?	?
Newcastle (West)	no	no	yes
Dewsbury	?	?	?
Leeds (N-E)	60 men	yes	yes
Howdenshire	no	no	no
Bedford	'decreasing'	yes	yes
Luton	30	yes	?
Reading	40–400	yes	yes
Newbury	'vague idea'	yes	?
Carlisle	1–2	no	?
Plymouth	'nothing definite'	yes	yes
Darlington	100	no	no
Ilford	'small'	?	?
Bournemouth	no	no	no
Southampton	'not very large'	yes (+section)	no
St Albans	ca.30	yes	yes
Folkestone	ca.150	yes	yes
Borough of Hythe	?	yes	no
Ashford	?	yes (+woman organizer)	no
Gravesend	200	yes	yes
Tonbridge	'weak'	yes	yes
Ashton under Lyne	50–100	no	yes
Wavertree	'fair'	yes	yes
Withington	no	yes	yes
Southport	200	yes (+section)	yes
Hampstead	no	'some women'	yes
Brixton	ca.30	no	?
Streatham	ca.30	yes	?
Brentford and Chiswick	'small but active'	yes	yes
Harrow	no	?	?
Twickenham	'small but active'	yes	?
Wellingborough	ca.50	?	?
Kingston on Thames	ca.30	yes	yes
Richmond	'small'	no	no
Wimbledon	ca.100	yes	yes
Sutton	6 active men	yes	yes
Central Hull	?	yes	yes
Middlesbro'(East)	60–70	yes	?
York	80–160	yes	no
Doncaster	'about 60, several young women'	yes	yes
Ripon	no	yes	?
Llandaff and Barry	20–92	?	?

District/Constituency	Membership estimates	9(a) Women	9(b) Youth
East Fife	?	?	no
Edinburgh	no	yes	yes
Edinburgh (West)	?	yes (+canvassing)	?

LP/FAS/34/267–399: File of reports of no branches

District	Membership	9(a) Women	9(b) Youth
Hallam (Sheffield)	?	yes	?
Brightlingsea	150	yes	?
Clacton	70	yes	?
East Islington	?	no	no
Wallasey	aa.120	yes	yes

constituted 24 per cent of members. While taking into account that the 'Questionnaire' was circulated only this one time, and that the sample was highly selective because not all party officials replied, the Labour Party's impression of the BUF in the summer of 1934 was that it was overwhelmingly a party of youth, which ably recruited and organized women.

With only these random sources on membership available, researchers studying the demographics of the BUF have relied on the willingness of former members to come forward and give testimony. Brewer's study of 'Mosley's Men' in the West Midlands is based on a sample of fifteen respondents, only one of whom is female. As his title blatantly suggests, Brewer has not included gender as one of his analytical categories. While he has admitted that the BUF was open on equal terms to men and women, he has nonetheless reached the debatable conclusions that 'in general, however, women members were few. This accords with the generalization observed throughout the world that women mobilize politically much slower than men irrespective of what party it may concern.'[16] In a numerically more ambitious project, Stephen Cullen has studied a sample of forty-three former BUF members, only four of whom were women. While Brewer takes his lack of sources as substantiation for his claims of women's support, Cullen sees in his sample that it 'is a considerable distortion of actual male/female balance within the movement ... . An educated guess might put female membership at a quarter to a third of the total.'[17] By collating the various figures mentioned, an even safer assessment would be that women represented 25 per cent of BUF participants and members.

Leadership and Controversy: The Women's Section and the Structure of Women's Organization

As a reflection of the ceaseless turn-overs in membership and conflicts within the leadership, the persistent urgency for retrenchment, and differing interpretations on the proper application of 'fascist' techniques, the BUF underwent frequent structural reorganization. These factors, contributing to internal instability and dissension, affected the women's organization at every stage. Furthermore, the women were certainly not immune to the scandals within the movement, and their full integration in the partisan politics, 'familial' squabbles, and factionalism is evidence for their inclusion.

How did the BUF institutionalize women's support for British fascism? What can the evolution of the organizational and hierarchical structure tell us about the male leadership's commitment to women's full and equal participation? The Women's Section of the BUF was first established in March 1933, under the leadership of Maud Lady Mosley (holding the titles of Director of Organization of the Women's Section and Chairman of the Central Council of Women's Branches) half a year after the launch of the movement. That the mobilization of women seemed to have been an afterthought was not the result of the absence of debate on female participation before 1933. Already in the New Party

> there was much discussion (much of it heated it was said) at Mosley's headquarters whether Youth Clubs should be mixed or confined to the male sex. The latter conception won the day, but not until the advocates of mixed clubs had expressed their criticism forcibly and urged that to confine the clubs to young men would be emulating the Hitlerist organization.[18]

The short-lived New Party did not organize women as methodically as the BUF was to do, nor did the early stages of Mosleyite fascism accept that women should be placed on the front lines of battle and be exposed to the 'broken bottles and razor blades with which our communist opponents have conducted the argument.'[19] However, the New Party was already cognisant of the efficiency of women in political organization. The prominence of Lady Cynthia Mosley in launching the New Party in the spring and summer of 1931 and in the General Election campaign of 1931 attests to this fact.

Why the politically inexperienced 'Ma' Mosley, and not Lady Cynthia, the former Labour MP and Mosley's long-time political partner, took up the directorship of the Women's Section can be traced to two factors.[20] First, Lady Cynthia Mosley clearly was not a fascist enthusiast, having been a genuine supporter of the Labour Party and showing signs of disquiet with her husband's conversion to fascism. Secondly, before she could be reconciled to Mosley's fascism, Cynthia Mosley died of pleurisy on 16 May 1933, at the age of thirty-four. Ready in the wings, Maud Mosley announced: 'When my son married Lady Cynthia, she took her place by his side. Now she is dead there must be someone to help him in his work and I am going to do my best to fill the gap.'[21] Consequently, the early life of the Women's Section was characterized by a mother's protectiveness for her son, rather than symbolizing the equal partnership between husband and wife in a political team which could then be projected on the national level.

In the first instance, premises at 233 Regent St. in London were placed rent free at the disposal of the BUF by a sympathizer and were used for a time as an enrolment depot and women's headquarters. By January 1934 the Women's Section was moved to 12 Lower Grosvenor Place, also the headquarters of the Youth Section, with Esther Lady Makgill – wife of Sir Donald Makgill who was co-founder of the January Club – serving as the Officer in Charge, and Mary Richardson acting as her assistant. Having their own headquarters was crucial for maintaining the women's interest and recruitment levels in this period as the *Fascist Headquarters Bulletin* (1933), under the heading of 'Lady Members,' stipulated that 'ladies are no longer allowed access to NHQ premises, except to attend mixed classes and concerts and at such times as may be from time to time authorized.'[22] Beginning in March, the Women's Section began fortnightly publication of *The Woman Fascist*, described as an 'enterprising little paper which will deal with news and problems peculiar to women members.'[23] In April of 1934 Mary Richardson replaced Lady Makgill who was forced to resign after being suspended as a result of serious deficiencies in the funds of the Women's Section. One of Richardson's early initiatives was the creation of a National Club for Fascist Women, opened at the headquarters of the Women's Section on 24 April 1934. The first sign of the ebbing away of the Women's Section's independence came when, in 1934, women's headquarters were again moved, this time to a former chapel adjoining the National Headquarters at 33 King's Road, and formally opened on 7 December by Oswald Mosley. In autumn of that year *The Woman Fascist* had already ceased publication, and it was promised that women's issues and news would be integrated into the BUF's main publications.

Maud Mosley had her offices first at the Grosvenor address, and later in the Black House. While she remained an active leader, responsible for paper-sellers, secretaries, and even stewardesses and was very energetic in her visits to provincial branches, Maud Mosley worked in parallel with the other women leaders. As we will see, this lack of definition in the women's hierarchy led to much conflict and discontent. By July 1935, with the first round of reorganization of the executive structure of the movement, Neil Francis-Hawkins temporarily assumed charge of the Women's Section, along with his other duties as Director General of Propaganda.

Personal antipathies, professional incompatibility and conflicts of interests characterized the Women's Section in the period up to 1935. Special Branch was very concerned with the shifts in BUF leadership and its reports offer one version of an administrative history of activities at National Headquarters. According to these, it is clear that women left their mark on the national organization by contributing to the management and mismanagement of the movement. It must also be assumed that it was precisely because the Women's Section contributed to the exacerbation of conflicts that, after 1935, its independence was eroded and it came to occupy a subservient position in the hierarchy.

Fascism and the Criminal Mind: Sex and Scandal

The first scandal to agitate the Women's Section was when Lady Makgill was caught embezzling party funds. A chartered accountant had to be engaged to examine the books and go through the various transactions. Recalling the incident, 'Ma' Mosley later wrote to her son that 'Lady Makgill did nothing but use the premises for her own business and told her secretary "If Lady Mosley were fool enough to sweat over county branches she could."'[24] While the depth of Lady Makgill's ideological commitment to fascism and her work ethic are open to question, her difficulty in remaining within the bounds of the law concerning financial transactions was a more enduring character trait. In July 1937 the communist *Daily Worker* had pleasure in bringing attention to the fact that Lady Makgill

who has just been sentenced to six months for seven charges of using worthless cheques to obtain goods and money on false pretences ... helped in 1933 to organize the women's section of the BUF. She seems to have done so pretty casually. What she said to the reporter was: 'I helped to organize the women's section of Sir Oswald Mosley's Fascists, though Heaven knows I'm no believer in Fascism'.[25]

Ironically, while criminal activity led to Lady Makgill's expulsion, the BUF was not untainted by the past criminal activity of its members, and her successor, Mary Richardson, was described by Special Branch as 'an ex-Suffragette, who has convictions for wilful damage, arson, assault on police etc., incurred with her "votes for women" activities.'[26]

That in the early years the BUF was hampered by sex scandals and the free reign of criminal elements can be partially accounted for by Lord Rothermere's recruitment campaign on the BUF's behalf in 1934, his deployment of an arsenal of gutter press techniques to stimulate recruitment, and his cheap shots at women's sexuality. Rothermere's bellow 'Hurray for the Blackshirts' was proceeded by the *Sunday Dispatch's* equally enthusiastic declaration 'Beauty Joins the Blackshirts.'[27] In May 1934 the *Sunday Dispatch* offered a prize of five pounds for the photograph of the most beautiful woman Blackshirt – in uniform, and the *Evening Standard* requested postcards to be sent in responding to the question: 'Why I Like the Blackshirts.'[28] Before Rothermere withdrew his support – shortly after the disastrous publicity spawned by the violent debacle at the Olympia Rally of 7 June 1934 – his newspapers were plastered with photographs of Blackshirted women practising ju-jitsu, marching, and saluting. Among the thousand words these pictures must have spoken, Young Communist Leaguers interpreted them as coquettish invitations to young men, 'come up and see me sometimes, look at the girls we've got.'[29] Indeed, political opponents delighted at the free reign of criminal elements in the BUF and the Communist Party related:

A glance through the newspapers of the past year show that a list of ripe and juicy specimens whom no decent and reasonable British workman would trust. The parade includes a pimp, whom a Portsmouth magistrate (not knowing he was dealing with a coming leader of Fascist Britain!) had sentenced to three months! Following him came Burglar, would be but unlucky burglar, and a collection of others which reeks of scandal and unpleasant things. A mob of young bucks raided the offices of the *Daily Worker* at night and attacked an old man of 67! It was not liked at Fascist Headquarters, either, when in the recent Brighton Trunk Murder trial Kay Fredericks was revealed as a BUF member.[30]

Sex scandals added spice to the strain of criminality. In April 1934 the reputation of women fascists was tarnished by allegations of sexual licentiousness at the Brixton Branch. The Brixton Branch had to change address 'in consequence of complaints lodged respecting the loose character of members of both sexes attached to the Branch. The Brixton Road address was in filthy and unsanitary condition, and it was reported to the landlord that men and women fascists were habitually sleeping there together.'[31] Significantly, four women were expelled from the movement because of their 'immoral conduct' – Misses Ward, William, Dixie and Mrs Welsh – while the men, who must by necessity have acted as accessories to their offences against propriety, were not expelled.[32] Along the same lines, the 'Labour Party Questionnaire on Local Fascist Activities' claimed that in Stoke 'loose women appear to be plentiful ... "it only wants a red light on the door!"'[33] With these incidents in mind, the common taunt to women members selling BUF literature on the streets as 'Mosley's whores' can be seen in context.[34]

Sexual scandals were not particular to the rank and file, and in December 1934 Special Branch reported on an affair between Mrs Joyce, William Joyce's first wife, and E.H. Piercey. It was reported that Piercey and Mrs Joyce were on 'more than ordinarily friendly terms,' and that 'the matter has been brought to a head owing to the fact that Mrs Joyce is about to be confined, and it is freely alleged that Piercey is responsible for her condition.'[35] As we have seen, women members were expelled for sexual misconduct, while Piercey was tactfully reappointed as Chief Inspector of Branches, away from London, so that the scandal could be avoided. Whereas there is evidence to suggest that one Michael Hay was expelled from the BUF for sodomy, heterosexual over-zealousness did not call for censure.[36]

The questionable ethics of women members and their precarious position in the BUF did not end there. In January 1935 there were reports of 'dissension between the Women's Section and the department dealing with organization which is controlled by F.M. Box. The head of the former (Lady Mosley) has complained that Major A. Cleghorn, when visiting branches in North East England recently, insulted some of their best people, with the result that they were leaving the movement.'[37] Within a week the situation became acute when Oswald Mosley appointed Richardson to take charge of part of the Lancashire area. Box and Lady Mosley were so opposed to this executive decision that Box had written out his resignation which he intended to present if Richardson was not withdrawn. As Lady Mosley wrote to her son in February 1935, 'then came Miss R. with her dishonest inefficiency, later backed by

Miss S. and Miss A. – in sullen opposition to me. I was a stumbling block to collaring the machine and all its resources.'[38] That this was partly a family squabble was demonstrated by the fact that 'Lady Mosley has been instructed by her son not to go to that county to annoy Miss Richardson. Lady Mosley would like to resign, and would do so if it were not that such an action might cause damage to the movement and harm the prestige of her son.'[39] By March of 1935, when the BUF embarked on its first major scheme of reorganization, it was reported that Lady Mosley was about to resign. Their conflict formed part of a larger scale feud within the increasingly dysfunctional British fascist family.

Lady Mosley's grandmotherly gentility was not necessarily suited to the rigours of fascist politics. However, her commitment to her son and to his movement was exemplified by her persistent meddling, moral hauteur and some considerable courage. While it was suspected that she was the source of Nazi officials' antagonism towards the BUF – having stated in an interview with a French journalist that 'Hitler was the greatest enemy of the BUF since people in this country would not join on account of the brutal methods in Germany'[40] – her public role in the BUF left her vulnerable to the brutal methods of BUF opponents in Britain. When she was visiting the Edinburgh and Dumfries Branch of the Women's Section in the summer of 1934, a Communist poster commanded 'Give Maud Some Bouquets,' an invitation to throwing stones. As one District Inspector later recalled, Lady Mosley 'entered fully into the life of the movement and was popular with the girls; she kept a motherly eye on some of the less staid and prettier ones and warned them of the hungry looks being cast in their direction by appreciative Blackshirts and by one high ranking officer in particular.'[41] But in the end, it was her sense of being unappreciated for her work and motherly concern by her own son, and even her belief that he made a fool of her in public, which motivated 'Ma' Mosley's resignation.

Maud Mosley's last words on the atmosphere of the Women's Section during her tenure made clear the urgent necessity for a purge of disreputable elements: 'Intrigue the whole time. Insubordination from people whose word you preferred to take to mine and who would disappear from the movement by your instructions. No, Tom, it is not quite good enough. There is a limit to one's endurance.'[42] The challenges to one's endurance exacerbated by mixing family life and politics were avoided thereafter: Mosley's second wife, Diana, was never an active member in the BUF.[43]

The First Purges: Reorganization and Retrenchment

Anne Brock-Griggs, the woman who rose to prominence in the national organization following the over-heated atmosphere of 1935, was credited with the fact that her 'advice has been instrumental in smoothing out friction on many occasions.'[44] And it was very much as a reaction to internal discord that a new constitution, rules and regulations were first announced in January 1935. The BUF was originally organized into areas, regions, branches, sub-branches and groups and further sub-divided at the local level into companies, sections and units. If there were enough women members a separate female branch was established.[45] The new organization was intended to give the BUF a broader base, to enforce discipline more effectively, and to build election machinery. The country was divided now into Northern and Southern zones with Anne Brock Griggs serving as Women's Organizer (Southern) and Olga Shore as Women's Organizer (Northern). While there were two women leaders, their authority over the women's organization was supreme. Divided now between Blackshirt and Political organization, with the Leader as the head of both, women's organizations were placed under the control of the Director of Political Organization, with the exception of the 'Special Division,' representing women who served as Blackshirts.[46] From the letters of concern written to the *Blackshirt* in the weeks following the announcement of these changes, it was clear that not all the revisions were favoured by women, especially those pertaining to women who had served in the Blackshirt divisions.

Not only did the reorganization of January 1935 serve to purge criminal elements, but it also, perhaps inadvertently, motivated the resignation of those unable to concede to the absence of democracy within the BUF. It was paradoxical that a British fascist should have been taken aback by the BUF's internal dictatorship and centralization of command, but that was indeed the case with Mrs H. Carrington Wood, a women's organizer in North London. She related that in response to the scheme of re-organization 'several women met at the house of one of the members to discuss proposals which would ensure the advancement under Fascism of the position of women in the country.' They proceeded to draft a petition which four of the women were to present to Sir Oswald Mosley. When it became known at National Headquarters that this meeting had taken place it was ruled out of order because, as Carrington-Wood explained, 'it was democratic ... . [I]t is the audacity and interference of a gang of bumptious men who have no respect for anyone who is not willing to serve as a tool to satisfy their own selfish ambitions.'[47] Carrington-Wood's resignation was as much a reaction against anti-democratic rule, as it was a protest against the false promises made to women members, who were now placed in increasingly dependent positions. To clear up any remaining confusion as to the movement's ideological character, the BUF was rechristened the British Union of Fascists and National Socialists in the autumn of 1936, thereafter the BU.[48]

The Second Purges: The Exacerbation of Dissent

When the Public Order Act banning the wearing of political uniforms and quasi-military organizations became law on 1 January 1937 the BU reorganized again, drafting a new constitution and changing titles and designations. Under the new constitution, women were to serve as Woman District Leader, Senior Women Team Leaders and Women Team Leaders. The system whereby England and Wales were divided into two zones – Northern and Southern – was abolished. The year of 1937 also inaugurated a winter of discontent for the BU, consisting of a round of resignations due in large part to a 70 per cent reduction of expenditures and the discharge of the majority of the staff at headquarters. While women no longer played decisive roles in the intrigues surrounding the bids by various 'authoritarian personalities' to win Mosley's favour, some were vocal in their disappointment with the direction of the movement, and others joined the rebel camp. Miss Black of the Accounts Department told a Special Branch informant of the deplorable conditions in her department where no proper balance sheets were kept. The various subsidiary companies were in a state of chaos, and the accountants simply arrived at some figures to satisfy Mosley. Miss Shaw, at one time attached to headquarters and now in charge of all women's work in the Northern Administration, said 'every thing is b—y bad, they couldn't be worse, and if we don't make drastic improvements the whole movement in the North will blow up.'[49]

Conflict and dissent among women members was of a perceptibly more politically and ideologically motivated character after 1935, culminating in the mutiny of women such as Olga Shore,[50] Women's Organizer (Northern), and Sylvia Morris and Mercedes Barrington, both BU prospective parliamentary candidates, to William Joyce's and John Beckett's National Socialist League (NSL). The creation of the NSL was triggered by a split between the supporters of Neil

Francis-Hawkins and his Organization bloc which advocated the growth of the militant Blackshirt semi-military mentality, and Joyce's Policy-Propaganda bloc, whose vision it was to develop the election machinery and win recruits with propaganda in factories and workshops.[51]

In March 1937, Miss Walters, formerly employed in the BUF mailing department, hosted a 'bottle party' for the disenchanted, attended by the Joyces, Goulding, E.B. Hart, and Miss Cutmore. Together suspecting that the reduction of staff was a conspiracy on the part of the Organization bloc to gain full control, they believed that 'the true National Socialists had been driven out of the movement and that they were being victimized because they tried to enlighten the Leader as to the true state of affairs in the organization.'[52] Later, when A.K. Chesterton resigned, he depicted those who remained after the upheaval in the following manner.

> Add a couple of nondescript women avidly nursing what they believe to be great and luminous career. Subtract two men of real political sense, whose influence is steadily on the wane, and in the residue behold the master-builders of 'Greater Britain.' Only Mosley can contemplate this circus with becoming gravity.[53]

Following from what was implied by Chesterton, the women who rose to prominence in the BU after 1937 were devoted to the movement and to the idea of the infallibility of their Leader. The growing fanaticism of women in this period leading up to the war was exemplified by their militant activities on behalf of their own Women's Peace Campaign and by their planned operation to undermine war-time morale.

Women Fascists for Peace and in War

Women's participation grew significantly in importance from 1938 to 1940 when the BU increasingly became an anti-war movement. As the leadership structure disintegrated progressively due to further retrenchment, the desertion of leading figures, and the eventual military call-up of many male members, women members came into their own both by taking over from the men and by establishing a virtually all-female pressure group. The tone of women's propaganda became decidedly more revolutionary; Anne Brock Griggs wished to stress that it was the business of women to take charge of a street block system and 'to bring and to maintain in the homes of the people the responsibility for their country's destiny ... . The revolution is won on the streets and maintained on the streets.'[54] The BU's 'National Campaign for Britain, Peace and People' was launched by September 1938. Awaiting Chamberlain's return after Munich, British mothers demonstrated with a poster parade in Whitehall; their pickets read 'Our Children Were Young In 1914 – Have We Brought Them Up For War'.[55] These relatively benign appeals to protect mother and child were sharply contrasted by the malignance of women's disaffection and their plans for infiltrating other organizations in order to disseminate Mosley's peace gospel.[56]

Women fascist revolutionaries were encouraged to carry on a crusade of demoralization among British women. Women were to act as subversive elements in other organizations, turn appeals to sentiment on their head, and spear-head a campaign that can only be described as 'peace mongering.'

> In shops, with Parents' groups at school, in the Co-operative Societies, in ARP, Women Citizen's Associations, Women's Institutes, as a member of any local organization, a woman has endless opportunities to inspire a solid resistance to the narcotic of false sentimentality... . Letters to the local Press are of great importance and even more opportunities will arise in the next few months, as the flow of Jewish refugee children increases and nauseating sentimentality is poured out from Press and pulpit.[57]

Notably, however, one of the few recorded incidents of BU women infiltrating another group was when they organized interruption of a peace meeting hosted by the Women's League Against War and Fascism, an association contending for the mantel of British female pacifism. At Kingsway Hall on 31 January 1940, BU women angrily demonstrated against

> ... the fake peace aims of Communism ... . As the lights went down for the performance of a one-act propaganda play leaflets were showered down from the gallery, and a number of women rose from the body of the hall and pushed their way onto the stage. The audience sat quietly while one of the women addressed them, charging the communists with hypocrisy in advocating Peace, when they had been most active in creating the spirit of hatred against the German people, and declaring that Mosley and the BU alone had been consistent in their work for peace. Disorder then broke out, as women on the platform protected their speaker from attacks on her.[58]

On this occasion the women were dragged off the platform by three men, after the communists had called in the police.

A more organized form of government opposition was inaugurated when BU women launched their Women's Peace Campaign at a public meeting at Holborn Hall on 28 February 1940. Anne Brock Griggs, Olive Hawks and Miss Steele delivered addresses, and this was the first large scale indoor meeting to be organized, addressed, and stewarded entirely by women.[59] This meeting was followed by week-end rallies on the afternoon of 3, 10, and 17 March, throughout parts of London. At a women's peace meeting on 13 April 1940, Mary Allen, ex-suffragette and Commandant of the Women's Auxiliary Service who had openly joined the BU in December 1939, gave an address. An unsympathetic witness to her speech reported that Allen had spoken 'facetiously of the "kitchen front", "grotesque words" she said and spoke disparagingly of the idea that women could help in a war which she thought to be unjustifiable ... she said "I am not in favour of peace at any price. We do not agree with this war."'[60] Allen was joined on the platform by Oswald Mosley, whose patronage at this women's meeting was seen as the climax of their six-week long campaign.

The intention was that the Women's Peace Campaign would not be confined to London but spawn satellites among the provincial branches, and that the money they raised should be sent to the Women's Peace Campaign Fund at 16 Great Smith Street. These smaller campaigns did not seem to materialize. In Bournemouth, where the branch was run by three women members, Florence Hayes, Iris Ryder and Joan Griffin – who dubbed themselves the 'Holy(?) Trinity'[61] – the women still played only supporting roles at BU peace meetings. In February 1940, for instance, Miss Hayes opened a large meeting in Poole addressed by Hugh Ross Williamson, former Labour Party prospective parliamentary candidate for East Dorset.[62]

Indeed, the case of the Bournemouth Branch was an especially interesting one for our investigation of women's full participation in the BUF. These three strong-willed women ran the branch and consigned the male District Leader to insignificance. There were certain disadvantages in an all-female branch, however, and as early as 14 November 1937 Hayes wrote to Robert Saunders: 'please can you come over in December – say 11th?... We are so handicapped by having no men speakers.'[63]The hazards of an all-female branch were aggravated during the war, and the women had to contend with the window of their BU shop being painted on two separate occasions in October 1939, once with white and then with red paint. Shortly thereafter, Joan Griffin wrote to Robert Saunders how 'the painting of our shop windows has now developed into window smashing ... and as the Insurance Company refuse to take us back on their books again, the landlord has given us a month's notice so once more we are on the move.'[64] In November 1939 the women secured premises for their District Headquarters in a basement shop and 'reverted to the cave-man', as the BU went underground both literally and metaphorically during the war.[65]

Similarly, as Louise Irvine recalls: 'In Birmingham we did not have a separate women's organization for peace, but worked generally together. We had a series of lunch-time meetings in the Bull Ring while we were still pushing for a negotiated peace, and women members could attend these, selling literature. We got quite a lot of support at these meetings.'[66] London continued to be the locus of the most militant BU activity.

The London-based Women's Campaign was very much an all-female effort. While Mosley spoke in the campaign, his near ignorance of their activities attests to the fact that women were left to their own devices in the operation of a pressure-group agitating for peace. When questioned about Olive Hawks' peace pamphlet 'Women Fight For Britain and Britain Alone!', Mosley's evasive response to the Advisory Committee intimated his distance from the women's branch of the movement.

> **A.** Yes she is a HDQ official. She is the women organizer and I should think that it was issued for their campaign, I should think so.
>
> **Q.** That is an appeal of the strongest kind to the women of this country to say to them 'Do not continue to support the war; on the contrary join the BU.'
>
> **A.** It is an appeal to them certainly to demand peace, but I do not think you can say fairly that there is any appeal to weaken the war effort, unless in some form there is an appeal to people engaged in war work at any time to slacken in that work.
>
> **Q.** When I say 'weaken the war effort,' I daresay you would agree with me that in the last resort the morale of the civilian population counts for more than anything else.
>
> **A.** That is the whole conception, of course, of totalitarian war.
>
> **Q.** And the women in particular.
>
> **A.** Yes.
>
> **Q.** When I say 'weaken the war effort,' this leaflet does, by implication say to them 'our children,' which is the greatest appeal you can make, 'your

children are going to suffer in this useless thing, stop it, join BU.'

A. Yes. Of course, that was issued, I presume, in the women's campaign, I think some time earlier this year.[67]

Open to question is whether Mosley's response indicated that he did not follow the activities of his women members closely, or that, under the circumstances, he was hoping to mislead the Committee and protect his followers. Either way, it seems clear that the women's organization had a life of its own and some independence from the male leadership.

Maintaining the momentum of female power and aggression unleashed by their peace campaign, during the early stages of the war BU women began to replace men in leadership positions. In the event of men up to age thirty being called up, the women were exhorted to prepare to take upon themselves the burden 'which the men are temporarily to lay down' and 'to fit themselves to shoulder the sternest tasks of District Organization and propaganda, and to mobilize the women of this country for peace.'[68] Under these conditions, when Leonard Jarvis, Temporary District Leader in Normanton, joined the army on 2 December 1939, his sister Mrs Lister took over his BU post.[69] Likewise, in Limehouse, Gladys Walsh (née Libiter) became District Leader when the men were called to war. As war-time D/L Walsh was in a position to observe first-hand the public's reaction to BU propaganda. Asked whether the public response was any different once Britain was at war and if audiences tended to be 'sucked in by the enormous government propaganda', Walsh responded: 'Yes, definitely it did. Although, really speaking, people more or less ignored it. You had fewer people stopping around at meetings. I suppose they were afraid of stopping around in those days. But it was a wash-out those few months. There were no proper meetings, there was nobody to organize them.'[70] Although it was never the intention that women should rise to generalized leadership positions, the original design was side-stepped when a real crisis emerged: the fixed ideology of male authority became defunct in the face of necessity.[71]

The pattern whereby women rose to greater prominence in extreme-right circles during the 'phoney war' period was not unique to the BU. Captain Ramsay's Right Club, founded in May 1939, and appealing to anti-Semitic and pro-Nazi elements among the British elite, had originally been organized along the lines of male authority. Ramsay's secret membership list, complied in 1939, showed that only men served as wardens and stewards, although Ramsay's list also identified 135 male and 100 female subscribers and supporters.

However, by 1940, a contingent of women activists 'appear to have become the mainstay of the Club, as opposed to being mere foot-soldiers.'[72] Further, when negotiations were underway for collaboration between Ramsay's Right Club, Admiral Domvile's The Link, and Mosley's BU in November and December of 1939, women were also well represented at these meetings, including Mary Allen, Norah Elam, Fay Taylour, and Mrs Whinfield.

The main crisis the BU had to face was not so much the temporary loss of men to the armed forces, but the internment of male leaders under DR 18B. Again, it was the women who stepped into the men's shoes and administered the organization in their absence. Special Branch was under the impression that following Mosley's internment 'deputies have taken over the jobs of the leading Fascist "officials" and carry on the work of the movement secretly. In order to fool the authorities a number of women took over men's work, but in reality they did nothing more serious than collect money to buy comforts for their interned menfolk.'[73] This appears to have been somewhat of a misdiagnosis, however, as there is a great deal of evidence to suggest that male members of the BU entrusted the women with many sensitive tasks in this period.

Mrs Norah Elam, ex-suffragette and BU prospective parliamentary candidate, took charge of part of the BU funds for a short period before and after war was declared, due to fears that the headquarters might be bombed, and even that Mosley might be assassinated. Her flat was raided in December 1939, and when her offices of the London and Provincial Anti-Vivisection Society were raided by Police, found in her possession was 'a list containing the names of eight members of the BU, together with a letter from Oswald Mosley stating that Mrs Elam had his full confidence, and was entitled to do what she thought fit in the interest of the movement on her own responsibility.'[74] Norah Elam was already detained in May 1940 when Diana, Lady Mosley took charge of paying salaries during the five-week interval between her husband's and her own detention. Although she had played an inactive role in the movement since 1935, Maud, Lady Mosley was entrusted with shares of New Era Securities, the BU's publishing company, and Sir Oswald pleaded with the Advisory Committee: 'she holds those shares. Please do not put her in jail because she is quite innocent. She did it as a favour to me.'[75] Innocence, however, was a very relative term in the spring and summer of 1940, and nearly one-hundred BU women were interned as suspected Fifth Columnist under Section 18B(1A) of the Defence Regulations. Their story will be told in the final chapter.

The Sexual Division of Labour: Women's Activities and Women's Work

From the above discussion of the institutionalization of women's support in the BUF it is clear that sexually discriminatory rhetoric and structural gender segregation did not prevent women from participating fully in the construction of the movement. Gisela Bock has observed that gender-based difference has to be separated from the question of gender-based hierarchies, and that 'a sexual division of labour does not necessarily imply a sexual division of social rewards and of power.'[76] Even as the BUF hierarchy seemed to place women in subordinate roles vis à vis male members, and women leaders were subordinate to male leaders, there is something to be said for the fact that there was power-sharing between men and women on many levels, and both sexes were rewarded for their devotion, political commitment and enthusiasm.

There were few activities from which women were excluded in the BUF, but there were areas in which their expertise was considered of particular utility. In public, women acted as Blackshirts and stewards, were involved in violent confrontations, spoke at meetings, raised funds, sold newspapers, marched, canvassed, and stood as candidates in elections the BUF contested. Behind the doors of BUF headquarters and branches, they organized children and youth groups and occupied salaried posts.[77]

The BUF's idealized conception of women suggested their necessary commitment to the diffusion of sex antagonism as part of their political work. Anne Brock Griggs explained how 'Fascism requires that women equally with men should offer a disciplined co-operation in the welding together of an ordered state, and Fascism will lay on all citizens of the state the duty of working in harmony, not in the interests of any section or class, but for the benefit of all its people.'[78] As a voluntary organization, the only means of enforcing discipline was to deny the privilege of wearing the black shirt to those who did not fulfil commitments of giving five nights a week to the movement. BUF propaganda was sure to emphasize the attractiveness of the woman in uniform so as to create envy in those excluded from the band: 'Fifty good-looking, stalwart girls stand smartly to attention ... blackshirted ... they are – and the uniform heightens their look of efficiency.'[79] It would be tempting to nick-name BUF women the 'blackskirts', but for the fact that the women's uniform was a black blouse, black beret and a grey skirt.

Actions Speak Louder than Words: Countering Women with Women

The BUF's politics of provocation and its penchant for violence was as much a drawing card with women as with males. Women were trained in ju-jitsu and as stewards for meetings 'for no male member of the BUF is permitted to use force upon any woman; and women Reds often form a highly noisy and razor-carrying section at fascist meetings. Thus we counter women with women.'[80] The eroticization of brutality and the flagrant excitation value of images of violence among women seemed to appeal to women as much as it must have aroused the male imagination and transfixed the male gaze. In 1933 it was pointed out that while only fifty women were being trained to be sent into the fray of political strife, they were chosen from an overflow of volunteers. With pride in their growing numbers and sovereignty, one woman wrote how

> in March 1933, we numbered 17. To-day, women's sections [are] working side by side with male branches ... . At first we were few. There was no possibility of holding our own meetings without the help of men. But today that is changed. Not only do we have our own speakers but we steward our own meetings as well, and it is in the role of stewards that the Propaganda Patrol is best known.[81]

While the tabloid press fully exploited the innuendo of young women in uniform, trained in physical fitness and self-defence, the *Sunday Dispatch's* beauty competition of 1934 seemed to be taking things too far. As Mosley was relieved to point out, Rothermere 'was staggered not to receive a single entry; and I was embarrassed to explain that these were serious women dedicated to the cause of their country rather than aspirants to the Gaiety Theatre Chorus.'[82] Women Blackshirts were attempting to develop an image of sternness and fearlessness. In fact, as Nellie Driver has pointed out when describing BUF marches, 'no speaking was allowed; no waving to friends and relations on the pavements– eyes forward, silent and grim. No lipstick of make-up was permitted to the women.'[83]

While women also served in more traditional auxiliary-type corps – there were classes for ambulance, bandaging and a blood-transfusion team – they were integrated into the para-military structure and involved in violent incidents, both defensive and offensive. They had their own Women's Defence Force, members of which held the St John's Ambulance certificate and were trained in ju-jitsu, and by 1937 their own Women's Drum Corps.[84] Although the BUF sanctioned women's defensive belligerence, women stewards were entreated to retain the accoutrements of their femininity, and Robert Saunders warned an eager recruit 'that it is against the regulations of the Movement for our women to wear trousers while on active duty.'[85]

To the dismay of the public and to those in the hall, the notorious Olympia Rally of 7 June 1934 was witness to both violence inflicted on and by women. One writer to *The Times* related that 'men and women Fascists were to be seen going away after the meeting with bandaged heads.'[86] In contrast, the anti-fascist novelist Margaret Storm Jameson testified that 'in one case a young woman was carried past me by five Blackshirts, her clothes half torn off, and her mouth and nose closed by the large hand of one ... I mention her especially because I have seen a reference to the delicacy with which women interrupters were left to women Blackshirts. This is merely untrue.'[87]

In October 1934 the BUF's Miss Needham was slashed with razor blades on the forehead, left shoulder and chest.[88] In December 1934, Margery Aitken, leader of the BUF's Women's Defence Force, appeared in court following scenes of violence at a meeting in Manchester. Testifying against one of the anti-fascists accused, Aitken described how 'she warned Miss Taylor who, however, refused to be quiet and seized a steward by the hair and spat at him. She also seized [Aitken] by the hair and kicked her. Witness added that she had to strike defendant in self-defence.'[89] On the same occasion when Mosley suffered a serious head injury caused by a projectile at a meeting in Liverpool in September 1936, 'a woman fascist was felled by a stone which struck her on the head, causing a wound requiring nine stitches.'[90]

The recollections of Yolande McShane, who became Women's District Inspector for all Merseyside, offer a different picture from the Press reports regarding the violence with which BUF women were confronted. During a particularly violent meeting at the Liverpool stadium in 1936, when the communists were out in force with razor-studded potatoes, knuckle-dusters and bicycle chains, McShane remembered how 'all the women Blackshirts were taken out of the rear entrance into police vans, driven to safety and then the vans returned – to the fray.'[91] While this latter example was more in keeping with Mosley's earliest pronouncements on the necessity of shielding women from political violence, it is clear that women were at one and the same time protected and allowed to take their own initiative when it came to participating in riotous assemblies. Indeed, it was also in Liverpool, 'a "rough city" at the best of times, [that] two of our best stewards there were a strapping big Irish girl, Monty Monoghan, and a tiny Maltese women, Flo Santos. They knew how to work together in rough houses.'[92]

Expounding the Creed of Fascism in their Own Words: Speaking and Oratory

It is not implied that violence was practised for its own sake. Violence was always secondary to the primary reasons for women's public appearances: speaking and propaganda work. Women were clearly meant to be the publicists for Mosley's 'Greater Britain,' and the instigators of fascism. As the *Fascist Week* explained: 'Fascism in Britain knows that its women members go a long way to help the cause; and that it is a woman's influence that has converted so many male members.'[93] The BUF encouraged women's public visibility, and in Irene Clephane's view 'among the oddest spectacles of the day is that of young women dressed in black shirts, standing on the pavement edges offering for sale the literature of the fascists, one of whose aims is to deprive women of the very freedom which makes it possible to stand unmolested as they do.'[94]

In the beginning, Lady Makgill tried to recruit more female speakers, stressing that women would be useful for disseminating 'personal propaganda,' and that 'the Old Gang parties have done an immense amount of work through "word of mouth" propaganda in every club and meeting place throughout the country.'[95] At their own meetings and in debate, the women had to be proficient in their knowledge of fascism, and study circles were set up alongside speaker's classes for this purpose. (Those with a different kind of vocal talent could take part in the Women's Choir, conducted by Mrs Pfister.) Their elocutionary skills were tested in December 1934, for example, when they met with the Women's International League of Democracy for a debate on 'Democracy vs Fascism.'

Women's addresses were not confined to their own meetings as they shared the platform and warmed-up the crowd for male colleagues. When the Women's Propaganda Section was formed in Manchester in 1935, it was reported that 'an experiment made by getting women speakers to open the ordinary Blackshirt meetings in Stevenson Square, is causing much interest ... .Women's speakers' classes are being held regularly in Manchester, and before long it is hoped to send the ladies to Blackburn, Bolton, Preston and elsewhere.'[96]

Indeed, it was by proving themselves to be inspiring speakers and ready to travel, that many of the women ascended the rungs of the BUF hierarchy.

Before joining the staff of the BU in 1935 as Woman Propaganda Officer, Anne Brock Griggs had been a speaker at outdoor meetings in London and the Home Counties.[97] The young Doreen Bell, whose first activity was selling the *Blackshirt* in Bognor, Sussex, was 'discovered' once she started to attend BUF speaker's classes. 'So great and obvious were her talents in this direction that she was invited to join the staff of the BU as a speaker,'[98] filling the post of Woman Staff Speaker. Her work was concentrated in the North, recruiting at Women's Exchanges in Manchester in 1936. When speaking at Duckett Street, Stepney, after the LCC elections, Bell was introduced as 'an example of enlightened womanhood.'[99] While much of women's propaganda covered the topics of women and fascism, Bell spoke about her work in the industrial North, the civil war in Spain, unemployment and trade unionism.

The BUF's intensive East London campaign of 1936–37 was brought to fever-pitch by the presumed oratorical talents of Anne Brock Griggs, Doreen Bell, Olive Hawks, Mrs Carruthers and Miss Good, who were all credited with having a 'stimulating effect upon massed audiences.'[100] The women were apparently as uninhibited as the men in making anti-Semitic references in their discourses, and for tactical reasons they had to be entreated to censor their speeches. As Neville Laski, President of the Board of Deputies of British Jews, explained: 'Mrs Anne Brock Griggs is now to concentrate on East End women, and will NOT mention the word "Jew"(as all speakers have now been warned). There will be plain clothed members at all meetings to use the word instead, as coming from the public, and to rouse others.'[101] The East End was also the setting for the first ever Women's Propaganda March in May 1936, led by Olga Shore and following a route from Bethnal Green to Victoria Park where Brock Griggs addressed the marchers.

Mascots of Female Emancipation Under Fascism: Canvassing and Candidature

Women's efficiency in propaganda work was channelled into the closely allied tasks of canvassing and electioneering. Indeed, the first branch to put the Street Block Organization into operation was the Women's Section, which began canvassing the Abbey Division of Westminster as early as February 1934.[102] Like public speaking and stewarding meetings, canvassing was a challenging occupation which demanded facility for persuasion. Naturally, the feminine presence on the door-steps of the nation went some way towards disarming public apprehensions of BUF hooliganism and disorderliness. Dorothy Parkyn described what the BU woman canvasser had to contend with, and recognized that her public appearance proved that 'we are not thugs (this is a very prevalent idea).'[103]

Women canvassers and candidates were a great asset to the movement as tokens of the liberality of the BUF towards the fairer sex. How could it still be alleged that the BUF was modelling itself on the German Nazi Party – which denied women the right to stand as NSDAP candidates and sit in the Reichstag – when ten of their one-hundred prospective parliamentary candidates were women? When he presented Mrs Elam at a meeting at the Town Hall, Northampton, in November 1936, 'Sir Oswald Mosley said he was glad indeed to have the opportunity of introducing this first candidate, and it killed for all time the suggestion that National Socialism proposed putting British women back into the home.'[104] The contrast with Nazi methods was always a conscious one, as was the BU's pride that 10 per cent of their parliamentary candidates were female – a higher percentage than any of the three British parliamentary parties. For the 1935 General Election the Conservatives had put up 19/585 female candidates (3.2 per cent); Labour 35/552 (6.3 per cent); and the Liberals 11/161 (6.8 per cent).

In November 1936, the BU began to announce its prospective parliamentary candidates. The ten women were: Mrs Norah Elam (Northampton), Miss L.M. Reeve (Norfolk), Sylvia Morris (Holland with Boston), Mrs Muriel G. Whinfield (Petersfield), Lady Pearson (Canterbury), Doreen Bell (Accrington), Miss L.A. King (Ilford), Miss M. Barrington (Fulham West), Olive Hawks (Camberwell), and Dorothy Viscountess Downe (North Norfolk). These were ten women of widely different background and an examination of the information given about them in the BUF press is an indication both of the types attracted to fascism and those traits the movement valued in its women.

Four had been engaged in war work between 1914 and 1918: Elam recruited in 'Red' South Wales and worked in a munitions factory; Lady Pearson had been Commandant of the Hertfordshire VAD Hospital; Barrington did war work in the last two years of the war and welfare work in East London; and Viscountess Downe ran the RFC Auxiliary Hospital. Six of the ten were unmarried, and could thus claim membership in the generation of surplus women. Four of the ten had had previous affiliations with the Conservative Party, Whinfield having been chairman of the Alton Women's Unionist Association for five years before she became disillusioned with the Tories and joined the BUF, and Viscountess Downe having been president of the Conservative Women's Association in Scarborough for eight years after which she became chairman of the Conservative Women's Association of King's Lynn. Only Bell was accredited with having socialist sympathies preceding her conversion to fascism. Only one had previously stood as a parliamentary candidate: in 1918 Norah Elam had stood unsuccessfully as an Independent. Five were professional women: Reeve had started in domestic service and rose to becoming an estate agent; Morris was a freelance journalist; Whinfield was a business woman; King controller of the *Daily Mail's* Women's Canvass Staff; and Hawks had worked for the Amalgamated Press and was currently in the BU Research Department. The women who had no professions were noted for commitment to volunteer work and philanthropy. Two, Elam and Barrington, were ex-suffragettes. In class complexion the majority were middle-class, with the notable exception of the two women from gentry families: Lady Pearson, sister of Henry Page-Croft, and Viscountess Downe, a wealthy East Anglia landowner. Finally, three were young women still in their twenties: Doreen Bell, Olive Hawks and Sylvia Morris signalled the BUF's appeal to youth.

The potential popularity of fascist women with British voters was never tested at the national level as no general election was called before the war. At the local level, however, both voter preference and the BU's sincerity in running female candidates was brought under some scrutiny. The BU contested six seats in East London for the London County Council election of March 1937, and Anne Brock Griggs stood for Limehouse.[105] Key to Brock Grigg's election platform were the issues which the BU considered women's domain. Interweaving more than a fair amount of anti-Semitic slander, Brock Griggs campaigned on the issues of housing, slum clearance, and the incorruptibility of Mosley's political character.[106]

The BU failed to have any member elected to the LCC: in Bethnal Green, Thomson and Clarke polled 23 per cent; in Limehouse, Brock Griggs and Wegg-Prosser 16.3 per cent; and in Shoreditch, Joyce and Bailey 15.8 per cent.[107] Gender did not seem to effect the number of votes cast for BU candidates. The LCC results were a great disappointment for the BU, and especially for Mosley as 'his hopes in relation to Limehouse were based on the returns of the Canvass Officers of that ward, which had led him to believe that Wegg-Prosser and Anne Brock-Griggs would poll many more votes than they actually did.'[108] Despondency over the results, and the accusations at NHQ that Mosley had been wilfully misled and that the election machinery was 'hopelessly bad' was followed by the discharge of many members of the paid staff – including two of the candidates, Joyce and Thomson – and a 50 per cent reduction of minor officials. Anne Brock Griggs was not as discouraged as her male colleagues; she was retained as a member of staff and thereafter became the BU prospective parliamentary candidate for South Poplar.

That the consequences of the LCC election was the weakening of the movement in spirit and in numbers goes some way to explaining why the BU did not *officially* contest the London Municipal elections of 1 November 1937. The BU did run candidates in that Municipal election. Fifty-six fascists were nominated in ten Boroughs (eighteen wards) all in East London with the exception of St Pancras, Mitchum and Croydon. Four of the fifty-six were women, and the women's share of the total votes cast for BU candidates was proportionally high.[109]

Practising What they Preached?: BUF Women in Salaried Posts

The BUF demonstrated its sincerity in upholding the principle of the equality of the sexes in the number of women candidates representing the movement. The question remains as to whether their continual advocacy of equal opportunity, abolition of the marriage bar, and equal pay for equal work were applied to their own employment policy and staffing. Ideally, 'fascism regards the principle of equal pay for equal work, as vital to the recovery of national prosperity. Since their entry into industry women have received lower wages than men for the same work. This amounts to victimization and, apart from the injustice to women, causes the displacement of men.'[110] The theoretical commitment to these principles was not without ambiguity – equal pay was posited as a remedy for women undercutting men's wages – and this ambivalence was borne out within the movement.

Special Branch reports on BUF personnel and headquarters staff show that in 1934 few women occupied paid posts, and the leaders of the Women's Section do not appear to have been remunerated. Women employees occupied secretarial posts: Miss Monk as assistant to the Leader, Miss Ann Cutmore as Deputy Leader Dr Forgan's secretary, and Miss Vernon as clerk under the chief of staff.[111] Reports of 1935 show that of the 154 paid employees at NHQ only 11 were women, but their salaries were commensurate with those paid to men.[112] In 1936 both Miss Olga Shore, Women's Organizer, and Mrs Anne Brock Griggs, Women's Propaganda Officer, were paid a salary of £260 per annum, the same wage as paid to Miss Black, cashier. For the sake of comparison, the highest salary of £416 was paid to Ian Hope Dundas, second in command to the Leader.[113] By March 1939, after many rounds of contentious staff reduction, eleven of the forty-eight paid employees were women, and Anne Brock Griggs earned £260 plus £160 for expenses, and Olive Hawks £120.[114] Significantly, seven of these eleven were unmarried. Consequently, while deviation from the ideal of equal pay was not glaring, it must be balanced against the percentage of women employed, the prevalence of unmarried female staff, and the traditionally-feminine clerical tasks they performed.

Who Were the Women Fascists?: Political Backgrounds

As a survey of the BU's prospective parliamentary women candidates suggests, there was no single type of woman most likely to support the BUF in the 1930s. Nonetheless, the most frequent political route taken was from Toryism to fascism, and it is clear that the BUF was in competition with the Conservative Party to recruit a well-defined type of woman. From its advent in Britain, fascism had the greatest affinity with the Conservative Party, attracted women with radically conservative beliefs who sought to play more militant and pro-active roles than those offered by the Conservative Associations, and during the 1920s women in the British Fascisti were advised to vote Tory in elections. From the 1934 responses to 'The Labour Party Questionnaire,' we see that British fascism did not tend to tempt Labour women away from socialism, but made special appeals to Conservative women.[115] Pugh has found that Conservative MPs fears about the loss of young patriots to Mosley in the 1930s was 'corroborated by the urgent requests made by the Primrose League habitation for guidance on the whole subject of Fascism.'[116] A favoured venue for BUF women's meetings were the conservative Women's Institutes, and in April 1936, for example, Mr FitzGerald, District Organizer in Dorchester, explained that 'as the villages are greatly influenced by the Women's Institutes, I was wondering if Mrs Brock Griggs could come and speak to one or two large ones.'[117] Perhaps because the BUF was seen to target Conservative women, Sir Reginald Bennett, the Secretary of the Primrose League, publicly declared his strong opposition to Mosley when he stated that 'British people will not submit to a dictatorship of either Right or Left.'[118]

Of the older generation of women, politically formative experiences were most often gained in the Conservative Party. In June 1934 Mrs Hugh Rayner OBE, Chairman of the Women's Branch, Conservative Party, Whitechapel, and a member of the Metropolitan Area Council of the Party, joined the BUF, as did Mrs Haig-Thomas and Miss C.W. Craig, sisters of the late Earl Haig.[119] Miss Jean Cossar, who joined the Newcastle branch in 1934 after approving of a BUF poster advocating 'Britain buys from those who buy from Britain', had formerly been Women's Organizer for the Conservative Association in Wansbeck and later for the South Hackney Conservative and Unionist Association. While it was clear that Cossar was attracted to the BUF because she perceived a stronger affirmation of her conservative principles in fascist propaganda, the other women who had been tutored in the Conservative Party broke their ties with Toryism more aggressively.

Mercedes Barrington, who had assisted the Conservative Party at elections since 1918, 'became disgusted with their ineffectuality and turned to Fascism as the only solution.'[120] Similarly, Dorothy Viscountess Downe 'left the Conservative Party in disgust ... and joined the BU, in which movement she saw hope for the future of Britain, which she could not see in any other Party.'[121] Mrs Whinfield gave a 'scathing attack on the so-called National Government'[122] when she explained her reasons for resigning from the Women's Conservative Association.

Relying on the BUF press alone, it would appear that these women severed all ties with the Tory Party before throwing in their lot with Mosley. While it is clear that BUF women were disenchanted by the Conservatives, some women were members of the BUF and the Conservative Party simultaneously, an indication, perhaps that they regarded the BUF as a pressure group whose political goals were not at variance with those of extremist sections of the Tory Party. Indeed, in 1934 T.C.R. Moore, Conservative MP for Ayr Burghs, wrote in the *Daily Mail* that 'the Blackshirts have what the conservatives need,'[123] arguing that the Conservatives had a great deal to learn from the BUF's success with British youth, and expressing the hope that the two parties would soon unite.

From the other side of the spectrum, Mary Richardson had joined the Labour Party in 1916. In 1922 and 1924 she stood as a Labour and then an Independent Labour candidate in Acton, on both occasions losing to the Conservatives. In 1931 she stood for Labour in Aldershot, again without success. Untypically, Norah Elam was disillusioned with party politics as early as 1918, when she unsuccessfully stood as an Independent. Her repulsion by party politics was expressed in terms of the greatest vehemence, seeing that party women 'once again wear the primrose in the memory of the Jew Disraeli, the rosette in honour of Sir Herbert Samuel, the red emblem in commemoration of Karl Marx; they have turned again as handmaidens to the hewing of wood and drawing of water for the party wirepullers, and they add to all this futility the cross upon the ballot paper once in every five years.'[124] The BUF was the storm-centre of variously motivated political discontents among women of the older generation, and fascism seemed to represent for them a new genre of political organization: a non-party party.

Many women, particularly those of the younger generation, underwent their political initiation rites in the BUF. Unity Mitford and Diana Mosley were politically baptized by fascism. Other young women came from families with affiliations with the Conservative Party, and the BUF offered to them the revolutionary edge absent from conservatism. Dinah Parkinson explained that 'I belong to an old Conservative family, and before my conversion to BU I was an ardent, if youthful Tory... But one day I ceased to let myself being hypnotized as [Tory women] are to-day.'[125] Yolande McShane, eighteen when she joined the BUF, came from a staunch Conservative family and she found it astonishing that 'I did not know socialism existed, only what my father called "Those damned Communists".'[126]

Notably, with the exception of Olga Keyes' conversion from communism to fascism, there were few women who crossed over to the BUF from the enemy 'Red' camp,[127] although there were some who had previous sympathies with socialism and the Labour Party. Doreen Bell was first moved by socialism, and Louise Irvine's father had been a dedicated Labour man who would tell his teen-age daughter 'you might be another Margaret Bondfield one day.'[128] Conservative or Labour background notwithstanding, a prevalent explanation given by young women for their attraction to the BUF was fascism's promise to alleviate social hardship.

Whether they were victims of the Depression or concerned middle-class women with a social conscience, the BUF gave vent to female philanthropic instincts. For Nellie Driver, a young woman who had been discharged from employment in a candy factory and who joined the BUF in 1935, later to become Women's District Leader in Nelson, 'family hardship and the suffering of the people around me ... caused me to rebel against prevailing poor social conditions.'[129] From a vastly different economic and class background, Yolande McShane, who had been sending contributions to East End charitable foundations since she was a child, 'found Mosley's ideas attractive – they seemed to promise a better life for the very poor.'[130]

Age, Class and Fascist Families

As these examples suggest, the women were divided along two main axes: age and class. On the one hand, youth was seen as an asset, and it was pointed out that in spite of their tender age many women rose quickly in the ranks. On the other hand, the movement was handicapped by the high proportion of young people; in 1937 in Liverpool 'impartial investigation tends to show that the members are all young men and women and of little material use to the movement.'[131] Considering that the terms of abuse for the governing classes were interchangeably the 'old gang' and 'old women,' it seems striking that women over the age of thirty should have tolerated the BUF's revolutionary ageism.[132] However, the young women had the effect of down-playing the BUF's age discriminatory rhetoric by accepting the older women, particularly the colourful ex-suffragettes, as role models.[133]

Furthermore, tensions were quelled in some cases when the generation gap was bridged by mother and child joining together. For example, Muriel Whinfield joined with her son Peter, and in Dorset Mrs A.L. Wiltshire joined with her two sons. Yolande McShane (née Mott), Nellie Driver, Gladys Walsh (née Libiter), Blanche Greaves (née Mann) each joined with their mothers, and the mother-daughter team of Agnes and Nancy Booth were both interned under DR 18B. When Mrs Mitt Sanford requested enrolment forms from the Dorset West Branch for herself and her daughter, she explained how both wished 'to join a party which upholds the strength, common sense and especially modesty and decency, in this age of disgusting vulgarity and democracy.'[134]

While generational conflict among the women was averted, the BUF was not entirely able to diffuse class conflict. The BUF vacillated on the class issue, exemplified by the assertion that 'although active and patriotic members of the middle-classes, who have learned to place service before self, are welcome within the Fascist ranks, yet Fascism has arisen in violent opposition to those bourgeois liberal standards upon which middle-class supremacy has been based.'[135] While the general impression has long been held that BUF women were predominantly middle-class, the movement attempted to gain a cross-class following. They offered at one and the same time certain concessions to middle and upper-class women who were accustomed to genteel politics – such as 'At Homes', the January Club, garden parties, bazaars opened by Baroness Ravensdale, and luncheons at the Criterion Restaurant – while also appealing to women in menial trades, domestic servants and victims of sweat-shop bosses.[136]

The BUF's indecisiveness on class and bourgeois capitalism was illustrated by praise for those prominent fascist women who were professionals or in business. Olga Shore was lauded as 'an excellent example of the generation of women who have turned from the ties of Victorianism to the wider world of business,'[137] and Muriel Whinfield was 'the best type of professional woman, who has turned to politics in a genuine effort to help solve the problems of this country.'[138] As the examples of women being entrusted with the BU finances early in war attest, women's business proficiency was exploited to full effect.

Gender Co-Operation or Male Supremacy?

Complementing the principle of the equality of the sexes was the ideal of co-operation between men and women in building a 'Greater Britain.' Men and women shared motivation for joining the BUF and the dominant themes for both sexes were recurring nightmares of the Great War, unflinching patriotism, dreams of economic recovery and social welfare concerns. As Irvine recalled, 'in many ways the women were not considered as a separate section, being encouraged and accepted to take part in any activities they could.'[139] Nellie Driver spoke of the great comradeship that existed among member of the BUF, and remarked that 'it was always the same, the men treated me as one of themselves, as a good comrade, and the only time they seemed to realise I was a woman was when danger threatened, and they put me in the middle for protection.'[140] Along the same lines, Blanche Greaves admitted that 'although one had these wonderful titles, like W/D/L and that sort of thing, it didn't really mean a lot, to be perfectly honest. You were there so you did it,'[141] and rigid segregated hierarchies were by-passed in practice.

These memories of the equalization of gender relations must be qualified, however. Gladys Walsh recalled how in the East End of London 'they were really gentlemen. In fact, I remember once one of the lads said "Bloody" something, and he was told to be quiet with the ladies present.'[142] When Robert Saunders was slated to meet the socialist Miss M.L. West in a debate on the proposition that 'the Fascist State is preferable to the Socialist State,' the BUF's Florence Hayes teased him by saying: 'rather annoying to be opposed by a women – you have to be polite!'[143] Although it should be appreciated that BUF women did not protest against the attempted resurrection of chivalry, fascist men impeded any genuine cross-gender solidarity by treating women with polite deference.

At the benign level of organization, however, the BUF was no more segregationist and anti-feminist than the other political parties, and it is with these contemporary comparisons in mind that we must be careful not to denounce fascist women as willing handmaidens to their own subjugation. As mass organizations, both the Conservative and Labour parties made special appeals to women and effectively organized women's patronage during the inter-war period. After 1918, the Conservative party adopted the principle of one third representation of women at all levels of party organization and continued to mobilize its female support through the Primrose League and the Women's Conservative Associations.

The Labour Party constitution of 1918 incorporated the Women's Labour League (founded 1906) fully into the party 'transforming its branches into "women's sections" of local party branches, giving women full party membership, a party official, the Chief Woman Officer, and four members on the National Executive Committee of the party, to be elected by the annual party conference.'[144] By the late 1920s much of the local party work was conducted by Labour's 1,800 women's sections, who together claimed a membership of 300,000 women by 1929. (Labour's nomenclature was certainly similar to the BUF's). During the 1930s Labour women paid the price for gender cohesion with the loss of gender identity and 'they were loyal party workers, concentrating on issues of interest to women voters without challenging male control of the policy-making structure.'[145] More significantly, as Melville Currell points out, still in the post-war period, 'that there are segregated, women-only associations alongside the major party organization implies the institutionalization of inequality, and their lack of executive function or autonomy underlies this.'[146]

If nothing more, the BUF had not institutionalized inequality to a higher degree than the main stream parties in the 1930s.

While falling into the pattern of the organization of women in the British party system, the BUF also proposed an alternative to what they considered the parties were offering to British women. They alleged that 'the Labour Party appeals first and foremost to the bread and butter side of Socialism ... . Conservatism, which is to-day merely a more respectable sort of Socialism, appeals to love of security, an appeal to which women are particularly vulnerable.'[147] Beyond assurances of mere material provisions, the BUF's pledge was that women would find spiritual regeneration and community in fascism.

Fascists in Love: Relationships Between Men and Women

The intensity of fascism's spiritual appeal, coupled with the aestheticization of politics through the BUF's uniforms and regalia, inevitably led to a sexually charged atmosphere. There can be little doubt that romantic considerations impelled some women to follow men into the ranks, and vice versa. The politically inexperience Eugenia Wright joined the Carlisle Branch when she was only 14 years old because she was 'smitten with a handsome lad who was very charming ... and looked great in uniform.'[148] In 1991 Mr Greaves explained why he joined the BUF in Kingston: 'Because I met a young lady, I fell in love with her, and I have been married to her now for 52 years.'[149]

Fortifying the ideal of male–female co-operation, marriages and love affairs frequently occurred within the movement. The wedding of Ian Hope Dundas, son of the Admiral Sir Charles Dundas, to Pamela Ernestine Dorman, niece of Ernest Shackleton, was rich in party symbolism, with Mosley serving as best man, and the bride wearing a gown 'trimmed with golden fasces.'[150] In March 1934 there was another fascist wedding in London at which the bride, Miss Edith Bowers Hill, 'wore the short grey flannel skirt and regulation Blackshirt of the Fascist organization [and] Mr O'Hagan wore the Blackshirt uniform ... A bodyguard from Fascist headquarters in King's Road, Chelsea, attended the wedding, and gave the Fascist salute.'[151] The O'Hagans planned a honeymoon in Rome in order to pay their respects to Signor Mussolini. These weddings set the precedent for Mosley's own 'fascist wedding.' When Sir Oswald Mosley married Diana (née Mitford) in Berlin on 6 October 1936, Hitler was in attendance and thereby symbolically sanctified their union as one in National Socialism.

After the failure of his first marriage, William Joyce wed Margaret Cairns 'the daughter of a textile warehouse manager and an enthusiastic member of the BUF, a secretary and a trained dancer who often performed at cabaret shows given at festive gatherings of the North Country Fascists.'[152] More controversially, Anne Cutmore, Dr Forgan's secretary and a writer for *Action*, was reported to be John Beckett's live-in mistress in 1936[153] – they later married. In 1938 Doreen Bell married A.G. Findlay, the BU Director of Public Relations, and Mosley was present at the wedding. Also in 1938 Mosley's secretary, Miss Monk, was engaged to John Garrett, Organizer of National Transport at NHQ. In January 1940 Heather Bond, drum major of the Women's Drum Corps, married B.D.E. Donovan, Assistant Director General, and their wedding was also attended by the Mosleys.

Before the war, Louise Fisher became engaged to S.L. Irvine, the District Leader in Birmingham, and working for the movement gave them the opportunity of spending their spare time together. As she recalled, 'I am afraid that sex and human nature being what they are – feminism or no feminism – romances sometimes bloomed!'[154] There were also occasions when romances bloomed at the most inopportune times. Olive Hawks had married F.E. Burdett in 1940 and both were shortly after interned under DR 18B. When the opportunity arose for married couples to be moved from the segregated camps on the Isle of Man and be united in Holloway in December of 1941, it was recorded that 'there is an objection to the inclusion of the Burdetts because Mrs Burdett has an infatuation for Raven Thomson, one of the BU leaders, and according to a report from the Governor of Holloway last August, does not want to see her husband again.'[155]

Romances were an inescapable result of men and women working together in close proximity, but the male-centrism and male-gang mentality of the movement was exemplified by Mosley's reasons for keeping his own marriage to Diana secret. As he explained to the 18B Advisory Committee, 'there is a legend in the movement that if you marry you cease to do any work. I therefore meant to keep it quiet for some time so that if they find it out I could say "well, you see I have not changed at all, the movement has been just the same," and that period of annoyance and disappointment about my marriage would have passed over.'[156] Was Mosley's sole concern the potential reaction of his male cohorts, or did he know intuitively what most twentieth century film stars know: that when a dashing leading man marries, the devotion of his female *fanatics* wanes?

Notes on Chapter 2

1 My italics. Advisory Committee to Consider Appeals Against Orders of Internment, 3 July 1940, HO283/14/2–117. Mosley's non-pejorative use of the term 'fanatic' to describe his women followers can be accounted for by the new idiom of the European extreme Right after the First World War. Mosse has argued: 'Such [fascist] new men also spoke a new language, one which sharpened traditional modes of expression and integrated them into a manichean world picture of enemy and friend ... The word *fanatic*, which had a negative connotation earlier, was now used as an adjective to signify heroism and the willingness to fight.' George Mosse, *Fallen Soldiers* (Oxford, 1990), p.178. In regard to Mosley's statement here quoted, it is also interesting to note that his congratulatory remarks to his women followers have been celebrated by the present-day Neo-Nazi Movement. The web site of the Women's Frontier of the World Church of the Creator, based in the United States, in the section on 'White Leaders of the Past and Present: Their Views on Women,' includes Mosley's statement 'Without the women, I could not have got a quarter of the way.' See www.wcotc.com.

2 Quoted in Katherine Thomas, *Women in Nazi Germany* (London, 1943). See also Eileen Lyons, 'Those German Women: A Contrast Between Democratic and Fascist Methods,' *Blackshirt*, No. 164, 13 June 1936.

3 D.S. Lewis, *Illusions of Grandeur* (Manchester, 1987), p.78.

4 My italics. Martin Durham, 'Gender and the British Union of Fascists,' *Journal of Contemporary History*, 27, 3 (July 1992), 513–527.

5 Oswald Mosley, *My Life* (London, 1968), p.305.

6 Quoted in Stephen Cullen, 'Four Women for Mosley: Women in the BUF, 1932–1940,' *Oral History*, 24, 1 (Spring 1996), 49–59. In Cullen's article Louise Irvine is given the pseudonym 'Lorna.' Nellie Driver also admitted that it was the women who 'kept the H.Q. clean and tidy, [and] brewed tea for the men as they came in from active duty.' However, these recollections should be balanced against Driver's other observation that 'we had women who were quite capable of ejecting any male tough from a meeting, and others whose zeal was an example to the men.' Nellie Driver, *From the Shadows of Exile* (unpublished autobiography), University of Bradford, p.32.

7 During question period at a conference I spoke at on 13 October 1996, a member of the audience remarked on how the picture I drew of the BUF's treatment of women seemed to show that their attitude was very liberal. In reaction against any such suggestion, the questioner advised me that he was certain that had the BUF come to power, their liberality towards women would have 'gone out the window'. Not that I disagree with this unfulfilled prophecy, but the starting point of this study must be to challenge such predictable prejudice and pre-conceptions.

8   These figures taken from (in order of appearance): HO144/20142/107–122, HO144/20146/87, HO144/20147/378–87, HO144/21063/459–62, HO144/21281/8–12, HO144/21281/112–14.

9   G.C. Webber, 'Patterns of Membership and Support for the BUF,' *Journal of Contemporary History*, 19, 4 (October 1984), 575–605.

10 I asked Robert Row – BUF member in Lancaster during the 1930s and the post-war editor of *Action* – what was his impression of the proportion of men to women members in the BUF? He responded: 'As a rough guide, from my own observations, at the big Hyde Park rally in September 1934 I would say there was only one woman member for every 15 men, whereas at the even bigger Earl's Court rally in July 1939, there seemed to be one woman there for every 4 men. It is pretty certain that this rising proportion of women members was due to the approach of the war and feminine opposition to it.' Letter from Robert Row to the author, 14 March 1997.

11 HO45/24895/27

12 The figure of 1,150 is taken from the *Star*, 17 December 1945. The other details from HO45/24467.

13 The activities of the BUF branches outside Britain were negligible. However, it is interesting to note that in January 1934 the British Ambassador reported on the creation of a BUF branch in Berlin, founded by one Mr B.A. Owen, owner of an English language school, whose intention it was also to form a Women's Branch. (His Majesty's Ambassador at Berlin, 31 January 1934, HO144/19070/208–11). When the British Embassy in Rome reported on the activities of the Roman Branch at their celebration of the King's birthday on 3 June 1934 it was noted that of the 115 persons in attendance over half were women. (Foreign Office, British Embassy, Rome, Communique from Eric Drummond, 8 June 1934, HO144/20141/283).

14 HO144/20144/167–171

15 Robert Saunders' Membership List, 30 October 1939, Saunders Collection, Sheffield University, File E.1. It should be noted that of these fifteen women, five had husbands who were also members (33%), four were married women who joined alone (27%), and the remaining six were unmarried (40%). We also have the BUF Blackshirt Organization Treasurer's Report for October 1936, for the Dorchester Branch. This records the membership of fourteen men and five women (26%). Saunders Collection, Sheffield University, File A.5.. While these figures are enlightening, it should be pointed out that the Dorset West branch was not necessarily representative. For most of the 1930s Saunders was one of the few active members in his district, and it was not until May 1938 that the branch could find a woman, Mrs Gladys Stephenson, to fill the post of W/D/L. Due to the low level of female adherence in Dorset, Florence Hayes, W/C/O Wessex, assumed charge of organizing women in Saunders' district prior to 1938.

16 J.D. Brewer, *Mosley's Men: The BUF in the West Midlands* (Hampshire, 1984), p.5.

17 Stephen Cullen, 'The BUF, 1932–1940: Ideology, Membership and Meetings' (unpublished M.Litt. dissertation, University of Oxford, 1987). In a still more numerically ambitious project, for his study of the BUF in East End London and South-West Essex, Linehan had a sample of 311 local Mosleyites. Among his caveats, he admits that women are under-represented in his sample. Nonetheless, he concludes that 'due to the level of female participation within the BUF, and the mostly subordinate role and status of women within its organizational structure, female fascists rarely featured in the various contemporary documents of the movement to the same extent as their male counterparts.' Thomas P. Linehan, *East London for Mosley* (London, 1996), p.210. Arguably, however, it is not so much women's under-representation in the movement as it is women's under-representation in the historiography which has perpetuated the impression that women's membership was comparatively insignificant.

18 Cecil F. Melville, *The Truth About the New Party* (London, 1931), p.41. Melville continues: 'Sir Oswald Mosley himself, however, denies that there was any case of emulating the "male ideal" of the Hitlerists, or any thought of confining women to the exclusive functions of the kitchen and the breeding of heroic Mosleyites in the making. He says that women are politically useful, and that he intends to organize special women's sections. All of which is, after all, what Signor Mussolini and Herr Hitler have already done.' p.41.

19 Oswald Mosley, *The Greater Britain* (London, 1932), p.40.

20 The nick-name of 'Ma' Mosley may seem condescending, but it was a term of endearment in the BUF. Furthermore, the responsibility for this nick-name must be assigned to Maud Mosley herself. At a BUF women's meeting at Guildhouse, Eccleston Square, in January 1934 she was quoted as saying: 'Only my great belief in this movement has attracted me from my grandmotherly armchair to a stool in the office of a youth movement.' Quoted in 'Lady Mosley's Plea: Rallying Women to the Blackshirts,' *Daily Mail*, 31 January 1934. When she opened the headquarters of the St Pancras branch in Arlington Road in May 1934, she did so by unveiling a photograph of her son, after which she mused: 'He was once my little boy. Now he is our leader. I hardly know him nowadays. He is working himself to death in a great cause.' Quoted in 'Sir Oswald Mosley's Mother: Opens New Branch of Blackshirts,' *Daily Mail*, 8 May 1934.

21 Quoted in Nicholas Mosley, *Rules of the Game* (London, 1982), p.257.

22 HO144/19070/50–60

23 'The Woman Fascist: Paper for Women Members,' *Blackshirt*, No. 48, 23–29 March 1934. According to 'What the Blackshirts are Doing,' *Sunday Dispatch*, 17 June 1934, the *Woman Fascist* was being privately circulated and had 700 subscribers.

24 Quoted in Nicholas Mosley, *Beyond the Pale*, p.91.

25 *Daily Worker*, 9 July 1937.

26 HO144/20140/102–20

27 'The Blackshirt movement is essentially one of youth. The women's sections are adding – Beauty. The women and girls of Britain are flocking to the movement. Many of them are strikingly beautiful.' 'Beauty Joins the Blackshirts,' *Sunday Dispatch*, 29 May 1934.

28 'Why So Many Women Support the Blackshirt Movement,' *Evening News*, 18 May 1934.

29 'Point Six – Fascism Means the Enslavement of Women ... . If anything were needed to show how they regard women, we need only go back to Lord Rothermere's recruiting stunt in the "Sunday Dispatch" during May ... . This is just a typical gutter press use of sex.' Young Communist League, *10 Points Against Fascism*, [1934?]

30 J.L. Douglas, *Spotlight on Fascism: Facts about Fascism, Men Behind Mosley, Culture Killers, Landlords, Leader and Captain Kidd, The Plan to Goosestep over Europe* (London, [n.d.])

31 HO144/20140/250–52

32 It is interesting to note that Lady Mosley was present at a dance organized by the Women's Section of the Brixton Branch the summer following this scandal, no doubt in an attempt to rehabilitate the reputation of the Branch. It was reported how 'the spontaneous inspiration of her address, and the warmth of her presence made such a deep impression on all, that the spirit of comradeship and sacrifice created amid the cheers that acclaimed Lady Mosley will carry forward the Movement in the S.E. London Area with renewed vigour.' 'Lady Mosley Visits Brixton and Richmond,' *Blackshirt*, No. 68, 10 August 1934. Also significant is that the Brixton respondent to *Labour Party Questionnaire* of July 1934 reported how in Brixton 'they are all male members, young women visit their quarters but do not take part in their meetings.' Labour Party Questionnaire on Local Fascist Activities, National Museum of Labour History, Manchester, LP/FAS/34/174.

33 Labour Party Questionnaire on Local Fascist Activities, National Museum of Labour History, Manchester, LP/FAS/34/16.

34 See Stephen Cullen, *The British Union of Fascists*, 1932–1940, p.100.

35 HO144/20144/242

36 HO144/20144/142–43

37 HO144/20144/197–98

38 Quoted in Nicholas Mosley, *Beyond the Pale*, p.91–92.

39 HO144/20144/183–84

40 Quoted in Nicholas Mosley, *Beyond the Pale*, p.70–71.

41 Quoted in Nicholas Mosley, *Beyond the Pale*, p.25.

42 Quoted in Nicholas Mosley, *Beyond the Pale*, p.92.

43 'I took no part in BU before the war except for fund raising. I often went along to meeting, but never spoke at one, and never took part in a march; the other

day I read in a paper that I had been "seen" striding along in a march, a complete invention.' Letter from Diana Mosley to the author, 26 March 1996.

44 'British Union Personalities: No. 3 – Mrs Anne Brock Griggs,' *Action*, No. 40, 21 November 1936.

45 By May 1934, six of thirty-eight London branches had women's officers and twenty-one of fifty-nine provincial branches had a women's section and officer. See HO144/20140/102–120.

46 'Although in all cases women will be regarded as a constituency organization, with the exception of Special Divisions, they shall have power to operate in teams of 3 to 9 members and will be recognized as such provided they give two nights a week service of a political character to the movement. It must be clear, however, that no obligation rests with the women to form teams and shall be encouraged to be active as ordinary political members in women's wards, organizations etc.' 'National Women's Organization(1935),' HO144/20144/84–90.

47 'The Fascist Policy: A Disillusioned Woman: Bumptious Men,' *Hampstead and Highgate Express*, 3 March 1935. Individual initiative was not well regarded in the BUF, and, as another example of dictatorial control, members of the Dorset branch were censured by Major A.Cleghorn, Director of Political Organization, for holding an unauthorized meeting. Cleghorn wrote to the Mr FitzGerald, D/L for Dorset, on 5 November 1934: 'I would like to draw your attention to the irregularity of the proceeding as it is not for the members of a branch to indicate how the branch is to be run, that is your duty and any interference in your prerogative must be discountenanced by you ... . We cannot have members presuming to instruct those who have been set in authority over them.' Saunders Collection, Sheffield University, File A.1.

48 In November 1937 the movement took on the appellation 'British Union,' thereby dropping the 'of Fascists and National Socialists.' HO144/21064/44–50

49 HO144/21063/406–11

50 HO144/21281/59–62

51 'Private Document – For Personal Use and Information Only [1937]: The facts are as follows: 104 members of NHQ salaried staff had to be dispensed with for reasons of economy alone ... . Nearly all those no longer on the salaried staff have offered voluntary service in their spare time, which is gladly accepted, and will consequently be available to the Movement as speakers, writers of voluntary organizers. The exceptions among so many are Messrs. Beckett and Joyce who have not emerged in the same manner from this stern test of character. The defection of these two will cause the Movement not the slightest difficulty when it is made good by the energy of thousands.' Saunders Collection, Sheffield University, File A.2.

52 HO144/20163/232

53 A.K. Chesterton, *Why I Left Mosley*, HO144/21247/98–101.

54 'Organization and Revolution: Women can be Real Revolutionaries,' *Action*, No. 112, 9 April 1938.

55 Anne Brock Griggs, 'British Mothers Demonstrate: Save Our Children,' *Action*, No. 138, 8 October 1938.

56 An example of BU anti-war propaganda directed towards British women: 'Women! Your children suffer in war. Prices rise. Coal is scarce. 1.5 million of our people are unemployed. Their families are in need. Why are millions found for war and nothing to improve the lot of the people. Why is profiteering rampant. To continue the war must mean greater suffering for the people. Prosperity will not come with war. Remember last time ... . Don't wish for peace, work for it, since only through peace can Britain and her people be saved.' Published by Olive Hawks, 16 Great Smith Street, HO45/24891/213.

57 'The Individual as Revolutionary: Women's Part in British Union,' *Action*, No. 153, 28 January 1939. By September 1939 Special Branch reported that 'Unofficially, members (both male and female) are being urged to join the civilian defence units – Air Raid Precautions, Special Constabulary, Nursing Reserve, etc. and to carry out the propaganda of the movement within these organizations.' HO144/21429/16–20. In October 1939 Special Branch reported that 'Alexander Raven-Thomson's wife, who is of German birth, conducts a business in Haymarket W., which is now doing an extensive trade in ARP requisites, such as steel helmets. The bookshop formerly maintained by the movement at 85 Fetter Lane EC4, has also been taken over by Thomson for the sale of ARP material.' HO144/21429/100. After BU members were interned, 'Miss Hiscox said she thought all those women in our circle should apply to join Ambulance Units so that in case of invasion they would take ambulances to the camp and attempt to bluff their way in and release internees.' HO45/25741/73–80.

58 'Angry Women Occupy Communist Platform,' *Action*, No. 205, 8 February 1940.

59 It was in February 1940 that Special Branch reported that Brock-Griggs was 'slackening in her enthusiasm for the movement and it is believed that she will shortly resign from her post as Chief Woman Organizer.' HO45/24895/16–17. Under questioning by the Advisory Committee on 2 July 1940, Oswald Mosley said that Anne Brock-Griggs was 'dismissed from her appointment since the war on grounds of inefficiency.' HO283/13/2–125. Nevertheless, along with Olive Hawks, Norah Elam and Mrs Whinfield, she was one of the first BU women interned in May 1940.

60 Letter from Mary Penman, HO144/21933/316–17.

61 Letter from W/C/O Wessex, F.E. Hayes to Robert Saunders, 22 February 1939, Saunders Collection, Sheffield University, File A.4.

62 Related in a letter From Robert Saunders to D.F. Thompson, 18 February 1940, Saunders Collection, Sheffield University, File A.8. How did the fact that Britain

was at war effect the level and frequency of branch meetings? As Saunders wrote, 'we hope to hold 34 between now and August in West Dorset. This does not seem many beside the 111 we held in the 12 months prior to last August, but it is as many as we can possibly manage under war conditions.' Letter from Robert Saunders to Eric Burch, 18 March 1940, Saunders Collection, File A.8.

63 Saunders Collection, File A.3.

64 Saunders Collection, File A.4.

65 Letter from F.E. Hayes to Robert Saunders, November 24 1939, Saunders Collection, File A.4

66 Letter from Louise Irvine to the author, 8 June 1996.

67 HO283/14/2–117

68 'Women Peace Campaign,' *Action*, No. 202, 18 January 1940.

69 Communication from the West Riding of Yorkshire Constabulary, County Chief Constable's Office to General Kell, 17 May 1940, HO45/25726.

70 Interview with Gladys Walsh, Archive of the Friends of O.M. Already the leading figure in the BU's Nelson Branch, Nellie Driver, almost single-handedly, had to contend with the problems and impossibility of branch organization once war began, and especially how after the arrest of BU leaders, provincial branches had to fend for themselves in the absence news and visiting officials from NHQ. See Nellie Driver, *From the Shadows of Exile*, p.47.

71 Not only did women take over men's jobs, but some literally replaced their BU husbands. 'We have to mourn two members killed in action, by the irony of fate the first name on the first casualty list was one of them. Our sympathy goes to the widow of a senior officer of HMS *Courageous*, who joined our Movement the day after she buried her gallant husband.' Letter from R/I Wessex to Miss Hayes, 2 November 1939, Saunders Collection, Sheffield University, File A.4.

72 Richard Griffiths, *Patriotism Perverted: Captain Ramsay, the Right Club and British anti-Semitism 1939–40* (London, 1998), p.250.

73 File on Richard Allister Houston, Copy of Political Notes Found at 71, Chiswick High Road, July 1940, HO45/25713.

74 These names were thought to be those authorized to take over the movement upon Mosley's incapacitation. There were no women on this list. HO283/48/27. MI5 presumed that Elam's Anti-Vivisection Society, with offices in Victoria Street, was simply a BU front organization. This may have been the case, but confusion has arisen due to the fact that the main organization of this type was the British Union for the Abolition of Vivisection, with offices at 47 White-hall, London. On the one hand, there is no evidence that Elam was an activist in the BUAV, and the BUAV's organ hotly denied any connection with Mosley's British Union. See 'The Single Aim of the BUAV,' *The Abolitionist*, July 1940. On the other hand, Dr Margaret Vivien, a BU member, was involved with the BUAV and she spoke on their behalf. See *The Abolitionist*, 1 August 1935.

75 Advisory Committee to Consider Appeals Against Orders of Internment, 2 July 1940, HO283/13/2–125. Maud, Lady Mosley was never interned.

76 Gisela Bock, 'Women's History and Gender History: Aspects of an International Debate,' in ed. R. Shoemaker and Mary Vincent, *Gender and History in Western Europe* (London, 1998), p.29.

77 The BUF counted on the submission of its members to voluntary discipline, and three separate divisions were instituted to reflect the differing intensity of individual commitments. Division I members were the active Blackshirts; Division II members were those who were active but did not wear the uniform; and Division III members were non-active. Women tended to be recruited into the second and third divisions, but a W/D/L would automatically be promoted to the first division.

78 Anne Brock-Griggs, *Women and Fascism: 10 Important Points* (London, 1936).

79 'Women: Equal Pay for Equal Work – Spreading the Truth of Fascism,' *Fascist Week*, No. 2, 17–23 November 1933.

80 'Women: Equal Pay for Equal Work – Spreading the Truth of Fascism,' *Fascist Week*, No. 2, 17–23 November 1933.

81 'Women Blackshirts: Helping to Build a Greater Britain,' *Blackshirt*, No. 58, 1 June 1934.

82 Oswald Mosley, *My Life*, p.344.

83 Nellie Driver, *From the Shadows of Exile*, p.12.

84 Sutton D.L.Q. – response to the Labour Party Questionnaire on Local Fascist Activities mentioned that 'a Women's Defence Force has been formed.' LP/FAS/34/4. The respondent for Hallam (Sheffield) reported a 'Women's Defence Organization. Making no progress (adjunct of the Tory Party).' National Museum of Labour History, Manchester, LP/FAS/34/421. The Women's Drum Corps was a post-Public Order Act innovation, and therefore it is significant that the women somehow circumvented the law by wearing a uniform when performing.

85 Letter from Robert Saunders to Mrs Diment, 11 March 1937, Saunders Collection, Sheffield University, File A.6.

86 *The Times*, 8 June 1934.

87 Miss Storm Jameson in 'Vindicator,' *Fascists at Olympia: A Record of Eye-Witnesses and Victims* (London, 1934), p.12.

88 'Woman Slashed with Razor Blades,' *Blackshirt*, No. 79, 26 October 1934.

89 Quoted in Martin Durham, *Women and Fascism* (London, 1998), p.54–55.

90 *Yorkshire Post*, 28 September 1936.

91 Yolande McShane, *Daughter of Evil* (London, 1980), p.30.

92 Letter from Robert Row to the author, 14 March 1997.

93 'Women: Equal Pay for Equal Work – Spreading the Truth of Fascism,' *The Fascist Week*, No. 2, 17–23 November 1933.

94 Irene Clephane, *Towards Sex Freedom* (London, 1935), p.228. 'Like other fascist movements, the BUF's attitude to women was decidedly modern, and when

one considers the contemporary moral attitude to the idea of women standing on the street selling newspapers, one can see the "revolutionary" nature of the role of Blackshirt women in the movement.' Stephen Cullen, 'The Development of the Ideas and Policy of the BUF,' *Journal of Contemporary History*, 22, 1 (January 1987), 115–136.

95 Esther Makgill, 'How Women Members can Help: Secretarial Work and Canvassing Work in Plenty,' *Blackshirt*, No. 51, 13–19 April 1934.

96 'Blackshirt Women Speakers in Lancashire,' *Blackshirt*, No. 113, 21 June 1935. Interestingly, the fascist women of Manchester held the first all-women propaganda march on 4 October 1936, while the BUF was engaged in the Battle of Cable Street in East London.

97 When Brock Griggs rose to the position of Woman Propaganda Officer, she sent out the following communique to all Districts and National Inspectors. 'As it is important that we should increase out team of women speakers, it is more than ever necessary to be on the look out for potential women speakers among the members .... It is not a question of oratory, which is a rare gift. We want first and foremost a team of women speakers who can expound the creed of Fascism simply, and in their own words.' Saunders Collection, Sheffield University, File A.1.

98 'British Union Personalities: No. 17 – Miss Doreen Bell,' *Action*, No. 55, 6 March 1937.

99 Metropolitan Police Report, 28 July 1937, HO144/21086/264–265.

100 'Live Fascist Women,' *Blackshirt*, No. 177, 12 September 1936.

101 Letter from Neville Laski to Sir John Russell, Under Secretary of State, 20 September 1936, HO144/21060/207. Even so-called entertainment in the BUF was of an anti-Semitic nature. Dances were frequently advertised and both men and women could unwind to the tunes played by 'an Aryan Dance Band, "Jazz without Jews."'

102 *The Fascist Week*, No. 13, 2–8 February 1934.

103 Dorothy Parkyn, 'Canvassing Tonight?' *Action*, No. 105, 19 February 1938.

104 'Northampton Meets Prospective British Union Candidate,' *Action*, No. 41, 28 November 1936.

105 In the run-up to the election the BU scheduled 420 meetings in the Bethnal Green, Shoreditch and Limehouse constituencies, 18 of which were addressed by women members Mrs Carruthers, Mrs Bowie, Mrs Thomas, Miss Barrington, Mrs Whinfield and Miss Olive Hawks. HO144/21063/379–387.

106 HO144/21063/365–68.

107 In Bethnal Green Thomson polled 3,028 votes and Clarke 3,022; in Limehouse Brock Griggs polled 2,086 and Wegg-Prosser 2,086; in Shoreditch Joyce polled 2,564 and Bailey 2,492 votes.

108 HO144/21063/242–46

109 The total BU vote in the Municipal election was 7,374. Mrs Margaret Warnett, Kingsland Ward, 110 votes; Mrs Catherine Tisler, St Pancras No. 1 Ward, 113

votes; Lilian Wilson, Bethnal Green North Ward, 665 votes; and Margaret M.E. Johnston, Bethnal Green West Ward, 354 votes. HO144/20164/54

110 Anne Brock Griggs, *Women and Fascism: 10 Important Points.*

111 HO144/20142/76–78

112 Special Branch report, 11 March 1935, HO144/20144/135–139.

113 Special Branch report, 27 March 1936, HO144/20147/297.

114 HO144/21281/119. By May 1939, the BU's precarious financial position resulted in another round of staff reduction, and Olive Hawks and Anne Brock-Griggs were dismissed, although the latter stayed on as a volunteer worker. HO144/21281/125.

115 'Dewsbury: At a meeting referred to in the Press reports, out of eight ladies present the President of the Women's Conservative Association and another active member were included.' LP/FAS/34/82. 'Central Hull: One Lady Councillor independent, Mrs Hatfield has prominently identified herself with the local Fascists.' LP/FAS/34/227. 'Harrogate: They appear to confine their attention to younger members of the Tory Party, particularly those interested in sports, Rugby and Golf players .... A kind of half-hearted support is offered by the younger element of the Conservative Party!', National Museum of Labour History, Manchester, LP/FAS/34/24.

116 Martin Pugh, *The Tories and the People 1880–1935* (Oxford, 1985), p.191

117 Letter from Mr FitzGerald, D/O, to A.D.G.O. Administration Southern NHQ, Saunders Collection, Sheffield University, File A.5. Brock Griggs spoke at the Women's Institute County Hall on Saturday 20 June 1936, and this meeting coincided with a 'Great Peace Rally' in Dorchester, addressed by Vera Brittain and others. Both Alexander Raven Thomson and Mr MacNab also addressed BUF meetings at the Women's Institute County Hall in Dorchester on 15 October 1936 and 28 January 1937, respectively. On the afternoon of Friday 25 March 1938 Brock Griggs was back in Dorset to speak at a meeting of the South Dorset Branch of the National Council of Women. The W/D/L for Dorset West, Mrs Gladys Stephenson, was accredited with doing 'much good work among Conservative women.' Confidential, West Dorset, 22 April 1936, Saunders Collection, Sheffield University, File A.4.

118 'Primrose League and the Blackshirts: Sir Reginald Bennett Replies to Sir Oswald Mosley,' *Morning Post*, 21 May 1934.

119 'What the Blackshirts are Doing,' *Sunday Dispatch*, 17 June 1934.

120 'More British Union Candidates,' *Action*, No. 49, 23 January 1937.

121 'More British Union Prospective Candidates,' *Action*, No. 69, 12 June 1937.

122 'Reds Deny Women Speakers Free Speech,' *Action*, No. 38, 7 November 1936.

123 'The Blackshirts have what the Conservatives need,' *Daily Mail*, 25 April 1934.

124 Norah Elam, 'Women and the Vote,' *Action*, No. 6, 26 March 1936.

125 Dinah Parkinson, 'To a Woman Tory,' *Action*, No. 103, 5 February 1938.

126 Yolande McShane, *Daughter of Evil*, p.29–30.

127 Olga Keyes, 'Ex-Communist Woman Tells Why Fascism is the Only True Socialism,' *Action*, No. 141, 29 October 1938.

128 Quoted in a letter from Louise Irvine to the author, 5 June 1996.

129 Nellie Driver, *From the Shadows of Exile*, p.12.

130 Yolande McShane, *Daughter of Evil*, p.30.

131 HO144/20163/406–411

132 Among those aspects of the British Blackshirt mentality which most perturbed Winifred Holtby was this fixation on youth against age, observing that BUF men regarded 'women between the ages of– shall we say– 40 to 70 (silver-haired mothers being sacred anyway) with the disappointed aversion of one who, expecting a good hot meal, finds only the congealing substance of an under-boiled egg left too long in its shell.' Winifred Holtby, 'Shall I Order a Black Blouse,' *News Chronicle*, 4 May 1934.

133 See Stephen Cullen, 'Four Women for Mosley,' *Oral History*, 24, 1 (Spring 1996), 49–59.

134 Letter from Mrs Mitt Sanford to the Secretary of the BUF, Dorchester, 10 November 1936, Saunders Collection, Sheffield University, File A.2.

135 Alexander Raven, 'Aristocracy of Worth,' *The Fascist Week*, No. 13, 2–8 February 1934.

136 'There was conflict between those middle and upper class women supporters of the BUF who saw the movement as a bulwark against socialism and labour militancy and wanted a cheaper, more malleable servant work force, and the domestics themselves, who were attracted to fascism because it campaigned for their rights.' Tony Kushner, 'Politics and Race, Gender and Class: Refugees, Fascists and Domestic Service in Britain, 1933–1940' in eds. T. Kushner and K. Lunn, *The Politics of Marginality*, p.51.

137 'British Union Personalities: No. 14 – Miss Olga F.C. Shore,' *Action*, No. 52, 13 February 1937.

138 'Prospective British Union Parliamentary Candidates,' *Action*, No. 42, 5 December 1936.

139 Unpublished article sent by Louise Irvine to Leonard Wise, 'A Woman's Point of View', 12 November 1984.

140 Nellie Drievr, *From the Shadows of Exile*, p.30.

141 Interview with Blanche Greaves, Archive of the Friends of O.M..

142 Interview with Gladys Walsh, Archive of the Friends of O.M..

143 Letter from W/C/O West Hants F.E. Hayes to D/L Dorset, 29 January 1938, Saunders Collection, Sheffield University, File A.3.

144 Pat Thane, 'The Women of the British Labour Party and Feminism, 1906–1945' in ed. Harold Smith, *British Feminism in the 20th Century* (London, 1990), p.124. In 1914 membership of the Women's Labour League was *ca.* 5,000, by 1923 it was 120,000, and between 1927 and 1939 it was between 250,000 and 300,000. In the inter-war period women composed at least half the individual membership of the Labour Party.

145 Pamela Graves, *Labour Women* (Cambridge, 1994), p.187. Looking at BUF propaganda and reading the frequent fascist attacks on the disproportionate influence of 'Red' women as opponents at BUF meetings, the impression would be that the CPGB was more open to women's participation. However, Bruley has argued that 'there is little evidence in Britain of serious and systematic work among women and very few party women's groups ever got off the ground. Women's membership varied from area to area, but typically not much more than 10 per cent of the total ... . Very often women recruits to the party were the wives of party activists. Branch meetings were largely a male affair, held in the pub during the evening. Women's sections, where they existed at all, were composed largely of "party wives" and met in the afternoon. Typically they concentrated on fund-raising and organizing party socials and failed to raise political demands relating to women.' Sue Bruley, 'Women and Communism: A case study of the Lancashire weavers in the Depression', in ed. G. Andrews *et al.*, *Opening the Books* (London, 1995), pp.64–82.

146 Melville Currell, *Political Woman* (London, 1974), p.37.

147 Anne Brock Griggs, 'Womankind in National Socialism,' *Action*, No. 99, 6 January 1938.

148 Letter from Eugenia Wright to the author, 6 May 1997. It should be noted that these motivations did not tend to result in long-term commitments to the BUF, and Wright left the movement only weeks after joining. She deserted the BUF because she was shocked by its anti-Semitism, and because her attraction to the young blond lad went unreciprocated.

149 Mr Greaves was present when Jeffrey Wallder interviewed his wife. Interview with Blanche Greaves, Archive of the Friends of O.M.

150 'Fascist Chief of Staff Married,' *The Fascist Week*, No. 7, 22–28 December 1933. A photograph of the cake-cutting ceremony also exists, and is held in the Joyce Collection at the University of Sheffield Library. The cake was also in the form of a fasces and placed on a table draped with the Union Jack.

151 'Fascist Wedding at Chelsea: Blackshirt Bride and Bridegroom,' *Daily Telegraph*, 27 March 1934.

152 Rebecca West, *The Meaning of Treason* (London, 1949), pp.73–74. In his book *Twilight over England* (Berlin, 1940), Joyce wrote of his wife 'it was through National Socialism that we met; it was therefore only fitting that our decision to leave for Germany on August 25th 1939, was a joint decision.' HO45/25779/46.

153 HO144/21060/207

154 Letter from Louise Irvine to the author, 5 June 1996.

155 Letter from E.A. Newsam to Sir Moylon, New Scotland Yard, 6 December 1941, HO144/22495.

156 Advisory Committee to Consider Appeals Against orders of Internment, 2 July 1940, HO283/13/2–125.

Chapter 3

The Ideology of Feminine Fascism

The British Union of Fascists proposed radical alternatives to the main trends in Britain's social, economic, cultural, and political development during the inter-war period. To women, the movement proposed a revised image of femininity, remedies to the exploitation of cheaper female labour, spiritual regeneration, a return to family and to a narrowly defined national community, and novel political representation in the Corporate State of the fascist future. A feminine fascist identity was developed in opposition to the bourgeois and liberal-democratic status quo, while still embracing the militant spirit which animated women's suffrage campaigners earlier in the century. Although conversant with Fascist and Nazi ideologues on the Continent, writers in the British Union of Fascists sought to announce their own creed of fascist femininity. Claiming to represent 'true feminism' by recognizing the irreversibility of women's emancipation, the BUF's *feminine fascism* applauded those aggressive aspects of women's activism essential to the success of a nascent fascist movement.

The boundaries of BUF ideology were fluid, it was often experimental and volatile in response to the changing European scene. The evolution of the movement's policies towards women reflected this flux and improvization. Nevertheless, while women's issues were relegated to a female sphere and to a women's page in the newspapers, the vociferousness of women was striking. Further, the British fascist reliance on a sexually-referential idiom meant that few areas of BUF ideological discourse were free from the power struggles of sexual politics and not pervaded by a gendered language.

The difference between the fervent idealism of fascist ideology and the reality of the BUF's marginality was a central factor in creating tensions at the organization level, encouraging internal controversy, and giving free reign to the eccentricities of personality. The previous chapter was concerned with women's visibility in the BUF and it was demonstrated that by indulging in personality conflict, humourless fanaticism and even unlawful behaviour, women members were partially responsible for the still-birth of the BUF as a political force. In this chapter we will be concerned with women's audibility in the British fascist discourse, and it will be illustrated how the mixed messages and contortions of women's propaganda should likewise be seen to have contributed to the fact that the British fascist clarion call fell on deaf ears.

The Image and Idealization of the Fascist Woman

The idealization and reification of fascist womanhood in Britain was most often a reflection of the perceived strengths and character traits of women members, but there was a clear distinction between what was highlighted as appropriate female behaviour in a nascent fascist movement, and what would be expected of British womanhood in an established fascist state. The British fascist woman of the movement was praised for her vibrant health, her physical attractiveness, her charm and intelligence, her quick-wittedness and her strong character. She was presented as sober and tenacious, motherly but wary of sentimentality, and weary of British conservatism. [1] Her most valuable talents and contributions to the movement were her gifts for oratory, her faculty in disseminating propaganda, and her facility in recruiting new members. As early as 1933 *The Fascist Week* offered its thanks to those women who motivated men to join the BUF: 'Fascism in Britain knows that it is a woman's influence that has *converted* so many of its male members.' [2] Together these attributes suggested the utility of women to the movement, as women were to act as the publicists, the temptresses, and the vendors of fascism to a British market suspicious of fascism's machismo and masculine aggression. [3] And impress they did, leading one ardent left-wing feminist to contemplate why so many women were buying black blouses upon observing 'a healthy, vigorous-looking specimen of Fascist youth striding down the King's Road, Chelsea ... . This young Fascist was a tall, well-built woman in the early thirties, with close-cropped black hair, black beret, black blouse and a party badge.' [4] While very much written tongue-in-cheek, Holtby's description attested to the fascist use of woman as mascot.

94

Fascism's cult of violence for men was complemented by a cult of beauty and physical fitness for women. Together these two mystiques acted as substitutes for overt expressions of sexuality. As Wilhelm Reich contended, 'the effect of militarism is based essentially on a libidinous mechanism. The sexual effect of a uniform, the erotically provocative effect of rhythmically executed goose-stepping, the exhibitionistic nature of militaristic procedure, have been more politically comprehended by a salesgirl or an average secretary than by our more erudite politicians.'[5] Images of the fascist mass woman as cheer leader were scattered throughout the literature. Anne Cutmore remarked how during a march through Bethnal Green in June 1936 'onlookers cheer as the Leader passes and a woman throws a flower from a window,'[6] and reports circulated of girls of sixteen or seventeen giving the fascist salute from their windows as a Blackshirt procession passed through Limehouse in October 1936.[7]

The fascist woman was objectified and simultaneously desexualized in BUF portrayals. As we shall see, discourse on sexuality and sexology was reserved for male dialogue and diatribe, while female arousal was confined to public displays of ecstatic support and spectacles of joy through work. The British fascist masculine aesthetic of hard lines, classical angularity, and a virile rejection of softness or curvature, was also applied to women's 'body' politics. Segregated from men but displaying characteristics compatible with the masculine ideal, women Blackshirts camping at Selsey in the summer of 1937 were depicted in the following manner by an admiring male writer: 'Nothing silly or soft about these women. They are nothing if not practical (and no one had better go to the camp and suggest they are nothing) and the happy carefree way in which they made themselves at home, was so refreshing after one has had their fill of the simpering little brats that democracy and Jewish films have produced.'[8] The quintessential fascist woman provided an anti-thesis to overt Hollywood sex-appeal and democratic pliability.

The BUF's often repeated trope of decadent and diseased democracy thwarting healthy and vigorous fascism was placed in the context of women when 'Senex' proclaimed that 'fascists consider it a duty to keep fit. Far too many women consider it their privilege to be ill ... just ill enough to pamper themselves and evade their share of the family work.'[9] The BUF's women leaders were appreciated for their healthy look and Anne Brock Griggs, Women's Organizer, was described as 'tall and slim [and] she epitomises in her appearance the finest characteristics of English womanhood, embodying a keen and active brain, a gift for speaking, and able powers of oratory with an attractive physique.'[10] Similarly, Doreen Bell, Woman Staff Speaker, was complimented for being a 'young and charming brunette ... with great powers of oratory.'[11]

It was through oratory that women fascists best served their function as publicists and popularizers of the fascist message. The woman orator was a figure of vitality, and an able resister of violent attacks by opponents and hecklers. Not all women were equipped for the task of public speaking, however, and Diana Mosley admitted being temperamentally unable to make a speech in the 1930s, while Louise Irvine confessed that 'I never had the self-confidence or quick repartee to make a good speaker.'[12] Those women who did muster the courage to speak were permitted some humour, although it was by exploiting emotional sensationalism that they provided a veneer of decency and domestic respectability to an aggressively masculine creed. The Women's Propaganda March at Balham in 1936 was attended by frequent interruptions which were 'good-humoured, but the speaker's humour was better. Someone asked why they wore black shirts. "Because they don't run," came the instant reply. "We all know what happens when you wash a red shirt."'[13] Women's dominion over the domestic sphere was not promoted only to provide British women with superior instructions in colour-fastness. It was argued that 'the approach of women to speaking is in some important aspects different from that of men. Always the inspiration of women has a more personal derivation.'[14] Consequently, while the visibility of women speaking on public platforms may have attested to the BUF's inclusion of women in public life, it was still the case that women preserved their femininity by 'staying close to home' in both the form and content of their speeches.

Fascist Heroines and Hero-Worship

Ideals of 'pre-conquest' fascist womanhood could also be deduced from those historical and contemporary figures who served as the BUF's heroines. Hero-worship was most closely allied to another set of female tendencies indispensable to palingenetic fascism, namely faith, spiritual yearning and experiences of conversion. Against the preoccupation with women's private sphere, the BUF's heroines were all women who had broken through the bars of women's confinement to the home. The BUF harkened back to the Tudor epoch in Britain's history and Mosley spoke longingly of the reincarnation of 'Merrie England.'[15] The British fascist intention was nothing less than the re-invention of the common weal! In this light it was natural that the Virgin Queen should become an icon for fascist women, and Tudor times were seen to be 'the Golden Age of women's accomplishments ... Queen Elizabeth was an accomplished orator.'[16] It was this reverence for Tudor England which inspired Kathleen Texera to aver that 'Shakespeare would have been a Fascist.'[17]

Queen Elizabeth was chosen as role model for her command over the nation, while the next heroine was chosen because her life seemed to epitomise government betrayal and the corruption of finance capitalism, and provide historical justification for anti-Semitism. Lady Hester Stanhope, the Younger Pitt's housekeeper and favourite niece, had been an adventurer in the Middle East. She had amassed debts with Jewish money-lenders – 'Shylocks' – while in the Arab world, which the British government refused to repay. E.D. Hart used her example to elucidate the BUF's attitude towards women. 'Those women who, whether from choice or, as in the case of Lady Hester, from necessity, explore other walks of life, will find both assistance and encouragement. When, like her, they display the Fascist virtues of courage, self-reliance, and tenacity of purpose, we ascribe to them the honour which is their due.'[18] Notably, Queen Elizabeth and Lady Hester Stanhope were heroines and role models chosen for women by men.

The BUF's modern heroines were selected for overcoming the bounds of gravity. Flight was a very pervasive metaphor for the fledgling movement, enforced by the living memory of Mosley as RFC pilot, realized by the BUF's defence policy which called for rapid air rearmament, and materialized by Lord Rothermere's christening the bomber aircraft he had designed and then donated to the nation 'Britain First,' after the BUF slogan. As early as 1924 Mary Allen learned to fly at Stag Lane aerodrome, where her fellow pupils were Lady Baily and Lady Heath, while 'Amy Johnson was polishing up her flying at the aerodrome, having just taken her A Licence.'[19] In 1934 the BUF established a special Flying Club for women in Gloucestershire.[20] With the imminent approach of war, in July 1938, *Action* celebrated the accomplishment of the women aviators Amelia Earhart, Jean Batten and Fraulein Hanna Reitsch, the latter having attained the rank of Flying Captain in the German Air Force.

Of course, the hero who most inspired BUF women was Sir
Oswald Mosley himself, and it was in their devotion to their saviour
that female fanaticism was presented in boldest relief. Mosley
was figured as muse both to the nation and to aspiring poetesses
in the BUF. Joan Bond's ballad elegized the decadence of the age
before asking,

> Dwells there a man in this once happy realm,
> Loving his country with a selfless love,
> With strength and will to crush this fearsome force?
> In British Union liveth such a man
> And in his fate lies our fate, yours and mine,
> The fate of England! [21]

Messianic imagery, unrelenting references to destiny and spiritual
renaissance enlivened BUF texts. British fascism was freely
acknowledged to be a secular theology, and Mosley preached that
'Fascism comes to politics with the force of a new religion, and
draws from its adherents a spirit of sacrifice and self-abnegation
in the cause, the force which triumphs over all material things.' [22]
BUF adherents recalled their turn to fascism as a conversion
experience. Diana Mosley understood her first encounter with
her future husband both as a personal and an ideological epiphany:
'He knew what to do to solve the economic disaster we were
living through, he was certain he could cure unemployment. Lucid,
logical, forceful and persuasive, he soon converted me as he did
thousands of others.' [23] Similarly, the 18B Advisory Committee
perceived British fascism's effect on some women, and in the
case of Miss Baggaley Committee members could appreciate how
'it is not without pathos that National Socialism should have inspired
this rather colourless existence with all the force of missionary
fervour.' [24]

Both sexes were commanded to live out their fascist faith, and
allow their lives to be governed by the new spirit. Taking over
former sites of religious education and worship, BUF National
Headquarters were situated in the King's Road, Chelsea, in 'a
grey pseudo-Gothic ex-theological college which [was] ... dubbed
"Ecstasy Castle."' [25] Similarly, after vacating their own headquarters
in Grosvenor Place in 1934, the Women's Section was stationed
in a former chapel adjoining National headquarters. Mosley stipulated
that 'our organization must differ even in respect from ordinary
political parties in that all our members, men and women, must

be active. They are introducing a new creed to their country and to the world, and are expected to live as crusaders to that creed.'[26] Significantly, whereas members often referred to prior political and secular commitments of which they had been cured, there were very few examples of the women among Mosley's followers who brought attention to their affiliations to religious groups before they were converted to fascism, although there were instances where Christian rebirth transpired after leaving the BUF.[27]

Religion was acknowledged to be a traditionally female domain. The short-lived *Woman Fascist* carried articles on 'Women and Religion,' and women contributors to the *Blackshirt* placed added emphasis on the spiritual content of fascism. The Austrian-born Baroness Ella de Heemstra – wife of V.A. Hepburn-Ruston, mother of the actress Audrey Hepburn, and friend of Unity Mitford – expressed the spiritual enthusiasm of many women members when she wrote 'we who have heard the call of Fascism, and have followed the light on the upward road to victory, have been taught to understand what dimly we know, and now fully realize that only the spirit can cleanse the body, only the soul of Britain can be the salvation of Britain ... . Only on the unshakable foundations of spirit can a new world be rebuilt.'[28] As proselyte and proselytizer, the ideal fascist woman demonstrated nothing short of religious fanaticism to Mosley and his British creed. This survey of the linguistic and ideological exploitation of piety and quasi-religious fervour can serve to explain Mosley's surprisingly non-pejorative use of the term 'fanaticism' to describe the devotion of his women supporters.

Marketing Motherhood: Breeders of Race and Nation

The centrality of palingenetic metaphors contributed to the construction of the ideal fascist mother as the breeder and nurturer of a race reborn. Women's birthing function and the spiritual rebirth of the nation were easily conflated, as were the concepts of biology and destiny. 'Biologically, Fascism is right to begin with: believing that the secret of a nation's true greatness is the harmony of its organic life, discarding the selfish futilities of individualism for the sublime entity of the Corporate nation.'[29] Mothers fulfilled their biologically destined roles by acceding to demands for an increase in the birth rate, and accepting as an honour the importance given to their powers of procreation. As

a reward for returning with full force to their mothering role, the
seven BUF propositions were:

1. Education for women to seek advice before the birth of their
children.
2. More clinics, of a more efficient and attractive design.
3. More women doctors, who may be preferred by patients.
4. Better training, pay and hours for midwives.
5. More specialized training in obstetric work for doctors.
6. Improvement and extension of local hospitals to provide more
maternity beds, and also facilities for training doctors and midwives.
7. Convalescent homes and an extended home help service enabling
mothers to recuperate fully after the birth of their babies. [30]

While the BUF was on the defensive in its emphasis on women
as mothers, and argued with opponents who feared that the rise
of fascism would mean the return of women to the home, Mosley
confidently asserted that

> the future of the race depends on women and that future is of vital concern
> to Fascism which is not occupied like the other parties solely by opportunist
> policies of the present. Fascist Government is a trusteeship not only on
> behalf of the present generation but also on behalf of the past, and still
> more of the future. A creed which carries that conscious responsibility
> must care for the welfare of women. [31]

Whereas Mosley's utterance on motherhood betrayed a debt to
the Burkean heritage of Tory sublimity, attacks against moral
conservatism and 'Puritanism' catalysed a decided turn towards
maternal race consciousness.

The transcendence of racial thinking over the more antiquated
nationalist emblem of the mother as the guardian of morality
was exemplified by Rosalind Raby's advocacy of better care for
mothers of illegitimate children. Taking her cue from Italian
provisions for maternal and infant welfare, and the Nazi state's
tolerant attitudes towards illegitimate births in order to spearhead
a racial and demographic revival, Raby promised that under a
British fascist government 'the unmarried mother will be given
the opportunity to earn an honest living for herself and her child.'[32]
On the one hand, the fascist mother was celebrated for breeding
heroes and warrior sons. John Strachey – who had been Mosley's
close ally in the Labour Party and then in the New Party, but
who by 1934 was Secretary of the Co-Ordinating Committee for

Anti-Fascist Activities – gave voice to the way in which anti-fascists saw fascism's marriage of sex and war: 'Men must find in death and mutilation the true purpose of their lives, and women must rejoice to exhaust themselves in childbirth that ever new generations of men may take their places upon the battlefield.' [33] Along these lines, 'Ma' Mosley was considered to be a particularly admirable figure as 'the courageous support which [she] is giving her son's campaign is finding an echo in every mother's heart.' [34] Further, it was rhetorically asked whether the mother was not, in fact, 'the very spring that drives the machinery, the force that has made possible the public activity of man, the hero, the fighter?' [35] The conceptual framework of male–female complementarity was buttressed by this Nietzschean proposition that women proved their utility by breeding and nurturing future soldiers and heroes.

On the other hand, the zig-zag of BUF policy and the inevitable ideological modifications necessitated by the metamorphosis from fascist revolutionary militarism to the seeming oxymoron of fascist pacifism, meant that by the time the peace campaign took centre stage, the British fascist mother sought to protect her offspring from becoming cannon-fodder in another international conflict. As one woman member of the Yorkshire branch pointed out: 'I lost my father on the Somme in 1916. Why should I now spend my life raising a family to go soldiering since our politicians want another big war.' [36]

The Politicization of Domesticity

In contrast to the demands made on women in the movement, projections of womanhood onto the fascist future concentrated on the validation of a women's sphere, motherhood and housewifery. The politicization of domesticity and the domestication of politics were poised as means towards the pacification of the sex war. British fascism was confident in its claim that both the movement and the Corporate State would respond to the needs and desires of 'normal' women.

The movement furnished a woman's world complete with their own Women's Section, their own newspaper, their own page in *Action* and the *Blackshirt*, all-women social events and meetings, and feminine accessories which announced fascist faith in the form of broaches designed with the BU's lightning symbol and Blackshirt dolls for children. [37] The *Woman Fascist* appeared for a short time until the autumn of 1934, and provided women members with their own intellectual forum. After it ceased publication, a woman's page in the *Blackshirt* was promised in its place, and it was intended to cover news and views of special concern to female members. This exclusive page appeared only sporadically, however, as did the woman's page in *Action*, titled 'Woman's Worlds,' which began appearing nearly two years after the *Woman Fascist* was discontinued.

The initial intent was that the tone in which women's issues were explored and expressed should not be dictatorial or didactic, in other words, uncharacteristic of the rhetorical assuredness typical of men's texts. As Anne Brock Griggs explained at the launch of the 'Woman's Worlds' section in *Action*,

> in these columns, week by week, I shall comment upon current topics, both political and social. My views may not be yours, but they are subjects which most of us must sooner or later form an opinion. In another part of this page we shall deal with matters related to the home, in which we do not lose sight of the relationship between our homes and the larger landscape of the State. [38]

The type of questions she posed to those reading her page exemplified the extent to which women's work outside the home was downgraded in preference for securing female command over the home. Among those queries she hoped women would be eager to answer was: 'If you are a business woman, how do you arrange your housekeeping?' [39]

At the level of organization and party structure, the order of the day was a division of labour between men and women, with some space for gender co-operation. [40] On the intellectual level, the BUF advocated an ideology of separate spheres by asserting that 'Fascism sees women as complementary and equal to man, standing beside him in no less honourable a fight, living a no less noble life, achieving in domesticity things parallel and of equal importance with man.' [41] In the BUF's formulation, both women's domestic sphere and men's public sphere were political, and the health of the national community depended on harmonious relations and a sound home life. 'It will be seen that far from thrusting women out of public life into the home, Fascism, through the Corporate State, will enable the woman in the home to emerge into public life and take her place in the functional organization of the state.' [42] To obfuscate the meaning of the terms private and public, however, was not equivalent to equalizing the two spheres, and in this way BUF pronouncements on the place of women in the state were obviously insincere.

How can we account for such contradictory statements about the role of women in the future fascist state? This co-existence of opposing views exemplified the heterogeneity of opinion, the movement's bid to attract and recruit women espousing diverse convictions, the BUF's marginality, and the inevitable tension between the co-option of Continental Fascist and Nazi principles and the BUF's reliance on women as militant party workers.

By the gesture of professionalizing domesticity, the BUF sought to protect itself against charges of forcing women to be free from public life. Certain professions were considered particularly suitable for women, and these were all essentially occupations which were most closely allied to women's biological and caring functions. Education, town planning, architecture, medicine, obstetrics, midwifery, nursing, and social welfare were assigned to women as the fascists claimed that 'there are some jobs ideally suited to women, and only women can do those jobs – but there are many jobs women are now doing that are more suitable for men.' [43]

Women journalists also sought to demonstrate how the model of the state was only an inflated version of the structural dynamics of 'domestic' government. The very same skills and feminine discernment they applied to making a success of their housekeeping were seen as transferable to state level. As one women journalist explained:

> The political interest of women can be aroused, provided that they know that their vote can help themselves, because women are very practical minded. Generations of weekly budget balancing has made them bargain hunters. So women of Britain, in the political sales, the one genuine bargain not specially stocked for the sales, is the creed of the BU, the name above the firm is pure British, and is the one known, trusted, and beloved by thousands of patriotic Britons, Oswald Mosley and the BU. [44]

Fascism was promoted as a good buy 'because it proposes to apply just the principles used by any sensible woman in dealing with the affairs of her own family to the needs of the great family, the State.' Should women fear political responsibility when already saddled with direction of their homes, the 'Ordinary Woman' reminded them that 'any mother knows that you cannot solve the problem of the "difficult" child in the home by pretending that he does not exist or that he is not "difficult."' [45] Furthermore, women were presumed to be especially well qualified for power in a *fascist* state as a consequence of their experience in domestic management, and Agnes Booth wondered 'when will they realize that women are, in a quiet way, the Dictators of this or any country? In their youth they are subject to and later become the mistress of the home, and so in turn, Dictators.' [46]

The BUF's formula for politicizing domesticity was potentially totalitarian and certainly invasive of privacy. This was ironic given that the fascists made great currency out of state intervention in working-class homes, and never minced words over their abhorrence for the Means Test. [47] Goebbels quipped that 'the only individual with a private life in Germany is the person who is sleeping,' and, although Mosley repeatedly spoke of the British fascism's philosophy as public duty and private freedom, Big Brother's intrusive glare was coming into focus on the British home.

From the perspective of prescriptions for women in the fascist future it is clear that the BUF was far from adhering to any kind of feminist agenda. However, BUF decrees on womanhood do not need to be seen as narrowly misogynist. Instead of aggressively anti-woman, the BUF's gender ideology should be understood as an expression of *feminine fascism*. As Currell argues, 'the notion of a feminine ideology relates to certain subjects being regarded as specially suitable to women's abilities and specialist knowledge – health, education, motherhood, family welfare, housing etc. – that is, all problems which are considered to be of special interest to women.' [48] Certainly the BUF was not alone among political parties during the inter-war period in assigning women their own politicized private sphere, but it was the overwhelming stress on women's domestic nature in all things which raised the heckles of anti-fascist observers. Analysing British Blackshirt literature as early as 1934, Winifred Holtby saw as significant

> the emphasis laid on the exclusively feminine functions of wifehood and motherhood. Throughout history, whenever society has tried to curtail the opportunities, interests and powers of women, it has done so in the name of marriage and maternity ... . Today, whenever women hear political leaders call their sex important, they grow suspicious. In the importance of sex too often has lain the unimportance of the citizen, the worker and the human being. [49]

While it is incontrovertible that the BUF paid attention to women's demands, would we not be more convinced of the movement's stated commitment to the equality of the sexes if gender roles had not been so sharply bifurcated, and if men and women had been exhorted to follow their leader on the same terms? Perhaps much of this seems manifest, and gender apartheid should logically follow on to patriarchal supremacy. The complexity of the BUF's gender ideology becomes apparent at this turn in the argument, however, and by examining the movement's philosophy of the family and their 'family values' we shall see how the patriarchal model is not a perfect fit.

The Fascist Family: Mothers of the Nation

At first glance, the BUF espoused a set of principles that today we might easily recognize as the direct ancestor to the 'family values' discourse of the New Right. However, there was little evidence in the fascist literature of a family unit comprising father, mother and offspring; references to the 'family' were synonyms for woman and mother. 'National Socialism, of whatever expression, stands or falls by the virility of its manhood and the perfection of its womanhood.' The BUF's programme was explained as the restoration of 'the family to its true place as the unit of society. Woman will take her rightful place in the new order: she will be at liberty either to accept or reject the glorious heritage of her sex.' [50] Clearly, man proved his virility in public life, and woman reached her perfection within the confines of the family.

Although anything as stultifying and bereft of sex appeal as Victorian mores was regarded with suspicion, women were figured as the guardians of morality, decency, and respectability. Olive Hawks predicted that 'the fascist women of the future will be neither narrow Victorians, nor sexless "arty" spinsters. They will be afraid neither of their brains nor their womanhood, but will dedicate both to clean wholesomeness of Fascist morality, and the service of the State which they are helping to bring into being.' [51] While to be sexless was no asset, fascist women were repelled by pornography, sexology, and overt expression of sexuality, and saw their role as protecting their families against the tide of decadence, and defending the social order against the communist desecration of 'Christian' moral standards. In 1934, when Commandant Mary Allen was given a tour of the Secret Police Headquarters where Communist exhibits had been collected by the German police during the Reichstag fire, she was appalled to see 'all sorts of incredibly foul and blasphemous pamphlets scoffing at religion, decency, home life – in fact everything the normal man and woman hold sacred.'[52] Yearning after sensual pleasure was equated with liberal individualism and its deformed cultural progeny – decadence – and the fascist woman could perceive nothing but aesthetic morbidity in modern life and Modernist art forms. Joan Bond eulogized the passing of Beauty and claimed that

> I cannot find her [Beauty] in this jazzing world
> In this licentious heated atmosphere,
> This dizzy, tawdry painted crew
> All tired and overwrought and satisfied
> With frenzied life and hectic sensual pleasure.
> I would pray for a cold relentless wind
> To blow the foetid mists and dark deceptions
> From the strained eyes of youth
> And I would have a storm of cleansing rain
> To wash corruption from these human souls.[53]

Allen's crusade against pornography and indecency, and Bond's cold shower and anti-sensualist verse illustrated the fascist woman's fear of the liberty of expression and the consequences of sexual licence.

Women fascists wished to see the family as the microcosm for the state, and thereby celebrate themselves as the gate-keepers of the national community. Elizabeth Winch hoped for the return of prosperity, surmising that under the conditions of affluence British women would once again have the option of returning to the home. Her basic anthropological reading of early state formation expressed her longing for the integrated family: 'the State, under practically every government in the world, is only a sublimated expression of the Family. Man, woman, and their children are the nucleus: families, bound in marriage, develop into clans; clans join together for the protection of their own interests – and thus on the basis of the Family great nations are built.'[54] With the acceptance of the family as the lowest common denominator of social structure, BUF women rested assured that their functions would be honoured.

The Fascist Family: Where Are The Husbands and Fathers?

Little did Winch care to realize, however, that the prototype for the New Fascist Man would be anathema to family life. The fascist man was ambivalent about familial co-operation, and 'Senex' scorned the situation where 'no man, whatever his station in life, is getting a square deal if he comes home after his day's work to a badly cooked and inferior meal, because his wife has not produced a good one.' [55] Certainly it was in the interest of the man to protect the family unit, but his public duties took him far away from the ancestral home, and left him the minimum of time to fulfil fatherly functions. A.K. Chesterton's wife, Doris, an unrepentant Fabian Socialist and pacifist, illustrated the way in which fascism was responsible for the theft of husbands from their wives. Doris Chesterton's satirical mock-dialogue between 'FFW' (the first fascist widow) and 'SFW' (the second fascist widow) appeared in the fascist press in 1936.

> FFW: My dear, I had a call. I thought you'd understand, and perhaps help. The truth is – my husband has caught Fascism.
> SFW: Darling! Of course I understand, and I'm very sympathetic. My own husband is six months gone with it.
> FFW: Mine's got it on the brain.
> SFW: Ah! The worst place to have it. Most don't get effected beyond the emotions. That's bad enough, of course, but when it touches the brain!!! What are his symptoms?
> FFW: Well in the first place he never sleeps. He talks all night.
> SFW: Of Fascism, Fascists, and Fascist Policy? I know!!!...
> FFW: And he never stops to eat a regular meal – says Fascist business leave him no time.
> SFW: You must get used to that. My husband has lived on cigarettes and coffee for six months. [56]

Women were abandoned and left in the home as if widowed, while fascist husbands cavorted together in public spaces with other members of their 'boys-only' club.

The BUF's ideology of masculinity at one and the same time excluded women from an all-boys club, and enlisted them in the struggle to regenerate British manhood. The fascist future was unabashedly masculine and youth oriented. The prioritized relationships were those between male comrades, united in a brotherhood, exhibiting the *esprit de corps* and dedication of the best armies, and teaching their younger officers the virtues of service to the nation. 'Fascism will take Britain and make it the playground and the schoolroom of Britain's coming manhood,' [57] 'Lucifer' projected. With the stress placed not only on masculinity, but on young and pubescent manhood, it can be understood how women and female sexuality were marginalized. The BUF saw itself as the only real 'Party of Youth' in Britain and, thereby, claimed that 'it realizes that the future of our great land is in the hands of youth ... . Boys of the BU are taught first and foremost allegiance to the King and the Empire, and how to be good citizens.'[58] It goes without saying that a nation personified as the adolescent man would place woman, and the institutions of marriage and fatherhood in precarious positions.

The relationships between man and woman, and between mother and son were depreciated in favour of manly comradeship. Man's warlike instinct had long been seen as threatened by female interference, and intellectual proto-fascism had no doubt that the rebirth of manhood was contingent upon the repression of womanhood and the quashing of feminism. In Nietzsche's view 'man should be trained for war, and women for the recreation of warriors. The belief that women are equal, or merit education, is a sign of shallowness. They should be treated as property, slaves or domestic animals.'[59] Points nine and ten of Marinetti's *Futurist Manifesto* set the tone for fascist misogyny and the exclusion of women:

> 9. We will glorify war – the world's only hygiene – militarism, patriotism, the destructive gesture of freedom-bringers, beautiful ideas worth dying for, and contempt for woman.
> 10. We will destroy the museums, libraries, academies of every kind, will fight moralism, feminism, and every opportunistic or utilitarian cowardice.[60]

While BUF propagandists never dared be so explicitly misogynist, the fascist-futurist ideal of the exclusion of women from the masculine warrior-horde was disseminated more subtly through the channel of literary expression.

For a certain period *Action* printed short stories in every issue. Fascist literary expression was rather amateurish, and creativity was always employed to reinforce the didacticism of BUF propaganda. H. Shaw's 'The Gallery Ten' told the tale of two working men, Clem and Paul, whose friendship reached a crisis point when they both fell in love with the same woman, a new school teacher in their Northern England town. One day their jealousy over the woman reached fever pitch and a scuffle ensued. Once both had been exhausted by their impromptu wrestling match, the woman intervened: 'She went first to Clem. "Thee go to Paul, lass; he's the best," said Clem. Paul reached a hand to find Clem's.

"Nay, lad, wenches don't amount to much," he said; and the hands clasped with such firmness as remained.' [61] Susan Sontag would certainly be able to read all the signs of Nazi sexual sublimation in Shaw's 'The Gallery Ten,' a short story which incarnates the carnal dynamics of 'fascinating fascism.' Sontag has shown that 'the fascist ideal is to transform sexual energy into a "spiritual" force, for the benefit of the community. The erotic (that is, woman) is always present as a temptation, with the most admirable response being a heroic repression of the sexual impulse.' [62] The BUF's readership would not have had to read between the lines to grasp the fact that the movement espoused *masculine fascism*, an ideology expressing the transcendence of male comradeship over physical lust and heterosexual love, and a doctrine in which woman figured as the intruder on scenes of male Platonic love.

Sensing that male Blackshirts preferred the company of men, Jenny Linton attempted to convince her readership that 'the domineering woman is neither respected by nor respects that she would like to dominate. Fascism aims to create a happy relationship between men and women, and with some attempt to return to the old (and much lamented) standards where men (where necessary) assumed a chivalrous care over "the weaker sex."' [63] Linton's attitude – although not typical of the bulk of women's contributions to the newspapers – illustrated the concessions and sacrifices some women were ready to make in order to realize the triumph of masculine fascism in Britain. Female journalists who expressed such notions were certainly accomplices to their own subordination and to the entrenchment of the ideology of separate spheres.

Macciocchi has discerned that in Italian Fascism 'even the figure of the husband does not exist.' [64] So too, in British fascist literature the husband seems nowhere to be found. Remembering how Mosley concealed the very event of his own marriage to Diana Mosley in October 1936, and noticing that his own three children from his first marriage had very little to do with the BUF in the 1930s, it seems clear that propagating family values was not high on the Leader's agenda.

Some anti-fascists experimented with psychoanalytic techniques in order to come to terms with the unconscious dynamics of British Blackshirtism. In 1937 Lionel Birch diagnosed that as a result of Mosley's own troubled relationship with his father, the Leader wanted to get his own back and 'be the father, not of a family, but of an entire nation. And his Blackshirts are required to achieve, not the free comradeliness of brothers, but the enforced unity of sons.' [65] This appears to have been a misdiagnosis, however. Mosley was the 'Leader,' a comrade, and the self-proclaimed commander of the disenfranchized war generation. As he was born in 1896, and in his mid-thirties when he launched the BUF, few of his followers could have imagined him as a member of their fathers' generation. His status as a widower was convenient for him in that he had given evidence of his potency and proved his ability to relate to a woman (unlike Hitler). Nonetheless, as widower, no woman would distract him, and time would not be taken away from the cause by attending to the duties of his own nuclear family.

Significantly, after Cynthia Mosley's death, Oswald and Cynthia Mosley's three children were brought up by a nanny and their aunt; they were wards in Chancery, and Mosley did not even have guardianship. Nicholas Mosley's recollections of his childhood and his involvement in his father's politics illustrate the ways in which Oswald Mosley made a concerted attempt to recast himself as a single man with no time for family matters. As Nicholas Mosley has remembered:

> My father kept us out of politics absolutely. In the Labour Party days we were trundled out for the 'photo opportunities,' family values stuff ... . But when the fascist thing started he kept us out of it ... . The only time we were included was one awful time I still react with horror to the thought of, was when I was 15 and there was a fascist summer camp, on the south coast, Selsey, and all the fascist youths were in tents. It was a huge holiday camp of all 14 and 15 year old boys, some with their fathers there. My father suddenly said that he would like it if I went incognito to this camp. I filled with horror and terror; I was a very shy boy. I said okay, and I went along and I was called 'Smith' or 'Brian' or something like that, and I shared a tent with these other boys, only for a couple of nights. On the second day my father appeared in his car standing up and everyone gave the salute and they all still didn't know who I was, or pretended they didn't know who I was ... . Then they all went to bathe in the sea and my father didn't acknowledge me. The reason I remember this so well was that that was the only time in all those years where I played any part at all. [66]

Similarly, when in 1939 the Beaverbrook press wrote an article attacking Vivian Mosley, Cynthia and Oswald's eldest child, for her lavish income and lifestyle, the BUF press retorted: 'Miss Mosley is a ward in Chancery, whose every arrangement is in charge of her aunt, Lady Ravensdale, her father has nothing whatever to do with her present activities. Therefore the Beaverbrook malice shoots very wide of the mark as an attack on a man who has neither time or inclination for any social life at all.' [67]

Family life was effectively negated by the BUF's para-military ethic, and by the intellectual construct of the Blackshirt as a full-time professional soldier. For Christmas 1933 Mosley sent out the following message to his officers: 'A Vigil Before Battle: The marching legions move forward to a new day. The keeping of Christmas is an old English institution, and Fascists cherish old traditions that serve a good purpose in our national life. It is a break in the struggle and the "tears of things" dedicated to children and home.' [68] Only during a cease-fire did the male Blackshirt have leave to indulge in the comforts of home and take up any fathering duties that may have been neglected when he was in the line of 'Red' fire. In 1935 the anti-fascist, Hilda Browning, observed that

> German family life under fascism ... is a somewhat one-sided affair. Again and again we hear complaints that owing to service with Storm Troops, and other military training, demonstrations, the 'Kraft durch Freude' (League Strength through Joy), no time is left to the men for family life at all. Even the time of children is so taken up by the 'Hitler-Jugend,' military training in schools, camping, etc., that the 'mothers of the nation' have found it necessary to make a formal protest. [69]

Subscribers to the patriarchal paradigm for fascism would have us believe that the woman was man's property. More subtly, however, the whole family unit was confiscated by the fascist movement, and sold for parts.

Mosley rarely invoked the symbolism of the family, and his constant vituperation against old men, old women, and fathers made him no champion of the sanctity of blood relations. He spoke of sons, but clearly considered himself a member of the generation of sons: 'We seek to create a nation-wide movement which replaces the legislation of old women by the social sense and will to service of young men.' [70] Mosley appropriated the voice of rebellious youth, not controlling and demanding father.

Where was the fascist father in BUF propaganda? While the husband was an absent figure, the father was banished from the fascist family altogether after being convicted for betraying his offspring. Generational conflict was a central pillar upon which BUF propaganda was built, and the fathers were regarded as the old men who had sent their young to die in the trenches. In 1936 Mosley said, 'again our generation is challenged to save the ideal of which the old men cheat us once again.'[71] By 1940 Mosley explained to his followers that 'you are at war because a few old gentlemen, who had won power by promising something quite different, gave a guarantee to Poland, in a hurried week-end meeting, which might involve the death of a million Britons.'[72] Lionel Birch recognized the effect on massed gatherings when Blackshirt orators attacked fathers and old men. 'The member of the audience may easily feel that, anyhow, the speaker is verbally knocking the block off each of their fathers for them; and that is usually felt to be a public service. Most people, when children, have felt that, in one way or another, their parents were unworthy.'[73] The rebuke of the fathers was a cheap means of exploiting the spirit of adolescent defiance against elders. Young recruits were further reassured that 'class based on social snobbery and the accident of inheritance shall go ... . A man shall be valued by what he is and not what his father was,'[74] as the BUF sanctioned symbolic patricide.

Oddly enough, both men and women in the BUF indulged in what can be termed sexist revolutionary ageism. The Youth versus Age war took the place of the sex war, and both sexes called for a coup against the 'old women' and the rehabilitation of British manhood.[75] Anne Brock Griggs believed that 'it is evident that Financial Democracy has meant a retrogression, especially marked in the lessening of the real influence of women, with increasing vacillation and *effeminacy* in government.'[76] Responding to the *Evening News's* question 'Why I Like the Blackshirts,' it was a woman who wrote the following: 'They stand for the ideals of manhood: courage, honour and chivalry; and those ideals alone can save England from breaking faith with "those who sleep" in Flanders fields.'[77] The eccentric Lady Houston – who had funded the Pankhursts many years before – contemplated writing out a large cheque for the BUF because she admired their 'revival of English manhood.'[78] As these examples suggest, the fascist masculine linguistic saturated the whole ideological discourse of the movement and animated women's voices.

The Male Youth Gang Triumphs Over Patriarchy

It has been common to view the fascist state as the most developed and accentuated form of patriarchy. The patriarchal interpretation was born during the inter-war period, and reinforced by feminists critics after the war. During the 1930s feminists and psychoanalysts began examining the kinship dynamics which buttressed the authoritarian state, and saw in the family hierarchy the seeds of the patriarchal fascist state. Reich's sex-economy analysis took for granted that the 'family is the authoritarian state in miniature, to which the child must learn to adapt himself as a preparation for the general social adjustment required of him later.' [79] Taking into consideration Nazism's neo-paganism, Naomi Mitchson imagined that in 'the re-constituted Teutonic home, the patriarch is again supreme ... the immediate representative of the state is the German father, as like Wotan as possible. The German wife is owned by both the state and by her husband.' [80] Projecting feminist apprehensions of Nazi patriarchy into a distant dystopian future, Katherine Burdekin imagined a world in which woman was deemed the lowest life form. In Burdekin's *Swastika Night*, the deity, Holy Adolf Hitler, was not born from woman, but sprung from the head of his father, and was 'the perfect, the untainted Man-Child.' [81] Virginia Woolf preferred to combat the patriarchal daemons and the bogey of sexist repression in Britain itself before sending off her guinea in aid of anti-fascist pacifists. The early feminists of Woolf's grandmothers' and mother's generation were recognized for 'fighting the same enemy that you are fighting and for the same reasons. They were fighting the tyranny of the patriarchal state as you are fighting the tyranny of the fascist state.' [82] Her analysis of the regrettably universal pervasion of patriarchy led her to make an important distinction between a more general patriarchal tyranny over women, and fascist tyranny specific to certain European states.

The underlying patriarchal character of fascism was intimated again by post-war feminists. Kate Millett asserted that 'if one takes patriarchal government to be the institution whereby that half of the populace which is female is controlled by that half which is male, the principles of patriarchy appear to be two fold: male shall dominate female, elder male shall dominate younger.' [83] As we have seen, however, in the BUF's world view not only was woman banned from the male gang, but younger male was charged with the mission of insurrection against his elders. Can patriarchy exist where fathers have been rendered impotent?

Observing many of the exact same characteristics in the Nazi vision and the social structure of the German state as I have identified in the BUF's imagination and hierarchy, Silke Hesse has argued that 'rather than patriarchy, the very different structure of a gang of adolescent youths is the model of fascist society ... The adolescent is the unattached person. He has outgrown the family of his childhood and has not yet acquired new commitments; he is responsible for no one but himself.' [84] The model of the male youth gang accommodates the BUF's military formations and warlike spirit. In the patriarchal family women are segregated into their private sphere and subordinated by the dominant male. In the para-military gang, however, women are unaccounted for and excluded, and aspects of femininity are purged.

Women's Bodies and Reproduction: A Male Domain

The fascist fixation on the adolescent male combatant can begin to account for many of the BUF's responses to contemporary dialogues on sexuality. Commentary on birth control, sterilization, eugenics, and abortion was relatively sporadic in BUF literature, but when these issues were broached, it was the men who dictated opinion. The birth control issue was not considered in the light of women's rights or as a branch of feminine ideology but as a national concern allied to concepts of duty and race regeneration. Nonetheless, the BUF resisted deriving its own policies directly from Italian Fascist and German Nazi decrees on birth control and eugenics.

Sir Oswald Mosley announced the movement's policy on contraception, and, although an increase in the birth rate was regarded as urgent, it was never recommended that birth control should be prohibited as it had been in Fascist Italy by the Rocco Code (1927) or severely regulated as in Nazi Germany by the Law for the Protection of the People and the State (February 1933). BUF policy makers acknowledged both the concerns of religious groups and the priority of taking advantage of modern scientific advancements. From the perspective of technological progress, and showing himself to be eugenically-minded, Mosley decreed that:

> knowledge of birth control, like all knowledge which modern science affords, should be available to all who desire it. But again the new social sense of Fascism will secure the production of children by the fit, and the raising of the standards of life will further encourage it. At present birth control is known and practised by the relatively well off. It is largely unknown

and less practised by the very poor. The result is exactly the reverse of national interest ... . The unfit will be offered alternatives of segregation sufficient to prevent the production of unfit children, or voluntary sterilization – none will be sterilized against their will.' [85]

Although Mosley's mandate appeared stern and decided, the issue was not a sacred or sensitive one for him. In fact, later in life he remembered the ways in which a witty fascist speaker could turn a heckler's interruption to his own advantage: 'undergraduate heckling at university meetings: "Are you in favour of birth control?" "Well I was, but I am beginning to think it is about twenty years too late."' [86]

Mosley's flippancy aside, birth control was a solemn issue for many members, especially Catholic sympathizers, and it was in recognition of their support that the BUF never widely advocated eugenics. In his valuable research into the Catholic press's response to the BUF's creeping policy of eugenics, Durham has demonstrated that Mosley 'was attempting in part to steer a path that minimized criticism from Catholic circles which he had hoped would be sympathetic to fascism.' [87] It is clear from the correspondence columns of the BUF newspapers that potential Catholic supporters would never accept fascist social engineering. 'What is your attitude towards Birth Control? Is this doctrine to be allowed to be propagated *ad lib* by the enemies of the Church?' asked 'FEAR A' TEACH', a Catholic who was not yet a fascist but was expressing interest in the movement. The reply given: 'Birth Control is entirely a matter for the private conscience of the individual. The state will certainly encourage a higher birth-rate, but will not interfere with the private and intimate concerns of the family.' [88] Abortion was even more contentious, and while *Action* published Richard Gayus's position on the issue, the editors provided a disclaimer stating that they did not necessarily agree with all that the author said, but his point of view was worthy of consideration. Gayus took the view that abortion was 'the violence of divine law – the cheapening of life, the encouraging of licentiousness – the collapse of the domestic life as found in the average home.' [89] G. Sutton denoted birth control as 'that policy of despair,' [90] and suggested as the alternative to reproductive morbidity a scheme for the state endowment of motherhood. [91] Significantly, the dialogue on the legality, morality and justification for contraception was conducted by men with little regard to how women felt about the matter.

When women lent their voices to the dialogue on reproduction, they were encouraged to think racially and see as their domain the concomitant areas of maternal and infant mortality. Population decline caused a great deal of consternation, and women's imaginations soared beyond an increased birth rate to conceive of means of propagating a Super Race. Anne Cutmore saw that birth control was a threat to a demographic revival and differed from Mosley in her concern that family limitation would soon be practised by the poor and the working classes.

> Although birth control and artificial means of limiting population have not entirely permeated the mass of working class people, they must soon do so – when there will at once begin a more rapid decline even than that recorded today ... . This alarming shrinkage is true, not of Great Britain alone, but also of the whole of North-West Europe, so that what we really have to face is a steady decline in all sections of the white race. [92]

Anne Brock Griggs commented again and again on the research of Sir John Orr, and his *Survey of Adequacy of Diet in Relation to Income* (1936) became her Bible. Reflecting on his recommendations, she wondered, if income levels increased and dietary habits could be improved, whether 'we could breed a race which is several inches taller than at present? Science would seem to indicate that we can... Allowing for the limits of heredity, it seems to be not beyond the power of *man* to breed a super-race.' [93] The way in which reproduction and population control became part of the feminine fascist pantheon did not secure women mastery over their own bodies. On the contrary, BUF women were even more determined than the men in delivering the message of racialist pronatalism.

British Fascist Sexuality and Responses to Sexology

Perhaps predictably, when we consider how BUF's attitudes towards reproduction were largely decided by the men, it follows that the parameters of fascist sexuality were also set by male policy-makers. The dominance of the masculine principle in BUF ideology and the exclusion of women from the adulated para-military male gang inevitably suggests two possibilities: either the full recognition of male sexual dominance over women, or scorn for woman culminating in a cult of homosexuality. The construction of British fascist sexuality was derivative. The revolt against psychoanalysis, the labelling of Modern art as 'degenerate,' and the apparent homophobia central to German Nazism were all reiterated in the BUF's propaganda.

Sir Oswald Mosley's New Party had given expression to a much less reactionary sexual politics than his BUF. The New Party's *Action* was edited by the bisexual Harold Nicolson, just as the Brown Shirt ancestors of the Nazi Party had been commanded by the homosexual Ernst Roehm. While the proto-fascist New Party already announced the Mosleyite call to men and women alike to join in reviving British manhood, *Action* was a more intellectually open forum for the communication of various opinions of gender roles. The paper advertised Virginia Woolf's *The Waves*, William Faulkner's *Sanctuary*, and Havelock Ellis's *More Essays of Love and Virtue*. The form of *Action* foreshadowed the BUF's newspapers in that it featured a 'Women's Page' (edited by Olive Rinder and discussing cookery, housekeeping and family budgeting), but there was also place for the women to broach the topic of their sexual repression. For instance, E. Arnot Robertson described her education in a girls' public school and the double-standard between male and female education among the social elite, and realized that 'where I was the general attitude towards sex was not so harmless. It took me and others years to get over it. Sex, never directly mentioned, was shrouded in titillating horror.' [94] In contrast to some liberality evident in the New Party, BUF propaganda never gave voice to women's concerns about the taboo placed on the exploration of their sexuality.

The British fascist ideology gave vent to paranoia about decadent-Jewish sexual perversity, and attacked sexual deviance. From Oswald Spengler's *Decline of the West*, James Drennan appropriated his own diagnosis of urban decadence. Drennan quoted Spengler's passages on the 'Ibsen woman' who 'instead of children ... has soul-conflict,' and on the modern cult of homosexuality 'which has certain psychological origins in the despair complex, which is the basis of all the sterilities of the "intelligent woman," and the womanish man – like the man-woman – is the creation and victim of the city.' [95] The BUF's sanctions against homoeroticism must be balanced against the fact that 'quite a lot of the early BUF people were homosexual and there was a rift in the BUF between the homosexuals and the others ... I am sure the early head of operations, Francis-Hawkins, was homosexual. And quite a few of them.' [96] Homophobia is generally only once removed from homoeroticism and homo-sentimentality.

If homosexuality was a sensitive issue since some BUF members were inclined in that direction, few members were personally threatened by the inclusion of psychoanalysts, Modernist artists, and Bloomsbury intellectuals in the movement's demonology. Surrealist art was attacked for its eroticism, absence of decency, and its vulgarity. After visiting the International Surrealist Exhibition at the New Burlington Galleries in June 1936, Charles Munday recommended that 'a lot of cold baths and long runs in the country will be needed by most of the exhibitors (exhibitionists?) to get this sort of cloying putrescence out of their system.' [97] No doubt on the defensive since psychoanalytic techniques were used to try to discover the mechanisms of the type of mind who would subscribe to the BUF, Wilhelm Reich's theories were assailed through criticism of his political leanings and his exile from Nazi Germany. 'Reich was a German until Hitler came to power: now he is a Swede. A great fighter for the Socialist cause he has contributed for the enlightenment of the proletariat of that country a book called: *The General Psychology of Fascism*. In addition he has written for the same publishers two other great works. *Breaking Through Sexual Morals* and *The Sexual Fight for Youth*.' [98] In BUF literature the terms 'sexual' and 'sex lives' were unconditionally disparaging.

Britain's intelligentsia was branded 'Bloomsbury bacilli,' and any allusion to Bloomsbury was short-hand to describe a diseased modern culture. When Charles Greenwood attended a meeting of the British Sexological Society, he encountered 'variegated specimens of "Bohemicus Bloomsburyus" and the sum total was as prize a collection of Jewboys, Old Boys, Tomboys and Nice Boys as one could wish to avoid.' [99] Although some inter-war British feminists held D.H. Lawrence culpable for the strain of misogynist thought which culminated in fascism, [100] the BUF's literary critics resisted commandeering the Lawrencian tradition. 'Since D.H. Lawrence, most writers have shown a terrific interest in this side of human nature [sexuality]. But it is becoming boring. There are many things to write about other than passion.' [101] Refreshing our memory, the homo-sentimentality expressed in Shaw's 'The Gallery Ten' was considered a healthy thematic deviation away from scientific and literary explorations of sexual feeling.

Women's propaganda marched in step with the male rhetorical charges against socialist adversaries, fashionable sets, and emanations of popular culture. Just as it was their policy that during disorder at Blackshirt meetings women stewards should be sent to eject anti-fascist women, BUF propaganda countered women with women.

The fascists made great currency out of their male opponents' impotence by highlighting the anti-fascist practice of using provocative women to act as interrupters and hecklers at Blackshirt meetings. At Olympia on 7 June 1934, when a woman was ejected, Oswald Mosley remarked: 'It is typical of the red cowards to send a women to do the job they dare not do themselves.' [102] In a similar incident in Hampstead in October 1936, the anti-fascist 'she-males' stayed outside 'while the females sought to take advantage of their sex by coming inside and yelling nonsense and abuse at the speaker ... several of the loud-voiced termagants were escorted out of the hall by the women stewards.' [103] In this exchange of unpleasantries, it was typical for anti-fascists to describe the female Blackshirt as an Amazon woman.

Fascist women maligned Modernism, Bloomsbury, Bright Young Things, spinsters, mannish-women, the 'Red' woman who gave them trouble when stewarding meetings, and attempted to warn their female counterparts about the corrupting influences of women's magazines and cinema-going. Their attacks were most frequently gibes at the opponents' physical attributes or presumed sexual orientation. Watching a procession of Left-wing marchers 'representing the heights and depths of Bloomsbury's uninhibited parlours' on May Day 1936, Cutmore observed

> a fat woman with uncombed hair and a thick tweed jacket ... . Here is a deplorable girl, whose out of condition body, over-fat body and legs, shorts which reach just below her knee, and personality exudes external and internal grime, [and] make one think of one's common humanity and regret it ... . These are the rejects of a ruthless civilization – and only in their increasing numbers are they any menace. [104]

Similarly, the type of intellectuals who extolled Russia as a haven for feminism were described as 'bleating Bloomsbury's short-haired women.' [105]

The Bright Young Thing was regarded not as a flapper but a sapper of the nation's wealth and vitality. She was dubbed the 'Mayfair Parasite,' and the young Doreen Bell deplored 'the cocktail night-club girl of Mayfair, who rises at lunch time, and retires, worn out with the quest for pleasure.' [106] *Action* made a valid point when it observed that the content of popular women's journals underestimated female intelligence and doped readers with fashion news, stories on socialites, horoscopes and recipes. [107] Ironically, the BUF was also propagating an ideology of domesticity and evoked the feminine mystique, and there have been many examples in the texts so far sampled where the fascist man employed a rhetoric of condescension when addressing the fascist woman.

Cutmore deplored the 'little group of "advanced thinkers" who hold soirees to discuss their sex lives.' [108] Among the intellectually and physically inferior members of the Communist party, BUF writers caught glimpses of the 'subman' and 'subwoman' of the Britain breed. [109] In first desexualizing and then dehumanizing the political opponent, fascist women denied themselves a speaking part in the titillating drama of modern sexual politics. Furthermore, the potentially arousing concept of sex war was neutered by the movement's formula for achieving gender peace by way of the Corporate State and fascist employment policy.

Forging Gender Peace: The Panacea of the Corporate State

For women to qualify for the 'post conquest' positions of architects and builders of a masculine Britain, they would have to accept the Corporate State's treaty to bring sex war to a negotiated peace. Olive Hawks explained how fascism 'rejects the sex war as it does the class war: as it does the whole political theory of division. It is by unity of purpose alone that our nation can struggle through to greater things.' [110] Her appraisal did not quite mesh with the ethos of the Corporate State, a state organized according to economic sectors and professional specializations. More to the point, women in the Corporate State would have to accept the idealized attributes of domesticity, and see in their successful management of the home the indispensability of their servility for national reconstruction.

The model for the Corporate State recognized the role of women in the labour market, as consumers, and as wives, but it was the celebration of domestic government that was considered to be the most ingenious and marketable aspect of the fascist plan. 'In the Home Corporation, women who run a home or are employed in domestic work will be represented. This will be recognized as one of the most vital corporations in the Fascist State, and will give the career of the home-maker the status of the profession.' [111] Raising the occupations of mother and housewife to the status of professions in the state was yet another example of the BUF's politicization of domesticity.

The Corporate State would be bicameral, one house fulfilling the legislative function and the other the executive, each with twenty-three occupational groups represented; an unelected Cabinet whose members would be chosen by the Prime Minister; and a House of Notables to replace the hereditary House of Lords. A change-over to a one-party system was predicted in that 'Government will no longer represent a particular party in the state, but will consist of the best political and administrative brains chosen by the Fascist Prime Minister to advise him. It will submit periodically (at the time of a General Election) to a direct vote of confidence from the people themselves by universal plebiscite.'[112] The Corporate House of Commons would represent occupational groups, and the members would be directly elected by those possessing an occupational franchise. In this House, the much heralded Corporation for Married Women sat at the very foot of the hierarchy, immediately below the position given to professional men. In the other house, representing the National Corporations (whose members were to be elected indirectly), the Domestic Corporation again sat at the foot of the diagram. Raven Thomson, the draftsman of BUF's blueprint, pointed out how

> either as an employer or worker in industry, or alternatively, as a married woman, housekeeper or domestic servant in the home, every woman will possess their vote to send a representative to the Lower House. For every substantial block of women in industry there will be a woman representative in Parliament, while women in the home and in domestic service will be represented entirely by women.[113]

This presumed utopia for women really seemed to mean that the female population would form a state within a state; they would only be assured representation by other women in the domestic corporations; they would carry the disability of not being permitted to hold the offices appointed by the Prime Minister; they would cast votes only on issues which had direct bearing on their sphere and, in fact, women would get the political boot from the foot of the hierarchy.

The BUF tried to sell the Corporate State to women as a panacea for the crisis in women's socio-economic position. The fascists idealized an all-women world and expressed the belief that 'only when women represent woman will womankind attain its rightful influence.'[114] Without doubt, if women ruled only over women, men too would be left free to govern men, and the thwarting and emasculating influence of the 'spinster MP' would finally be eradicated. Nonetheless, Doreen Bell went as far as exclaiming that 'many ardent feminists have been induced by anti-Fascist propagandists to oppose the Movement, little realizing that through the Corporate State in BU many of the ideals for which they have fought so hard and sacrificed so much will be realized.' [115] In a state of specialists, women would be liberated from the struggle to conform to a man's world, and while Bell was not too far off the mark in remarking upon a certain compatibility between her dream state and some aspects of the New Feminism, she disregarded the underlying democratic context of British feminism. Winifred Holtby discerned that 'at present I feel and think like a citizen and an individual; if the Blackshirts were victorious, I should be expected to think only as a woman.' [116]

Women in the Labour Market: Given the Choice to Return to the Home

The BUF's plan for the Corporate State was accompanied by a number of apparently advanced proposals for ameliorating the position of women in the labour market. The ideology of feminine fascism upheld the principles of equal pay for equal work, the abolition of the marriage bar, the end of the exploitation of women as cheap labour, and promised that those women who so desired would be able to return to the home and leave the role of bread-winner to husbands and sons. However much their proposals seemed to resonate with inter-war New Feminist demands for the women worker in industry, BUF writers condemned the Open Door Council and similar feminist organizations for blinding themselves to the 'evil' conditions under which women worked.[117] On women's employment, the movement 'was highly ambiguous on where it stood [and] ... some BUF writers openly argued that the introduction of equal pay for women might well result in their widespread dismissal, to the benefit of the nation.' [118] The return to prosperity, the end of women undercutting men's wages, the specialization of women's employment, and equal pay were all double-edged swords, at once cutting away the Depression-era exploitation of cheaper women's labour, and, at the same time, severing women's ties with employment in the public sphere.

The plight of the woman worker – as prevalent a theme as any in the movement's literature – was interpreted as a direct result of the Slump. BUF writers examined the unemployment statistics to show how disgraceful a system was that sent women out to work while men were compelled to stay at home to care for the family. Democracy's effeminacy and the mock recovery from the Depression achieved by the National Government seemed to be illustrated by the unemployment statistics of November 1933.

> The most significant figures are those which show the total unemployment among women has fallen by 354,000, or 51.4%, during the same period. Thus the reduction of unemployment has been mostly secured by finding work for women. This is the real achievement of the Government: continued unemployment of men, but women driven into industry at cheap rates because the unemployment and low wages of their husbands makes it impossible otherwise to keep the home together. [119]

Of course, these figures were misleading, for after the passing of the Unemployment Insurance (No.3) Act (1931) – better known as the Anomalies Act – most married women were restricted from benefits and their numbers no longer figured on national insurance registers. [120] When it is remembered that Mosley used his opposition to this very bill as a vehicle for his resignation from the Labour Government in 1930, it should have followed that BUF journalists would have been attentive to these nuances when interpreting government-issued unemployment figures. However, the statistical reality was of far lesser importance to BUF critics than was the exposure of the threat to the nation's manhood by mass unemployment.

The lower rate of women's unemployment was seen as affirmation of democracy's emasculating effect on British manhood. In the artificial-silk industry in Congleton, Cheshire, depressed conditions led to a situation where 'men must weep and women must work... the women-folk go off on their daily tasks while the men have to stop at home, cook breakfast, nurse the baby, and do their domestic duties.' [121] Raven Thomson considered it 'a national scandal that female unemployment should have decreased so much more than male, in times of economic stress like the present. Elementary principles would suggest that if there must be unemployment, it should be the man rather than the woman who should be found work.' [122]

As Susan Pedersen has remarked, during the Depression 'loss of economic status and loss of familial status became inextricable – hence the common observation that men experienced unemployment as an assault on their manhood.' [123] Nor was this unique to the 1930s, and John Tosh has observed for the late nineteenth century that 'unemployment not only impoverished workers but gravely compromised their masculine self-respect (including their ability to demand respect from women).' [124] British fascists were not alone in observing this attack on masculine pride and dignity during the 1930s, and a wide range of social critics – such as J.B. Priestley, George Orwell, E. Wright Bakke and the Pilgrim's Trust – recorded this aspect of men's experience of life on the dole. The BUF went beyond merely chronicling this psychological phenomenon of male demoralization, and called for a crusade to rescue British manhood. In this general atmosphere of an onslaught on individual and collective masculine identities, the BUF's cult of masculinity was less an unrestrained bid for male dominance than a stop-gap ideological measure for male survival in the age of the Means Test. Capitalizing on the mood of opposition to the economic war on man's dignity, the BUF over-compensated the male worker by way of fascism's reactionary masculinism.

On the whole, women in the BUF complied with male dictates, and Anne Brock Griggs' support for equal pay was in recognition of the fact that 'since their entry into industry women have received lower wages than men for the same work. This amounts to victimization and, apart from the injustice to women, causes the displacement of men.' [125] She lamented the failure of Ellen Wilkinson's bill for equal pay in the civil service, debated in the House of Commons on 1 April 1936, but emphasized that 'it is not a feminist question, nor should it be viewed from that angle and exposed to the flippant back-chat in Westminster. The sweated labour of women in industry today is a serious menace to the standard of living. Red petticoats swirling in the House have unwittingly raised a storm.' [126] That the BUF's Chief Women's Organizer did not regard equal pay for equal work as a feminist issue is indicative of the fact that women were not intended to be the main beneficiaries.

The BUF's 'Black Petticoats,' however, were careful not to propose turning women out of work against their own will; returning to the home would be voluntary. The situation of the woman worker was demonized, and the forces of compulsion and coercion were assigned to Financial Democracy and the economic pressures which drove women into industry. 'Under Fascism women will not be compelled to resign, but encouraged to do so by the fact that, under the Corporate State and the scientific methods of raising real wages, men will be able to afford to marry women

– and women will not be compelled to earn their own living as they are at present.' [127] The BUF turned a negative into a positive – the prerogative of a movement leagues away from the centre of power.

To a greater extent than contemporary social critics, the BUF masculinized the highly emotive issue of mass unemployment. And yet it was the developed plan of the Mosley Memorandum that attracted women to the movement. Robert Row has remembered how the trinity of issues which motivated women to support the BUF were peace, jobs and getting rid of slums. Of his sample of women members at the Yorkshire branch in 1938, 'all said they followed Mosley, the only British politician to have sacrificed his career for the unemployed, and devised policies to create jobs with good wages combined with steady prices in shops.' [128] In Fascist Italy and Nazi Germany BUF women witnessed the fulfilment of the Mosleyite vision of national renewal, prosperity, and improved employment opportunities for menfolk and seemed little perturbed by the condition of their sex under the new regimes.

Responses to the Position of Women in Italy and Germany

For all of British fascist women's unswerving love for their Motherland, a glance towards the Fatherland which seemed to have realized the fascist dream temporarily averted their gaze from the economic and spiritual depravity of Britain during the Bleak Age. 'Fascist tourism' became somewhat of a vogue among Mosley's women supporters, and in addition to the sensational examples of Unity Mitford and Diana Mosley, rank and file members also indulged in travels to fascist dream lands. Anne Brock Griggs, Muriel Currey, Viscountess Downe, Mary Allen, and Rosalind Raby, each travelled to Italy or Nazi Germany. They returned with souvenir messages of German friendship towards Britain, and glowing reports of national efficiency, aesthetic grandeur, and 'happy women.'

The Nazi cure for unemployment was much discussed, and when the Viscountess Downe gave a speech to the BUF's King's Lynn Branch after returning from a trip to Germany 'she explained how unemployment has been reduced from 5 million to 2 million since the coming of the Nazis into power ... . The German sentiment towards Britain was one of friendship and the feeling of despair, which was universal during the post-war period, had given way to

hope.' [129] On the more controversial issue of women's employment
and enforced domesticity in the Third Reich, the BUF applauded
the setting up, in July 1934, of a Central Office for dealing with
the working women in the German Labour Front, bringing concerns
for their welfare under one centralized authority. Readers were
assured that 'no woman was relieved of her situation if it were
possible at the time to improve her standard of life, e.g. by providing
work for an unemployed son or husband.' [130] Britain's fascist women
appreciated the Nazi realization of the politicization of domesticity,
and they also envied the way in which German women had been
liberated from the intrigues of democracy.

Eileen Lyons asserted that in Germany 'all the girls and women
are happy, so far as it is humanly possible for all a multitude to
be "happy." They have plenty of liberty, and are not forced into
the home ... . The organization of women under the leadership
of Frau Scholtz-Klink is a wonderful achievement and one the
British women may look upon with envy.' [131] Even more did British
fascists envy the attention paid by the Nazi state to physical fitness.
On a fact-finding tour during 1934, Rosalind Raby's initial prejudice
against the German woman – which she claimed had been
conditioned by anti-fascist propaganda in Britain – was contradicted
by what she witnessed for herself.

> I had visualized the woman of Germany being relegated to a sort of Victorian
> era in which she could only justify her existence by producing a well-cooked
> 'schnitzel' or cannon-fodder for another war. But it is difficult to conceive
> of a Victorian era in which women participate equally with men in practically
> every branch of sport on a footing freer of convention and self-consciousness
> than in this country. [132]

BUF women craved what they saw as the order, dignity, moral
drive and aesthetic achievement of Hitler's regime. On 1 May
1936 – while Anne Cutmore was watching the procession of
British socialist 'submen' and 'subwomen' who negated 'the ideal
of simplicity, beauty and unity' – Brock Griggs was in Germany
luxuriating in the Nazi celebration of May Day. Brock Griggs
described scenes of '80,000 of Germany's youth ... gathered to
do honour to Hitler ... Round the stadium the red and black of
the standards contrasts with the splash of white made by the
blouses of girls ... . It is a feast of colour and an example of
orderly discipline.' [133] The theatrical magnificence entranced her;
the lively canvass of ordered humanity overrode any notice of

the forced segregation of the sexes; and when she pointed out with glee that Hitler had been an architect before he became the German Chancellor (she was the wife of an architect), her attitude exemplified the conquest of the Nazi aesthetic over reasoned observation.

Muriel Currey – Honorary Secretary for the London Group for the Study of the Corporate State, and one of a set of Britons who admired Fascist Italy from the 1920s, that included Major James S. Barnes, Harold E. Goad, and Francis Yeats-Brown – was the BUF's chief female enthusiast for the organization of womanhood in Mussolini's Italy. Also a fascist tourist, she travelled to the Abyssinian War in 1935, by permit of the Italian Government. [134] She praised the Fascist state for achieving the equality of the sexes without being obsessed by female suffrage, as British and American women were wont to be. 'The fact that women have not a parliamentary vote in Italy has blinded some ardent feminists to the importance and power of women in the Italian Corporate State.' [135] Currey pointed out that 90 per cent of teachers in Italy were women; that women were streamed into certain professions such as interior decoration and floral design where they would not have to compete with men; that women had their own Federation in the Confederation of Professional Workers; that no marriage bar applied to professions; and how valiant the Italian Government's efforts were in providing mothers and children with holidays and welfare facilities.

While BUF women were anxious to prove the superiority of the Nazi model to Financial Democracy in Britain, they did take into consideration certain aspects of divergence between the different national cultures. In Mosley's understanding, fascism 'is the new faith born of the post-war period in the last decade. It is not the product of Italy, nor of any other foreign country.' [136] BUF women were thus required to make a certain distinction, as British fascism had to be sold with the stamp 'Made in Britain.'

While the movement commonly accused feminists of being blind to realities, one BUF woman at least was aware of the negative publicity stemming from the Nazi tendency to emancipate women from emancipation. In the correspondence columns of the *Fascist Quarterly* – a journal not nearly as widely disseminated as the newspapers – the following exchange of ideas and anxieties took place. Olga Bonora was distressed by Irene Clephane's new book *Towards Sex Freedom*, which spoke alarmingly of women being eliminated from public life in the new Germany. Bonora wrote,

This book is a very good seller and therefore might prove dangerous to us, unless we, the Women of the Movement, are given even more assurances, to pass the neophytes and potential members, that our freedom will not be interfered with. Unfortunately, Hitler is dismissing women teachers from the girls' schools, as he considers women 'unfitted to teach.' They are also being excluded from many branches of sport, including flying. I know that we advocate freedom for women and the right to work, but could this statement be fortified? [137]

Anne Brock Griggs, in her capacity as Chief Woman Propaganda Officer, ventured to respond to Bonora's consternation and soothe her nerves. 'We do not as a rule compare British Fascism, especially in this respect, with its continental manifestations; for as you are aware from your first hand experience of Italy and Germany, a differing racial tradition in their attitude towards women makes comparison between these two countries impossible.' [138] This dialogue exemplified the extent to which BUF women were conversant with inter-war British feminism, and the degree to which they remained concerned to maintain the strides towards women's emancipation already achieved in Britain.

The milder forms of differentiating British women from the women of fascist countries came in the form of seeing Italian and German women as naturally more submissive. 'That German women have a greater love of home life than their British Cousins is a national characteristic,' [139] Lyons admitted. When Mary Richardson and Sylvia Pankhurst – fascist and anti-fascist ex-suffragette respectively – engaged in a press polemic in June 1934, Richardson defended the position of women in Italy, praised Fascist welfare centres, crèches and sanatoria, while allowing for the fact that 'the position of women in Italy has never been on par with that of British women. We have always been more independent and more politically minded than the women of Latin countries.' [140] In an attempt to dispel the illusion that the BUF was anti-feminist, E.D. Hart cared to remind his readers that 'there can be no stronger characteristic of the British nation than its recognition of the equal partnership of men and women. The British wife is neither the pampered goddess of America, nor the household drudge of Central Europe.' [141] As this last example suggests, the ideology of feminine fascism was two-tiered, and uncritical admiration for Fascist and Nazi models was balanced by respect for British women's own volition. Ironically, one way in which British fascist women proved their agency

128

and independence was by giving free reign to their own racial hatreds.

Motherly Hate: The 'Other' in Feminine Fascism

If the positive women in feminine fascism were fertile mothers, obliging wives and fanatical Blackshirt women, the negative women were a more motley crew of spinster MPs, conservatives, feminists, socialists, communists, international activists and pacifists. Together these negative women were accused of anti-national acts, broken spirits and their failure to represent the 'normal' woman of the British breed. Lionel Birch assumed that the 'Fascists have adopted Colonel Blimp's assumption that tolerance and the desire to reconcile are feminine un-British qualities.' [142] As this survey of opinion will indicate, there was nothing tolerant or conciliatory about the way in which feminine fascism rhetorically denigrated those it stigmatized as ' Other.'

Women MP's were considered as 'Other' in that the 'M' was missing. Democracy failed women because those few women who did sit in the House of Commons were seen collectively as unmarried and childless, and thus potentially abnormal. Mosley set the tone when he wrote: 'the field of women's interests is left clear to the professional spinster politician who used irrelevantly to be described as the member for "No Man's Land." It will not be surprising to those familiar with this distressing type that the interests of the "normal women" occupy no great place in the attention of Parliament.' [143] Abnormality could refer to either sexual or national out-groups, and Norah Elam, the ex-suffragette who had stood as an Independent in 1918, was disturbed by the fact that the first woman elected to the House of Commons was 'the Sinn Fein Countess Markieviecz, who though a notorious and avowed enemy of Britain, found it a perfectly simple matter under the democratic system to secure election to the Parliament of the country which she had openly boasted that she would destroy, disintegrate and discredit.' [144] To add insult to injury, the attack against the political woman was more truly an assault on democracy itself and an ethnically heterogeneous national community.

As much as the unrepresentative woman politician, the feminist had betrayed British womanhood. The feminist had done so not so much by serving only her sex to the exclusion of men, but paradoxically, when we consider the source, by selling out to party interests. Elam condemned post-enfranchisement women for having 'allied themselves with the very parties in the state which had treated them with such unprecedented contempt. They once again wear the primrose of the Jew Disraeli, the rosette in honour of Sir Herbert Samuel, the red emblem in commemoration of Karl Marx; they have turned again as handmaidens to the hewing of wood and drawing of water for the Party wirepullers.'[145] Elam did not seem to see the irony in her condemnation, and disregarded the fact that BUF women were wearing the Blackshirt in honour of Mosley, the former Labour MP, and acting as handmaidens to Mars by engaging in and condoning fascist violence. However, that emancipated women should join the democratic parties was less the point than that they unwittingly served the Jewish interest. When Brock Griggs declared that the 'ping-pong at Westminster will not breed an athletic race,'[146] perhaps she was being more candid by exposing feminine fascism's essential fusion between racialism, gender differentiation, and anti-democratic sentiment.

Tony Kushner has asked: 'was anti-Semitism linked to patriarchy or was it gender blind?'[147] Pondering the same problem from the perspective of women in the BUF, the questions that we must pose are as follows: were women in the BUF anti-Semitic? Were they as anti-Semitic as the men? Was the nature of women's anti-Semitism in any way distinctive? And, how was woman represented in anti-Semitic propaganda?

The answer to the first question is readily apparent, as women in the BUF indulged in some of the most malignant forms of hate propaganda. However, while the BUF's anti-Semitism was blatant, it was not necessarily part of the attraction of fascism for some women. Yolande McShane remembered that 'Mosley's policies were not racist; he was anti-Jew, but as I knew no Jew and Mosley seemed to object to their apparent monopoly of British money and business, it did not seem to me very important, compared with the promise of "equal opportunities for all."'[148] And yet fascism was a package deal, and scape-goating, xenophobia, and rhetorical violence against the Jews were inextricable from the British fascist ideological discourse.

There also seems to be little reason to doubt that women could be as racist as men. Feminine fascism did highlight certain areas of the anti-Semitic discourse, and particularly rampant were stereotypes of the predatory Jew exploiting women workers in the sweat shops, perpetrating sex crimes, and disseminating indecent literature. The evil machinations of Jewish interests were identified behind each area of social crisis which had been assigned to women's sphere. The self-ascribed role of fascist woman as mother of the race meant that it was judged that women were the most vulnerable to the Jewish corruption of culture, the desecration of the Christian family, and the thinning of the British racial blood line. One BUF critic asked: 'The instability of our homes, the pseudo-scientific study called psycho-analysis, the discontents occasioned in British families by the falsity of Hollywood sex-filled entertainment, the pernicious doctrine of Marxism, the destruction of the family by use of contraceptives: can it be seriously denied that all these things have originated from the Jew?'. [149] Anti-Semitism was always reinforced by arousing anxieties about sexual potency, and women were portrayed as the symbolic victims of a Jew-ravaged Britain.

In the feminine fascist imagination, the Jew was always male and in a position of authority over British women. (There were significantly few derogatory images of the Jewish woman). Mosley explained the origins of the BUF's anti-Semitism by the fact that 'our girls were dismissed from shops owned by Jews. Our people were persecuted. Our supporters were blackmailed by Jewish interests.' [150] The undue influence of the Jew was only possible in Financial Democracy, but his power transcended democracy and rendered the parliamentary system a farce. Eileen Lyons pointed out, 'one may be an ardent Tory, Socialist, or even Liberal, but is it going to get "Our Mary" out of the Jewish sweat-shop? Is it going to make the old Jew pay decent wages? No! Is not Financial Democracy afraid of the Rosenbaums, or perhaps it would be truer to say are not the Rosenbaums Financial Democracy?' [151] The use of 'Our Mary' connoted Jewish corruption both of the helpless common woman, and the first Christian mother. Women weakened and prematurely aged by work outside the home for 'slave wages' were described as 'broken on the financial rack,' [152] as the Jew became woman's captor and torturer. The allusion to torture administered by the Jew suggested the reliance on the medieval library of images, and, in particular, reawakened the (false) memory of blood libel. Jewish employers were also held responsible for preventing sympathetic British women from joining the BUF, and when Dinah Parkinson had a short exchange with a typist on the bus, the young woman scoffed: 'They held a Blackshirt meeting in Cheetham Hill recently. I longed to go, but I daren't. I know nothing about the policy, but I do know all the Jewish employers are scared stiff.' [153] There was some sadistic pleasure taken from the fact that Britain's working women could arouse the fears of their Jewish employers.

During the BUF's East London campaign, anti-Semitism was one of the main planks supporting the women's platform. The whole discourse surrounding slum clearance was buttressed by reference to Jewish corruption and domination: 'Fascism does not need the poisoned blood money of aliens to rehouse British people.'[154] Brock Griggs spoke of the 'evil force of finance, which flourishes as weeds do in the garden they destroy.'[155] At one of her meetings campaigning for the LCC elections, Brock Griggs spoke of corruption in housing, and argued that 'when the Tories were in power ... the head of the Housing Committee was a Jew – Levita, but 3 years ago when Labour came into office a great change took place, another Jew – Silkin was the head.'[156] BUF women contributed their voices to the movement's line of argument that only Jews should be conscripted for service as 'British life and wealth must not be sacrificed in Palestine.'[157] In regard to the same issue, the BUF played on male fears of the alien's sexual licentiousness and threat to White women by claiming that 'Jews are the international enemy, that Arabs are complaining that Jewish men are outraging Arab women in Palestine.'[158]

As Claudia Koonz has pointed out for the case of women in the Third Reich: 'at the grassroots of daily life, in a social world populated by women, we begin to discover how war and genocide happened by asking who made it happen.'[159] In Britain too, fascist women were by no means victims, and their Jew-baiting activities, their appeals to motherly protectiveness and their fear-mongering drove the anti-Semitic campaign at every turn. In its reaction to the 'Other', feminine fascism transformed motherly love into motherly hate.

Fascism and Feminism: A Marriage of Inconvenience

While BUF women aided and abetted the dissemination of hate propaganda against the alien and the negative political women, the place of feminism in the construction of their own self-image was more ambiguous. From this survey of the form and content of feminine fascism, it might at first appear that feminism belonged with the other fascist negations, and that only an anti-feminist reaction was compatible with the BUF's anti-modern resistance to intellectualism, Modernism, psychoanalysis and so on. The BUF rejected feminism as an all-female movement for women's further emancipation, while seeing in their own movement's women's policies the fulfilment of 'true feminism.' Martin Durham has attempted to pin down two distinct currents of thought in the BUF's view of women: 'a form of fascist feminism' militating against 'an unashamed traditionalism.'[160] I would argue, however, that no such dichotomy was in evidence. It was with a unity of purpose that BUF women supported the fascist creed largely on the terms set out by their male counterparts, identifying themselves first and foremost as fascists, and, in a distant second place, as women.

A contingent of BUF women labelled themselves feminists, revered the suffragette movement for its militancy, and saw no incompatibility between fascism and what they understood to be feminism. BUF women continued to apply the term to define their own ends. In praising the provisions made for women in Nazi Germany, Eileen Lyons stated that 'naturally their greatest effort is motherhood of the race. Why not? No matter how much the rampant "feminist" (the writer is one) may forget or deny it, the majority of women of every country are wives and mothers.'[161] BUF women made a concerted attempt to temper fascism's machismo by staking out a centrist position on the sexual-political spectrum. Olive Hawks saw that 'after centuries of oppression [women] are often going to unfortunate extremes to prove their independence from economic and moral custom. Fascism in this as in everything else, upholds neither the reaction or the anarchy.'[162] By 1936 the movement was relieved to announce that its Women's Organizer (Northern), Miss Olga Shore belonged to a generation of women who have turned from the ties of Victorianism to the wider world of business.' Although 'she is not an "ultra feminist," in that she would not demand equality for women in spheres in which they are not suited, she is a strong supporter of the idea of feminine emancipation.'[163] The BUF was most at ease with this take on the subject – a view that was non-threatening to the complementary ideologies of feminine and masculine fascism.

The responses of fascist women in Britain must be placed in the context of a mild anti-feminist back-lash during the inter-war period, the hegemony of the ideology of women's domesticity over the whole political spectrum, and the limbo of the nomenclature. Virginia Woolf noted that 'the word feminist, according to the dictionary, means "one who champions the rights of women." Since the only right, the right to earn a living, has been won, the word no longer has a meaning. And a word without meaning is a dead word, a corrupt word.'[164] The feminist Ray Strachey observed that 'modern young women know amazingly little of what life was like before the war, and show a strong hostility to the word "feminism", and all they imagine it to connote.'[165] Particularly among the younger fascist women, feminism did not speak to their concerns, and they scorned the sectionalism and narrowness of single-sex organizations. Louise Irvine's memories of her motivations for joining the BUF bear out Strachey's observation and also exemplify the way in which BUF women accepted the gains towards independent thought made by the earlier generation of women who fought for the vote:

> I was by no means a feminist, and do not consider myself ever to have been. But I do believe in being accepted as an independent, free-thinking individual and when I joined the BUF I think that was how women were accepted ... . In my own personal life and the women I mixed with feminism was not an issue.[166]

Irvine's attitude should be explained neither as anti-feminist reaction nor as traditionalism, but more simply as an absence of interest and detachment.

When evaluating the impact of feminist influences on BUF women, we must consider first and foremost the ideological priorities of joiners. Robert Row has claimed that

> three issues – peace, jobs and getting rid of slums – counted for more with our Yorkshire women members than what is popularly known as 'feminism.' But what is really meant by the word? If it means that working women are protected against exploitation and receive the same high pay as men, ... that as many occupational opportunities are open to women as to men, but also that the care of mothers and children becomes a special duty of the State, and Mosley's principle 'we want men who are men and women who are women' is always to the forefront, then I would say that the BUF was on the side of true feminism.[167]

Perhaps it is appropriate that the last voices we listen to on the subject of women in the BUF is a man's. Although *feminine fascism* was espoused by women, it was largely articulated either by men or in full recognition of masculine supremacy over the movement's policy. While feminism and fascism were divorced due to irreconcilable differences, I would argue that the marriage of feminine nature and fascism was a contented and companionate one. In their celebration of women's sphere, their ideological consent in occupying 'woman's worlds,' and their dream vision of the Corporate State as a panacea for the crisis in the political condition of women, Mosley's women summoned ample intellectual and emotional enthusiasm for their own position as they understood it.

Notes for Chapter 3

1   'The whole attitude of the Conservative Party is childish. Hours of valuable time is spent in idle talk, social parties, whist drives, and games for the young members of the Primrose League ... . The minute God, or politics, are mentioned, one is told to desist.' 'Why I Left the Tories: A Woman Explains,' *Action*, No. 119, 28 May 1938. Similarly, when Anne Brock Griggs attended a Primrose League rally at the Royal Albert Hall, she found nothing to praise in the political activism of Conservative women, and grew tired to 'see woman after woman pass, to see the same face eternally repeated; the face of the woman conservative worker.' 'Baldwin's Lips Unsealed: Anne Brock Griggs Reports His Speech to the "Primroses,"' *Blackshirt*, No. 161, 23 May 1936.
2   My italics. 'Women: Equal Pay for Equal Work – Spreading the Truth of Fascism,' *The Fascist Week*, No. 2, 17 November 1933. Mullaly's fictional prototype of a BUF adherent, Peter Fletcher, is first attracted to the movement when he sees an alluring woman Blackshirt. See Frederic Mullaly, *Fascism Inside England* (London, 1946), p.8.
3   Indeed, women members served as the 'window dressing' in BUF shops. In a circular of May 1936, *Scheme for Provincial Bookshops*, District Leaders were encouraged to: 'agree to find a competent person to look after the shop. In this connection Districts will find many lady members only too willing to take charge of the shop in the morning or the afternoon. The District Officer [male] ... should be on duty in the evening to deal with any requests for information made by the public during the day.' HO144/20147/23.
4   Winifred Holtby, 'Shall I Order a Black Blouse?,' *News Chronicle*, 4 May 1934.
5   Wilhelm Reich, *The Mass Psychology of Fascism* (Harmondsworth, 1970), p.66.
6   Anne Cutmore, 'In the Heart of an Empire: Great East London Welcome to Sir Oswald Mosley,' *Action*, No. 17, 11 June 1936.
7   'Sir Oswald Mosley in the East End,' *Manchester Guardian*, 15 October 1936.
8   'Women Enjoy the Camp,' *Blackshirt*, No. 227, 4 September 1937.
9   'Senex,' 'Chief Considerations of the Housewife,' *Fascist Week*, 16–22 March 1934.
10 'British Union Personalities: No. 3 – Anne Brock Griggs,' *Action*, No. 40, 21 November 1936.

11 'British Union Personalities: No. 17 – Miss Doreen Bell,' *Action*, No. 55, 6 March 1937.

12 Letter from Louise Irvine to the author, 8 June 1996.

13 Linda Shore, 'Mrs Brock Griggs at Balham: Great Work by Women's Section,' *Blackshirt*, No. 165, 20 June 1936. When we examine the titles of BUF pamphlets, this manner of addressing women directly and in the second person was very much in evidence. Of the twenty-three pamphlets issued free to all branches in April 1936, only three covered women's issues and each assumed a certain familiarity with the readership: '"Women of Britain, You Have the Vote but Have You Power?," "Women in Industry: Do You Work for Slave Wages", and "To Wives and Mothers."' HO144/20147/237.

14 'Women as Orators,' *Action*, No. 151, 14 January 1939.

15 From a speech by Oswald Mosley on 8 June 1937: 'From the ashes of the past, shall rise a Merrie England of gay and serene manhood and adorned by the miracle of the modern age and the modern mind.' *Mosley: The Facts* (London, 1957), p.91.

16 'Women as Orators,' *Action*, No. 151, 14 January 1939.

17 Kathleen Texera, 'Shakespeare Would Have been a Fascist,' *Blackshirt*, No. 104, 18 April 1935.

18 E.D. Hart, 'Hester Stanhope: A Noble Englishwoman,' *Blackshirt*, No. 180, 3 October 1936.

19 Mary S. Allen, *Lady in Blue* (London, 1936), p.86.

20 'What the Blackshirts are Doing,' *Sunday Dispatch*, 16 June 1934.

21 Joan Bond, 'The Lost Spirit,' *Action*, No. 164, 15 April 1939. It is interesting to note that a handful of women associated with the BUF were aspiring poets. Mary Richardson was an artist and made some attempts at verse, which she published as *Cornish Headlands and Other Lyrics* (Heffer, 1920). Olive Hawks wrote inspirational poetry for the BUF: 'We Live,' *British Union Quarterly* III, 3 (July–September 1939), and 'Chant for the People,' *British Union Quarterly*, 4, 1 (Spring 1940). Nellie Driver had 'one bad habit, writing verse in Lancashire dialect in local newspapers. Horrible stuff.' Letter from Robert Row to the author, 14 March 1997. Gladys Walsh felt unable to express her deep admiration for Mosley in prose, and in later life eulogized the Leader's passing in verse, for she admitted that 'when I feel anything deeply I write it in poetry.' Interview with Gladys Walsh, Archive of the Friends of O.M.

22 Oswald Mosley, 'Revolution of the Nation,' *Fascist Week*, No. 1, 10–16 November 1933.

23 Diana Mosley, *A Life of Contrasts* (London, 1977), p.95. Diana 'fell simultaneously for his [Mosley's] ideas and for his person. It was the passion of Juliet and at the same time the conversion of St Paul; emotion and conviction were inextricable.' Jonathan and Catherine Guinness, *The House of Mitford* (Harmondsworth, 1984), p.323.

24 Supplementary Report in the Case of Ethel Anne Baggaley, 9 June 1943, HO45/25710.

25 Winifred Holtby, 'Shall I Order a Black Blouse?' *News Chronicle*, 4 May 1934.

26 Oswald Mosley, *Fascism in Britain* (London, 1933) pamphlet.

27 In 1944 Yolande McShane (née Mott) 'became a follower of Christ.' Yolande McShane, *Daughter of Evil* (London, 1980), p.67. Nellie Driver was 'reborn' after her experiences in the BUF and her internment under 18B, and Florence Hayes of Bournemouth turned to spiritualism after her experiences as an 18B detainee. Although a very devout High Church Anglican before she joined the BU, only after her release from internment did Lucy Pearson decide: 'I feel after the war I should probably prefer to work with some religious organization for propounding the basis for a Christian Society rather than with the political organization which has the duty of implementing it.' Letter from Lucy Pearson to John Adams, 3 November 1940, Essex County Record Office, D/DU/758/42/2.

28 Baroness Ella de Heemstra, 'The Call of Fascism,' *Blackshirt*, No. 105, 26 April 1935.

29 E.D. Randall, 'The Flame of Fascism: Discarding Selfish Futilities of Individualism,' *Fascist Week*, No. 11, 19–25 January 1934.

30 Eileen Dewis, 'The Distaff Side,' *Blackshirt*, No. 179, 26 September 1936.

31 Oswald Mosley, 'Fascism Will End the Battle of the Sexes,' *Fascist Week*, No. 10, 12–18 January 1934.

32 Rosalind Raby, 'Daughters of Martha,' *The Fascist Quarterly*, 2, 1 (January 1936), 47–57.

33 John Strachey, *The Menace of Fascism* (London, 1933), pp.42–3.

34 Ann Preston, 'Our Blackshirt Sons,' *Blackshirt*, No. 59, 8 June 1934.

35 'Martha,' 'The Hand that Rocks the Cradle,' *Blackshirt*, No. 79, 26 October 1934.

36 Quoted in a letter from Robert Row to the author, 6 March 1997.

37 'Quartermasters Stores, BUF', Robert Saunders Collection, University of Sheffield, File A.1.

38 Anne Brock Griggs, 'A Woman's Outlook,' *Action*, No. 1, 21 February 1936.

39 Anne Brock Griggs, 'A Woman's Outlook,' *Action*, No. 1, 21 February 1936.

40 Even if activities were less segregated in practice than in theory, propaganda continued to suggest the division of male and female political interests. F.D. Hill, Business Manager, BUF Publications Ltd wrote to all District Leaders: 'Hitting hard at the political logic of our opponents, the distribution of these Silent Propagandists, will prove an excelled method of interesting the electorate …. More over, four of these deal with an important section of the electorate. The women! ... No. 111 "Fascism Means Real Freedom to British Women;" No. 112 "To Wives and Mothers;" No. 113 "Women in Industry:" No. 114 "Women of Britain."' Saunders Collection, Sheffield University, File A.1.

41 'Martha,' 'The Hand that Rocks the Cradle,' *Blackshirt*, No. 79, 26 October 1934.

42 Raven Thomson, 'The Corporate State and You: No. 11 – The Housewife,' *Action*, No. 24, 30 July 1936.

43 'Women: Equal Pay for Equal Work – Spreading the Truth of Fascism,' *Fascist Week*, No. 2, 17–23 November 1933.

44 Eileen Lyons, 'Women Fought for the Vote: What Have They Got – Nothing,' *Action*, No. 62, 24 April 1937.

45 'Why Fascism Appeals to Me, by an Ordinary Woman,' *Blackshirt*, No. 4, 1 April 1933.

46 Agnes Booth, 'Women and Dictatorship,' *Action*, No. 100, 13 January 1938.

47 'The second National Government was returned to power on a panic election frantically promising "to maintain the unity of family life." The Means Test still remains the cruel wrecker of homes shadowed by the sinister cloud of unemployment.' Anne Brock Griggs, 'Grand National Government,' *Blackshirt*, No. 154, 4 April 1936. Similarly, 'Fascism is determined to defend the family from the disintegrating influences which have been at work ever since politicians introduced the iniquitous "family means test", and encouraged wage cuts, which have forced mothers and daughters into the labour market.' A. Raven Thomson, 'The Corporate State and You: No. 11 – The Housewife,' *Action*, No. 24, 30 July 1936.

48 Melville E. Currell, *Political Woman* (London, 1974), p.31.

49 Winifred Holtby, 'Black Words for Women Only,' *Clarion*, 24 May 1934.

50 'The Problem of the Woman Worker: National Socialism Will Solve It,' *Blackshirt*, No. 146, 23 January 1937.

51 Olive Hawks, 'Ideals of Womanhood,' *Blackshirt*, No. 76, 5 October 1934.

52 Mary Allen, *Lady in Blue*, p.152. Much of Allen's career can be described as an anti-vice crusade. In her capacity as a policewoman, she campaigned against drug traffic, white slavery and pornography. She wrote 'Tackling the Vice-Dens of the East' (*Sunday Dispatch*, 11 December 1936), and her few contributions to *Action* consisted of 'End this Indecency' (No. 216, 25 April 1940), 'Indecent Photographs' (No. 218, 9 May 1940), 'Nude Exhibitionism' (No. 219, 16 May 1940).

53 Joan Bond, 'The Lost Spirit,' *Action*, No. 164, 15 April 1939.

54 Elizabeth Winch, 'Senseless Drudgery Will Go,' *Fascist Week*, No. 8, 29 December–4 January 1933–34.

55 'Senex,' 'Chief Considerations of the Housewife,' *Fascist Week*, 16–22 March 1934.

56 Quoted in David Baker, *Ideology of Obsession* (London, 1996), pp.126–27. The same sense of the wife being abandoned by the fascist husband rang true in the case of the Joyces. 'From the beginning, it is said, his life with the girl he married when they were both 21 had been a cycle of romantic ecstasy and

quarrels and impassioned reconciliations; he would turn anything into a fight. He took it for granted, too, that he should spend an amount of time with men friends, which must have made home life exiguous. During his time in service with Mosley his relations with his wife grew more and more purely quarrelsome, and in 1936, although they had two little daughters, this marriage was dissolved.' Rebecca West, *The Meaning of Treason* (London, 1949), p.73.

57 'Lucifer,' 'A Land Fit for Britons to Live In,' *Fascist Week*, No. 7, 22–28 December 1933.

58 Geoffrey Dorman, 'An Appeal to Youth,' *Action*, No. 60, 10 April 1937.

59 John Carey, *The Intellectuals and the Masses* (London, 1992), p.72.

60 Filippo Tommaso Marinetti, *Futurist Manifesto*, Paris, 20 February 1909. The Vorticists of the pre-war years were the British branch of the Futurist movement, and the movement's leading figures were Ezra Pound and Wyndham Lewis. Pound certainly had a strong connection with the BUF, and he contributed frequently to fascist publications. In November 1936 Special Branch reported that 'an endeavour is being made to win over D.B Wyndham-Lewis (author of *Left Wings Over Europe*) to the movement and to persuade him to become a contributor to *Action*.' HO144/21062/348–350.

61 H. Shaw, 'The Gallery Ten,' *Action*, No. 17, 11 June 1936.

62 Susan Sontag, *Under the Sign of Saturn* (New York, 1980), p.93.

63 Jenny Linton, 'Fascist Women Do Not Want Equal Rights With Men: They Desire Only The True Woman's Place In The Community,' *Blackshirt*, No. 80, 2 November 1934.

64 Maria-Antoinetta Macciocchi, 'Female Sexuality in Fascist Ideology,' *Feminist Review*, 1, (1979), 67–82.

65 Lionel Birch, *Why They Join The Blackshirts* (London, 1937), p.39.

66 Interview with Nicholas Mosley, Lord Ravensdale, by the author, 25 September 1996.

67 'Beaverbrook Press and Miss Vivian Mosley,' *Action*, No. 172, 10 June 1939.

68 Oswald Mosley, *Blackshirt Policy* (London, [1934?]), p.75.

69 Hilda Browning, *Women Under Fascism and Communism* (London, 1935), p.18.

70 Oswald Mosley, *The Greater Britain* (London, 1932), p.40.

71 Mosley speaking on 2 February 1936. *Mosley: The Facts* (London, 1957), p.83. The BUF's ageism was in tune with the fascist zeitgeist. Mussolini wrote of World War I: 'We who willed to enter the war, who ought to have seized power, we young men committed then a mistake for which we have paid dearly; we sacrificed our glorious youth to miserable old age ... I mean not only those who in actual years are aged. Some are born aged. I speak of those who are surpassingly old, who have become encumbrances. They have never understood, never grasped the reality of war.' Quoted in Margherita G. Sarfatti, *The Life of Benito Mussolini*, trans. Frederic Whyte (London, 1925), pp.245–6.

72 Oswald Mosley, *The British Peace and How to Get It* (London, 1940).

73 Lionel Birch, *Why They Join the Fascists*, p.15.

74 Oswald Mosley, *Tomorrow We Live* (London, March 1938), p.55.

75 In general, fascist women conceded that the temperament of male youth rebellion was omnipotent. In one incident, however, Anne Cutmore – a frequent contributor to BUF publications as well as their drama critic in later issues of *Action* – took vehement exception to G.E. DeBurgh Wilmot's article 'Our First Duty to CULTURE is to Destroy it,' as puerile, and responded a fortnight later with 'Assumed and Deliberate Barbarism is Decadence.' In her defence of culture she castigated the impulse to destroy civilization for the sake of destruction or to fulfil the male adolescent desire to find something to condemn. Cutmore believed that 'there are still men able to create works of such power and magnificence, of such overwhelming sincerity that they will irresistibly be draw the people towards them, leaving the poseurs "in all the squalor of an exploded sham."' Anne Cutmore, 'Assumed and Deliberate Barbarism is Decadence,' *Blackshirt*, No. 69, 17 August 1934. As women figured as the guardians of morality, so they too could serve as the trustees of culture and throw cold water on the rebellious young man's instinct to vandalise his father's 'civilization.'

76 My italics. Anne Brock Griggs, 'Womanhood in National Socialism,' *Action*, No. 99, 6 January 1938.

77 Letter from Mrs V. Sylvaine, quoted in 'Why so Many Women Support the Blackshirt Movement,' *Evening News*, 18 April 1934.

78 Oswald Mosley, *My Life* (London, 1968), p.347.

79 Wilhelm Reich, *The Mass Psychology of Fascism*, p.64.

80 Naomi Mitchson, *The Home and a Changing Civilization* (London, 1934), p.104.

81 Murray Constantine (pseud.), *Swastika Night* (London, 1937), p.6.

82 Virginia Woolf, *Three Guineas* (London, 1984), p.222.

83 Kate Millett, *Sexual Politics* (London, 1989), p.26.

84 Silke Hesse, 'Fascism and the Hypertrophy of Male Adolescence,' in ed. John Milfull, *The Attractions of Fascism* (New York, 1990), p.159. Mullaly's analysis of what motivated the fictional Peter Fletcher to throw in his lot with the BUF calibrates with this youth-gang model. For Fletcher the 'gang appeal was powerful. You could lose your old, muddled self and find a new identity in the movement.' Frederic Mullaly, *Fascism in England*, p.9.

85 Oswald Mosley, *Fascism: 100 Questions Asked and Answered* (London, 1936). As Lewis has pointed out, 'while the percentage of middle class people using mechanical methods of birth control increased from 9% to 40% between 1910 and 1930, the comparable figures for the working class were 11% and 28%.' Jane Lewis, *Women in England 1870–1950* (Sussex, 1984), p.18.

86 Oswald Mosley, *My Life*, p.290.

87 Martin Durham, *Women and Fascism* (London, 1998), pp.38–9.

88 'Four Questions Answered,' *Action*, No. 23, 23 July 1936.

89 Richard Gayus, 'Is Abortion Justified? The Rule of Two Laws,' *Action*, No. 128, 30 July 1938.

90 G. Sutton, 'Family Endowment,' *Action*, No. 209, 7 March 1940.

91 The BUF's claim to represent the concerns of feminism broke down at the point for, as Brian Harrison has pointed out, inter-war New Feminists were chiefly concerned with the achievement of three goals: birth control, women's emancipation leading to greater concern for welfare, and pressure for better-paid women's careers. See Brian Harrison, *Prudent Revolutionaries* (Oxford, 1987).

92 Anne Cutmore, 'Dwindling Britain,' *Action*, 26 December 1936.

93 My italics. Anne Brock-Griggs, 'Subman and Superman: Sir John Orr Vindicates the Housewife – But Indicts a System,' *Action*, No. 4., 12 March 1936.

94 E. Arnot Robertson, 'Stiff Upper Lippery: Stuff for Girls,' *Action*, Vol.1, No. 7, 19 November 1931.

95 James Drennan, *BUF: Oswald Mosley and British Fascism* (London, 1934), pp.190–1.

96 Interview with Nicholas Mosley, Lord Ravensdale, by the author, 25 September 1996. See also Trevor Grundy, *Memoir of a Fascist Childhood* (London, 1998), pp.112–13. Grundy has pointed out that in the post-war Union Movement, one of the chief organizers, Alf Flockhart, was convicted for 'interfering' with a man in a public lavatory, leading East End members to insist that Mosley expel him from the movement.

97 Charles Munday, 'Exhibition – or Exhibitionism: The Surrealists,' *Action*, No. 20, 2 July 1936.

98 Alfred Norris, 'Sex-Stuff and Socialism: "Left" Literature Flooding the Bookshops,' *Blackshirt*, No. 168, 11 July 1936.

99 Charles Greenwood, 'Sex Appeal to Bloomsbury Bacilli,' *Blackshirt*, No. 158, 2 May 1936.

100 Holtby described D.H. Lawrence as 'the self-appointed poet and prophet' of nationalism and leader-lust. Winifred Holtby, *Women and a Changing Civilization* (London, 1934), p.159. 'Behind the political antics of British Fascism, a literary cult associated with the names of D.H. Lawrence and John Middleton Murray, revived the idea of "auxiliary" women. In their peculiar vision no real meeting place for the sexes existed; it worshipped the instinct, emphasized sexual differences and functions, and encouraged much talk (by men) about women's "normal" place.' Vera Brittain, *Lady into Woman* (London, 1953), p.197.

101 H.E. Bates, 'Modern Fiction: A House of Women,' *Action*, No. 17, 11 June 1936. 'D.H. Lawrence. A great artist, you say. But only in a decadent age do people argue that life is well-served by an art which feeds upon deformity.' A.K. Chesterton, 'To the Intellectuals: You Shall Cater for a Sane and Virile Nation,' *Fascist Week*, No. 9, January 5–11, 1934.

102 'Fascists at Olympia,' *The Times*, Friday, 8 June 1934.

103 'More "Skirted" Shouting at Hampstead,' *Blackshirt*, No. 184, 31 October 1936.

104 Anne Cutmore, 'The Pity of it: May Day in London,' *Action*, No. 12, 7 May 1936.

105 'Soviet Anti-Feminism,' *Action*, No. 108, 12 March 1938.

106 Doreen Bell, 'Mayfair Parasite: Pampered Idleness,' *Action*, No. 119, 28 May 1938. In correspondence with Robert Saunders, D/L in Dorset, Mrs Mabel Sanford wrote on 9 June 1936: 'any decent minded person would deplore the scandalously loose behaviour of democracy in England with the partially dressed freaks of men, throughout the summer months, and the still less-dressed painted gezebels of women, in these days of so-called emancipation. All of these would have been under lock and key in stronger, and more moral Reigns.' Saunders Papers, University of Sheffield, File A.2.

107 'If women are to be worthy of the place in the life of the nation which we believe they can fill, it is up to them to kill this form of snob journalism stone dead by refusing to take the slightest interest in the flittering to and fro of the so-called society butterflies.' 'Press Dope for Women,' *Action*, No. 105, 19 February 1938. This point was made even more forcefully in the context of women's opposition to war: 'the first of the ways in which women can prevent the war-mongering poison of the gossip Press from doing its fatal work is by ruthless boycott of those "news"-papers which force sex and politics down the throats of their readers at the same gulp.' Olive Hawks, 'Women! You can Stop this War,' *Blackshirt*, No. 110, 26 March, 1938.

108 Anne Cutmore, 'The Pity of it: May Day in London,' *Action*, No. 12, 7 May 1936.

109 'With the subman National Socialists are unfortunately compelled to be familiar. It would now appear that the recreation of the tired razor-knight, the weary wielder of the barbed wire cudgel, is the subwoman.' 'The Subwoman,' *Action*, No. 38, 7 November 1936.

110 Olive Hawks, 'Ideals of Womanhood,' *Blackshirt*, No. 76, 5 October 1934.

111 Anne Brock Griggs, *Women and Fascism: 10 Important Points* (London, 1936).

112 BUF Speakers Notes, April 1935, HO144/20144/4–10A.

113 Alexander Raven, 'The Position of Women in the Fascist State,' *Blackshirt*, No. 72, 7 September 1934.

114 'Women in Parliament,' *Blackshirt*, No. 166, 27 June 1936.

115 Doreen Bell, 'Women's World: By Women for Men and Women,' *Action*, No. 199, 6 January 1938.

116 Winifred Holtby, 'Shall I Order a Black Blouse?' *News Chronicle*, 4 May 1934.

117 'The Problem of the Woman Worker: National Socialism will Solve it,' *Blackshirt*, No. 196, 23 January 1937.

118 Martin Durham, 'Women and the BUF,' in ed. T. Kushner and K. Lunn, *The Politics of Marginality*, p.6.

119 'Current Cant and Fascist Facts,' *Fascist Week*, No. 2, 17–23 November 1933.

120 'The anomalies regulations were largely ineffective in denying benefit to the

part-time or short-time workers protected by the unions, but they did success-fully strip the most vulnerable seasonal workers and married women workers of their insurance benefits ... . Fully 78% of claims made by married women, or over 200,000 workers, were disallowed in the nineteen months following the introduction of the regulations.' Susan Pedersen, *Family, Dependence and the Origins of the Welfare State* (Cambridge, 1993), p.303.

121 'Where Women are the Workers,' *Action*, No. 2, 28 February 1936.

122 Raven Thomson, 'The Corporate State and You – No. 11: The Housewife,' *Action*, No. 24, 30 July 1936.

123 Susan Pedersen, *Family, Dependence and the Origins of the Welfare State*, p.310

124 John Tosh, 'What Should Historians do with Masculinity?: Reflections on Nine-teenth Century Britain,' in eds. R. Shoemaker & M. Vincent, *Gender and History in Western Europe* (London, 1998), p.73.

125 Anne Brock Griggs, *Women and Fascism:10 Important Points*.

126 Anne Brock Griggs, 'Red Petticoats and Blue Stockings: Equal Pay – A Trivial Debate Which Raises Major Issues,' *Action*, No. 9, 16 April 1936.

127 'Current Cant and Fascist Facts,' *Fascist Week*, No. 2, 17–23 November, 1933. For all its seeming modernity, the BUF's policy on women's employment was probably derived from those promises made to women in Germany by the Nazi Party before it came to power. 'A 1932 appeal to employed women urging them to vote National Socialist indicated how the party tried to attract working and professional women. The appeal promised that all women – employed women, housewives and mothers – would be citizens of the Third Reich. No women would lose their jobs, but National Socialism would not allow women to be forced into employment. It would secure decent wages for men so that those women who wished to do so could stay at home. "But no woman who, out of personal preference, wants to take up a profession, will be prevented from doing so ... Germany, the great mother, embodied in National Socialism, loves and needs every one of its daughters: the one by her child's cradle and the one behind the counter, the one at the stove and the one at the lectern, the one in the factory and the one in the laboratory, everyone who works honestly and selflessly for the rise of the Fatherland." Leila J. Rupp, *Mobilizing Women for War* (Princeton, 1978), p.20.

128 Letter from Robert Row to the author, 6 March 1997.

129 'Viscountess Downe At King's Lynn Branch,' *Blackshirt*, No. 87, 21 December 1934.

130 'Working Women in Germany,' *Action*, No. 133, 3 September 1938.

131 Eileen Lyons, 'Those German Women: A Contrast Between Democratic and Fascist Methods,' *Blackshirt*, No. 164, 13 June 1936. In an interview with Claudia Koonz, Scholtz-Klink said about her role in the Nazi state: "'My own women's division concerned itself with women's responsibilities. We formed almost a state within a state. In my ministry I directed departments of economics, education,

colonial issues, consumer affairs and health, education and welfare. No man ever interfered with us; we did as we pleased." Her decision to create a separate bureaucracy for women had "nothing to do with feminism," she insisted, but sprang from her own intense pride in being a woman.' Claudia Koonz, *Mothers in the Fatherland*, p.xxiii. Sholtz-Klink visited Britain in an official capacity in 1936 and again in 1938. In 1938 she was welcomed at a dinner hosted by the Anglo-German Fellowship, and a range of British women's organizations were also represented. Interestingly enough, the BU's Women's Section does not seem to have sent a representative. See *Daily Telegraph*, 8 March, 1938.

132 Rosalind Raby, 'A Woman in Nazi Germany,' *Blackshirt*, No. 81, 9 November 1934.

133 Brock-Griggs, 'May Day in Germany,' *Action*, 14 May 1936. See also Joan Morgan, 'Hitler's Berchtesgaden: An Idyll of New Germany,' *British Union Quarterly*, 1, 1 (January–April, 1937), 66–7. Ann Seelig-Thomann, 'Germany and Her Women,' *British Union Quarterly*, 1, 4 (October–December, 1937), 52–6.

134 When in Rome applying for leave to go to Abyssinia, she was told that 'my application would be forwarded immediately to the Chief of Government, but did I understand that life would not be exactly comfortable, especially for a woman? It was the only occasion on which my sex was so much as mentioned, for Italians take an eminently sensible attitude that if woman is prepared to do the same work as a man, and accept the same conditions as a man, no unreasonable obstacles should be place in her way.' Muriel Currey OBE, *A Woman at the Abyssinian War* (London, 1936), p.15.

135 Muriel Currey, 'Women and the Corporate State: Equality of the Sexes in Italy,' *Blackshirt*, No. 58, 1 June 1934. See also Harold E. Goad and Muriel Currey, *The Working of the Corporate State* (London, 1934).

136 Oswald Mosley, *Fascism in Britain* (London, 1933).

137 *The Fascist Quarterly*, 1, 3 (July 1935), 164. It is interesting that Bonora picked up on the points relating to women in Germany in Clephane's book, when the author also wrote specifically about BUF women. See Irene Clephane, *Towards Sex Freedom* (London, 1935), pp.226–7.

138 *Fascist Quarterly*, 1, 3 (July 1935), 164.

139 Eileen Lyons, 'Those German Women,' *Blackshirt*, No. 164, 13 June 1936. In contrast to BUF women's observations of distinction, Mosse has analysed that 'there is a surprising similarity between English and German national stereotypes, their ideals of masculinity and the role of women ... . To be sure, Marianne is similar to Germania or Britannia as the chaste guardian of the nation.' George L. Mosse, *Nationalism and Sexuality* (New York, 1985), p.21.

140 Mary Richardson, 'My Reply to Sylvia Pankhurst,' *Blackshirt*, No. 62, 29 June 1934.

141 E.D. Hart, 'Square Deal for Women,' *Blackshirt*, No. 244, 8 January 1938.

142 Lionel Birch, *Why They Join the Fascists*, p.19.

143 Oswald Mosley, 'Fascism Will End the Battle of the Sexes,' *Fascist Week*, No. 10, 12–18 January 1934.

144 Norah Elam, 'Fascism, Women and Democracy,' *Fascist Quarterly*, 1, 3 (July 1935), 290–8.

145 Norah Elam, 'Women and the Vote,' *Action*, No. 6, 26 March 1936.

146 Anne Brock Griggs, 'Food or Usury?' *Fascist Quarterly*, 2, 2, (April 1936), 237–44.

147 Tony Kushner, 'Sex and Semitism: Jewish Women in Britain in War and Peace,' in ed. Panikos Panayi, *Minorities in Wartime* (Oxford, 1993), p.119.

148 Yolande McShane, *Daughter of Evil* (London, 1980), p.30. At one of her first, and indeed her last, visit to the Carlisle Branch, Eugenia Wright has described the form of the BUF meeting: 'Then we were invited – no! – instructed to march round the room chanting "The Yids, the Yids, we've gotta get rid of the Yids!" I asked who were "the Yids" and when told, refused to say it as I felt it was not the right thing to do.' Letter from Eugenia Wright to the author, 6 May 1997.

149 *The British Union Quarterly*, 1, 3 (September 1937), 105.

150 Advisory Committee to Hear Appeals Against Orders of Internment, 2 July 1940, HO283/13/2–125.

151 Eileen Lyons, 'Women Fought for the Vote: What Have They Got – Nothing,' *Action*, No. 62, 24 April 1937.

152 Anne Brock Griggs, 'Women Must Work: The Labour International Will Sell Them Into Slavery,' *Blackshirt*, No. 157, 25 April 1936.

153 Quoted in Dinah Parkinson, 'In a Manchester Sweat Shop,' *Blackshirt*, No. 156, 18 April 1936.

154 'How Britons Live: Anne Brock Griggs Describes the Building of a Super Race,' *Action*, No. 15, 28 May 1936.

155 Anne Brock Griggs, 'Food or Usury,' *Fascist Quarterly*, 2, 2 (April 1936), 237–44.

156 Special Branch report of a BUF meeting at Piggott St, Limehouse, HO144/21063/365–68.

157 Anne Cutmore, 'Conscript the Jews,' *Blackshirt*, No. 179, 26 September 1936. In a more unguarded moment, one BUF woman expressed the opinion: 'As far as driving the Jews goes, I expect that many know nothing about them or their powerful mischief. Very apparently nobody likes, or wants them, therefore they should be shipped to a distant no-man's land and get on together, which they appear able to do, and certainly not be dumped, by the informal interference of Britain, on the unfortunate Arabs, for whom we have the greatest liking and sympathy.' Letter from Mrs Mabel Helen Sanford to Robert Saunders, December 1936, Saunders Collection, Sheffield University, File A.4. Certainly there were many women among the 'Jew-wise' in such organizations as the Imperial Fascist League, the Nordic League, and the Right Club. See *Who's Who*.

158 HO144/21378/307

159 Claudia Koonz, *Mothers in the Fatherland*, p.3.

160 Martin Durham, 'Gender and the BUF,' *Journal of Contemporary History*, 27, 3 (July 1992), 513–27.

161 Elieen Lyons, 'Those German Women: A Contrast Between Democratic and Fascist Methods,' *Blackshirt*, No. 164, 13 June 1936.

162 'Youth and Womanhood Turn to Fascism,' *Blackshirt*, No. 70, 24 August 1933.

163 'British Union Personalities,' *Action*, No. 40, 21 November 1936.

164 Virginia Woolf, *Three Guineas*, p.221.

165 ed. Ray Strachey, *Our Freedom and Its Results* (London, 1936), p.10.

166 Letter from Louise Irvine to the author, 5 June 1996.

167 Letter from Robert Row to the author, 6 March 1997. Taking issue with the author's suggestion that feminism was a term which cropped up again and again in the BUF's publications, John Warburton, President of the Friends of O.M., wrote to me that 'women like my wife and her sister were the true feminists of that age. In short they believed in women's equality with the male *where they were equal* [his italics] which is a long way from what seems to be the "feminism" of today in a very wide field. Indeed, before they died they were horrified by the vast claims for equality in spheres where men and women could never be truly equal.' Letter from John Warburton to the author, 29 July 1997.

Chapter 4

The Legacy of the Suffragettes for British Fascism

In the political diaspora from the Edwardian suffragette movement some former militant women settled into the seemingly inhospitable territory of British fascism during the 1930s. Mary Richardson, Norah Elam (Mrs Dacre Fox), and Mary Allen each sought refuge and renewal in Sir Oswald Mosley's British Union of Fascists, importing with them the legacy of their militant feminist struggle in the pre-war period and their disillusionment with the post-war condition of the women's movement in the aftermath of female enfranchisement. These fascist women resuscitated the extra-parliamentary methods and militancy of their earlier suffragette struggle, while deciding that the vote was an 'empty vessel' and democracy a sinking ship. While the 'masculine spirit' of British fascism might well have been hostile to the enlistment of militant women, it was the irony in this case that the former suffragettes were welcomed amid much favourable publicity, held posts of prominence and trust in the movement's Women's Section, and found a forum in which to express their revisionist feminism. They were ideologically accommodated by the development of a BUF historiography in which the suffragette struggle was claimed as a precedent for fascist dissent.

Drawing attention to the activities of the ex-suffragettes in the BUF may well elicit a primary response of consternation, and some regret. How could three women who had fought in the vanguard of the Edwardian suffrage struggle migrate to an anti-democratic and masculine movement by the 1930s? How could their ideologies of feminism and their drives to emancipate women be tailored to complement the doctrine of revolutionary fascism? Was it merely intellectual acrobatics when they identified the objectives of their militant battle for female enfranchisement in a vehemently anti-democratic creed? Were Richardson, Elam and Allen traitors to feminism, just as Elam and Allen would be suspected of being Fifth Columnists and traitors to liberal-democratic Britain in 1940?

It would be convenient to characterize these women as renegades, and argue that the acceptance of the new fascist faith necessitated the renunciation of militant feminism, but for the fact that biography more often than not lacks coherence. By tracing the political choices of these three women; by examining the connections between some former suffragettes and the far-Right; and by asking how these three women negotiated the merger between their suffragette memories and their fascist aspirations, it will be argued that there was some logic in their personal progress from the Women's Social and Political Union (WSPU) to the BUF. Furthermore, perhaps the development of the fascist feminist type can tell us as much about the potential of Edwardian radical feminism as about the nature of the BUF's women's policy.

Broken Roads: From Militant Suffragism to Fascism

The pre-war activities of the BUF's suffragette recruits have been recorded in histories of the Women's Social and Political Union and in the BUF press itself. The story of their fascist activities is somewhat more obscure and must be pieced together from public records, personal memoirs, and their self-representation in the movement's publications. While the sources for retrieving their life stories change, it is remarkable to what extent character and temperament seem to have remained consistent over time. Like so many other suffragettes, they deemed their youthful experiences in the WSPU formative, and these defined their political psychology for the rest of their partisan lives.

To a greater extent than either Richardson's or Allen's, Mrs Dacre Fox/Norah Elam's (born ca.1878) activities and the political attitudes she espoused in the WSPU foreshadow her espousal of fascism. She had a distinguished suffragette record in thrice being imprisoned in Holloway for militant acts, and she had gone on hunger strike for which she received a medal with three bars from the leaders of the WSPU. In January 1914 she organized deputations to bishops, asking them to take action against the conditions imposed on suffragettes in Holloway. On 30 July 1914,

Mrs Dacre Fox was arrested at Buckingham Palace while attempting to present a letter from Mrs Pankhurst to King George V. Also in 1914, she was arrested on Lord Lansdowne's doorstep, where she had gone to bring public attention to bear on the government's unequal treatment of violent resisters to Irish Home Rule and suffrage militants.[1] After war was declared, however, she 'followed the Pankhursts into apostasy,'[2] channelled her suffrage vigilance into energetic recruitment for the war effort, and became a key figure among those ex-WSPU members who developed a creed that can best be described as nationalist feminism.

After the First World War, Mrs Dacre Fox – eager to taste the fruits of the Sex Disqualification (Removal) Act – stood unsuccessfully as an Independent candidate for Richmond, Surrey. From the vantage point of the 1930s, she explained that in 1918 'my own distrust of Party politics made me chary of turning in this direction, and I preferred to stand as an Independent, going down with all the other women candidates on this occasion, save one.'[3] Temporarily putting aside her revulsion with traditional party politics, she became a member of the Conservative Party from which she and her second husband, Dudley Elam, defected to join the BUF in 1934. Dudley Elam had been Chairman of the Chichester Conservatives, he was a retired civil servant from the Ministry of Health, and he became an unpaid receptionist at the BUF's National Headquarters. Norah Elam became the BUF County Women's Officer for West Sussex, a prospective parliamentary candidate for the British Union in 1936, and she was a frequent contributor to BUF publications from 1935 to 1940.

Elam's status in the BUF and the sensitive tasks with which she was entrusted offer some substance to the BUF's claim to respect sexual equality. While, in principle, the movement was segregated by gender and women in positions of leadership were meant to have authority only over other women, Elam was quite evidently admitted to Mosley's inner circle. As Mosley explained to inquisitive detectives from the Special Branch in 1940, because of his fears that National Headquarters might be bombed and even that he might be assassinated by an angry mob, it was Mrs Elam who 'took charge of part of our funds for a short period before and after the declaration of war. There was nothing illegal or improper about this.'[4] As further evidence of the high esteem with which she was held by Mosley, when Norah Elam's offices at the London and Provincial Anti-Vivisection Society were raided on 18 December 1939, the police found in her possession a list containing the names of eight members of the BU, 'together with a letter from Oswald Mosley stating that Mrs Elam had his full confidence, and was entitled to do what she thought fit in the interest of the movement on her own responsibility.'[5] The Elams were also among those most prominent BU members who, during the 'phoney war', regularly attended secret meetings convened for the purpose of organizing collaboration between the various extreme right 'patriotic societies'.

Norah Elam was the only ex-suffragette to be interned in Britain, as her second foray into anti-government plotting landed her in Holloway as an indisputable 'political prisoner.' (During her previous internments, she, along with other suffrage prisoners was refused the status of political prisoners.) She was interned under Defence Regulation 18B (1A) on 23 May 1940 as part of the first group of BU officials to be arrested. Olive Hawks, Muriel Whinfield, and Anne Brock Griggs were also among those first women arrested. Elam was somewhat exceptional for declining to make an objection and an appeal before the 18B Advisory Committee, but Diana Mosley did much to advocate her release. When Diana Mosley was visited in Holloway by her lawyer, Sir Walter Monckton, on 26 April 1941, she brought forward the cases of the older women internees, and spoke of Elam: 'She has an old husband who is not very strong, has been interned and had a very bad time at Stafford and some other prison – she is worried that she may have to go to the Isle of Man.'[6] Elam was released some time thereafter, and was at liberty when, in 1943, she was among the very few former members of the BU to be granted a visit with the 'Leader' and Lady Mosley, when the couple was interned together in Holloway prison. On the occasion of this visit, it was reported that the Elams were escorting Unity Mitford, who was staying with them at their home at 5 Logan Place S.W.[7] Elam was also active in the furtherance of the aims of the 18B Detainees (British) Aid Fund, and thereby had the opportunity to re-apply the tactics she had used during suffragette days when she had agitated for the release of her fellow dissidents.

Although her road to fascism was much less coherent than either Elam's or Allen's, Mary Richardson (1883–1961) was the most infamous of the three ex-suffragettes and she rose to the highest position in the women's hierarchy of the BUF. Some early temperamental affinities between suffragettism and fascism were evident in Richardson's case, however. Richardson remembered how she reacted the first time she stewarded a meeting for the

WSPU at the Albert Hall in the following manner: 'I cannot remember a single word of what was said on that, for me, so memorable occasion. But at the time the words did not matter. In some strange way I was inspired by the atmosphere of the great gathering. "We will fight," I kept repeating to myself.'[8] And fight she did, in self-abnegation and with millenarian fervour. She shone in the spot-light of WSPU publicity and built her reputation on the extreme nature of her militant acts. By October 1913 she was a suffragette 'mouse,' evading re-arrest under the Prisoner's Temporary Discharge for Ill-Health Act, and when she and Rachel Peace were again imprisoned, both on remand for arson, they were the first to suffer from the reintroduction of forcible feeding. More than seventy years after these events, Anne Page, a younger member of the BUF, remembered Richardson as 'one of the most militant suffragettes, [who] was arrested nine times in 1913 and 1914 and was one of the first two suffragettes to be forcibly fed. She achieved notoriety by jumping on the running board of King George V's carriage to present a petition and by slashing the *Rokeby Venus* in the National Gallery.'[9] Indeed, Richardson's most nefarious stunt as a militant was vandalising the *Rokeby Venus* in March 1914, an act of protest against Mrs Pankhurst's recent arrest in Glasgow. On 30 July 1914 Richardson was released from Holloway for an appendix operation.

While certain aspects of Elam's suffrage activities prefigured her espousal of fascism, the opposite was true for the case of Mary Richardson. There was a story that when Richardson was breaking windows in the West End before the war, she had known Benito Mussolini, at that time the editor of the socialist journal *Avanti!*. She opposed the fascist movement from its Italian inception in 1922, and wrote Mussolini a scathing letter after his March on Rome in which she accused him of betraying his principles. In reply, he sent her a prophetic telegram with the words 'Some day, perhaps, your eyes will be opened.'[10] She had become a member of the Labour Party in 1916, and stood as a candidate for Parliament three times, losing to the Conservative incumbent on each occasion: she contested Middlesex, Acton, in 1922 as a Labour candidate, the same constituency in 1924 for the ILP, and fought Hampshire, Aldershot, in 1931 for Labour.

In December 1933, it was announced Richardson had joined the Blackshirts, and she explained that what attracted her was 'its policy of Imperialism, and action combined with discipline [which] raise the movement above comparison with the present party system.'[11] By January 1934 she was made assistant to Esther, Lady Makgill, leader of the BUF's Women's Section, and she took over as Chief Organizer of the Women's Section by May, when Lady Makgill was forced to resign after being caught embezzling funds. Richardson opened a National Club for Fascist Women at 12 Lower Grosvenor Place, the headquarters of the Women's Section, on 24 April 1934. In 1935 Richardson came into conflict with 'Ma' Mosley and F.M. Box. While the public records suggest that these personal antipathies motivated her defection, more recent research has uncovered the real reason behind Richardson's and the BUF's parting of ways. According to Durham, Richardson was expelled from the BUF in February 1935 for having organized a meeting protesting the unequal remuneration of women employed by the movement, and Richardson herself claimed that 'all the best women left when I was expelled.'[12] While Richardson had achieved high rank in the BUF, among the three ex-suffragettes, she was the only one who questioned the sincerity of the BUF's women's policy, and the only one who eventually became disillusioned by fascist assurances of fair play for women.

Of the three BUF ex-suffragettes, although Mary Allen (1878–1964) was a card-carrying member for the shortest time, her guilt by association with the fascist movement in Britain can be traced back the farthest. As a young woman Allen was 'converted' to the suffrage cause after hearing a speech delivered by Annie Kenney, the ex-mill hand. The ideal of near-religious conversion to the cause that was shared by suffragette and fascist women alike certainly came true in her case, for she 'abandoned home, parents, friends and comfort to follow a vision,'[13] and follow a leader. In July 1909 she was arrested, with thirteen other women, for breaking the windows of the Home Office, and fined £5 plus 2/6d costs or a month in the Second Division. She chose prison, and after a sixty-hour hunger strike she was released. On 13 August 1909 Allen accompanied Keir Hardie and the Home Secretary, Herbert Gladstone, on a tour of inspection of conditions in Holloway. After her second term of imprisonment and another hunger strike she fell ill, and Mrs Pankhurst personally forbade her to risk imprisonment again. Her days as an active militant over, she became an organizer for the WSPU in Edinburgh.

Allen is best remembered for her pioneering work with women police, her mannish attire and preference to be addressed as 'Sir' at her headquarters,[14] her obsession with women in uniform, and her moral alarmism directed at all branches of the 'vice racket.'

Allen would explain that her experience of the treatment of women in Edwardian prisons demonstrated to her the urgent necessity for women in the police force. Rather than renounce her political rite of passage through the law-breaking WSPU, she asserted that

> I have never ceased being thankful that I was a rebel against law and order before I became head of an organization of policewomen. For just as it is the axiom that the ex-poacher makes the finest gamekeeper in the world, so it is true that Suffragette experience has been invaluable to me over and over again.[15]

She spent the Great War as Margaret Damer Dawson's sub-commandant in the Women's Police Force, received the OBE in 1917 for her war service, and became commandant upon Damer Dawson's death in 1920. The war over, she was not prepared to obey the Metropolitan Police Commissioner's instructions that her Women Police must disband, and founded her own Women's Police Reserve (re-christened the Women's Auxiliary Service in 1923). After 1918 she was persistently characterized as an eccentric mannish-woman, and a public nuisance.[16] In May 1921, along with her 'unofficial women police,' she was fined and ordered to pay costs for the unauthorized wearing of a uniform similar to that of the Metropolitan Police.

Her political ambitions undeterred by public and official censure, she stood as a Liberal candidate for the St George's Division of Westminster in 1922, focusing her campaign on women police and the importance of the uniformed officer. Not surprisingly perhaps, she came in at the bottom of the poll with only 6.5 per cent of the votes. She spent most of the inter-war years globe-trotting to promote women police, and visited Germany, Spain, France, Brazil, Poland, and Egypt in her capacity as 'Commandant.' In November 1933 she formed the Women's Reserve to enrol women to serve in the event of a national emergency, this time arousing the exasperation and hostility of Lady Londonderry, the President of the Women's Legion. Lady Londonderry judged that it was neither 'necessary [n]or desirable at the present moment to start an entirely new organization, which has no recognition from the authorities, and which would be run ... practically on Fascist lines. It would only lead to unnecessary overlapping.'[17] It was interesting that Allen chose as the motto for the Women's Reserve 'For God, King and Country,' the very same slogan used by Lintorn-Orman's British Fascists.

Allen's open admiration for, and collaboration with, fascism both at home and abroad, and her virulent anti-communism dated from as far back as 1926. In that year she mobilized her women against the strikers and accepted recruits to her Women's Auxiliary Service from the British Fascists. Also in 1926, at the International Police Congress and Exhibition in Berlin, she met General O'Duffy, the leader of the Irish Blueshirt movement, by whom she was very much impressed. In 1933, with her Women's Auxiliary Service, she visited the British Fascists Ltd, and in April 1934 she addressed a meeting of the BUF's January Club. In January 1934, shortly after the Reichstag fire, she visited Germany 'to learn about the truth of the position of German womanhood,'[18] and to encourage the Fuehrer to re-establish women police in the Third Reich. She was given an audience with Hitler and Goering. Allen was very impressed by Hitler, entranced by his oratory, and spell-bound by his visionary eyes. She 'recognized in him an enduring blood-brother of the ordinary decent people of Europe, whatever their nationalities, who want peace for their trade and safety for their children.'[19] Indeed, in her autobiography, *Lady in Blue* (1936), Allen devoted more space to her interview with Hitler and to her tour of the exhibition of Communist weapons at the Secret Police Headquarters in Berlin than to any other episode in her proud career as a crusader for women in blue. In 1936, as General Franco's guest, she visited Spain where, it was alleged, she preached the doctrine of a Fascist International and 'had made complete arrangements with the British Fascist party and its sympathizers to stage meetings of protest, if and when the British Government showed any symptoms of sympathy for the Republicans.'[20] It was not uncommon that European dictators should exploit some British women's enthusiasm for fascism for maximum propaganda value, and Allen was certainly one such ambassador who returned to Britain with messages of friendship from Hitler and Franco.

Allen's road to fascism was logically sign-posted, and the progress from women in blue to women in black was not a grand leap.[21] Allen's 'coming out' as a member of the British Union was untimely, as she joined soon after the declaration of war in the autumn of 1939. She occupied a seat of honour at a luncheon for the movement's London Administration in March 1940, and she addressed a BU Women's Peace meeting at Friend's House on 13 April 1940. It was also maintained that in March, April, and May of 1940 she attended secret meetings convened by leaders of Britain's pro-Nazi and anti-Semitic organizations to prepare plans for a fascist *coup d'état*.[22] She explained that she had joined the BU because she agreed with its policy for peace and its concentration on the interests of the British Empire.[23] She also testified that she had been associated with the fascist movement through her friendship with Norah Elam, whom she had known since the militant suffrage movement.[24]

An order under Defence Regulation 18B(1A) was made against Allen and served on 16 June 1940, and while she was never interned, her activities were restricted under 18B(2). At her appeal before the Advisory Committee she revealed her deep resentment against a system which had never paid her due credit: 'I believe I have earned more than I have been given ... . There are always people who live to found movement after movement but nothing is done for them.'[25] Looking back upon her life's work, mourning the absence of official recognition, and afflicted by the 'grave injustice' of the Defence Regulations imposed by the Home Secretary, perhaps she took some small comfort in the fact that she had broken the windows of the Home Office as early as 1909. Such considerations aside, a final irony to Allen's martial patriotism was achieved when five Metropolitan Women Police were placed in charge of alien and fascist internees on the Isle of Man.

Elam, Richardson, and Allen shared more than pride in their ordeals as pre-war militant feminists, and certain similarities in their post-suffrage experiences offer clues to the type of militant woman who was susceptible to the lure of revolutionary fringe fascism. The BUF's ex-suffragettes had all been unsuccessful in their bids to be elected to parliament, and felt first hand the disappointment that arose from the failure of any suffrage campaigner to benefit from the constitutional right they had fought for so tirelessly. Elam spoke with deep regret when she recalled how the first woman to be elected to the House of Commons was the Sinn Fein Countess Markievicz, and the first to take her seat the American Lady Astor – the presence of both outsiders being an affront to her nationalist feminism. All three ex-suffragettes had made some attempt at accommodation with the very parties which had treated militant women 'with such unprecedented contempt,'[26] as they were all members of one of the main political parties before they opted for the abolition of the entire decadent party system and the over-throw of 'Financial Democracy.' While none had been active in a feminist organization during the inter-war period, each identified the fulfilment of her own national service-oriented feminism in fascism. From a psychological perspective, to varying degrees of intensity, each believed that she was owed more than she had received for her dedication to the women's suffrage struggle, and that this inheritance had remained wanting. In their ultimate rejection of liberal democracy, each in her political life personified the disillusionment and the disappointed hopes of politicized women in post-suffrage Britain.

From Women's Rights to the Women on the Political Right

Focussing attention on the BUF's seemingly anomalous recruitment of the ex-suffragettes either provokes a disturbed reaction from those who see treachery to feminism in their political allegiance, or is dismissed as an accident of history and the eccentricity of personality. However, links between pre-war militant feminists and the British Right emerged as soon as the 'votes for women' banners were lowered. Richardson's, Elam's, and Allen's eventual conversion to fascism was not such an aberration when we examine the post-suffrage passages taken by a number of their WSPU heroines, and when we remember how many of their revered WSPU leaders turned decisively against socialism and towards vigilant nationalism from the outbreak of the Great War. Christabel Pankhurst recalled how 'war was the only course for our country to take. This was national militancy. As Suffragettes we could not be pacifists at any price.'[27] The BUF's former suffragettes each remembered supporting the Pankhursts' decision to transfer the energy exerted on anti-government militancy to loyal and patriotic service in war. Mrs Dacre Fox's conversion from suffragettism to nationalism was clear from the very beginning of the war, and at a Brighton meeting on 21 September 1914 she urged 'the young men of the nation to answer Lord Kitchener's call for fresh reinforcements.'[28] After her release and pardon in the summer of 1914, Richardson reminisced how Mrs Pankhurst 'pleaded with us to be loyal to the Government and to the country. Some of us felt a little bewildered. But her eloquence did much to persuade us she was right.'[29] Similarly apprehensive but loyal, Allen obeyed the Pankhursts' command to 'cease fire,' and described how 'we were to drop our private struggle with those in power, and offer ourselves as the first volunteers to help the Government in its dark hour. I won't pretend we liked it! We were heart and soul in our fight to gain recognition for women.'[30] For Allen, suffragette credentials convinced her that she was over-qualified to enlist for more staid auxiliary work. Instead of taking up a post offered to her at the Needlework Guild, she was among the first to enrol in Margaret Damer Dawson's Women Police Volunteers, because, as she wrote later, 'I wanted action.'[31]

A rightward turn among some suffragettes became even more definite as the Great War progressed. Pandering to nationalist zeal, the WSPU's journal, *The Suffragette*, was renamed *Britannia* on 15 October 1915. In late 1917 and 1918, Emmeline and Christabel Pankhurst, and Flora Drummond preached against communism and striking during war-time in South Wales, the Midlands and on Clydeside. They were accompanied by Norah Elam on these expeditions, who was later credited by the BUF for placing 'her services at the disposal of the Government [at the outbreak of war]. Mrs Elam had a distinguished war record – recruiting in "Red" South Wales, working in a munitions factory, and was a member of several Government Committees.'[32] In 1918, together with Annie Kenney and Flora Drummond, Christabel Pankhurst formed the Women's Party, and her own campaign propaganda borrowed freely from the agenda of the Right as she championed heavy German reparation payments, opposed Irish Home Rule and trade unionism, and confined the feminist content of her platform to the advocacy of improved housing. Christabel failed narrowly to win the Smethwick seat, the very seat which Oswald Mosley was to hold for Labour in 1926 and again in 1929.

During the General Strike of 1926 Emmeline Pankhurst – the one-time member of the Independent Labour Party – took a firm stand against trade union agitation and informed Lady Astor that she wished to organize relief work. On 1 May 1926 'Commandant' Mary Allen picked up the telephone at the temporary headquarters of her Women's Auxiliary Service at Rochester Row only to hear

> the voice of Mrs Emmeline Pankhurst, my own former Suffragette leader, putting her services entirely at my disposal. During the strike she organized meetings and concerts in slum areas where the wives and children of strikers, open as they were to subversive propaganda and likely to feel the pinch of hunger, provided a dangerous explosive material ready for the first agitator match.[33]

In 1927, Emmeline Pankhurst was adopted as the Conservative candidate for Whitechapel and St George's, by which time 'her concern for empire, her distaste for socialism and her support for Baldwin had displaced feminism from her list of priorities.[34] Although Mrs Pankhurst died before she could contest the seat, Christabel predicted that 'she might well have been elected to Parliament by acclamation and agreement between voters of all parties and no party, as a sign of political reconciliation between men and women, between the post-war and pre-war eras.'[35] Christabel's hopes for the form of her mother's success were reminiscent of that paradoxical absence of regard for the democratic process, constitutionalism, and the exercise of the vote already in evidence within the WSPU's internal government.[36] In striking contrast to the political sympathies and activities of the socialist Sylvia Pankhurst, Adela Pankhurst Walsh was a founding member of the Australia First movement, and she was interned in March of 1942 under Regulation 26 of the National Security Act, in circumstances parallel to the detention of suspected Fifth Columnists in Britain.[37] In their radically varied political choices during the inter-war period, the dispersal of the Pankhurst women over the political spectrum bore many resemblances to another notorious family of distinguished women who were similarly splintered by extremist politics, the Mitford sisters.

Reactionary responses to inter-war politics among former suffragettes were not confined to members of the Pankhurst family. In April 1926, Flora Drummond, the 'General' of the WSPU, organized a march of thousands of women which demanded an end to strikes, and in 1928 she formed the anti-communist Women's Guild of Empire which 'pioneered the idea that women should be mobilized against the trade unions.'[38] When she was Lady Byron, the eccentric Lucy Houston was an active supporter and a generous contributor to the WSPU, and her biographer has deduced that it was Mrs Pankhurst and Mrs Pethick-Lawrence 'who taught her the value of propaganda, mob appeal, and the mass meeting.'[39] During the inter-war period Lady Houston was firmly placed on the fringes of British fascist politics; she flirted with the idea of contributing to Mosley's BUF on several occasions, and she was the owner of the *Saturday Review* which consistently apologized for fascist dictators. In light of these examples, Richardson, Elam and Allen could each convince herself that she was remaining faithful to her suffragette mentors in her own rightward journey across the political landscape.

The cross-fertilization between suffrage militancy and British fascist politics was a persistent feature throughout the inter-war period and pre-dated the formation of the BUF. The first fascist organization in Britain was founded in May 1923 by Miss Rotha Lintorn-Orman (1895–1935). It was telling that New Scotland Yard mistook this eccentric, ultra-patriotic ex-servicewoman for 'an ex-suffragette' who ran her organization 'with the assistance of some very "harmful" lunatics.'[40] Clearly, the notion was that Edwardian suffrage militancy could be effortlessly metamorphosed into post-war nationalist chauvinism. While there was no evidence to suggest that Lintorn-Orman herself had been a suffragette (she was busy leading Girl Scout troops in Bournemouth since 1909) female members of her British Fascists did volunteer for service with Mary Allen's Women's Special Police during the General Strike of May 1926,[41] when they must have worked alongside the recruit Allen was most proud of, Mrs Pankhurst.

Traces of proto-fascism have been identified in the suffragette movement, and the Pankhursts' rule over the WSPU has been characterized as a dictatorship. Cecily Hamilton argued that the WSPU was 'the first indication of the dictatorship movements which are by way of thrusting democracy out of the European Continent.' Emmeline Pankhurst 'was a forerunner of Lenin, Hitler and Mussolini – the leader whose fiat must go unquestioned, the leader who could do no wrong.'[42] In 1938, Emmeline Pethick-Lawrence admitted with some regret that developments in the WSPU 'bore a certain resemblance to the dictatorship so common in the world today ... . It is so-called upholders of democracy who create, when they are false in their principles, and when they attempt to crush their opponents, dictatorships.'[43] Both movements have been acknowledged to depend on the leadership principle, hero-worship, quasi-spiritual inspiration, palingenetic imagery, and Romantic longings for national regeneration; both encouraged the development of women's skills for self-defence, and gave vent to female aggression and rebelliousness; and both were accused by rivals of criminality, lunacy, fanaticism and tyranny. Both movements also aestheticized politics, and there are grounds to argue that the BUF borrowed freely from these militant forbears for its own development of propaganda techniques and design. For instance, at the Women's Exhibition at the Princess Skating Rink in Knightsbridge from 13 to 19 May 1909, the WSPU sold dolls draped in the movement's purple, white and green, and offered lessons in ju-jitsu to its members. During the 1930s the BUF sold dolls dressed in the traditional blackshirt and trained its women in ju-jitsu so that they could defend themselves against communist disrupters.

Militant enthusiasm was the main psychological characteristic that was perceived to be shared by adherents to both extra-parliamentary movements. When Winifred Holtby noticed a young woman donning a black blouse walking sturdily towards BUF headquarters, she reflected 'how that enviable sense of exaltation is not the exclusive property of the Blackshirt movement. It has been observed in Catholic converts, Salvation Army recruits, militant suffragettes, communists, Jacobites, jingoes and pacifists alike.'[44] In *Wigs on the Green*, Nancy Mitford mocked the militant spirit that animated suffragette and woman fascist alike, and satirized the humourless devotion to a charismatic leader which drove otherwise idle women to become earnest and ridiculous. Eugenia Malmains (Unity Mitford), member of the Union Jackshirts (BUF), mounted her soap-box to preach: '"The country must be purged of petty vice before it can be fit to rule the world.".... "That's a fine girl," said Jasper. "If she had been born 20 years sooner she would have been a Suffragette."'[45]

On a more serious note, it was remarkable how the suffragette struggle was claimed as a precedent for dissent by fascists and anti-fascists alike. Anti-fascist hecklers who were attacked mercilessly by Blackshirts at the Olympia meeting of 7 June 1934 were described as latter-day suffragettes. One writer to the editor of *The Times* observed that 'organized interruption provokes organized terrorism as we saw during the Suffragette campaign, when women were treated by Liberal stewards almost as badly as the Fascists treated their hecklers.'[46] Similarly, an ILP witness to the Olympia rally noted how 'twenty years ago the women Suffragists interrupted Cabinet Ministers to arouse public attention to their demand for the right to vote. To-day, Socialists and Communists are interrupting the leader of the Fascist movement to arouse public attention to the character of Fascism.'[47] From the fascist camp, *Action*'s radio critic, commenting on Flora Drummond's appearance on the BBC's 'I Saw the Start,' commended her for bringing to light 'two occasions in which women were thrown out and brutally assaulted at meetings of the Liberal Party, the Party which nowadays turns pale pink at what it is pleased to call "Blackshirt brutality."'[48] Ironically enough, even Cicely Hamilton – ex-suffragette and anti-fascist who had earlier drawn parallels between forms of dictatorial control in the WSPU and in the fascist movement – was nonetheless reminded of the treatment of women during militant days when she witnessed opposition to the women's contingent in a BUF march. Hamilton wrote:

I noticed, by and by, that the crowd's idea of insult had little altered since
the early days of the century; when the women's contingent passed us by,
the jibes to which it was subjected by certain of my neighbours were the
same as the jibes with which we who fought the battle for the suffrage
were familiar in the days of long ago. Where were the prams, and who
was looking after things at home? With the humorous suggestion that women
were joining the Blackshirt ranks because they were looking out for husbands!
Spite attainment of the vote and all the vote implies; spite the freedom
claimed by the younger generation; the tradition that woman's place is in
the home and nowhere else, is evidently one that dies hard.[49]

Rights to the suffragette legacy were fiercely contested in the
heated atmosphere of extremist politics during the 1930s.

Devotees and Detractors: The Reception of the Suffragettes by BUF Women

While the above survey of the uses and abuses of the suffragette
legacy goes some way to explain how the BUF could accommodate
the support of the ex-suffragettes and exploit their zeal for its
own purposes, there were forces within the movement which
militated against such a comfortable co-habitation. Competing
with the inheritance from the suffragettes, through Oswald
Mosley's marriage to Cynthia Curzon, the BUF derived its
patrimony from the Edwardian anti-suffragists. The Edwardian
Radical Right had been divided on the issue of female suffrage,
as Lords Curzon and Cromer led the anti-suffragist charge, while
the quintessential Tory Die-Hard, Lord Willoughby de Brooke,
reacted with dismay at the Liberal Government's treatment of
militant women and urged the Unionists to support votes for
women. Speaking at an anti-suffrage demonstration in Glasgow
on 1 November 1912, Lord Curzon asserted that 'the interest
of the State must necessarily override the interests of any class,
section, sex, or community inside it.[Cheers] If the interests of
women were opposed to the interests of the State, then I say
fearlessly the interests of the State must prevail.'[50] Looking ahead
to the BUF's response to the narrower interests of feminist
organizations and fascism's emotional call for the cessation of
sex war and sex antagonism in the name of co-operation within
the national community, we can see how the movement also
integrated this anti-suffrage heritage.

With such mixed ideological parentage, it was understandable how many younger fascist women either rejected their suffragette forebears or reacted with ambivalence to the militant women of an earlier generation. The most extreme reaction came from Jenny Linton who commented that 'there is no place in Fascism for the militant woman, and in daily contact with the true Fascists she would readily find that she had made her life very uncomfortable.'[51] Linton made capital of the psychological dissimilarities between the bullying militant and the acquiescent fascist woman, and the same basic sentiments were reiterated by Dinah Parkinson. In 1938, Parkinson recounted the following confrontation with an anonymous suffragette:

> Recently, I met an ex-suffragette of the militant type. 'I'm too old to bother about newfangled ideas,' she said, when I began to explain the aims of BU, although she listened intensely ... And then she talked of her activities with the suffragettes. I was very interested and intrigued, although I cannot say I agreed with her entirely, because like a great many woman who have taken part in a purely feminist cause, she seemed to labour under the prejudice against men. This idea is as annoying to the woman Blackshirt as that of the type of man who believes that a woman's duty is to look ornamental and do very little else, and who immediately labels as 'bluestocking' any woman who takes an intelligent interest in public affairs.[52]

From the vantage point of inter-war extremist politics, the unrepentant suffragette was depicted as old-fashioned and resistant to change, while BUF women identified the modern fascist ideal as the acceptance of the principle of 'equal but different.'

Although the unidentified militant woman received pejorative notice, the younger women did seem to regard the survivors of the suffragette movement as role models. 'Pauline's' reminiscences of Mary Richardson illustrate the high regard in which the suffragettes were held by younger followers:

> She was a fiery speaker particularly at street corner meetings and used to plaster her hair down with Grip-fix so it would not blow about on these occasions. She had been with Emily Davidson[sic], the suffragette who threw herself under the King's horse at the Derby and was killed. This one escaped to Epsom Station where a sympathetic station master hid her in the ladies' loo until the hue and cry were over. She lived in a ground-floor flat in Cheyne Walk and was a magnet to us young people.[53]

This same reverence and deference to her elders is evident in the recollections of Louise Irvine, who was interned with Elam in Holloway: 'I was a little in awe of her – she was of course a much older woman, and highly intelligent and erudite.' Irvine remembered that 'Lady Mosley sometimes invited me to her cell with a few others for a small friendly get-together. All sorts of topics – art, music, literature etc. were discussed, and Mrs Elam was invariably there ... . I was never close enough to her to hear about her suffragette experiences, but she was certainly a staunch member of BUF.'[54] Irvine's suggestion that Elam advocated her present fascist views more fiercely than she informed fellow prisoners about suffrage days is significant. The younger fascist women seemed less influenced by the feminist content of previous WSPU activity than by the sensationalism and defiance which motivated suffragette acts of militancy. The militant temperament *tout court* served as a precedent for their own rebellion against the establishment. Asked how his mother responded to feminism at the time when she was a member of the BUF, Francis Beckett has explained Anne Cutmore's views thus: 'I doubt whether Anne ever used the word feminism – was the word much in use in her generation? – but she held strong feminist views and had been strongly influenced by the suffragettes.'[55] The fascist suffragettes were applauded and embraced for their discerning conversion to fascism, while simultaneously providing the younger women with an exciting lineage of *feminine* militancy.

The younger women appear to have been encouraged in their attitudes towards feminists and unconverted suffragettes by the BUF's ex-suffragettes themselves. Elam was certainly not a defender of her former allies, as she collaborated in the creation of the negative image of the militant woman. Elam wrote: 'with few notable exceptions, we find these extinct volcanoes either wandering about in the backwoods of international pacifism and decadence, or prostrating themselves before the various political parties, which for years they denounced as cesspools of corruption and chicanery.'[56] An enduring theme in Elam's fascist journalism was the wrong turns taken by former suffragettes after the struggle was over. By arguing for the complementarity of pre-war feminist endeavour and post-war fascism, Richardson, Elam and Allen differentiated themselves from those women who had never woken up from the suffrage dreams of sexual equality to the nightmare of imprisonment and maltreatment.

Connecting Roads: From Feminist to Fascist Militancy

Reassuringly, the majority of inter-war feminists lamented the resemblances and fought against fascism at home and abroad,[57] Richardson, Elam and Allen relished the thought of continuity between their militant feminism and fascism, and went to great lengths to prove the benefits of this relationship. In 1934 Mary Richardson engaged in a press polemic over the treatment of women under fascism with her former sister-in-arms, Sylvia Pankhurst. Richardson counted on the endurance of her own and Sylvia Pankhurst's shared memories, pointing out that they had been close associates in the WSPU, had worked together in Bow and were confined to Holloway at the same time. However, she was still at pains to convince Pankhurst that the two movements resembled one another in activity and in the public responses they elicited.[58] She implored Sylvia to 'remember' the indignities of forcible feeding; the shame of the actions of the mob on Black Friday; the militants' proud use of 'force and bludgeons, of dog whips, truncheons (carried and used by Mrs Pankhurst's bodyguard), stones in their multitude, and bricks and hammers;'[59] and that when suffragettes were attacked they had no other choice than to offer violent but valiant resistance. Richardson explained how: 'I was first attracted to the Blackshirts because I saw in them the courage, the action, the loyalty, the gift of service, and the ability to serve which I had known in the Suffragette movement. When later I discovered that Blackshirts were attacked for no visible cause or reason, I admired them the more when they hit back and hit hard.'[60] Familiar with the inner-workings of both movements, the BUF's ex-suffragettes cultivated the discourse of proto-fascist militant feminism to fullest effect.

Elam constructed her own comparative history of the two movements and found much common ground, postulating Mosley to be the latter-day Mrs Pankhurst, and fascist dictatorship the perfection of WSPU voluntary discipline and service.

> In this conception of practical citizenship, the women's struggle resembles closely the new philosophy of Fascism. Indeed, Fascism is the logical if much grander, conception of the momentous issues raised by the militant women of a generation ago. Nor do the points of resemblance end here. The Women's Movement, like the Fascist Movement, was conducted under strict discipline, and cut across all party allegiances; its supporters were drawn from every class and Party. It appealed to women to forget self-interest; to

relinquish petty personal advantage, the privilege of the sheltered few for the benefit of the many; and to stand together against the wrongs and injustices which were inherent in a system so disastrous to the well-being of the race. Like the Fascist movement, too, it chose its Leader, and once having chosen gave that leader absolute authority to direct policy and destiny, displaying a loyalty and devotion never surpassed in the history of this country. Moreover, like the Fascist movement again, it faced the brutality of the streets; the jeers of opponents; the misapprehensions of the well-disposed; and the rancour of politicians.[61]

Reflecting upon the unfulfilled legacy of the pre-war women's struggle and the laxity of British women's commitment to national service by the 1930s, Mary Allen became convinced that 'it is women, perhaps, who are in need of a dictator – but, I hasten to add that I am not qualifying for that unenviable post.'[62] The BUF's ex-suffragettes regarded feminism and fascism as analogous political impulses, and saw in their conglomeration the potential for the resurrection of the spirit of *their* earlier suffragette struggles.

Suffragette Experiences in Publicity and Memory

Rather than having to discard their suffrage identities in order to wear the new blackshirt, the ex-suffragettes were encouraged to call upon the past to propagate the fascist future. As a reward for the publicity value of their support, the BUF gave the ex-suffragettes publicity. The movement featured their personal histories and represented them as heroic agitators in a feminist revolution. Mary Richardson was advertised as 'a pioneer worker for the "rights of women,"'[63] an 'ex-suffragette and a leading protagonist for women's emancipation ... . During the seven years prior to 1914, Miss Richardson took an active part in the suffrage movement, for which she was sentenced to terms of imprisonment totalling more than three years.'[64] Notably, however, while the BUF's newspapers publicized Richardson's souvenirs from the WSPU, such as the medal she possessed that had been given to Mrs Pankhurst by the 'Women of America' and the first petition carried to the House of Commons demanding the female franchise, conspicuously absent from the distinctions listed were her acts of arson and her slashing the *Rokeby Venus*. Perhaps this omission can be partially accounted for by the high esteem in which Diego de Velazsquez was held by the BUF. For instance, when A.K.

Chesterton spoke of fascism's construction of the man of action, he located the nascent spirit of fascist masculine endeavour in the life work of Shakespeare, Beethoven and Velazsquez.[65] It followed that propagandists did not elect to honour Richardson's literal and figurative assault upon one of fascism's cultural heroes.

Norah Elam was described as 'one of the leaders of the Women's Suffrage Movement in pre-war days, [who] served three terms of imprisonment and endured several hunger strikes.'[66] Elam provided further favourable publicity for the BUF by being one of its prospective parliamentary candidates. Beginning in 1936 the BUF announced its list of one-hundred candidates, and took gleeful pride in the fact that ten of the first hundred were women, a higher percentage than any other party in Britain. When Mosley presented Elam to her prospective constituents at the Town Hall, Northampton in November 1936, 'he was glad indeed to have the opportunity of introducing this first candidate, and it killed for all time that suggestion that National Socialism proposed putting British women back into the home. Mrs Elam, he went on, had fought in the past for women's suffrage ... and was a great example of the emancipation of women in Britain.'[67] With the emphasis placed on their pre-war activities, the ex-suffragettes served as mascots for the BUF's women's policy, and their membership was fully exploited to drive home, before a sceptical public, the distinctions between British and continental variants of fascism.

The personal and conceptual relationship between suffragettes and fascists was mutually beneficial. In addition to the movement praising their suffragette past, the BUF provided a forum in which the women could record their memories of suffrage days and secure for posterity their top billing in the WSPU. When Mrs H. Carrington-Wood, a North West London Organizer for the BUF, resigned from the movement in 1935 – alleging that 'the promises made on Fascist platforms and in Fascist literature are inadequate to appease the anxiety of the womenfolk, who naturally do not want to risk going back to where they were before the days of the Suffragettes' – it was Norah Elam who took vehement exception to her charges, and derided her for 'exploiting the Suffragettes.' From Elam's perspective, only the women who had engaged in the earlier struggle had licence to evoke the memory.

> But what really 'gets one's goat' is the exploitation of the fight made by women such as myself who suffered imprisonment and the horrors of the hunger and thirst strike, in order to vindicate our principles in the days of

the Suffragette battle ... those of us who bore the heat and burden of that day have, at any rate, earned the right to challenge those who now want to make capital of the sacrifices of militant women.[68]

For Elam, suffragette experiences had been developmental and she was keen to share her own memories with younger fascist women, especially once her life had come full circle and she was again back in Holloway where, for instance, in 1942, Officer Baxter recorded the following exchange between Diana Mosley and her mother, Lady Redesdale:

> Lady Redesdale [sic] said she wanted to go see the lady in Logan Place(meaning Mrs Elam) and Lady Mosley said 'Oh do, she is such a sweet dear soul and you will probably find her in the midst of a large tea – she is very fond of her food, which makes her all the more marvellous as she was here in the Suff. time and went on hunger strike three times and Mrs Pankhurst gave her a medal with three bars and she is so proud of it; the officers in those days were so different to now, they absolutely tortured those poor women – do get her to tell you all about it, it's so interesting and six of the officers couldn't bear it, and all resigned on the same day stating as their reason that they hadn't joined the service to torture women so they left' (I was one of the officers at that time, so I was rather amused).[69]

Lady Mosley's reaction epitomized how Elam's part in the history of British feminism was appreciated by her fascist peers. It also suggested the manner in which Elam had kept alive and recycled her memories of the WSPU through fascism.

The persistence of their suffragette memories was also exemplified by the content of their contributions to the BUF press. While each ex-suffragette had explained her attraction to the BUF as respect for its policy of imperialism and patriotic action, it was rare that they wrote on gender-neutral subjects or transcended the confines of 'feminine politics.' With only a few exceptions, all three women limited their journalistic output to articles on women's issues, suffrage-related memories, and the barrenness of inter-war feminist politics. Their fixation on their earlier political lives seemed to carry over to their propaganda activities within the movement. Mrs Gladys Walsh (née Libiter) was a young member of the BU's Limehouse branch from 1936, and she remembered how: 'we also had one of the Suffragettes ... I can't remember her name. But I know she came down and gave a sort of lecture about the Suffragette movement.'[70] Both Elam and

Allen spoke of a new ideal of gender co-operation in political life, but by restricting themselves to women's issues they in effect fortified the fascist segregation of male and female political spheres.

The Suffragettes in BUF Historiography

The BUF went beyond applauding individual militant actions by granting the pre-war militant suffrage movement as a whole a prominent place in its own historical memory. It was not considered 'too far-fetched to suggest that just as before the war the anti-parliamentary movement of Ulster Loyalists had within it the germ of a Fascist revolution, aborted by the war, so the Women's Suffrage movement might, uninterrupted by the same cause, have been the direct inspiration and forerunner of the Fascist movement in Great Britain.'[71] BUF historiography had the greatest reverence for the Golden Age of Tudor Government and it was claimed that this had also been 'the Golden Age of women's accomplishments ... . The reaction of anti-feminism came after, coincident with Puritanism, and the rise of Parliamentary power.'[72] Through this process of conceptualization (or misconceptualization), British fascists did not only profess to be the rightful inheritors of the suffragette legacy, but they also asserted the BUF's claim to represent 'true feminism.'

Doreen Bell gave voice to a *leitmotif* in the BUF's women's policy when she explained how 'many ardent feminists have been induced by anti-Fascist propagandists to oppose the Movement, little realizing that through the Corporate State in BU many of the ideals they have fought so hard and sacrificed so much will be realized.'[73] The negotiation of a merger between fascism and 'true' feminism was facilitated by charges of decadence and ineffectuality in the inter-war women's movement. Within the BUF, the most vociferous critics of contemporary feminist organizations were the ex-suffragettes themselves.

'J'Accuse': Indicting the Contemporary Women's Movement

The ex-suffragettes indicted inter-war British women for every political sin imaginable. In the same breath, Elam characterized other former suffragettes as 'empty volcanoes;' castigated younger women for not appreciating the monumental achievements made for their freedom by militant women a generation ago; accused individual feminists for colluding with the party system; at one and the same time scoffed at women for acting as accomplices to war-mongers and for serving international pacifism; faulted feminist organizations for the narrowness of their efforts in the interest of a single-sex; and portrayed the whole female population as obtuse for believing that 'a woman is free because she also votes, or that democracy can offer anything but the careful and organized exploitation of men and women who suffer it to exist.'[74] Days after the Munich crisis, the self-avowed anti-Semitic ex-suffragette borrowed the Dreyfusard rhetoric to exclaim 'J'ACCUSE: Failure of the Women's Movement,' as Elam wondered 'where is there to-day an organized body of women which is protesting against the intrigues of democracy?'[75] Similarly, Allen had exhibited signs of deep disenchantment with organized feminism before she joined the BUF, and, from the vantage point of a policewoman, she shuddered at many of the immoral choices made by modern women.[76] In the face of war, Allen articulated the essence of feminized fascism when she advised 'that women drop for good and all the tiresome reiteration of "Women's Rights" and substitute for it "Women's Responsibilities."'[77] Perturbed by the retreat of British women from action into decadent individualism, Elam and Allen renewed their demand for 'deeds and not words,' this time to light the flame of fascist revolution.

On the one hand, while fascists were implored to surpass rhetorical invectives by seeking out physical confrontation, verbal attacks on women's organizations provided the best outlet for fascist women's venom. Fascist women took exception to a communication issued by the Six Point Group to raise funds for Spanish feminists, and asserted instead that 'we women of BU believe that the supporters of the feminists movement prefer dabbling in international politics to ventilating the legitimate grievances of their own countrywomen.'[78] This inhumane feminine fascist isolationism was even more marked when the BU assailed Lady Baldwin for her drive to aid alien refugee children through the Baldwin Refugee Fund, and the fascist women were confident that 'most parents will heartily endorse BU's oft-repeated declaration that British children must come first.'[79]

On the other hand, the triumph of deeds over words became the order of the day when women Blackshirts reinforced their rhetorical attacks by disrupting the meetings of competing women's organizations. In March 1937, the British Union fought the LCC elections, and out in protest against their campaign was none other than Flora Drummond with her Women's Guild of Empire. Elam described Drummond's own operation to encourage East End women to vote against the BU as an 'anti-fascist circus,' and she reproached the Guild for being 'obsessed with the crazy idea that putting a feminine cross on a ballot paper is the sure weapon of the modern age.'[80] When women Blackshirts interrupted one of Drummond's meetings at the Bethnal Green Library, they made their exit with cries of 'Hail Mosley!'[81]

Women's Discourses on the Vote

The ex-suffragettes' offensive action against women's organizations, contemporary feminism, and even against female philanthropy was motivated by their deep disillusionment with the outcome of female enfranchisement. Their subjective sense of lost promise and even betrayal culminated in an uncompromising rejection of parliamentary democracy. Discourses on women and the vote in the BUF were clearly predicated on the assault on the democratic system as such. The arguments were essentially tautological, as fascism would, in effect, dispense with parliamentary suffrage, both male and female.

The vote was variously described as an 'empty vessel,' 'merely a symbol,'[82] 'a barren girl,'[83] and Anne Brock Griggs subtitled her prescriptive pamphlet *Women and Fascism: 10 Important Points* with the defeatist statement 'You Have the Vote – Yet You Are Still Powerless.' Looking at developments abroad, Muriel Currey averred that 'the fact that women have not a parliamentary vote in Italy has blinded some ardent feminists to the importance and power of women in the Italian Corporate State.'[84] The notion was that there was a definite incongruity between sign and signifier, and the symbolism of the female franchise had been undermined by the conquest of Financial Democracy. Rarely, however, was it acknowledged as ironic that the BUF intended to come to power constitutionally, by appealing to male and female voters, and use democracy to defeat democracy.

Against this absolute rejection of the exercise of democratic rights, the BU's blatant opportunism became apparent when the Women's Peace Campaign was launched. When it came to the anti-war campaign, the female franchise took on a renewed significance and was represented as having a positive and pro-active role to play in the bid for peace: 'Rise Up! the remedy is in your hands. You have the vote for which an earlier band of

170

brave women fought. Use your right, it is not too late. Demand peace.'[85] In general, however, woman's political rights under the democratic system were stigmatized, and the BUF followed the ideological patterns of continental fascists when they called for emancipation from democratic emancipation.[86]

In light of the BUF's dismissal of any respect for the franchise, it was ironic that the fascist suffragettes embraced their title as 'suffragettes' and retained identification with a cause that was anathema to the political destiny they prescribed for Britain during the 1930s. More clearly, they were working through issues of revisionary feminism in the BUF, divorced from the context of a democratic idiom, principles of representation, and liberal tolerance.[87] Over three decades of political activism, the former suffragettes in the BUF managed a monumental shift from an extra-parliamentary struggle for rights for inclusion in the democratic process to a willingness to employ democratic methods in order to overthrow parliamentary democracy. Ridden with paradox as this shift might seem, the fascist ex-suffragettes demonstrated that there was a certain logic in this progression.

Notes on Chapter 4

1   To Lord Lansdowne, Dacre Fox wrote: "'I have come to take refuge with you, as you yourself have delivered several speeches endorsing and inciting to violent resistance to Home Rule and yet the government do not attack you. I am confident, therefore, that under your roof I shall have the same immunity from arrest and imprisonment that you yourself enjoy."... He replied that it was impossible for him to allow her to take refuge in his house, in which, moreover, she would still be within reach of the law.' Quoted in Dame Christabel Pankhurst, *Unshackled* (London, 1959), pp.272–3.

2   Andrew Rosen, *Rise Up, Women* (London, 1974), p.250.

3   Norah Elam, 'Women, Fascism and Democracy,' *Fascist Quarterly*, 1, 3 (July 1935), 290–8. In 1918 she came second in the poll, winning 3,615 votes (20.2%) and losing to C.B. Edgar, a Conservative Coalitionist.

4   HO45/24895/9–12. It is presumed that the eight names, all men, were those who were entrusted to become leaders of the British Union when and if Mosley himself was put out of commission.

5   HO283/48/27

6   HO144/21995/99

7   From the Governor, H.M. Prison, Holloway G.2 Division, 25 March 1943, HO45/24891/342.

8   Mary Richardson, *Laugh a Defiance* (London, 1953), p.5.

9   Anne Page in ed. J. Christian, *Mosley's Blackshirts: The Inside Story of the British Union of Fascists 1932–1940*, (London, 1986), p.16.

10   'Ex-Suffragette Joins the BUF: Mussolini's Predictions,' *Fascist Week*, No. 7, 22–8 December 1933. I am grateful to Jeffrey Wallder for the information about Richardson's acquaintanceship with Mussolini in the pre-war era. This anecdote suggests that Richardson visited Italy before the war, as Mussolini only visited Britain on one occasion in 1922 to attend an international confer-ence in London on the subject of German reparations. Mussolini never returned, and his impression was that 'London is a nightmare to anyone from Italy. All that grey grime penetrates everywhere, into your clothes, your room and even into your trunks; there's no getting away from it ... . I hope I'll never have to go back to England.' Quoted in Rachele Mussolini, *My Life with Mussolini* (London, 1959), p.50.

11   'Ex-Suffragette Joins the BUF: Mussolini's Predictions,' *Fascist Week*, No. 7, 22–8 December 1933.

12   Quoted in Martin Durham, *Women and Fascism* (London, 1998), p. 63.

13   Mary Allen, *Lady in Blue* (London, 1936), p.15.

14   '"Commandant" Mary Allen who, at her headquarters, is addressed as "Sir", was wearing a long dark blue tight-fitting tunic, dark blue breeches, black top-boots and a peaked cap which sat on her close-cropped grey hair with just a shade of Beatty angle.' *Daily Herald*, 8 November 1933.

15   Mary Allen, *Lady in Blue*, p.74.

16   After Allen's appearance before the Advisory Committee, G.H. Stuart Brunning submitted a Dissident Report on 30 November 1940, and described her in the following manner: 'That Mary Allen is a terribly conceited woman, a crank with a tremendous grievance, is true. That, in trailing round in a ridiculous uniform she gives false impressions is also true, and I feel that she is an unmiti-gated nuisance. These things, however, are not the business of the Committee and I cannot see enough in her short BU connection to justify even the mild restrictions imposed on her.' HO144/21933/244.

17   Lady Londonderry, 'Letter to the Editor,' *The Times*, 12 December 1933.

18   *Evening Standard*, 29 January 1934.

19   Mary Allen, *Lady in Blue*, p.150–1.

20   HO144/21933/244

21   Levine has pointed out that while Mary Allen was alone among policewomen to become a fascist, it was not uncommon that many former suffragettes who had become policewomen 'keenly and rapidly disengaged themselves from public association with the suffrage issue, a dissociation which tended to loosen the bonds of feminist identification apparent in pre-war campaigns on this issue.' Philippa Levine, '"Walking the Streets in a Way No Decent Woman Should": Women Police in World War I,' *Journal of Modern History*, 66, March 1994, 34–78.

22 HO144/21933/330–331.

23 The peace campaign waged by Britain's extreme right also attracted another former suffragette, Dr Maude Royden. Although a leading pacifist, Royden became active in the British People's Party in July 1939, when she was a speaker in support of BPP candidate St John Philby in the Hythe by-election. She 'can hardly have been unaware of the company she was keeping. Not only did the Conservative and Liberal candidates repeatedly point out the Fascist connections of the BPP, but a pamphlet produced by the BPP during the campaign, *Alien Money Power in Great Britain* ... was clearly anti-Semitic.' Richard Griffiths, *Patriotism Perverted* (London, 1998), p.57. A statement issued by the British Council for Christian Settlement in Europe was signed by, among others, Dr Maude Royden, Mrs H.M. Swanwick, Laurence Houseman, and Lady Stalbridge. HO45/25729.

24 HO144/21933/404–430.

25 HO144/21933/404–430.

26 Norah Elam, 'Women and the Vote,' *Action*, No. 6, 26 March 1936.

27 Dame Christabel Pankhurst, *Unshackled*, p.288.

28 Andrew Rosen, *Rise Up, Women!*, p.250.

29 Mary Richardson, *Laugh a Defiance*, p.190.

30 Mary Allen, *Lady in Blue*, p.24.

31 Mary Allen, *Lady in Blue*, p.25.

32 'Prospective BU Parliamentary Candidates: The First Twelve with their Prospective Constituencies,' *Action*, No. 40, 21 November 1936.

33 Mary Allen, *Lady in Blue*, pp.93–4.

34 Brian Harrison, *Prudent Revolutionaries* (Oxford, 1987), p.35.

35 Dame Christabel Pankhurst, *Unshackled*, p.297.

36 On 19 September 1907 – precipitating the split which formed the Women's Freedom League – WSPU headquarters issued the following letter sent to all organizers: 'We are not playing experiments with representative government. We are not a school for teaching women how to use the vote. We are a militant movement and we have to get the vote next session ... . It is after all a voluntary militant movement; those who cannot follow the general must drop out of the ranks.' Quoted in Antonia Raeburn, *The Militant Suffragettes* (London, 1973), pp.40–1.

37 See Verna Coleman, *Adela Pankhurst: The Wayward Suffragette* (Melbourne, 1996).

38 Martin Durham, 'Suffrage and After,' in eds. M. Langan and B. Shwarz, *Crises in the British State 1880–1930*, (London, 1985), p.185.

39 J. Wentworth Day, *Lady Houston D.B.E.: The Woman Who Won the War* (London, 1958), p.29. Her eccentricity was already well developed by the Edwardian period when she concocted the 'parrot plot' for the WSPU. 615 parrots were trained to scream 'votes for women' and were to be sent to the House of Commons. The plan never got off its perch.

40 2 February 1924, PRO 30/69/221.

41 'The Work of the Women's Units During the Strike,' *The Fascist Bulletin*, No.41, Vol. 3, 29 May 1926.

42 Cicely Hamilton, *Life Errant* (London, 1935), p.68.

43 Emmeline Pethick-Lawrence, *My Part in a Changing World* (London, 1938), preface.

44 Winifred Holtby, 'Shall I Order a Black Blouse?,' *News Chronicle*, 4 May 1934.

45 Nancy Mitford, *Wigs on the Green* (London, 1935), p.195.

46 Letter to the Editor – Hamilton Fye, 'Fascist Meeting at Olympia,' *The Times*, 13 June 1934.

47 'Behind Fascist Brutality,' *New Leader*, XXVI, New Series, 22, Friday, 15 June 1934.

48 Bluebird, 'Brutal Liberal Assaults on Women,' *Action*, No. 80, 28 August 1937.

49 Cicely Hamilton, *England as Seen by an Englishwoman* (London, 1938), pp.73–4.

50 Quoted in Brian Harrison, *Separate Spheres* (London, 1978), p.43.

51 Jenny Linton, 'Fascist Women do not Want Equal Rights with Men: They Desire only the True Woman's Place in the Community,' *Blackshirt*, No.80, 2 November 1934.

52 Dinah Parkinson, 'Ideals of Womanhood,' *Action*, No.109, 19 March 1938.

53 Quoted in Stephen Cullen, 'Four Women For Mosley: Women in the BUF, 1932–1940,' *Oral History*, 24, 1 (Spring 1996), 49–59.

54 Letter from Louise Irvine to the author, 6 May 1996.

55 Letter from Francis Beckett to the author, 24 May 1997.

56 Norah Elam, 'Suffragette in Anti-Fascist Circus: Flora Drummond Tries Bluffing the Women,' *Blackshirt*, No. 230, 25 September 1937.

57 For feminist reaction to fascism see Johanna Alberti, 'British Feminists and Anti-Fascism in the 1930s,' in ed. Sybil Oldfield, *This Working-Day World* (London, 1994), pp.111–22, and Phyllis Lassner, *British Women Writers of World War II* (London, 1998).

58 Although Richardson tried to evoke the memories of their collaboration, there seems to be some evidence to suggest that Richardson supported Christabel's decision that Sylvia's East London Federation should be cut off from the 'parent' body. Writing to Sylvia from Paris on 7 November 1913, Christabel made it clear that once the ties were severed between the WSPU and the Herald League, Mary Richardson would no longer be made available to speak on Sylvia's platforms: 'Before you were approached to speak at the Herald League Albert Hall meeting, I had been asked whether Annie Kenney or Miss Richardson wd. speak. I said no. Upon getting this refusal from me – which was also a refusal to have the WSPU represented on the platform, they approached you and got your consent to speak.' Quoted in Andrew Rosen, *Rise Up! Women*, pp.218–19.

59 Mary Richardson, 'My Reply to Sylvia Pankhurst,' *Blackshirt*, No.62, 29 June 1934.

60 Mary Richardson, 'My Reply to Sylvia Pankhurst,' *Blackshirt*, No.62, 29 June 1934.

61 Norah Elam, 'Fascism, Women and Democracy,' *The Fascist Quarterly*, 1, 3 (July 1935), 290–8.

62 Commandant Mary Allen & Julie Helen Heyneman, *Woman at the Cross Roads* (London, 1934), pp.136–7.

63 Olive Hawks, 'Youth and Womanhood Turns to Fascism,' *Blackshirt*, No.70, 24 August 1934.

64 'Ex-Suffragette Joins the BUF: Mussolini's Predictions,' *Fascist Week*, No. 7, 22–28 December 1933.

65 A.K. Chesterton, 'Return to Manhood: Regiment of Old Women Routed,' *Action*, No. 21, 6 July 1936.

66 'Prospective BU Parliamentary Candidates,' *Action*, No. 40, 21 November 1936.

67 'Northampton Meets Prospective BU Candidate: Mosley's Great Meeting,' *Action*, No. 41, 28 November 1936.

68 'Fascism Will Mean Real Equality: By an Old Suffragette,' *Blackshirt*, No. 96, 22 February 1935.

69 From the Governor of Holloway, 6 February 1942, HO45/24891/444.

70 Interview with Mrs Gladys Walsh, copyright 'The Friends of Oswald Mosley.'

71 'Women as Orators: The Woman's Part in British Union,' *Action*, No. 151, 14 January 1939.

72 'Women as Orators: The Women's Part in British Union,' *Action*, No. 151, 14 January 1939.

73 Doreen Bell, 'Women's World: By Women for Men and Women,' *Action*, No. 199, 6 January 1938.

74 Norah Elam, 'Women, Fascism and Democracy,' *Fascist Quarterly*, 1, 3 (July 1935), 290–8.

75 Norah Elam, 'J'ACCUSE: Failure of the Women's Movement,' *Action*, No. 138, 8 October 1938.

76 'A convinced militant suffragette myself, I cannot help feeling that we started a fire that has consumed far more than we had envisioned.' Commandant Mary Allen & Julie Helen Heyneman, *Woman at the Cross Roads*, p.56.

77 Commandant Mary S. Allen, 'Women's Responsibilities,' *Action*, No. 220, 23 May 1940.

78 'Feminists Duped by Reds: Emma Goldman's Appeal,' *Action*, No. 166, 29 April 1939.

79 'Mother's Day for Aliens,' *Action*, No. 169, 20 May 1939. It was recorded that on 14 January 1939 'the Theatres and Cinemas of London gave special performances to raise money for the Baldwin Fund for Refugees from the recent German pogroms, and the fascists seized the opportunity to stage another demonstration. Members of the BUF invaded the Theatres and Cinemas, stink bombs were thrown, slogans shouted, assaults were made on individuals and

panics created.' Elizabeth A. Allen, *It Shall Not Happen Here* (London, 1943), p.13.

80   Norah Elam, 'Suffragette in Anti-Fascist Circus: Flora Drummond Tries Bluffing the Women,' *Blackshirt*, No. 230, 25 September 1937.

81   Norah Elam, 'Women's Anti-Fascist Circus,' *Blackshirt*, No. 234, 23 October 1937.

82   Norah Elam, 'Fascism, Women and Democracy,' *Fascist Quarterly*, 1, 3 (July 1935), 290–8.

83   F. Alderidge, 'Women Demand Results: Valueless Vote,' *Action*, No. 121, 11 June 1938.

84   Muriel Currey, 'Women and the Corporate State: Equality of the Sexes in Italy,' *The Blackshirt*, No. 58, 1 June 1934.

85   A.K. Wood, 'Stop this War: To British Women, Wives Mothers, Daughters and Sisters,' *Action*, No. 186, 23 September 1939.

86   'Emancipation of women from the women's emancipation movement is the first demand of a generation of women which would like to save the Volk and the race, the Eternal-Unconscious, the foundation of all culture, from decline and fall.' Alfred Rosenberg quoted in ed. George L. Mosse, *Nazi Culture* (New York, 1968), p.40.

87   To varying degrees, all three ex-suffragettes exhibited sympathy for the BUF's policy of racialism and anti-Semitism. Elam's anti-Semitic remarks are quoted in Chapter Three. Richardson wrote articles condemning the anti-Christian act of profiteering and usury, and saw the freedom of British workers threatened by 'the wage-slavery of the Orient.' Mary Richardson, 'New and Old Rome,' *Blackshirt*, No. 75, 28 September 1934. When Allen's home in Nanquindo Valley, St Just, was searched by officers of the Special Branch in 1940, found were copies of many anti-Semitic pamphlets and books, including the works of Arnold Leese, leaving little doubt of her views on the 'alien menace.' HO144/21933/345–46.

Chapter 5

Mosley's Women and Mosley's Woman:
The Leader's Sexual Politics

Observing the British Union of Fascists from near or afar, it is difficult not to receive the impression that the movement was simply a cult in veneration of one man: Sir Oswald Ernald Mosley (1896–1980). Thus far this study has concentrated on the roles women played in the BUF, the representation of the feminine in fascist propaganda, and rank-and-file gender relations. The questions that remain to be posed are how Mosley's own personal relationships with the women of his family and his class impacted upon the development of his sexual politics; how his mental construct of the 'normal' British woman dictated the boundaries of feminine fascism; and to what extent his renowned sex-appeal heightened female interest in the BUF. The divergence between his libertine behaviour with his own women and his prescriptions for the mass woman in the sex-war-torn arena of public life exemplify the complications and contradictions in the Leader's sexual politics. Mosley's stern adherence to a culture of a masculine Britain, and his self-fashioning as a world protagonist of Elizabethan, Byronic, or Nietzschean proportions not only bolstered the hero-worship of his dedicated followers, but also facilitated the derision and parody of his many detractors. Together, the attention paid to his public persona by supporters or adversaries secured Mosley's celebrity status in the popular imagination of his self-proclaimed 'war generation.'

Sir Oswald Mosley was a figure of literary stature and a personality of tragic-heroic dimensions; he was an exemplar of the aristocratic rebel who took a turn towards fascism as a revolt against the decline of his own class, and because of a sense of personal displacement and deracination – or so he has been variously portrayed by his contemporaries and critics. Thus the women in his life provided the 'love interest' in the story of an egotistical dandy, rogue-rebel, *enfant terrible*, or buccaneer, thirsty for public distinction. His mother was allegedly his central formative influence and compensated for the absent father by her adulation and unwavering support for her 'man-child.' His capitalizing on the atmosphere of free love in the circle of Bright Young Things is said to have complemented his inconsistencies in politics and his inability to remain faithful to any party. Mosley's feelings of responsibility for the early death of his first wife and steadfast political partner was followed by a definite protectiveness towards his second wife – this evolution happened to coincide with his intellectual journey from socialism to fascism. These were relationships with women that would have aroused the interest of any spectator of the scene: Mosley was a 'leading man' on the verge of gothic villainy. His success with women allowed him to synthesize a politics of provocation with one of sexual excitation. The feminine influences in Mosley's private and public life were central to his story and led to a sexually charged atmosphere in which British fascism flourished during the 1930s.

Is the interest of historians and biographers in the private lives and sexual drives of 'Great Men' merely retrospective voyeurism, or can we discover something vital about the psychology of extremism from the manner in which firebrands or would-be demagogues related to the opposite sex? It is the contention here that private behaviour, ability to relate to women, and the varying heights of the pedestal upon which leaders of men placed their women, all informed their political thought on the woman question. Although such a claim might well be contentious, it must also be kept in mind that the popular fascination with this dimension of sexual politics never diminishes. It is commonly agreed that sex and power are mutually corrupting, and that a man's behaviour in the bedroom impacts upon his masculine assertions in the boardroom.

Certainly, Mosley would have been the last person to accept such an approach and line of enquiry. It may seem ironic, yet understandable, that a man so well endowed with the characteristics that fuel the interest of psychoanalysis should have reacted so vehemently against the interpretational techniques of (popular) psychology. Freudian psychology and communism were twin bogeys in Mosley's world view: 'sexual determinism is not very different in essence from economic determinism,'[1] he stated, expressing distaste for psychoanalysis, which he characterized as feminine. His resentment of the manner in which he was interpreted by his critics revealed his profound understanding of the emphasis placed on childhood experience and sexual behaviour in the diagnosis of political personality: 'Every sob-sister in the popular press feels she is competent in a breathless little article of slipshod appraisal and spiteful disapprobation to analyse the alleged complexes of every giant and dwarf who traverse the world scene.'[2] Undoubtedly, Mosley ranked himself with the giants, felt threatened by the pettiness and incomprehension of the 'old women' in Parliament, by a 'hag-ridden Britain,'[3] and by the 'Mrs Grundy' types who allegedly held sway over public morality, and remained virtually unchallenged by the 'spiritually castrated young gentlemen'[4] among the BUF's Red opponents. But did he maybe protest too much?

Women Behind the Fascist Throne

From the earliest interrogations into the characters of Mussolini and Hitler, scholars and journalists alike have endeavoured not to overlook the manner in which these men treated and regarded women. On the eve of war, Rosita Forbes interviewed both Hitler and Mussolini, and wished to know 'by whom are these dictators influenced? In their secret lives are there women who play a part, for the safety or destruction of our civilization?'[5] She found that behind this essentially masculine form of government, Mussolini took counsel from his daughter, and Hitler had been most moved by the death of his mother. Recognizing the female influences and women behind these fascist thrones has served either to humanize the subject of biography by identifying typical male yearnings and capacity for love alongside the desire for totalitarian dominance, or to further demonize the demagogue by suggesting parallels between his behaviour with women and his crimes against humanity. Gossip about leading men's tastes in female companionship has also had the effect of bursting the bubble of inflated dictatorial egotism.

In an ambience of fascist high-seriousness, Mussolini's biographer and some-time mistress, Margherita Sarfatti, understood that

> my book is essentially a woman's book. It is taken up largely with details which you, perhaps, will dismiss as 'gossip'. But, for my part, I have read too much of history to disdain gossip. It is only through visualizing the

protagonists that we come to understand the nature of great events. The story of Rome lives in the recorded actions and thoughts, loves and quarrels, of individuals.[6]

Although Sarfatti presumed that women were both the producers and consumers of biographical banter, her approach still lent validity to the supposition that intimate deportment was inextricably linked to civic action. In *A Life of Contrasts*, Diana Mosley was similarly self-deprecating about womanly curiosity in the private life of her notorious acquaintance, Adolf Hitler. She prefaced her recollections of Hitler's politesse and her descriptions of his ease among women of her own class with the claim that her memories were 'only what the French call *la petite histoire*', while still admitting that 'even in small matters the truth is sometimes interesting.'[7] Within fascist circles, interest in private life was deprecatingly labelled a feminine fixation, one to be explored in female narratives, and antithetical to the preoccupations of the fascist man of action. The relegation of women to the private sphere was, in effect, reinforced by granting the female dominion over gossip and *in camera* history.

Beyond the hagiographical accounts offered by fascist women, biographical studies of Mussolini and Hitler tend to accept the close correspondence between private life and public persona. Mussolini's relationships with women are most often cited to expose his hypocrisy. Although he had many mistresses, Mussolini acted the family man, and when Italian women were granted a limited local franchise in 1925, for example, 'if he had has his way, he would have withheld the vote from women living in open adultery.'[8] In striking contrast to Nicholas Mosley's iconoclastic portrait of his own family, Vittorio Mussolini respected standards of fascist *machismo* and the idealization of women in his portrayal of his father's indiscretions. The Duce's son remembered his mother as his father's 'brave and loyal companion, keeping in the background when things were going well and returning to his side as soon as there was more fighting and suffering to face.'[9] George Mosse has tried to show how Mussolini's and Hitler's contrasting expressions of intimacy were symptomatic of the substantially dissimilar national cultures of respectability underpinning Italian *avant-gardist* Fascism and moralistic German National Socialism. 'Hitler, unlike Mussolini, could not have afforded to keep a series of mistresses, however discreetly; this was not a way of proving one's manliness in Germany.'[10] Masculine and macho fascism was personified by the

Duce himself, and it was this example which Mosley tended to emulate, by his very nature as much as by design.

Records of the rumours and confirmed reports about Hitler's sexual behaviour range from the sensationalist and salacious to the psycho-historical and scholarly.[11] Descriptions of Hitler's sexual conduct vary from anecdotes about his sado-masochism and misogyny to diagnoses of syphilitic impotence and asexuality. Alan Bullock has confirmed Diana Mosley's observation that 'Hitler enjoyed and was at home in the company of women ... . If ladies were present at table he knew how to be attentive and charming, as long as they had no intellectual pretensions and did not try to argue with him.'[12] Bullock also gives some consideration to two hypotheses which may offer an explanation for Hitler's habits of abstinence and prolonged bachelorhood: that Hitler was affected by syphilis which he contracted as a youth in Vienna, and that he was incapable of normal sexual intercourse. Conjecture about Hitler's relations with women fortifies Bullock's study in tyranny in so far as 'egotism is a malignant as well as an ugly vice, and it may well be doubted whether Hitler, absorbed in the dream of his own greatness, ever had the capacity to love anyone deeply.'[13] John Carey gives voice to a stereotypical analysis when he remarks that Hitler deemed that 'motherhood was the only proper occupation for [women], and if they did not have children they tended to go off their heads. He did not like to see them grapple with ideas, which were man's domain.'[14] The Fuehrer's degradation of the female intellect and his objectification of women are seen to have determined the direction of Nazi women's policy and to have expedited the exclusion of women from public life in Germany.

Although the existing evidence about Hitler's encounters with women behind closed doors can never be corroborated, it has been widely observed that he reinforced political pageantry with sexual metaphor in developing the Nazi aesthetic. The Hitler myth has been fortified by portraying the Fuehrer as a conjurer with hypnotic powers and spell-binding eyes, particularly effective for arousing the enthusiasms of his female audiences. When the Baroness Ravensdale attended the 1936 Nazi Party Congress she was impressed that 'when Hitler spoke he raised the crowds to their greatest height of ecstasy.'[15] According to Susan Sontag, 'Hitler regarded leadership as sexual mastery of the "feminine" masses, as rape. (The expression of the crowds in *Triumph of the Will* is one of ecstasy; the leader makes the crowd come).'[16] Sexual politics should be understood not only as the record of the sexual activity of political figures and the impact on popular perceptions of unreliable pillow-talk, but as the projection of sexual imagery and urges onto the political landscape.

It was indicative of Mosley's own manipulation of the techniques of sexualized politics that he went so far as gendering his depictions of the European dictators. Of his first meeting with Hitler in April 1935, Mosley remembered how he had been able to resist the Fuehrer's much vaunted hypnotic powers: 'He was simple, and treated me throughout the occasion with a gentle, almost feminine charm.'[17] Ascribing feminine characteristics to a man was a common technique of ridicule in the BUF's subversive propaganda. Further, Nicholas Mosley recalls that his father disliked Hitler, and would call him that 'terrible little man'. In old age, 'one of the sayings he liked to bring out over the dinner table was that Italy, being a feminine country, had fallen in love with Mussolini, a man; whereas Germany, being a masculine country, had fallen in love with Hitler, a woman.'[18] Mosley is a rich subject for a study of the politics of gender as his discourse, in private and in public, was informed by the binary opposites of sex.

Mosley's Women: The Reluctant Marriage Between Private Life and Politics

While much inquiry has been made into trying to determine who were the men who provided Mosley with his intellectual influences and backed him in his political enterprises, less attention has been paid to the women who informed his political choices, provided the emotional background to his political impatience, and followed his star. Beneath Mosley's iron-clad masculine exterior rest layers of female influence and guidance. In keeping with his conception of the new fascist man, Mosley wished to draw a clear line of division between private and public life. His success in achieving this segregation, however, was never absolute.

When paying some fleeting notice to Mosley's domestic arrangements during the 1930s, Skidelsky has observed that 'public and private life were kept in rigidly separate compartments. No fascist lieutenant ever came to Denham,'[19] the ancestral home where his three children were being raised by their aunt Irene Ravensdale, a nanny, and a French housekeeper. Nicholas Mosley sees more nuances here, and believes that my father never consciously equated sex and politics. I think his style and the way he always talked was to completely separate them. I remember his favourite character in history was Caesar, because he thought Julius Caesar could dally with Cleopatra, but as soon as the call came from politics or battle he could drop it and stay away ... . Sexuality and women were for relaxation and dalliance. But at the same time, he didn't really quite do that, you see. He didn't live that out. He did risk a lot of his politics by his overt relationship with Diana while still married to my mother.[20]

In contrast to his frequent assertions of superior masculine restraint, it was testimony to Mosley's fallible virility that he could never achieve a clean divorce between his personal and political ambitions. Nicholas Mosley has also suggested that 'in some way it was probably his zest for life – even his sexual drives – that helped to render him politically ineffectual ... Tom, with the cutting edge of his personality, seemed often to be almost knowingly self-destructive.'[21]

Sir Oswald Mosley, known as 'Tom' to his family and close acquaintances, was born under the sign of Scorpio on 16 November 1896 to Katherine Maud and Oswald Mosley. The first of three sons, he was heir to a Staffordshire baronetcy. His parents soon separated due to the uncontrolled and over-indulgent sexual habits of his father, which contrasted so strikingly with the principled Christian ethics and forthright common-sense exemplified by his mother. In his troubled relationship with his father, Mosley was typical of the young men of his age and his circle, and exhibited many traits in common with the Bright Young Things, or the 'Children of the Sun' of the Missing Generation. The young Mosley rapidly replaced his father in his mother's home – becoming her 'man-child' – and he remained 'passionately devoted'[22] to her until her death in 1948.

On the one hand, Mosley had a share in a lineage of lechery, his father and grandfather having both left their wives and pursued numerous extra-marital relationships. On the other hand, his positive relationship with his mother was strengthened by the fact that his was a 'broken home' where there was also 'an atmosphere of strife between preceding generations,' since his father had also had a conflictual relationship with his own father. This helped to determined Mosley's peculiar dependence on female presence. 'I have a tendency to rely on some obliging woman to do small things for me which I feel she can do as well or better than I can, and are a waste of time for me to do; a conceit which obliging women are happily quite tolerant about. It arises clearly from being the man of the house too soon.'[23] Mindful of the implications to be derived from this dependence on women, Mosley was anxious not to be labelled a 'mother's boy.'

Perhaps to protect his male ego, he claimed that as a child 'I did not suffer from lack of male influence. The company of one or the other grandfather was constant, and no one could have been more male than these two.'[24] In the same concern to protect his masculine reputation against presumptions based on the 'family romance' being enacted in his childhood home – with the added variables of a traditional public school education at Winchester, and military training at Sandhurst – Mosley was careful to dissociate himself from any foray into homosexual experimentation.[25] He set out to affirm his maleness from the earliest age, providing his mother with 'gratuitous advice and virile assertions on every subject under the sun,'[26] and he first injured his leg in a crash when as a young recruit in the Royal Flying Corps in 1915 he was showing off his new gravity-defying skills in front of his mother. Running – but never limping – through his fascist rhetoric, and projected onto the hierarchy of his fascist movement, it was clear that the masculine principle dominated his thought.

The simultaneous experiences of war and sex launched Mosley on his political career. The haunting memories of the trenches and of his fallen comrades saddled Mosley with his life's mission to represent the decimated war generation, while his early success with women of his class presented him with the first platforms from where to preach his message. Mosley was invalided out of the army in March 1916. Following his military service he worked for the Ministry of Munitions and the Foreign Office in 1917–18, and concurrently plunged into the whirl of High Society life. From the flat he took in Grosvenor Square, he gained entry into the houses of the great hostesses of his day: Maud (Emerald), Lady Cunard; Sibyl, Lady Colefax; Maxine Elliott; Nancy, Lady Astor; and Mrs Ronnie Greville. In fact, it was through his popularity with the women of the elite that he first made contact with prominent men, such as F.E. Smith, Asquith, Lloyd George, and Winston Churchill. 'He had looks, presence and manners to succeed – and he did.'[27] He became the lover of Margaret Montagu, Catherine D'Erlanger, and Maxine Elliott, as it was the convention in his circle that a young man should be initiated into sexual maturity by older married women. 'His success with women gave him confidence with older men: confidence with politicians of course added to his success with women.'[28] From the start, Mosley's political and sexual self-image were in lock-step. The true marriage between his public and private life was very much based on his sexual impulses.

Cynthia Mosley: 'Of My Husband's Party'

In 1918, Mosley joined the Conservative Party; he stood in the Coupon Election of December 1918 as the Conservative-Coalitionist 'soldier candidate' in Harrow, and when he was elected he was the youngest MP in the House of Commons. Mosley remained neither a Conservative nor a bachelor for very long. By 1919, his political partnership with Lord Curzon's daughter, Cynthia (Cimmie), was established after the two met in Plymouth while they were both working for Lady Astor's campaign to become the first woman to sit in the House of Commons. Their extravagant Society wedding took place on 11 May 1920, six months before the young-man-in-a-hurry defected from the Conservative benches to sit as an Independent due to his indignation over the outrages perpetrated by the Black and Tans in Ireland. Their married life coincided with the most diversified phase of Mosley's political and sexual development, and many of the elements of his more progressive thought on the woman questions can be attributed to Cynthia's influence and the political camps into which they ventured together.

If he saw his mother as 'a paragon of virtue,'[29] Cynthia too 'was a good woman in the true, natural sense of the word.'[30] Cynthia, however, was of a more radical bent than her mother-in-law, and easily enlisted for the march of post-suffrage women into inter-war politics. It was indicative of the couple's openness to the new breed of political women that not only did they fall in love under the spell of Lady Astor's first electoral campaign, but they also chose Nancy, Lady Astor and Violet Bonham-Carter to be godmothers to their first son Nicholas (born 1923). If 'Ma' Mosley was typical of the Victorian woman, Cynthia was a strong example of the emancipated woman ready to serve her husband as well as the interests of the national community. Her influence over Mosley was not confined to the private sphere, as Cynthia's public-minded rectitude often buffered the impact of her husband's erratic political decisions and provocative charisma.

Cynthia was born in 1898, the second of three daughters to George Lord Curzon and Mary Leiter, a Chicago heiress of Dutch descent.[31] Cynthia's early education followed the conventions of her class – nannies and governesses. Her mother died in 1906, and her upbringing was monitored by her father, the former Viceroy of India, ardent Tory imperialist, and anti-suffragist. Nonetheless, her formal education was superior to that of Mosley's second wife, Diana (née Mitford). While the Mitford girls were not encouraged to go to school due to Lord Redesdale's conviction that women did not require much education,[32] in 1916 Cynthia went to boarding school at Eastbourne, and during the war (winter of 1917–18) she worked as a clerk in the War Office, followed by a short welfare course at the London School of Economics and social work in the East End of London. Lady Cynthia's idealism and humanitarianism directed her towards the Left: in 1924 she joined the Labour Party with Mosley with relative ease, dedicated herself to advocating the protection of the rural environment, and preached an emotional variant of Christian Socialism.[33] Indeed, she was never content with her husband's last hue on the political spectrum, and she has come down to us as an angelic figure, who, had she lived, might have acted as a bulwark against some of her husband's more distasteful fascist excesses.

Mosley saw Cynthia as 'someone with whom in partnership he might set out to alter the world.'[34] Her loyalty to her husband was constant, and she endured with dignity the social ostracism of the Tory elite who could never quite tolerate her class betrayal. In 1928 she confided to a journalist that 'Lady Astor is one of the few friends who will still see me,' and it was reported that 'virtually all her former Society acquaintances have now turned a cold shoulder to the renegade, avoiding shaking hands with her.'[35] Although persistently attacked by the Left for her wealth and luxurious lifestyle, which jarred with Labour's austerity, she could say with some justification that 'we are not Socialists for fun... We work for a better and happier England. Our enemies say we want to destroy the fine building of the British State. We say that the building is not so fine, since wages are low, houses bad, and unemployment terrible.'[36] Her elder sister, Irene Ravensdale, remembered: 'in the 1920s my sister's political development was astonishing. In her devotion to him [Mosley], she had made herself into an admirable speaker; after a maiden speech which I attended at Harrow, when she told a women's meeting: "I cannot speak, I only ask you to send my husband in at the top of the poll, as polling day is his birthday."'[37] She was her husband's junior partner in social and political life, and Cynthia became one of the thirty-six women who served as

MPs during the inter-war period. When she was elected for Stoke-on-Trent and he for Smethwick in the 1929 General Election, the Mosleys were only the second husband-and-wife team ever to sit in the House of Commons.

Cynthia Mosley was preoccupied by social and class issues, and the thrust of her maiden speech in support of the Widows', Orphans', and Old Age Pensions Bill was to demolish the Conservative prejudice that people were demoralized by being given 'something for nothing.'[38] Although one of the new breed of women MPs, Lady Cynthia Mosley espoused a weak version of feminism, a brand which domesticated politics so that the role of women could be seen as indispensable, rather than weighing in for the furtherance of female emancipation. She employed a line of argument that was characteristic of Labour women, conceding that women's place was in the home but 'that was the very reason why we should take an interest in politics ... politics were the bread and butter of life.'[39] While the Curzon daughters had no evident sympathy for their father's stand on the woman question, they rebelled by exemplifying the potential of women in public life in pragmatic terms, rather than developing a programmatic ideology of feminism. For example, while the Baroness Ravensdale was engaged in the long struggle to have peeresses sit in the House of Lords in their own right and worked for the Union of Women Voters, she still acknowledged that 'I owe much to the courageous feminists of the past age who were victorious in so many fields for our advancement, but I confess that a lot of redoubtable, determined feminists together frightened me into fits, and I served their cause poorly.'[40] This emphasis on women in politics, as opposed to feminist politics, was to be emulated by BUF attitudes as women were invited to join in the struggle to build a masculine Britain where their sex would be honoured and their domestic needs paid high regard. It is evident that Mosley was not exposed to radical feminism through the political women in his life, but his generous tribute that Cynthia had been his 'steadfast, ever loyal and able colleague in the tough existence of politics,'[41] revealed a more progressive vision than mere notions of the 'power behind the throne'.

Cynthia followed her husband into apostasy from socialism, defected to the New Party, and played a central role in the early days of campaigning when he was ill with pneumonia.[42] Their political partnership became more tenuous, however, with the beginning of Mosley's fascist career. Accounts conflict as to how

Cynthia made the intellectual and emotional transition from her heart-felt socialist convictions to Mosley's new-found fascist initiative. Her son supposes that

> she wouldn't have done anything against my father, never spoken out about him. But I don't think she would have ever become part of the fascist movement. She did not play much of an active part in the early days of the fascist movement ... . She certainly wouldn't conceive of being head of the women's movement.[43]

Harold Nicolson, never a believer in her intellectual capacities, made the following entry in his diary on 15 February 1931: 'Poor Cimmie cannot follow his [Mosley's] repudiation of all the things he had taught her to say previously. She was made for society and the home.'[44] Nicolson also recorded Cynthia as stating that she wished to put a notice in *The Times* dissociating herself from her husband's fascist venture. She was certainly distressed and confused by the situation. At the time of the launch of the BUF in October 1932, Vera Brittain's diary recorded H. G. Wells' account of how

> on the day of the crisis, after Mosley had gone, Cynthia drove herself over to the Casino [in Antibes], danced deplorably in public, and then got drunk and smashed up her car driving it home. Wells gave this as an instance of the Mosleys' inability to exercise self-discipline even in a time of crisis, but it sounded to me much more as if Lady Cynthia had been driven to desperation and simply stopped caring what happened or what she did.[45]

Countering these glimpses into her psychological state, there is evidence to suggest that in time Cynthia might have reconciled herself to Mosley's 'modern movement'. Her sister remembered how 'in the last year of her life she was searching for designs for a Fascist flag – he [Mosley] wanted to make Sousa's March, the Stars and Stripes, into a Fascist anthem, with words by Osbert Sitwell.'[46] She 'devoted many hours daily, in her failing health, to working out an elaborate card-index system in the offices of the Movement.'[47] She accompanied Mosley on a visit to Rome in April 1933, on which occasion they were both present at a march-past of Mussolini's fascists. Also in April, she was spotted at a Fabian meeting addressed by a Communist speaker. She was grilled by a reporter on her conspicuous presence there, to which she responded

'My God ... can't I hear other political views without adopting them?'
And then she put the real kibosh on the *Sunday Express* by proving her
100% political consistency: – 'I am a member of my husband's Party.' There's
political loyalty for you.[48]

Through her husband's political and sexual infidelities, and her
own ill-health, Cynthia continued to demonstrate a determination
to remain her husband's junior partner, no matter what the enterprise.
She was of her husband's party, and she knew it.

Cynthia's real legacy to the BUF was the effect upon her husband
of her early death, rather than her limited activities in building
the new organization. It can be argued that her death at the age
of thirty-four from peritonitis, rather than any achievement as a
fully politicized woman, had the greatest subjective influence on
the development of Mosley's fascist women's policy. Mosley's attacks
against political women became increasingly caustic after she died,
and he warned against the over-taxing of the strength of a woman
who was both politician and mother. (We could also speculate
that Mosley's defeat as New Party candidate for Stoke-on-Trent
in 1931 by Mrs I. Copeland (Conservative) may also have contributed
something to his radical turn against political women.) At one
and the same time he had no use for the 'spinster MPs' and
doubted the potential for the normal woman, the wife and mother,
to play a full political role. He spoke from his own experience
when he said that 'any normal mother of children who secures
election to parliament imposes an impossible burden on her physique
if she seeks to discharge both her duty to her children and to
her constituents.'[49]

As Diana Mosley explained, 'since Cimmie's death M. had been
haunted by the idea that she had worn herself out by political
activities beyond her strength. My work for him had been entirely
connected with business and not at all with propaganda.'[50] With
the passing of Cynthia, Mosley's views on the place of his women
in politics shifted from the desire to have his partner at his side
and in public view to a jealously guarded confidentiality surrounding
his relationship with Diana. This new protectiveness was exemplified
by his wish that his marriage to Diana on 6 October 1936 should
remain secret in order to shield her against the abuse Cynthia
had suffered as a result of his politics. When the news of his
second marriage finally broke in November 1938, Mosley explained,
'My first wife was subject to the most blackguardly abuse from
some sections of the press and it was my desire that no woman

should again be subject to such treatment merely because she happened to be married to me.'[51]

Consistent Inconsistency: Mosley's Political Promiscuity

Arguably, Cynthia's health had been undermined as much by Mosley's romping from bed to bed as from party to party. Mosley's egotism could be dualistic, and responsive to the complementary feminine influence in public life. Against this optimistic appraisal of their political partnership, however, it was also perceived that Mosley's vanity was individualistic and absolute. Cynthia's lack of radicalism was attributed to her 'being sacrificed to the hurried ambitions of her husband. Everyone liked her, and not only her lovely face: everyone felt her sincerity; we should have written off Tom much sooner but for her,'[52] remembered Mary Agnes Hamilton, a fellow Labour MP in MacDonald's 1929 Government. In his cavalier treatment of Cynthia, the first indications of Mosley's style of Gothic villainy came into view. Hamilton could see him as a victimizer of women, and this image was echoed by two other prominent Labour women. Beatrice Webb's view of Tom was that 'with such perfection there must be some rottenness somewhere.' Likewise, Ellen Wilkinson wrote: 'The trouble with Oswald Mosley is that he is too good looking ... he is not the kind of nice hero that rescues the girl at the point of torture but the one who hisses at last we meet.'[53] The distrust that Mosley engendered was very much a result of his morally questionable activities in private life; he undermined his political respectability by acting the playboy, a drawback even in the free-love atmosphere of progressive politics during the 1920s.

Accounts abounded of Mosley's philandering during the 1920s and the early 1930s. 'There are different opinions about how long Tom was faithful to Cimmie after their marriage: her sister imagined possibly a few years: Tom's second wife, Diana, suggested a few months.'[54] Nicholas Mosley has argued that his father played by the unwritten rules of the game of upper-class society in his pursuit of other women, and that he at least remained consistent by confining his choices to women from his social set.[55] Sir Oswald never considered women of the middle- or working-classes worthy of his attention, particularly in matters of sexual intimacy. In private life, among his own women, 'sexually he wasn't a chauvinist. All these attitudes, he made advances to women he thought were equal to him. That is the opposite of the chauvinism that pounces on everyone.'[56] He only pursued women of the greatest prestige, and even when a member of the Labour Party, belonging to a circle where the principles of easy free-love reigned, 'Tom did not take advantage of this situation. He had a brief walk-out with one of the wives at the ILP summer school: but soon after he coined the witty slogan – "Vote Labour: Sleep Tory" – and reverted to type.'[57] Inevitably, his indulgence in the newfound sexual freedom of the elite circles he and his wife inhabited was not well regarded by Cynthia.

His sexual indiscretions were immense, and his slight respect for Cynthia was exemplified by the apparent attitude that his sexual drives had no ethical boundaries: he had love affairs with her younger sister Baba (Alexandra) soon after Cynthia died, and he confessed to an affair with her step-mother, Grace Curzon, shortly before his wedding. While he might have reserved these privileges for the aristocratic man, he was enough of a product of his Lost Generation that he could concede that women should have an equal share of freedom in sexual matters. When the full extent of his philandering was revealed to Cynthia, he suggested to her that she, too, gratify herself by pursuing extra-marital affairs, something she was incapable of even contemplating.[58]

His inability to remain faithful when infidelities could flatter his vanity was mirrored in his political promiscuity during the 1920s. In the 1930s this personal restlessness was also reflected in one of the central premises of his philosophy of British fascism. 'The fascist principle is private freedom and public service,'[59] he asserted. This differed markedly from the Nazi assertion, as articulated by Goebbels, that 'the only individual with a private life in Germany is the person who is sleeping.' But this was not the kind of 'sleeping' Mosley wanted to protect or felt compelled to defend. He grounded his strong defence of Edward VIII during the Abdication Crisis on the same theoretical premise:

> The recompense of this country for 25 years faithful service is the denial of every man's right to marry and to life in private happiness with the woman he loves. Let the man or woman who has never loved be the first to cast a stone. Certainly we will not see stones cast at him or his lady by a decadent society, large sections of which, in recent times, have condoned and even flaunted some of the vilest vices known to humanity.[60]

While the leader of the BUF had many motives to defend the King – not least Edward's developing sympathy for fascist regimes

– the subjective and self-referential origins of Mosley's intellectual position were not difficult to trace.

Mosley's consistent volatility in his choices of both political allies and lovers blended well with the dynamics of fascist personality and its burgeoning hero myths. Sarfatti identified Mussolini's great originality in the fact that 'while on the surface he may seem changeable, yet in reality his nature is unalterable and forms a harmonious whole. In some respects he may appear a romantic.'[61] Mosley played the same game of double-think when in 1932 he claimed that 'if anything, I am disturbed by the fact that through 14 years of political life, and more than one change of Party, I have pursued broadly the same ideals ... . In a world of changing facts and situation, a man is a fool who does not learn enough to change some of his original opinions.'[62] Mosley's mercurial behaviour met little resistance from fascist ideological flux.

Diana Mosley: The Leader's Fairy Princess

Mosley's reputation as a playboy was on the ebb once he had committed himself to fascism. He maintained that he had abandoned social life in order to expend his full energies on the fascist struggle, 'that his total commitment to his fascist movement would be a fitting memorial to his late wife [and] he told his followers at their headquarters – "From now on this will be my home."'[63] However, it was during the early days of the BUF that Mosley first met Diana Guinness, and so began a more muted political partnership that would serve him well throughout his long career as a fascist. His ambition to conquer the most prestigious and attractive women in his social set reached its apotheosis when he won Diana, the trophy of the Bright Young Things, heir-apparent to Emerald Cunard's society throne,[64] and starlet of the debutante world. Mosley became the 'Father Superior'[65] to his new mate, as Nancy Mitford tellingly described his relationship to her sister.

Diana's first partisan commitments were to fascism. Even when married to Bryan Guinness (1929–33), whose father Walter Guinness (Lord Moyne) was the Conservative Minister of Agriculture, she had been vaguely anti-Tory, but essentially apolitical. Her political baptism came when she met Mosley. 'From Diana's point of view, Mosley and his beliefs lent each other credibility; to most of her friends, on the contrary, each made the other more suspect. It seemed very much as if the fairy princess had been carried off

192

by the demon king.'[66] To the contemporary spectator it might have appeared that Mosley had only kidnapped Diana's heart, but their intellectual sympathies had as much to do with their strong attraction to one another and future alliance as did the physical fact of sex appeal. In fact, Diana was repelled by the legends surrounding Mosley's demonic charm, and, as she later remembered, 'like everyone else, I also knew of his reputation as a lady killer, but this did not predispose me in his favour.' [67] As a rule, Diana kept a low profile in British fascist politics for after Cynthia death, Mosley 'became so concerned about me that he stopped me doing many things I well could have done. If I was ill he thought I was going to die; he imagined it might be a result of the tension caused by his own life of struggle and strife.'[68] Only in Germany, as Unity Mitford's sister and as an accepted member of Hitler's inner-circle, did she find an active outlet for her fascist convictions.

It was really only when Mosley began his affair with Diana that he broke the rules of the game and offended sexual mores by accepting that Diana leave her husband, take her two small children, and set up house as his mistress. 'Tom seemed to be claiming simply that he had the right to have two wives – a state of affairs traditionally indeed held to be taboo.'[69] It was partly due to the scandalousness of their affair that Diana remained on the side-lines of BUF activity. At first,

> he didn't think of leaving [Cynthia]. He just wanted everything as men are apt to do ... . So when he first met Diana he did not want her in the lime-light, he wanted her in the background ... . After my mother died that feeling carried on with him. He saw her as his fairy princess [and] he wanted to keep her safe in this extraordinary fairy castle in Derbyshire.[70]

On 11 April 1933, it became public that Diana was suing Bryan Guinness for divorce. Just over one month later, on 16 May, Cynthia Mosley died.

While Diana's activities on behalf of domestic fascism were negligible,[71] she was well integrated into the intrigues of international fascism and Nazism. She first gained access to the Nazi elite through her British connections: at an affair hosted by Mrs Richard Guinness she met Putzi Hanfstaengl, her 'first drawing-room Nazi.'[72] It was he who invited Diana and Unity to the first Nuremberg Parteitage in 1933. Again in 1934, the two sisters attended, and this time Unity found that it was 'a jamboree of her dreams.'[73]

By the time they attended the 1936 Olympic Games in Berlin, Unity and Diana were already part of Hitler's inner circle, and it was through Diana's friendships with Magda Goebbels and the Fuehrer that she was able to arrange the secret wedding ceremony for 6 October 1936.[74] Her relationships with leading Nazis could well have been innocent, but for the fact that, as Mosley admitted, 'it was a habit of Hitler to convey to me his view of events through Diana.'[75] Taking advantage of her favour in Nazi circles, Diana also represented Mosley's business interests in Germany when she sought backing for his scheme of radio advertising concessions for Sark, Ireland, and Germany.[76]

In early August 1939, Diana and Unity went to Bayreuth for the Festival, after which Hitler invited the sisters to luncheon. On this the last occasion Diana ever saw Hitler, 'he told us war was certain, Britain determined to fight. Although since the Polish guarantee, war had seemed very possible, this confirmation from Hitler gave us a feeling of despair ... . I told him I thought my husband would continue to speak for peace as long as it was legal to do so.'[77] Once interned under Defence Regulation 18B, Diana Mosley was questioned:

> **Q.** Have you ever reflected during your detention why you have been detained?
> **A.** Yes, often.
> **Q.** What conclusion did you come to?
> **A.** It was because I married Sir Oswald Mosley.
> **Q.** You are probably right. There is something in that. There are very few people in the country holding the view you hold.[78]

In an unguarded moment the Advisory Committee may have given voice to this perception, but Diana Mosley was certainly much more suspect for her close relations with the leaders of warring nations than the majority of small-fry BUF men and women rounded up during the Fifth Columnist scare of 1940. Shockingly, even her sister Nancy and her former father-in-law warned the authorities that Diana should be interned. Walter Guinness wrote to the Home Office: 'It has been on my conscience for some time to make sure that the Authorities concerned are aware of the extremely dangerous character of my former daughter-in-law, now Lady Mosley,'[79] and he enclosed a summary of conversations which his grandson's governess had recorded when taking the child to visits with his mother. Diana Mosley may well have been the cloistered fairy princess within the walls of a lonely Wootton Lodge in Derbyshire, but she parted with the conventions of the acquiescent mistress when she acted as Mosley's informal diplomat in Nazi Germany.

It is also significant that Mosley's attempt to separate his private life with Diana from his public life in the BUF not only faltered on occasion, but even back-fired. It had been his choice that their wedding should be clandestine, both to shield her from public abuse suffered by the women intimately allied to him, and because 'he said that in our movement people might be apt to think, as he was just married and so on, he perhaps would not work so hard for them, and would spend so much time and so on, and he thought it would be better if they did not know anything about it.'[80] One need only look closely at the chronology of events leading up to their nuptials to see how the BUF was affected by Mosley's private life.

On 4 October 1936, two days before he was scheduled to be in Berlin for his wedding, the BUF was arming to fight the Battle of Cable Street in their stronghold in the East End of London. Why did the Battle of Cable Street deteriorate into a fight between anti-fascist demonstrators and the police, rather than becoming the much anticipated pitched battle between the fascists and their many opponents? Why did Mosley meekly concede to the Commissioner of Police, Sir Philip Game's command that the Blackshirt marchers surrender their plan to parade through the East End? 'What did my father think he was doing. A big demonstration in the East End and then due to be married in Goebbels' house … . Why didn't he just march through Cable Street? … But then, of course, had he been arrested he wouldn't have been able to get to Berlin the next day for the wedding.'[81] Nicholas Mosley has acknowledged that the decision to turn around, to obey the Police and react in deference to Sir Philip Game was out of character for his father. Mosley's anxiety over missing his flight to Berlin the next day may well have changed history.

Mosley as the Aristocratic Rebel

The distinctions Mosley made between his own women and the objectified woman of the masses was symptomatic of his enduring loyalty to his own class identity. Mosley spoke fondly of his childhood home at Rolleston, a 'truly feudal survival', and he idealized the relationship between master and servants on the estate as the real 'classless society.'[82] His biographer has suggested that Mosley's entire life 'can be seen as an attempt to reintegrate his background into the mainstream of twentieth century English life at the time when English society itself was starting to be threatened by the forces which had earlier destroyed his family position.'[83] David Cannadine has seen Mosley's career as a prime example of the manner in which the British aristocracy negotiated its own decline and fall, and he has deemed that 'Mosley's fascism was deeply rooted in his own rootless experiences as a landed gentleman.'[84] From Mosley's vantage point, his aristocratic identity was not at odds with his leadership of a populist movement. He strongly felt that a natural affinity existed between the lowest and highest classes, and identified a common enemy in bourgeois culture and its attendant stifling Puritanism.[85]

The BUF endeavoured to solve the dilemma of an aristocratic-led fascist movement by cultivating the theory of an elite of merit, rather than one of heredity. Ideologues differentiated between aristocracy based on social class and manners, and a modern elite made up of new fascist men. Raven Thomson explained that 'Fascism gains its strength by an alliance of the true aristocrats of intellect and of action, of blood and of character, with the workers of hand and of brain, producers of the nations wealth.' And it followed that 'the true aristocrat, the born leader of men, has no need for class distinction to maintain his natural superiority.'[86] The class that Mosley had betrayed, first by becoming a member of the Labour Party and then by embracing fascism, was decried as decadent and effete. The construction of the Corporate State would entail the dismantling of the House of Lords, and the degenerate peerage was cautioned that 'no longer will the country house of the decadent plutocracy stand empty for three-quarters of the year while their owners disport themselves in the night clubs of Europe, while the peasants, because they have no land, are relegated to the care of the "local authorities."'[87] Although Mosley had himself sought recreation in those very night clubs,[88] he was spared the taint of decadence by being lauded as a natural aristocrat of merit and a born leader of men.

While the BUF made the class compromise of calling for a meritocracy of nobility, Mosley's aristocratic manner and appearance remained a liability. His dandified comportment encouraged much ridicule and served for some to explain the still-birth of the fascist idea in Britain. 'The leader of the BUF is so obviously not a man from the ranks come forward to lead the people. He stands but ill-disguised a patrician in Black shirt clothing, and that so faultlessly tailored.'[89] By way of warning that the real threat of a fascist coup would come from within the National Government, Ellen Wilkinson dismissed the significance of Mosley by recognizing that he 'is unpopular with his own class. Yet he is too scornfully aristocratic to be beloved by the masses.'[90] The history of British fascism and the aristocracy is conspicuous for the absence of noble followers of the BUF. Why was it that Mosley failed to convert his own declining class to his modern movement? How was it that his example of extremism was at once emblematic of the restlessness of his Lost and Missing Generation, of the Children of the Sun and of the Auden Generation, of the Bright Young Things and of the Mayfair Flappers, while he was exceptional among fitful notables to embrace a British variant of the continental fashion?[91]

We can approach an answer to these questions by first understanding Mosley as the quintessential aristocratic rebel, as Bertrand Russell described the type:

> The aristocratic rebel, since he has enough to eat, must find other causes of discontent ... . It may be that love of power is the underground source of their discontent, but in their conscious thought there is a criticism of the government of the world, which, when it goes deep enough, takes the form of Titanic self-assertion, or in those who retain some superstition, of Satanism.[92]

The aristocratic rebel wins distinction through a process of self-creation towards becoming a figure of supreme charisma; paradoxically, he is a leader without followers. Pondering the question of why so few members of his father's own class identified themselves with the BUF, Nicholas Mosley suspected:

> I certainly don't think he ever resented any of his aristocratic friends for not following him or letting him down. What was very odd about him as a politician was he always felt himself as a one-man-band, and he didn't care much about who was following him. Which is strange for a politician: one thinks politics is the art of the possible. It wasn't for him.[93]

That Mosley made scant attempts at winning the support of the women of his own social set was yet another indication of his aspiration to draw a line of demarcation between his experiences in social life and his activities in the fascist movement. Nonetheless,

197

there was a significant handful of notable women who were attracted to fascism, for, as Nancy Mitford gibed, 'aristocrats are inclined to prefer Nazis, while Jews prefer Bolsheviks.'[94]

Mosley's Women: Fascism as Foreplay

As the example of Diana Mosley suggests, British women of the elite were more likely to satisfy their curiosity about fascism on the Continent and mix in the international set than to implicate themselves in the déclassé British fascism of the streets. In social life, articulating sympathy for fascism was as much a means to provoke and titillate one's companions as it was an expression of a carefully pondered ideological stance. Griffiths has observed that 'there is no doubt that, from an early date, the European dictatorships had an aura of glamour for certain members of London high society.'[95] The same London hostesses who had launched Mosley on his political career a decade before were, by the 1930s, searching for new stars to follow and more thrilling vogues.[96]

There were many examples of women among Mosley's social set who found fascism recreational. As early as 1932, Virginia Woolf recorded that Alice Keppel, famous courtesan and Edward VII's mistress, had 'immense superficial knowledge, and [was] going off to Berlin to hear Hitler speak.'[97] In High Society discourse 'pro-Nazism seems to have been part of that superficiality.'[98] In 1933 Emerald Cunard was pro-Hitler and arranged to go to Germany. It was Lady Cunard's entertaining technique to 'drop some bombshell, or make some outrageous statement purposely; that at once flung the guest into seething argument and dispute.'[99] By indulging in her risqué 'machine-gun' conversational tactics in the presence of her Royal guest, Emerald Cunard was rumoured to have been responsible for poisoning Edward VIII with pro-Nazism. Lady Cunard certainly did much to make the German Ambassador, Joachim von Ribbentrop, welcome among her circle of friends and she was often spotted with Ribbentrop at the Opera, while Lady Astor's reputation was tarnished by allegations of pro-Nazism because she had frequently entertained the Ambassador at luncheons at Cliveden. On 29 May 1936, public attention was aroused when the 'millionairess Mrs Laura Corrigan, who had taken Crewe House for the Season, gave a lunch party in honour of the sinister Herr von Ribbentrop. That afternoon, Mrs Corrigan, Ribbentrop and Lord Londonderry left to spend a long Whitsun weekend at the Londonderry stately home in Northern Ireland, Mount Stewart.'[100] During the Fifth Columnist panic of 1940, Lafitte speculated that far fewer traitors could be found among the refugees than among figures in 'Mayfair drawing-rooms where Ribbentrop was once welcomed.'[101] In these circles, women who 'flirted with fascism' could flirt using fascism to arouse those they pursued.

Fascist Italy and Nazi Germany became playgrounds for the wealthy and were among the tourist attraction of the era.[102] Tours to fascist states provided vicarious experiences of authoritarianism, and presented a welcome visual contrast to the bleak age of Depression in Britain. Nuremberg was the most popular destination, and notables as politically diverse as Lady Diana Cooper, the Mitford sisters, Irene Ravensdale, Baba Metcalfe, Sir Frank and Lady Newnes, Lord and Lady Redesdale, and Mrs Ronnie Greville all attended Nazi rallies.[103] The Nazis encouraged the interests of British aristocrats and they 'realized the potential of so many well-connected young English people in their midst. If their first impressions of Germany were favourable ... then their return home was likely to filter youthful Nazism through the English upper-classes.'[104] It was no accident that the first members of his entourage Hitler wished Mosley to meet were three aristocratic women with English connections. In order to put Mosley at ease during their first meeting in April 1935, Hitler invited the Duchess of Brunswick, Frau Winifred Wagner and Unity Mitford, unaware that the last of these already knew Mosley.[105] Indeed, no young aristocratic woman fulfilled the Nazi wish for a well-connected propaganda agent as efficiently as did Unity Mitford[106] – daughter of a peer, Winston Churchill's cousin,[107] and Sir Oswald Mosley's sister-in-law.

Whereas fascism was foreplay for many women in British High Society, for Unity Mitford it was the climax. She shared with the London hostesses of her day the inclination to shock and *épater les bourgeois*, but during her debut Unity's 'efforts to brighten up the social scene gained few adherents ... . As a result Boud was considered a little eccentric by her contemporaries.'[108] She was unique among her set for seeking liberation from social constraints through Blackshirt violence in Britain. As Claud Phillimore, one of Unity's friends during her fascist phase, recalled: 'She had quite a masculine streak in her. She would go off to

BUF meetings in Oxford, donning her blackshirt which couldn't be taken seriously. She enjoyed doing it to provoke.'[109] On another occasion, as part of a BU contingent at a 'Save Peace, Save Spain' rally organized by the Labour Party on 10 April 1938, Unity luxuriated in the frenzied atmosphere. Fully apparelled in her fascist uniform, emblazoned with a Nazi badge, Unity was set upon by supporters of the meeting. As she reported, 'the crowd got very angry and started saying insulting things. A man tore off my badge... I hit him in the face. Then a woman said something insulting about Hitler. I hit her too.'[110] Arguably, her temperamental affinities with fascism were profound, but her intellectual grasp was limited. While her impetus was frivolous, Unity's commitment to Anglo-German friendship ran deep and she attempted suicide in September 1939, as Germany and England became declared enemies.

The BUF itself attracted two sets of aristocratic women: the members of Mosley's family and a handful of notable ladies who saw a truer expression of their conservatism in the British brand of fascism. The BUF was generally ambivalent about aristocratic women, and starting with the New Party, special criticism was reserved for titled women who debased their class by advertising soaps, cigarettes, etc.: 'A title was once, and still is to some, esteemed an honour; who degrades it to a commodity degrades not only herself but her class.'[111] As the BUF became more radically populist, and its membership militated increasingly against privilege, the attacks on women of the elite also intensified. By 1938, Doreen Bell wailed against the 'Mayfair Parasites' and their pampered idleness, and complained that 'the cocktail night-club girl of Mayfair, who rises at lunch time, and retires, worn with the quest of pleasure ... neither adds to the prestige of the nations by her behaviour nor the wealth of the nation by her work.'[112] Again, the irony was that the BUF was led by a former Mayfair dandy who had married the luminary of the Bright Young Things.

The BUF made a few attempts to attract and accommodate women of the elite. Against the image of the BUF as a brawling band of hooligans, the movement hosted respectable social occasions where upper-class women could feel welcome. Baroness Ravensdale and Alexandra Lady Metcalfe, Cynthia's two sisters, filled the gap that Cynthia had left, and both attended meetings of the January Club.[113] The January Club, set up to appeal to the Establishment, was described as 'essentially a man's affair',[114] but a ladies' dinner was scheduled for 17 May 1934 where guests were entertained by a debate between Sir Oswald Mosley and Sir Charles Petrie on 'Roads to Fascism.' Although Irene Ravensdale was openly associated with the BUF, she later asserted that she had no sympathy for Mosley's politics, found his anti-Semitism painful and terrifying, and that she had only attended his meetings at Albert Hall and Olympia 'out of a curious loyalty to my dead sister, in case some awful incident should happen to this new dictator whom I found I was quite incapable of fathoming or supporting.'[115]

In 1932, Mosley first aroused the curiosity of Lady Houston, proprietor of the *Saturday Review*, when he addressed a lunch-hour meeting at the Cannon Street Hotel. Lady Houston proceeded to draft a cheque for 100,000 or 200,000 pounds (the reports conflict as to the precise amount) to Mosley and the BUF, but she tore it up due to insulting remarks published against her in the fascist press.[116] In attendance at the Blackshirt wedding of Ian Hope Dundas (son of the 26th Chief of Dundas) to Pamela Ernestine Dorman in December 1933, were Maud, Lady Mosley, Lady Laird-Clowes, Miss Shackleton (representing Lady Shackleton), Lady Makgill, and Madame Sarnolea. *The Fascist Week* presented this list of guests in the same format as *The Times* displayed the guest lists for important Society functions.[117] Mosley would also frequently speak at garden parties hosted by such wealthy and well-connected supporters as the Viscountess Downe, an East Anglia landowner, and Lady Pearson, sister of Henry Page-Croft (later Baron Croft). Maud, Lady Mosley hosted 'At Homes' either at Women's Headquarters or, for instance, 'Lady Dalton very kindly put her house at the disposal of the BUF for an "At Home."'[118] Attendance lists compiled by Special Branch of the British Union's annual London Administration luncheons, held at the Criterion Restaurant, testify to the fact that a small number of titled women lent open support to the movement.[119]

Despite some celebrated examples, women of the elite were generally conspicuous for their absence from the BUF. Nonetheless, anti-fascist opponents preferred to believe that at Olympia Mosley was 'revealed with his mask off – an angry, screeching maniac, only applauded by his ladies in evening dress, who come to watch fascist brutality in order to pander to appetites which everything else decadent in the world can no longer satisfy.'[120] Mosley's popular image and literary persona were bolstered by these frequent references to his ominous sex-appeal.

Mosley Between the Sheets: The Leader's Literary Persona

It may at first seem problematic to read Mosley's life and career as text. However, among Mosley's most outstanding accomplishments were two forms of literary artistry. In the first instance, 'he was madly in love with his own words,'[121] and he won support or notoriety for the puissance of his oratorical style. He wove a rhetoric of Romantic resonances into the political literature he produced, a distinctive if not anachronistic feature in an age of journalistic textual styles. Secondly, Mosley had an image of himself as the self-created hero, an auto-didact, and subtly made reference to his debt to traditions and types in literature. Why are these points significant when trying to determine Mosley's appeal to women? In Britain, the woman was historically figured as the reader of novels, serials, and popular literature. Any man who created a persona that revealed a romantic or Byronic inheritance would have a particular appeal to women. And as Harold Nicolson remarked, Mosley 'is a romantic. That is his great failing.'[122] Furthermore, Mosley's style and appearance was often compared to that of a film star, and women were also figured as the most avid consumers of the new medium.

For his critics, Mosley's 'political Douglas Fairbanksism' was a ready and amusing target. He was seen as 'a dandy, whether in civilian clothes with top hat and gold-knobbed cane, or in Fascist uniform – to which Low added the ballooned sleeves of the Renaissance. His meetings rivalled the appeal of cinema.'[123] He was described as the 'Rudolf Valentino of Fascism – tall, dark, slim, straight, elegant, with fierce challenging eyes and that air of being a romantic figure which captures so readily the fancy of young persons with nothing much to do or think about.'[124] After covering the Earl's Court meeting of 1939, the Beaverbrook reporter Frank Waters noted in his diary how 'the audience howled, hugging itself. [Mosley] knew exactly when to make it laugh, when to cheer, when to jeer and sneer. A top-line variety star could hardly have shown greater versatility.'[125]

From character assassination to hero-worship, Mosley exploited his icon status to good effect among his adoring fans in the BUF. For instance, foreshadowing the garish memorials to popular entertainment icons, the Bethnal Green branch of the BUF boasted 'a large-size oil-painting of Mosley, festooned for the occasion [of his visit] with coloured lights ... . Here also the leader settled down to the task of signing scores of photographs of himself.'[126]

The Leader's birthday was ceremonialized by members of the BUF, and in November 1937, for example, Florence Hayes was organizing a whist drive to celebrate the occasion.[127] Albert Potter and his wife, both BUF members in Norfolk, owned a transport café which they decorated with 'portraits of the King and Queen ... [and] photographs of Mosley and fascist posters.'[128] It was difficult not to admit that what Mosley possessed was sex-appeal of the Hollywood variety, and he himself admitted that what he offered to working class audiences, through the BUF's uniforms, emblems, marching and other spectacular methods was 'glamour as the films have it.'[129]

Mosley's cousin, James Lees Milne, left a revealing but unflattering portrait of Mosley when speaking at his last meeting at Stoke, mindful of the sexual impulse which informed his political mannerism.

> The posturing, the grimacing, the switching on and off of those gleaming teeth, and the overall swashbuckling, so purposeful and calculated, were more likely to appeal to Mayfair flappers than to sway indignant workers in the Potteries. I did not then and do not now, think that the *art of coquetry* ought to be introduced into politics.[130]

Mosley used an erotically charged and flirtatious oratory, fitted to seducing the women of his class and of the populace, and reflective of the risqué intonations of High Society dialogue. It was no accident that BUF women were prone to 'idolize him,'[131] and that Mosley should have been the object of women's infatuations, such as in the case of the middle-aged Lucy Pearson, who, Diana Mosley admitted, 'had a crush on my husband.'[132] This idolatry did not cease even after the war, and in the Grundy household the mantelpiece was adorned with a photograph of Mosley in black fencing uniform, and Mrs Grundy could not believe her luck when at a post-war meeting she enthused 'I touched him. Now I've got the strength to carry on.'[133]

Paradoxically, Mosley himself expressed only disdain for literature and the imaginative arts. When he was interviewed by Rom Landau in 1939, he argued that 'there is little literature in this country today, nothing but literary sterility. And I believe it is inevitable that it should be so. In an age of action we cannot expect literature to be anything but sterile.'[134] And yet, he lived his life as art, as fascists are wont to do – after all, Mussolini's favourite maxim was 'I shall make my own life my masterpiece.'[135] Mosley was the self-created hero, or villain, whom others chose as the subject of fiction; his contribution was to build the myth surrounding his figure. Nietzsche wrote that 'active, successful natures act, not according to the dictum "know thyself"; but as if there hovered before them the commandment: will a self and thou shall become a self,'[136] and Mosley fulfilled these prescriptions.

Mosley's literary persona was intensified by his promiscuous sexual behaviour and his reputation as a playboy. Aldous Huxley based the character Everard Webley on Sir Oswald in *Point Counter Point* (1928). Huxley was prophetic of Mosley's fascism, and incisive in his portrayal of Mosley's extra-marital relations and the manner in which he pursued other women. In an attempt to seduce the married Elinor, Everard declares, 'You don't know what love can be ... . You don't know what I can give you. Love that's desperate and mad, like a forlorn hope. And at the same time tender, like a mother's love of a sick child. Love that is violent and gentle, violent like a crime and as gentle as sleep.'[137] His intensity in his relations with women, his sexual power and prowess, his early fascination with the criminality of love, and his equal dedication to a life of political provocation and sexual seduction were well noted by his contemporaries. Huxley also suggested a marriage between sexuality and violence in the Webley/Mosley mind, a sadistic streak in his character which aligned with the tradition of the strangely alluring Gothic villain.

Webley/Mosley's hunger for an exuberant sex life exposed something menacing in his character and psychology. Huxley's Webley 'despised women, resented them because they wasted a man's time and energy. She [Elinor] had often heard him say that he had no time for love-making. His advances were almost an insult – the proposition one makes to a woman of the streets.'[138] The women with whom the flesh-and-blood Mosley had affairs also took note of his somewhat vulgar and deprecating manner, and it was Georgia Sitwell who confided to Diana later in life – 'Of course we all went to bed with him but afterwards we were rather ashamed.'[139]

Mosley's enduring desire to be viewed as the quintessential man of action, as a public figure of hard-facts and earnestness, was easily subverted by parody. He was spoofed by P.G. Wodehouse in *The Code of the Woosters* (1937), where he appeared as Roderick Spode, leader of the Black Shorts, and secret designer of ladies' underclothing under the name of Eulalie Soeurs, of Bond Street. Mitford-speak branched out into 'Leadertease' by nick-naming him T.P.O.L, the Poor Old Leader, and P.O.F., the Poor Old Fuehrer, both terms of endearment in the Mitford cannon. However, by 1940 Nancy Mitford had dubbed him 'Sir Oswald Quisling.'[140] Mosley appeared also in H.G. Wells' *The Holy Terror* (1939) as the thinly veiled Lord Horatio Bothun, leader of the Popular Socialists, whose members wore purple shirts and brown belts. Wells' Lord Horatio was the 'sedulous student and ape of the Italian and German adventurers,' for whom what could 'have been more natural than for the rejected romantic leader of the Reds to invert himself in another swift transformation, become an anti-Red, and stretch out his strong right arm to protect the rich old ladies of the land from the Red Horror.'[141] In Winifred Holtby's anti-fascist dystopian play, *Take Back Your Freedom* (1939), Mosley was obviously one of the sources for the composite figure of Arthur Clayton, founder of the People's Planning Party, son of a domineering mother who herself serves as Honourary Commander of the Women's Legion of his Grey Guards, and 'the matinee idol among politicians [who] packs his meetings with hysterical women because he has four straight limbs and a good complexion.'[142]

In public life, Mosley and his Blackshirts were noted for their dearth of humour. Mosley's former ally in the New Party, Harold Nicolson later argued that 'a sense of humour cannot prosper either in a totalitarian and classless society or in a society in the process of revolution.'[143] The fascist mind was defined by its lack of self-irony, which, in turn, encouraged subversion through mockery: perhaps humour was the most effective antidote to fascism. Nancy Astor gave voice to a typical feeling when she told a National Government rally in 1935 that 'British people could not stand fascism – it was too farcical, if ever it came we should all die laughing.'[144] If high seriousness is the hallmark of fascism, then 'humour is the evidence of freedom.' Reflecting on the resurgence of the fascist mentality in late twentieth century European culture, U2's lead singer, Bono, prescribed humour as the only effective antitoxin:

> we stumbled upon the same thing that the Berlin Dadaists discovered, which is the idea of undermining the machismo of fascism. People underestimate its sex appeal, and our duty was to kind of dampen their hard-on with the cold water of humour. Fear of the devil leads to devil worship, but if you mock the devil he'll run.[145]

In the end, by playing the role of Nietzschean superman and humourless dictator to rave reviews, Mosley's 'main service [was] to keep Fascism insignificant in Britain.'[146]

Mosley's public speeches betrayed a great debt to the High Romantic tradition, while his rhetoric lacked the self-doubt which had made Byronic posturing more palatable. Byron and the fascist politician shared cosmetic resemblances,[147] and Mosley was certainly attracted to the Byronic hero of the poet's serious mode. To his children Mosley would 'quote some of the *Childe Harold* bits,'[148] and shortly after the war he identified Byron as a British representative of his own Hellenic and Elizabethan revolt against the hypocritical mercantilist tradition of the English Cavalier–Puritan.[149] The more purple passages in Mosley's speeches testify to his debt to this Byronic tradition of sublimity. Mosley spoke of his generation's fortune to be young 'between storm and storm,' and he pitied those who had lived through lotus years for

> 'never having stood on the topmost pinnacle of sacrifice where thunder threatens and lightning strikes. They have never felt on their brow the beckoning wind of the future, nor seen with their eyes the land that is to come ... . They have never felt the fierce fires of danger, and of suffering urging forwards and upward the spirit of humanity.'[150]

However, while Mosley could assert that his 'shall be the epic generation whose struggle and whose sacrifice shall decide whether men at last shall know the dust or shall grasp the stars,'[151] the Byronic hero was humbled by the realization that he was 'half dust, half deity'[152] and, in the end, Byron's satirical vision would exonerate him from being identified as the direct ancestor of the fascist hero.

Mosley's Woman: Generic Genders

Mosley expressed a colourful and sublime idealism about the women of his class and the mission of his reified generation. However, when he descended to the terrestrial level, the typology he developed to describe the common people was at best unimaginative, and at worst condescending. His son remembers that his father read Otto Weininger's *Sex and Character*, and 'used to talk about that book, in a rather whimsical way,'[153] but Mosley's vision of gender was uncomplicated and straightforward. He decreed that 'the part of women in our future organization will be important, but different from that of men; *we want men who are men and women who are women.*'[154] He claimed that he understood the needs and *a priori* drives of British womanhood, and his oft described 'normal woman'

206

did 'not seek, [nor] have time for, a career in politics.'[155] He painted a picture in which his normal women, as mothers of the race, had been victimized by dreams of feminine political grandeur, and by the false promise of professional women politicians who were in no way 'qualified to represent the mother of the nation ... [and] whose one idea is to escape from the normal sphere of women and to translate themselves into men.'[156] In keeping with his protective feeling for Diana, he hoped to shield women from 'the genialities of broken bottles and of razor-blades with which our Communist opponents have conducted the argument.'[157] In exchange for women's political ambitions, Mosley promised that 'Fascism in Britain will maintain the British principle of honouring and elevating the position of women. We certainly combat the decadence of the present system which treats the position of wife and mother as inferior ... . But women will be free to pursue their own vocations.'[158]

The normal woman was partnered with the 'ordinary man,' to whom Mosley appealed by advocating the demolition of the spirit of D.O.R.A., and the dismantling of the governessing and mothering state. As British fascists, he explained, 'we seek to create a nation-wide movement which replaces the legislation of old women by the social sense and will to serve of young men.'[159] His symbol of working-class life was the public house, and he spoke frequently of safeguarding private freedom by revoking licensing hours. At a meeting at the Chelsea Town Hall on 26 April 1937, for example, he was asked 'Q. What is your attitude towards D.O.R.A. and the licensing hours? A. We are against a grandmother in the Government of the nation. We believe in governing this nation by the methods of a man and not of a woman and therefore we oppose all these petty restrictions in the liberty of the individual.'[160] In his vision of the ordinary folk, he imagined that 'men talk in the workshop, the women talk at the wash-tubs, and everyone talks in the pub at night.'[161] Mosley became quite accomplished at playing to the gutter in his bid to capture the populist momentum.

Mosley was taken to task for the BUF's apparently reactionary categorization of gender roles. Winifred Holtby was certain that Mosley could find his women who were women 'at their quintessence in the slave markets of Abyssinia or in the winding alleys of a Chinese city.'[162] As another sceptic opined: 'every Blackshirt who stands on the street to-day is a menace not only to the honour of women, but to their disfigurement and maltreatment in the brutal dungeon they will create in the absolute exclusion of the slightest respect for sex.'[163] Mosley was confident enough that this was not the case that he quoted Bromley's melodramatic statement, taken from the *Daily Herald*, in the *Fascist Week*.

The tone and direction of Mosley's contribution to the gender debate in fascism was consistently defensive. As early as 1934 he defended the Nazi record on women's employment, and the National Socialist subsidy for marriage, deciding that this was 'a "piece of tyranny" under which, I imagine, many young English women would be quite glad to suffer.'[164] Throughout the 1930s he modified his position only very slightly by adding emphasis to the fascist assurance that 'women, whether in home or industry, will hold a high and honoured place in accord with British tradition and will receive full measure of representation and weight in the counsels of the State.'[165] During his appeal before the Advisory Committee in 1940, he was again prosecuted for the BUF's designs for women in the Corporate State and compelled to demonstrate how British fascism intended to deal with the female population in a manner distinct from the Nazi exclusion of women from professions. He described to Violet Markham how women 'have their Industrial Corporation, their Professional Corporation and – *this is one of my own ideas* they have not it in Germany – a special Corporation for the married women with children.'[166] While this last claim might have indicated that Mosley played a central role in formulating the BUF's women's policy, his speaking-part in the dialogue on feminine fascism was minor.

As the ideologue of the movement, Mosley's comments on the woman question tended to be theoretical, and the practical details of women in the organization concerned him far less than did the Utopian model of his future government. The appointment of 'Ma' Mosley as leader of the Women's Section was a case in point. As Nicholas Mosley mused, 'I can't think why he thought my grandmother could [be the head of the women's movement]. That is certainly one of the strange things – quite an important thing. An indication that certain bits of the organization he wasn't taking seriously. What he was taking seriously was the heraldic message, the legend.'[167] Furthermore, Mosley's ambivalence about the organization of women in his movement was testimony to his extreme masculinism, rather than to a virulent anti-feminism. As his son Nicholas also remarked, 'I can't remember him ever talking about feminism. He wouldn't have been against it, he just would have thought if it happens it happens, okay.'[168] Diana Mosley has reiterated that impression:

Mosley was not a 'feminist' but he did believe every woman should have a Marshall's baton in her knapsack. In other words, equal chance to get to the top in any profession she might choose ... . As to equality of the sexes being reconciled with fascism, I cannot see any problem here. Both sexes include weak and strong, stupid and clever, funny and humourless. I think the emphasis should be on the quality of the individual.[169]

Mosley's sexual politics were conditioned by his own sense of masculine supremacy and the imminent triumph of the masculine sensibility. While individual women could join in the struggle to establish his masculine Britain, by necessity, the feminine had to be purged.

Mosley's Masculine Movement

The mystique surrounding Mosley the Leader was reinforced by the cult of masculinity which laid the foundation for BUF ideology and organization. Certainly, the BUF did not hold the exclusive rights to ideals of masculine supremacy, the new fascist man, and a *mannerbund*. Essential to generic fascism was 'extreme stress on the masculine principle and male dominance, while espousing an organic view of society. Exaltation of youth above all other phases of life, emphasizing the conflict of the generations, though within a framework of national unity.'[170] Nonetheless, the BUF adapted the masculine cult to British conditions and the specific sexual politics of their own leader.

Mosley's stress on masculinity was obsessive, his fear of softness and pliability alarmist. His fascism was 'the steel creed of an iron age' – the most potent force. Supported by a family tradition of Royalist dissent, he identified as the historical precedent for the BUF's attitude to the manly 'the Merrie England of gay and serene manhood;'[171] his band of new man would have to measure up to the brawny figure of the Elizabethan yeoman. 'Our young, hard Fascism springs from the hard facts of a testing and turbulent age ... it brings also a new type of manhood to government,'[172] he ejaculated. Philosophically, fascism was appreciated as 'the last orgasm of an over mature and already sentient European civilization.'[173] Mosley warned potential adherents that 'we want men, not eunuchs, in our ranks ... . In fact, in our movement we seek to create in advance a microcosm of national manhood-re-born.'[174] Obtrusive fascist male sexuality was translated into the techniques of fascist violence. At the Olympia meeting there were reports that a man was ejected "'minus his trousers. His private parts exposed" ... (a favourite Blackshirt trick was to cut the braces or belts of interrupters so that, in the days before skin-clinging clothes, they had to hold up their trousers and could not use their hands for fighting.'[175] The Blackshirts compounded their own sense of virility by symbolically castrating the opponent, asserting hegemony over heterosexual potency.

British fascist sexuality was measured against the effetism and decadence of Modernist intellectuals and the 'old women' who ruled Britain. A.K. Chesterton recommended the merits of sublimation before explaining how 'in an age of health sex and its mutual benefits are taken as a matter of course. Under Fascism, which holds introversion suspect, an atmosphere will be created favourable to health. The bladder of lunatic obsession with sex will be pricked.'[176] Chesterton challenged the legitimacy of the British ruling class not by criticizing policies, but by imagining each figure in government as a shape-shifting hermaphrodite:

> Mrs Baldwin, the PM, offers to masculinity only the odour of a pipe. Mrs MacDonald, the Lord President of the Council, differs only from orthodox femininity by talking eternally without ever saying a word. Tart Miss Eden pits her flapper brains, without the accompanying charm, against the real men like Mussolini and Hitler. The nation whirls and faints amidst these oppressive feminine vapours.[177]

Such adolescent sarcasm and puerile witticism was the only available lighter side to over-blown fascist rhetoric.

Through the starry-eyes of his followers, Mosley was the anti-type to the effeminate, loquacious, and perverse member of the ruling class in Depression-era Britain. Defying the matriarchal hold on his nation, Mosley was a man who 'thinks and feels for Britain as a man, and all true men, all true women, recognize his lead and follow him unfalteringly through ordeals which only they can face and they can survive.'[178] He was portrayed as a model of virility and masculine endowments as 'his tall athletic frame, with its dynamic force and immense reserve of strength; his unconquerable spirit, with its grandeur of courage and resolve [made him] an outstanding leader of men.'[179] As a 'leader of men' it was Mosley's task to define the new fascist men who would follow him; it sufficed that the women serve as the cheer-leaders.

By 1932, after the humiliating defeat of his New Party, main-stream politics could no longer sate Mosley's masculine appetite. The BUF was formed in Mosley's image as a para-military organization in which the Leader could finally synthesize his two great talents and life-long ambitions – to be a leader of his generation and to become a 'professional man.' In the BUF Mosley 'reverted to type and lived in the spirit of the professional army where I began; I was half soldier, half politician.'[180] The new British fascist man was Mosley in miniature, also 'half soldier and half politician, partly a tough warrior in hard and practical tests, and partly an inspired idealist who marched for the stars with his feet firmly on the ground.'[181] With Mosley busy in the occupation of moulding his followers to his Spartan and athletic likeness, there was scarce intellectual energy left to design the new fascist woman.

On the one hand, when Mosley was absorbed in the creation of the new fascist man, his own women and his 'normal woman' were relegated to the background. On the other hand, Mosley's masculine fascism was not auto-erotic. It depended on the compliance of the women in his private life, and was sustained by the enthusiasm among some British women for the sexually charged atmosphere in which their hero was worshipped. While his opponents type-cast him as the villain of his generation, to his followers he was the only hero, and his masculine assertions fed the flames of their ardour. The young Blanche Greaves, Women's District Leader in Kingston, saw him as 'a wonderful person, as a one off person, you had one in a generation. Some people might have thought it was Churchill, but I thought it was O.M.'[182] As Gladys Walsh remembered, 'he was one of the great leaders of all time, I think. And above all things, he was a man.'[183]

Notes on Chapter 5

1   Quoted in Robert Skidelsky, *Oswald Mosley* (London, 1975), p.476. In his post-war philosophical treatise, Mosley explained how psychologists may be 'fair judges of the neurotics who pass through their consulting rooms, but very poor judges of Statesmen whom they have not ever seen. Their experience has been concerned with disease, not with the problems of astounding vitality.' Oswald Mosley, *The Alternative* (Ramsbury, 1947), p.281.

2   Oswald Mosley, *My Life* (London, 1968), pp.21–2.

3   Oswald Mosley, *The Greater Britain* (London, 1932), p.36.

4   A.K. Chesterton, *Oswald Mosley, Portrait of a Leader* (London, 1937), p.114.

5   ed. Rosita Forbes, 'These Women Make History 1: Women Around the Dicta-
    tors,' in *Women of All Lands* (London, 1939), pp.30–5.
6   Margherita Sarfatti, *The Life of Benito Mussolini*, trans. Frederic Whyte (Lon-
    don, 1925), p.346.
7   Diana Mosley, *A Life of Contrasts* (London, 1977), p.123.
8   George L. Mosse, *Nationalism and Sexuality* (New York, 1985), p.157.
9   Vittorio Mussolini, *Mussolini: The Tragic Women in his Life*, trans. Graham Shell
    (London, 1973), pp.59–60. In her own account of their marriage, Rachele
    Mussolini made similar claims of her role in Mussolini's life as a strong sup-
    porter in the background of his public life. She also attributed his infidelity to
    the emotions he excited in women, and not to his own philandering nature: 'I
    do not deny that he had some love affairs, but the fanatical devotion he inspired
    made them readily comprehensible, and he was always the first to tell me about
    them. Sometimes his contrition was positively comic.' Rachele Mussolini, *My
    Life with Mussolini* (London, 1959), p.78.
10 George L. Mosse, *Nationalism and Sexuality*, p.156. While some critics argue
    that Mussolini tried to portray himself as a stern family man, more recent
    research has drawn attention to the fact that Mussolini was also developing a
    competing image of supreme virility, and his propagandists tried to build a
    myth of immortality around the Duce. His birthdays, his illnesses and the fact
    that he had become a grandfather were not to be published in the Italian
    press. He kept his head close shaven to hide any signs of grey. 'No references
    were made to his family life, to his role as a husband or father. The image of
    the family man would presumably soften his virility. Interestingly, none of
    the directives cited by Cannistraro excludes information about the lovers and
    amorous exploits he was "known" to have.' Barbara Spackman, *Fascist Virilities*
    (Minneapolis, 1996). pp.2–3. See also Maria Fraddosio, 'The Fallen Hero: The
    Myth of Mussolini and Fascist Women in the Italian Social Republic (1943–
    5),' *Journal of Contemporary History*, 3 (1996), 99–124.
11 See Ernest R. Pope, *Munich Playground* (London, 1943); Albert B. Gerber, *The
    Life of Adolf Hitler* (Philadelphia, 1961); Glenn B. Infield, *Eva and Adolf* (New
    York, 1974); Hans Peter Bleuel, *Sex and Society in Nazi Germany* (Philadelphia,
    1973). As Barrow has noted, 'Hitler's sex life, or lack of one, remained a
    subject of world-wide interest.' Andrew Barrow, *Gossip* (London, 1978), p.92.
12 Alan Bullock, *Hitler: A Study in Tyranny* (Long Aire, 1964), pp.391–2.
13 Alan Bullock, *Hitler: A Study in Tyranny*, p.396.
14 John Carey, *The Intellectuals and the Masses* (London, 1992), p.203.
15 Baroness Ravensdale, *In Many Rhythms* (London, 1953), p.196.
16 Susan Sontag, *Under the Sign of Saturn* (New York, 1980), p.93. There is a
    parallel in the case of Mussolini whose 'only sensual pleasure was sex. He had
    always had affairs, perhaps because they satisfied his lust for power. He be-
    lieved that the masses, like women, admired masterful men. Mussolini enjoyed

seducing and mastering women, but he enjoyed even more seducing and mastering the masses.' Jasper Ridley, *Mussolini* (London, 1997), p.170.

17 Oswald Mosley, *My Life*, p.365. Although he tried to burst the myth of Hitler's hypnotic powers, it was also noted that Mosley had similarly bewitching powers over his audiences. As James Lees Milne observed: 'He had in him the stuff of which zealots are made. His eyes flashed fire, dilated and contracted like a mesmerist's. His voice rose and fell in hypnotic cadences.' James Lees Milne, *Another Self* (London, 1984), p.97.

18 Nicholas Mosley, *Beyond the Pale* (London, 1983), p.70.

19 Robert Skidelsky, *Oswald Mosley*, p.339.

20 Interview with Nicholas Mosley, Lord Ravensdale, by the author, 25 September 1996.

21 Nicholas Mosley, *Rules of the Game* (London, 1982), p.180.

22 Oswald Mosley, *My Life*, pp.21–2.

23 Oswald Mosley, *My Life*, p.21.

24 Oswald Mosley, *My Life*, p.21.

25 'Apart from games, the dreary waste of public school existence was only relieved by learning or homosexuality; at the time I had no capacity for the former and I never had any taste for the latter. My attitude to homosexuality was then much less tolerant than now, because I have long taken the view on basic grounds of liberty that adults should be free to do what they wished in private, provided they do not interfere with others.' Oswald Mosley, *My Life*, p.35.

26 Oswald Mosley, *My Life*, p.21.

27 Robert Skidelsky, *Oswald Mosley*, p.67.

28 Nicholas Mosley, *Rules of the Game*, p.8.

29 Oswald Mosley, *My Life*, p.7.

30 Oswald Mosley, *My Life*, p.11.

31 Cynthia's somewhat uncertain maternal ancestry was a sticking-point for the BUF during the 1930s. Time and again Mosley's speakers were questioned as to the Leader's late wife's Jewish forebears, as it was assumed that her grandfather, Levi Zeigler Leiter, must have been a Jew. Although the *Dictionary of American Biography* states that Levi Leiter was a descendant of James Van Leiter, a Dutch Calvinist who came from Australia in 1790, Cynthia's ancestry was still considered ambiguous. For example, 'at the meeting at Luton a question was asked regarding an *attack* [my italics] published in the *Sunday Referee*, stating that Lady Cynthia Mosley was Jewish. The Leader replied that his late wife's father was the late Lord Curzon, who had nearly 1000 years of British ancestry, and her mother was American, not of Jewish, but of Dutch descent.' 'Attack on Late Lady Cynthia Mosley,' *Blackshirt*, No. 151, 13 March 1936. Mullaly argued that 'it is a debatable point whether Mosley would have been in the position, in later years, to have whipped up his notorious anti-Semitic campaign, had it not been for the tragic death of his first wife in 1933 ... she herself was of Jewish extraction.' Frederic Mullaly, *Fascism Inside England* (London, 1946), p.16.

32 When Diana Mitford asked her father if she could learn German, upon the recommendation of Prof. Lindemann, Lord Redesdale responded: "'Certainly not." "Oh Favre why not? After all, Tom is learning it." "That is different. Tom is a boy."' Diana Mosley, *A Life of Contrasts*, p.58.

33 Speaking in Glasgow in 1925 Lady Cynthia explained: 'Socialism ... represented the first time that the principles of Christianity had even been brought into politics. She thought the fundamental reason for the failure of the present system of government was that it contravened the very principles of Christianity itself.' 'Labour's Lode Star: Lady Cynthia Mosley's Clyde Baptism in Glasgow,' *Bulletin and Scots Pictorial*, 9 November 1925.

34 Nicholas Mosley, *Rules of the Game*, p.26.

35 'Cut by Society: Lady Cynthia Mosley's Complaint,' *Daily Telegraph*, 15 August 1928.

36 Quoted in 'Cut by Society: Lady Cynthia Mosley's Complaint,' *Daily Telegraph*, 15 August 1928. No matter how much she tried to demonstrate her sincerity as a Labour convert, the press had a field day in showing up the contradictions between the Mosleys' smart-set behaviour and the lip-service they paid to socialist principles. See 'Mrs. Mosley Moves: Luxury Hotel to a Boarding House: Smethwick Comedy,' *Daily Express*, 7 December 1926; 'The New Socialism,' *Morning Post*, 29 July 1927.

37 Baroness Ravensdale, *In Many Rhythms*, p.137.

38 *Hansard*, HC, 31 October 1929, Vol. 231, cols. 417–22.

39 Quoted in Martin Pugh, *Women and the Women's Movement in Britain 1914–1959* (London, 1992), p.171.

40 Baroness Ravensdale, *In Many Rhythms*, p.98.

41 Oswald Mosley, *My Life*, p.111.

42 Part of the first contingent of MPs to resign in the 'Mosley Secessions,' she 'met the Party Executive Committee on Saturday, the 14th February [1931], and, in reply to a question, expressed dissatisfaction with the position of the Labour Party. At a public meeting in the evening, in reply to a question on the report appearing in the press respecting resignations, she said that resignation was contemplated but she would not say anything definite without consultation with her husband.' PRO30/69/381.

43 Interview with Nicholas Mosley, Lord Ravensdale, by the author, 25 September 1996.

44 ed. Stanley Olson, *Harold Nicolson: Diaries and Letters 1930–1964* (London, 1980), p.23.

45 ed. Alan Bishop, *Vera Brittain, Diary of the Thirties 1932–1939* (London, 1986), p.93. Entry for 5 October 1932.

46 Baroness Ravensdale, *In Many Rhythms*, p.141.

47 *In Memory of Cynthia Mosley*, [date?], p.5. Joyce Papers, University of Sheffield.

48 'My Husband's Party,' *London News*, April 1933.

49 Oswald Mosley, 'Fascism Will End the Battle of the Sexes,' *Fascist Week*, No.
    10, 12 January 1934. What was also indicative of Mosley's shift of vision on
    the woman question was the way Cynthia was increasingly idealized in BUF
    propaganda, and honoured for her maternity and womanly virtues. For in-
    stance, the BUF published the elegantly bound volume, *In Memory of Cynthia
    Mosley* [1935?], filled with excerpts from her parliamentary addressed on the
    Rural Amenities Bill and the Widow's, Orphans and Old Age Pensions Bill,
    with tributes by an array of eminent persons, and adorned by a Madonna-like
    portrait of her holding her youngest child.

50 Diana Mosley, *A Life of Contrasts*, p.176.

51 Quoted in Nicholas Mosley, *Beyond the Pale*, pp.146–7.

52 Mary Agnes Hamilton, *Remembering My Good Friends* (London, 1944), p.181.

53 Quoted in Nicholas Mosley, *Rules of the Game*, p.114.

54 Nicholas Mosley, *Rules of the Game*, p.33.

55 It is claimed that Mosley did not wish to dominate or exploit women and that
    he enjoyed competition between equals. 'I claimed that in that respect, for
    nearly all his life, he actually did play according to the strange upper-class game.
    He never took advantage of women who might have been glamorized by his
    power. He only ran after people of his own set. That set at the time was a very
    free-living, what might be called an immoral set, but those were its morals: a
    man ... only made advances to married women of their social background who
    would know what the rules were.' Interview with Nicholas Mosley, Lord
    Ravensdale, by the author, 25 September 1996.

56 Interview with Nicholas Mosley, Lord Ravensdale, by the author, 25 Septem-
    ber 1996.

57 Nicholas Mosley, *Rules of the Game*, p.96.

58 'Certainly my father tried very hard not to be hypocritical about this. All the
    letters he wrote to my mother kept on saying "I know I have been flirting with
    so and so, but it doesn't matter, it is trivial." My mother said "alright, I under-
    stand what you are trying to say and understand it is trivial to you and should be
    trivial to me but it isn't, I can't help it," and then she minded. My father
    couldn't ever come to terms with that because he felt genuinely that she shouldn't
    have minded ... . But if she had gone off I am sure he would have minded.'
    Interview with Nicholas Mosley, Lord Ravensdale, by the author, 25 Septem-
    ber 1996.

59 Oswald Mosley, 'The Philosophy of Fascism,' *Fascist Quarterly*, 1, 1 (January
    1935), 38–43.

60 Oswald Mosley, 'Stand by the King: Defeat Financial Democrats' Attempt to
    Smuggle King Edward from his Throne,' *Action*, No.42, 5 December 1936.

61 Margherita Sarfatti, *The Life of Benito Mussolini*, p.245. In the same vein, Mus-
    solini, 'who began his life as a Socialist, has passed through many stages of
    opinion in the course of his evolution. But his evolution may be likened to an

ascending straight line. This is his true consistency; and it would be absurd to quote any stage of his past, against his present. The same may be said of the political doctrine underlying Fascism. Fascism never possessed a ready-made philosophy. It arose as a Party of action.' James Strachey Barnes, *The Universal Aspects of Fascism* (London, 1928), p.30.

62 Oswald Mosley, *The Greater Britain* (London 1932), p.16. In his autobiography/apologia, he wished to explain his political about-turns, particularly the sudden intellectual conversion in 1945–46 from fascist nationalism to Europeanism, in the following manner: 'At my worst, I have never made any claim to infallibility, which I leave to those responsible for the present condition of the world. After the war I faced fresh facts, learnt from my mistakes, and felt free to become a European.' Oswald Mosley, *My Life*, p.287.

63 Nicholas Mosley, *Beyond the Pale*, p.4.

64 'One of her [Emerald Cunard's] special favourites among the beautiful women she regularly invited was Lady Mosley. Lady Mosley (who according to Sir Oswald Mosley, was nicknamed "Golden Corn" by Lady Cunard and designated by her to take over the leadership of London society in due course) saw something else in her friend besides social skill and wit.' Anne Chisholm, *Nancy Cunard* (London, 1979), pp.158–9.

65 Letter to Diana Guinness from Nancy Mitford, 25 April 1935, in ed. Charlotte Mosley, *Love from Nancy: The Letters of Nancy Mitford* (London, 1994), p.96.

66 Jonathan and Catherine Guinness, *The House of Mitford* (Harmondsworth, 1984), p.324.

67 Diana Mosley, *Loved Ones* (London, 1985), p.156.

68 Diana Mosley, *A Life of Contrasts*, pp.165–6.

69 Nicholas Mosley, *Rules of the Games*, p.242.

70 Interview with Nicholas Mosley, Lord Ravensdale, by the author, 25 September 1996.

71 An exception to the rule of Diana's non-intervention in British fascist politics was one occasion on 27 October 1935, when she made a spectacle of herself at a demonstration in Hyde Park held by the British Non-Sectarian Anti-Nazi Council. She was the only one in the audience to vote against a resolution calling for economic sanctions, and she gave the fascist salute.

72 Diana Mosley, *A Life of Contrasts*, p.107.

73 Diana Mosley, *A Life of Contrasts*, p.117.

74 That Diana and Magda Goebbels (1901–45) should have been good friends is understandable when we consider some parallels between Magda and Joseph Goebbels' relationship and that of Diana and Oswald Mosley. Magda's background was in high society, and she was converted to Nazism by a speech delivered by Goebbels in Berlin. She divorced her first husband and became Goebbels' secretary. Their wedding took place on 12 December 1931, and their Berlin home became a magnet to Hitler and to top Nazi officials. However,

Goebbels was also a 'noted philanderer, sometimes carrying on liaisons in the bedroom next to hers.' Sharon Cosner and Victoria Cosner, *Women Under the Third Reich* (Westport, 1998), p. 57.

75 Oswald Mosley, *My Life*, p.368.

76 Part of the Government's case against Mosley in 1940 was that the BUF was under foreign influence, and that through the Museum Investment Trust Ltd., formed as a holding company, 'it was alleged that in the months of June and July 1938 Sir Oswald Mosley entered into association with persons concerned with a wireless broadcasting station to be erected in Germany.' HO45/24891/34–65. For a detailed history of Mosley's preparation for the wireless concession and Diana Mosley's role as a facilitator of the business arrangements see W.J. West, *Truth Betrayed* (London, 1987).

77 '1939 As Seen by Lady Mosley,' *Comrade*, No.18, April/May 1989.

78 Advisory Committee to Consider Appeals Against Orders of Internment, Witness: Diana Mosley, 2 October 1940, HO144/21995/15–36.

79 HO144/21995/76–77.

80 Advisory Committee to Consider Appeals Against Orders of Internment. Witness: Diana Mosley, 2 October 1940, HO144/21995/15–36. It should also be noted that when their marriage was finally made public in November 1938, the BUF press did its best to welcome the beautiful Diana into the movement with open arms. Instead of accepting a wedding gift from his followers, Mosley made the gesture of asking that a wedding fund be set up to take in donations and subscriptions for the movement. This seemed part of his attempt to play down the impact his marriage would have on his single-minded dedication to his British Union. See 'Wedding Fund Opened – All Will be Given to British Union,' *Action*, No.147, 10 December 1938.

81 Interview with Nicholas Mosley, Lord Ravensdale, by the author, 25 September 1996.

82 Oswald Mosley, *My Life*, p.11. See also Robert Skidelsky, *Interests and Obsessions: Selected Essays* (London, 1993), p.207.

83 Robert Skidelsky, *Oswald Mosley*, p.23.

84 David Cannadine, *The Decline and Fall of the British Aristocracy* (New Haven, 1990), p.549.

85 Nicholas Mosley has explained: 'One of the things both I and Skidelsky talk about was his idea that there was a natural bond between the aristocracy and the working classes, so-called, because of this old country myth of the aristocracy and horses and grooms, and dogs and shooting and the land. My father had a genuine feel about that and there is something in it... He had a gut-feeling of fascism having this natural bond between the aristocratic leader and the mass of people. They would have a natural sympathy with one another, and a natural antagonism to financiers and puritans ... . He felt that both the aristocracy on the one side and the working class on the other had a natural way of ignoring

middle class values.' Interview with Nicholas Mosley, Lord Ravensdale, by the author, 25 September 1996.

86 Alexander Raven, 'Aristocracy of Worth,' *Fascist Week*, No. 13, 2–8 February 1934.

87 'Lucifer,' 'A Land Fit for Britons to Live in,' *Fascist Week*, No. 7, 22–28 December 1933.

88 During his appearance before the Advisory Committee to Consider Appeals Against Orders of Internment, on 3 July 1940, Mosley was questioned on his frequent visits abroad: 'A. For 20 years past, exactly 20 years, I have been an addict of foreign travel. I can tell you why. When we were young and silly we were a quarrelling class, the Conservative Party, and the only fun we could have was abroad. If we had our fun here they could have said look at the rich Socialists and our photographs would have been in all the papers.' HO283/14/2–117.

89 Lewis Broad and Leonard Russell, *The Way of the Dictators* (London, 1935), p.290.

90 Ellen Wilkinson and Edward Conze, *Why Fascism* (London, 1934), p.64. 'In England, Miss Wilkinson said, Fascism would not come through collections of people who took Sir Oswald Mosley's half-crowns and dinners – Fascism in Britain was coming through Lord Trenchard, and his officer-class police force.' *Report of the National Conference of Labour Women*, West Hartlepool, 23–25 May 1933, The Labour Party, Transport House, p.64.

91 'Byronic, Napoleonic, Nietzschean, Mosley was certainly the nearest thing to a political leader of the British *Sonnenkinder* found and his politics expressed their temperament, in its emphasis on athletics and fighting, and uniforms, military comradeship, rough practical jokes, the worship of young male heroes and nostalgia for a primitive past.' Martin Green, *Children of the Sun: A Narrative of "Decadence" in England After 1918* (New York, 1976), p.252.

92 Bertrand Russell, *A History of Philosophy and Its Connection with the Political and Social Circumstances from the Earliest to the Present Day* (London, 1946), p.747.

93 Interview with Nicholas Mosley, Lord Ravensdale, by the author, 25 September 1996.

94 Nancy Mitford, *Pigeon Pie* (London, 1982), p.43. Orwell was under the same impression: 'The British ruling class were not altogether wrong in thinking that Fascism was on their side. It is a fact that any rich man, unless he is a Jew, has less to fear from Fascism than from either Communism or democratic Socialism.' George Orwell, 'The Lion and the Unicorn: Socialism' in eds. Sonia Orwell & Ian Angus, *The Collected Essays, Journalism and Letters of George Orwell: Vol. 2, My Country Right or Left, 1940–1943* (Harmondsworth, 1971), p.92.

95 Richard Griffiths, *Fellow Travellers of the Right* (London, 1980), p.168.

96 Indeed, well-connected women such as Wallis Simpson and Pamela Jackson (née Mitford) could have their dresses made by Anna Wolkoff, William Joyce's

clandestine war-time correspondent. See A.W. Brian Simpson, *In the Highest Degree Odious* (Oxford, 1992), p.148.

97 ed. Anne Oliver Bell, *The Diary of Virginia Woolf: Vol. 4 1931–35* (London, 1982), p.80. Entry for 10 March 1932.

98 Richard Griffiths, *Fellow Travellers of the Right*, p.170.

99 Baroness Ravensdale, *In Many Rhythms*, p.88. Mosley described Lady Cunard as 'a bright little bird of paradise … . If talk flagged and the taciturn great would not perform, she would wake the company up with a direct frontal attack.' Oswald Mosley, *My Life*, p.75.

100 Andrew Barrow, *Gossip*, p.82.

101 Francois Lafitte, *The Internment of Aliens* (London, 1988) p.174

102 It is certainly noteworthy that the fact that Italy and Germany were under fascist regimes did not repel English travellers. On the contrary, exploring the new regimes could be a motive for travel. In 1929, Cresswell remarked how 'tourists returning from Italy were apt to be faced with one invariable question: "Have you seen the Pope?" Today the question has come to be: "Have you seen Mussolini."' C.M. Cresswell, *The Keystone of Fascism* (London, 1929), p.19. In her prime, the fictional Miss Jean Brodie is simultaneously enamoured by images of the Italian Renaissance and the Italian Fascisti, and takes all her summer holidays in Italy, and later in Germany. Upon her return one year she brings her pupils a picture 'of Mussolini's fascisti,' and tells them that "'Mussolini is one of the greatest men in the world, far more so than Ramsay MacDonald and his fascisti."' Muriel Spark, *The Prime of Miss Jean Brodie* (London, 1961), p.44. The 1999 Zefferilli film, *Tea with Mussolini,* likewise portrays a number of English women's love affairs with Florence and Italian artistic splendour during the 1930s and through the war, and the Scorpioni refuse to return to England even when the two countries are at war. Even the staunchly anti-fascist Nancy Cunard had a strange fascination with Italy: 'she missed it whenever she was away, yet no sooner was she back than she longed to be elsewhere. Her visits, though numerous, were therefore never a long duration. Besides, the Mussolini regime appalled her and some of its more puerile manifestations even affected her personally.' Daphne Fielding, *Emerald and Nancy* (London, 1968), p.80. The idea that Germany was a playground for women of the British elite was confirmed by Nichols' experiences that 'in the thousands of mile I travelled throughout [Germany] the only drunken people I observed were two English society women at a cocktail bar in Berlin.' Beverly Nichols, *News From England/ or A Country Without a Hero* (London, 1938), p.90.

103 When Mosley was questioned on BU members attendance at the Nazi Party Conferences in Germany, he explained that the members of his movement did not go with his consent. He did reveal, however, that official invitations were sent to the BU for the Nuremberg Party Festival through Lady Dyer. See HO283/ 13/2–125. Diana, Lady Cooper described her uncomfortable experience at the

Nuremberg Conference in 1933 in her autobiography, and although she admitted that 'the organization impressed us,' she and Duff Cooper were 'only too delighted to leave the hall quarter-way through [Hitler's] oration.' Diana Cooper, *The Light of Common Day* (Harmondsworth, 1959), p.123.

104 David Pryce-Jones, *Unity Mitford* (London, 1976), p.121.

105 Diana Mosley, *A Life of Contrasts*, p.125.

106 On the one hand, Unity was a 'direct pipeline to the British leaders and Hitler used her for propaganda purposes and for sounding out the British leaders about the approaching international conflict.' Glenn B. Infield, *Eva and Adolf*, p.166. On the other hand, 'Joachim von Ribbentrop and Unity have hated each other cordially, ever since Ribbentrop was Nazi ambassador to the Court of St James. For Unity and Ribbentrop quarrelled about the methods of advancing the Fascist movement in England.' Ernest R. Pope, *Munich Playground*, p.117.

107 On 5 March 1938 Unity wrote to her 'Dear Cousin Winston' about the justice of Hitler's Anschluss. As she told him, with and air of authority: 'I really do think that you, in common with most English people, are very misinformed about Austrian affairs, which are consistently misrepresented in the British press.' Letter from Unity Mitford to Winston Churchill, The Chartwell Trust, The Churchill Archive, Cambridge.

108 Jessica Mitford, *Hons and Rebels* (London, 1960), p.59.

109 Quoted in David Pryce-Jones, *Unity Mitford*, p.79. Nancy Mitford's treatment of Unity in *Wigs on the Green* (1935) testified to what degree the young fanatic could not be taken seriously. Nancy Mitford's satirical *roman a clef*, in which the BUF appeared as the Union Jackshirts, Mosley as Captain Jack, and Unity as Eugenia Malmains is often understood to be a staunchly anti-fascist novel. However, Nancy was also a short-time member of the BUF, she and her husband Peter Rodd purchased blackshirts and attended some meetings, and it was only after Diana's humourless reception of *Wigs on the Green* that Nancy's flirtation with fascism finally ceased. She had amended the novel after Diana and Sir Oswald reacted to the many scenes in which the 'Lead' appeared, but ended up exasperated by the family censorship. She wrote to Diana: 'I also know your point of view, that Fascism is something too serious to be dealt with in a funny book at all. Surely that is a little unreasonable? Fascism is now such a notable feature of modern life all over the world that it must be possible to consider it in any context, when attempting to give a picture of life as it is lived today...' To Diana Guinness, from Nancy Mitford, 18 June 1935, in ed. Charlotte Mosley, *The Letters of Nancy Mitford: Love from Nancy*, p.100.

110 Quoted in David Pryce-Jones, *Unity Mitford*, p.233.

111 Geoffrey West, 'Aristocrats,' *Action*, Vol. 1, No. 1, 8 October 1931.

112 Doreen Bell, 'Mayfair Parasites: Pampered Idleness,' *Action*, No. 119, 28 May 1938.

113 Lady Alexandra (Baba) Metcalfe, married to the Prince of Wales' former equerry, 'Fruity' Metcalfe, filled the gap that Cynthia had left in more than one

way. 'As I have made fairly clear in the second volume of my book – it was certainly very common knowledge, but I was a bit diffident because people were still alive – what he also did after my mother died, but not before, was have an extremely heart-felt relationship with her younger sister, my aunt Baba Metcalfe. He did, after my mother died, have this relationship which carried on in parallel with Diana through the thirties. So that was risky enough, that was quite a difficult juggling act to keep up.' Interview with Nicholas Mosley, Lord Ravensdale, by the author, 25 September 1996.

114 *Evening News*, 5 May 1934.

115 Baroness Ravensdale, *In Many Rhythms*, p.144.

116 Lady Houston was another of the very eccentric women who were attracted to fascism. She had 'a little Belgian griffon dog, which she called Benito after Benito Mussolini, whom she admired mainly because he had dosed the Italian Socialists and Communists with castor-oil. In one of her letters to the Duce, she invited him to come over here and treat the English Reds and Pinks in the same fashion.' Richard Griffiths, *Fellow Travellers of the Right*, p.25.

117 'Fascist Chief of Staff Married,' *The Fascist Week*, No. 7, 22 December 1933.

118 'Lady Mosley Attends Hampstead 'At Home,''' *Blackshirt*, No. 85, 7 December 1934.

119 On 29 February 1939, 430 persons attended, including Lady Downe, Lady Lucas, and Lady Maud Mosley (HO144/21281/112–114). On 5 March 1940, 480 persons attended, including Lady Cuncliffe, Lady Domvile, Dowager Viscountess Downe, Lady Mosley, and Lady Pearson (HO45/24895/22–24). While the BUF's success in attracting titled women was more marked in its breach than in its observance, other organizations of the far Right were more successful in enlisting this class of women. The Right Club ledger (*ca*.May 1940) listed 141 men and 100 women. Women subscribers included: Hon. Mrs Ramsay, Princess de Chimay, Lady Ronald Graham, Lady Brindley, Lady Saltman, Princess Blucher, Lady McKins, Hon. Lady Clark, and Viscountess Selby. Copy of the Right Club ledger with Brian Simpson.

120 *Daily Worker*, 6 June 1934.

121 James Lees Milne, *Another Self* (London, 1984), p.97.

122 ed. Stanley Olson, *Harold Nicolson: Diaries and Letters 1930–1964*, p.36. Entry for Rome, 6 January 1932.

123 E. Tangye Lean, *The Napoleonists* (London, 1970), p.315.

124 A.J. Cummings, 'Mosley as Fascist Valentino: His Albert Hall Stage,' *News Chronicle*, 23 April 1934.

125 Frank Waters' Journal, 15 October 1939, Frank Waters Papers, McMaster University, Box 8, F.1.

126 'Among His Own: The Leader Visits East London Districts,' *Blackshirt*, No. 183, 24 October 1934. The adulation of Mosley's portrait became somewhat of a BUF tradition. When Mosley was still interned under DR18B, his supporters

who were at liberty organized a birthday party in his absence and 'the room was decorated with the BU standards of Westminster and St George Branch – at one end of the room was a large picture of Sir Oswald Mosley illuminated by lamps.' HO45/25702.

127 Letter from W/C/O West Hants to D/L Dorset, 14 November 1937, Saunders Collection, University of Sheffield, File A.3.
128 Richard Reynell Bellamy, *The Memoirs of a Fascist Beast*, unpublished manuscript.
129 Advisory Committee, 22 July 1940, HO283/16/2–65. That Mosley has been chosen as the subject of a four-part biopic (produced by Marks and Gran, starring Jonathan [beef] Cake, and broadcast on Channel Four between 19 February and 5 March 1998) is further testimony to his star-quality and Hollywood-appeal. *Mosley* is, in effect, an exploration and exploitation of the Leader's sexual politics, and soft-pornographic bedroom scenes take up nearly as much screen time as illustration of his political career.
130 My italics. James Lees Milne, *Another Self*, p.97.
131 Diana Mosley, *A Life of Contrasts*, p.176.
132 Letter from Diana Mosley to Brian Simpson, 26 December 1989. Original with Brian Simpson.
133 Trevor Grundy, *Memoir of a Fascist Childhood* (London, 1998), p.32
134 Rom Landau, *Love for a Country* (London, 1939), p.68.
135 Margherita Sarfatti, *The Life of Benito Mussolini*, p.76. It should also be noted in this context that the Mitford daughters who went to the Left were the ones who produce literature, while Unity and Diana were the subjects of literature and lived their lives during the 1930s as a saga.
136 Freidrich Nietzsche, *The Nietzsche Reader*, trans. R.J. Hollingdale (Harmondsworth, 1977), p.232.
137 Aldous Huxley, *Point Counter Point* (Harmondsworth, 1961), p.281.
138 Aldous Huxley, *Point Counter Point*, p.282. In keeping with Mosley's lack of interest in literature, he never read Huxley's novel. 'As far as I know Huxley hardly knew my father, but they must have bumped into one another in those days. In fact, after the war, when I read *Point Counter Point*, I said to my father "what about you and Aldous Huxley, how well did Huxley know you? You know there is this character Everard Webley?" and my father had never heard of it ... . He certainly never read it, he didn't read novels ... . He couldn't understand why anyone would write fiction when there was extraordinary things to write about fact.' Interview with Nicholas Mosley, Lord Ravensdale, by the author, 25 September 1996.
139 Quoted in Nicholas Mosley, *Rules of the Game*, p.155.
140 Nancy Mitford certainly hoped that Nazism could be undermined by a good dose of Mitford humour. 'Sister Nancy was so determined to "save" Unity from Hitler that she forged a family tree that included a Jewish ancestor and

sent the document to Himmler, who soon discovered it was faked.' Glenn B. Infield, *Eva and Adolf*, p.165.

141 H.G Wells, *The Holy Terror* (New York, 1939), p. 110. Upon the formation of the BUF Mosley wrote to Wells, and sent him a copy of *The Greater Britain*, in hopes that Wells would see the fulfilment of his wish for a 'Liberal Fascisti' in Mosley's new endeavour. See Warren Wagar, *H.G. Wells and the World State* (New Haven, 1961), p. 196. Wells clearly rejected and mocked Mosley's fascism, as is evident in his reaction to the Albert Hall meeting of 1934 which is recorded in Wells' *Experiment in Autobiography* (New York, 1934), pp.669–70.

142 Winifred Holtby and Norman Ginsbury, *Take Back Your Freedom* (London, 1939), p.41. As a bachelor and latently homosexual character, the Clayton figure is also based on Hitler.

143 Harold Nicolson, *The English Sense of Humour and Other Essays* (London, 1956), p.35.

144 *Kilmarnock Standard*, 6 July 1935. Quoted in Brian Harrison, *Prudent Revolutionaries*, p.97.

145 William Gibson, 'Turning Money Into Light,' *Details*, (February 1994), p.69.

146 Mary Agnes Hamilton, *Remembering My Good Friends*, p.182.

147 Mosley self-consciously tried to match Byron's masculine feats: in 1925 Bob Boothby believed that 'this was the period when Mosley saw himself as Byron rather than Mussolini. He was certainly a powerful swimmer and used to disappear at intervals into the lagoon [in Venice] to commune with himself.' Robert J.G. Boothby, *I Fight to Live* (London, 1947), p.171. His son remembered that on a family trip to Venice in 1930 or 1931, 'my father set out to swim from the city of Venice to the Lido, which is an enormous swim, because Byron had done it... that was the time that he was behaving rather badly.' George Gordon, the 6th Lord Byron, had occupied a similar position in the British consciousness during the 1820s as Sir Oswald Mosley did in the 1930s: both were 'new men' on the fringe of respectable society, and both failed to convince their contemporaries in their social caste to rebel against the tradition that bolstered their status. Byron made himself master of the Satanic school, showed disdain for the aristocracy which gave him birth and privilege, and grudgingly admired the enemy, Napoleon. Mosley too was characterized as 'a genuine experimentalist looking for a good plan – a Napoleon itching for any campaign.' Letter from George Catlin to Winifred Holtby, 5 April 1931, Vera Brittain Collection, McMaster University, File 6. Mosley made himself the leader of British fascism, reacting in what would have seemed a predictable way to the decline and fall of the British aristocracy, and astounded his contemporaries by setting up the leaders of Fascist regimes in Europe as his role models. Both men were estranged from their fathers; both eventually rejected the positions and opportunities open to them as a consequence of their origins; and yet, both maintained a strong bond with their

aristocratic identity. Both sought vent for their energies and dedication to the principle of action in travel and recourse to foreign models of conduct. In fact, Mosley travelled to Italy in 1932, to learn from Mussolini's fascism, with Christopher Hobhouse, a descendant of John Cam Hobhouse, the Napoleonist friend of Byron. Both were obsessed with their sexual potency, and Mosley too could well have been described as 'mad, bad, and dangerous to know.' Both men were egregious for their womanising; both exhibited the traits of the Gothic villain (the first vampire was modelled on Byron); and both men had a predilection for the women of their own class. As a 'footnote,' both walked with a pronounced limp, which they compensated for by frequent virile assertions. (Ironically, while H.G. Wells' described Lord Horatio/Mosley as a romantic personality, he added the detail that he was 'Byron without the limp.' H.G. Wells, *The Holy Terror*, p.109.) Consequently, even by the standards of physical appearance, the two men, notorious for their romance and restlessness, could be allied in the public imagination.

148 Interview with Nicholas Mosley, Lord Ravensdale, by the author, 25 September 1996.

149 'Why was that continuity of the Hellenic tradition, which is the soul of Europe, driven from the place of rebirth, in the soil of England, to live again and to live for ever in the German genius of Goethe and Schiller – which was both preluded and followed by all that is finest in the spirit of France – and was reflected again in the revolt of Byron, Shelley and Swinburne.' Oswald Mosley, *The Alternative*, p.27.

150 From a speech Mosley delivered on 1 November 1934 in *Mosley: The Facts* (London, 1957), p.95.

151 Oswald Mosley, *Tomorrow We Live* (London, 1938), p.72.

152 Lord Byron, *Manfred* (I,ii,40).

153 Interview with Nicholas Mosley, Lord Ravensdale, by the author, 25 September 1996.

154 Oswald Mosley, *The Greater Britain*, p.41.

155 Oswald Mosley, *The Greater Britain*, p.41.

156 Oswald Mosley, *The Greater Britain*, p.41.

157 Oswald Mosley, *The Greater Britain*, p.40.

158 Oswald Mosley, *100 Questions Asked and Answered* (London, 1936).

159 Oswald Mosley, *The Greater Britain*, p.40.

160 Special Branch transcription of a meeting held by the BUF at Chelsea Town Hall, 26 April 1937, HO144/21063/50.

161 Special Branch verbatim report of a speech delivered by Mosley at the conference of senior headquarters officials, 17 January 1939, HO144/20146/95–110.

162 Winifred Holtby, *Women in a Changing Civilization* (London, 1934), p.193.

163 Quoted in Oswald Mosley, 'Spirit of the Blackshirts,' *Fascist Week*, No. 3, 24 November 1933.

164 Oswald Mosley, 'Fascism Will End the Battle of the Sexes,' *Fascist Week*, No. 10, 12–18 January 1934.

165 Oswald Mosley, *Tomorrow We Live*, p.16.

166 My italics. Advisory Committee to Consider Appeals Against Orders of Internment, Witness: Sir Oswald Mosley, 3 July 1940, HO283/14/2–117.

167 Interview with Nicholas Mosley, Lord Ravensdale, by the author, 25 September 1996. While the choice of his own mother was an arguably sign of his lack of interest, Lady Mosley served his cause well. As one former member recalled: 'Whereas most of us were somewhat overawed by Mosley himself, we were perfectly at ease with his mother, who was easily approachable and motherly.' Anne Page in ed. J. Christian, *Mosley's Blackshirts* (London, 1986), p.15.

168 Interview with Nicholas Mosley, Lord Ravensdale, by the author, 25 September 1996.

169 Letter from Diana Mosley to the author, 5 April 1996. Diana Mosley's comments to me contradict somewhat her own record of Mosley's responses to a short questionnaire in a little journal she possessed called *All About Everybody*. Among the eight questions she would ask her respondents was '4. Do you believe in the equality of the sexes.' To this Mosley answered in the negative. Diana Mosley, *Loved Ones*, pp.10–11.

170 ed. Stein Ugelvik Larsen et al., *Who Were the Fascists* (Bergen, 1980), pp.20–1.

171 From a speech delivered on 8 May 1937 in *Mosley: The Facts*, p.91.

172 Oswald Mosley, 'Steel Creed of an Iron Age,' *Fascist Week*, No. 2, 17 November 1933.

173 James Drennan, *BUF: Oswald Mosley and British Fascism*, p.16.

174 Oswald Mosley, *The Greater Britain*, p.39.

175 Robert Skidelsky, *Oswald Mosley*, p.373. A corroborating account of these fascist techniques is given by Leonard Wise, an East London shopkeeper. He recollects: 'I liked the story of the Blackshirt speaker in Tottenham who was persistently heckled by a Red with the cry "What about Olympia?" "What about Olympia?" asked the speaker sarcastically. "What abaht the bloke wot got thrown down four bleeding flight of stairs, 'ah bleeding trousers torn off, 'is arse, and then got arrested by the police for disorderly conduct?" "You can't believe all the lies you read in the newspapers," replied the speaker." "Newspapers be buggered! " came the reply. "I WOZ THE BLOKE."' ed. J. Christian, *Mosley's Blackshirts*, pp.4–5.

176 A.K. Chesterton,'To the Intellectuals: You Shall Cater for a Sane and Virile Nation,' *Fascist Week*, No. 9, 5–11 January 1934.

177 A.K. Chesterton, 'Return to Manhood: Regiment of Old Women Routed,' *Action*, No. 21, 9 July 1936. Ironically, as his biographer has noted, 'Chesterton enjoyed a happy marriage to a Fabian Socialist and pacifist, and displayed a complete lack of misogyny, enjoying close working relationships with many women.' David Baker, *Ideology of Obsession: A.K. Chesterton and British Fascism* (London, 1996), p.202.

178 A.K. Chesterton, 'Return of Manhood: Regiment of Old Women Routed,' *Action*, No. 21, 9 July 1936.

179 A.K. Chesterton, *Oswald Mosley: Portrait of a Leader*, p.164.

180 Oswald Mosley, *My Life*, p.303.

181 Oswald Mosley, *My Life*, p.305. In his post-war thinking, Mosley developed a somewhat modified typology of men. He devised three categories: the 'Will to Comfort' man (democracy), the 'Will to Power' man (self-serving authoritarianism), and the 'Will to Achievement' man or the 'Thought Deed' man. The latter was the ideal type and would bring to being his new European idea. See Oswald Mosley, *The Alternative*, pp.289–95.

182 Interview with Blanche Greaves by Jeffrey Wallder, from the Archive of the Friends of Oswald Mosley.

183 Interview with Mrs Gladys Walsh, from the Archive of the Friends of Oswald Mosley.

Chapter 6

Behind Bars and Barbed Wire:
Women's Experiences of Internment
Under Defence Regulation 18B, 1940–45

During the Second World War the British Union was outlawed, its publications banned, and 747 of its members interned under Defence Regulation 18B(1A). The first legislative steps in defence of the realm were taken with the Emergency Powers (Defence) Act, which was passed by both Houses of Parliament on 24 August 1939; and an Order in Council affecting the freedom of political discussion and the Press came into effect on 1 September 1939. Further changes were provoked by the German invasion of Denmark and Norway in May 1940, coupled with the discovery on 22 May 1940 of subversive activities on the part of Tyler Kent, a cipher clerk in the American Embassy, and Anna Wolkoff, a leading member of the MP, Captain Maule Ramsay's Right Club. An Order in Council immediately amending Defence Regulation 18B was made on 22 May 1940, and under 18B(1A) the Home Secretary was empowered to detain any person who posed a threat to national security by being a leader or member of any organization that was presumed to be under foreign influence or control.

Caught in the snare of the Defence Regulations, BU members were quick to identify a government conspiracy, and Mosley was convinced that the Labour Party had made the passage of 18B(1A) and his own imprisonment, conditions of their entry into the government.[1] While the Defence Regulations promulgated by a 'democratic' government made victims out of BU members by denying them their civil liberties, it must also be pondered how British Fascists would have acted had the tables been turned. As early as 1932, Harold Nicolson recorded that Mosley could not 'keep his mind off shock troops, the arrest of MacDonald and J.H. Thomas, their internment in the Isle of Wight, and the rolls of drums around Westminster.'[2] Conversely, during the war, some civil libertarians opposed the internment of British fascists under 18B 'notwithstanding the fact that some of the people concerned would mete out similar treatment to Socialists if they had the upper hand.'[3]

While the stories of the British fascist women caught in the net of Defence Regulation 18B are often tragic and invite pathos, their trying war-time experiences should not completely obliterate the fact that they played pro-active roles in the movement prior to 1940 and, indeed, throughout the Second World War. Certainly the legality of 18B(1A) was highly contentious; the bureaucratic administration of the Defence Regulations bordered on the Kafkaesque; the treatment of male and female rank-and-file members of the BU was unnecessarily punitive; the behind-the-scenes machinations of MI5 and the security services led to some arbitrary arrests and many fanciful denunciations; and the Fifth Columnist panic which necessitated the internment of Britain's home-grown fascists appeared to be a symptom of mass hysteria. However, the experiences of BU women must be seen in the context of the round-up of German, Austrian and Italian enemy aliens, many of whom had come to Britain in search of political asylum and refuge from Nazi persecution. The history of British fascist women behind the bars of Holloway Prison and the barbed wire of the camps on the Isle of Man was one of a reversal of fortune: in 1940 the persecutors and would-be collaborators became the victims.

A substantial body of literature has accumulated concerning the functioning of the Defence Regulations, the role of MI5 in counter-espionage work directed against the extreme Right in Britain, and the legal history of 18B. A similarly abundant historiography and collections of testimony record the plight of enemy aliens detained under Royal Prerogative.[4] Existing research, however, has not focused on other developments which will be considered here – the internment of British women; the interesting, albeit short and short-sighted, history of women caught by the surveillance eye; the relationship between women and the intelligence establishment; the treatment of British fascist women and their children during wartime; and the impact of incarceration on women's political convictions and beliefs about the state.

Women Caught By The Official Eye: The Relationship Between Women and the Intelligence Establishment

On 23 November 1933 the decision was taken at a conference in the Home Office that systematic intelligence should be gathered about the BUF by local constabularies, the Metropolitan Police, Special Branch and MI5.[5] In the period before the escalating threat of war, the intelligence establishment observed fascist women in their contingent roles in the BUF and as side-line participants in the chronic feuding at headquarters. Reports made mention of a handful of women who figured prominently at the national level of activity but, more generally, British fascist women were regarded as the lunatics of the lunatic fringe. With the exception of tabulating the number of men to women at some fascist meetings – a practice not followed when recording the composition of communist meetings – Special Branch appeared to be gender-blind and somewhat negligent about monitoring the activities of the BUF's visible minority of women. It also seems that during the 1930s MI5 only recruited men as agents and moles – 'P.G. Taylor' (alias) and W.E.D. Allen most prominent among these – although there is some reason to believe that information reported by a few loose-lipped females confirmed to the authorities the gradual financial sinking of Mosley's fascist ship.[6]

The richer information concerning individual women and MI5 reflection on the consequences of female anti-democratic militancy did not bear much documentary fruit until the end of the 1930s. In an effort to justify orders of internment, the official sources began to explain the chronology and particulars of individual fascist activism. While these later sources disclose elements of personality, ideological stands and sets of mentalities, they reveal as much about the observer as the observed.

On the one hand, the documentary evidence to be garnered from sources relating to cases of internment are invaluable as they offer information on the extent of commitments to fascism and the tenor of anti-war sentiments, and thumb-nail character sketches. On the other hand, these sources fall short of identifying the issues which most absorbed the 18B detainees themselves: what we have in the case files of 18B internees is, in fact, the Home Office's 'shopping list.' Naturally, the Advisory Committee to Consider Appeals Against Orders of Internment was anxious to discover an individual's potential for subversive activity, and the intensity of anti-government opinion. This was only one side, however, as adherence to fascism was not solely a negative reaction to the current political system. Furthermore, in responding to the provocative questions asked by the Advisory Committee, BU appellants were on the defensive, and the veracity of their testimony cannot be relied upon. After Lucy Pearson's first appearance before the Advisory Committee, her non-political sister suggested 'if I'd been in your shoes I should have said anything in order to get out.'[7] It is safe to assume that many women temporarily buried their fascist hatchets in their bids for release.

While many women suffered incarceration for their fascist beliefs, others were instrumental in administering the Defence Regulations, and still others were involved in feeding information to the security services. The relationship between women, British fascism, and the intelligence establishment became considerably more intimate and intrusive with the coming of war. Some BU women who could not blindly collude with the movement's strategy for undermining war-time morale turned police informant, and Olga Bonora, herself an Air Raid Warden, felt obliged to report on the movements of Charles Frederick Watts of the BU's Westminster St George Branch. Upon a visit to that branch in October 1939 she had seen a number of steel helmets and white metal ARP badges. She 'had asked Watts how they had come to be there. He told her ... it was intended to take them to various branches in the East End and that during air raids fascists would wear them. They would pose as air raid wardens and in the general confusion proceed to "beat up" all the Jews they could find.'[8] More covertly, it has been alleged that Mosley's own secretary, Miss Margaret Monk, sent regular reports about the BU to Special Branch.[9] Neither Bonora nor Monk were ever interned.

In 1938, Charles Maxwell-Knight was appointed head of B5b division of MI5, a section newly created to supervise the placing of agents in subversive organizations. As a result of Maxwell-Knight's belief in women's special aptitude to act as *agents provocateurs*, he recruited three female agents, Marjorie Amos, Joan Miller and Helene Louise Munck, to infiltrate Captain Ramsay's Right Club. The young Joan Miller, formerly a salesperson at Elizabeth Arden, was assigned the task of posing as a disgruntled War Office employee so as to win the confidence of Anna Wolkoff, a prominent member of the Right Club. As Miller remembered, 'I got to know Anna too, and whenever I spoke to her I put on a show of opposition to Britain's involvement in the war and support for the Fascist cause – not too emphatically at first, of course, but more openly as time went on. I invented a pre-war romance with a Nazi officer to account for these aberrant views.'[10] The testimony of Maxwell-Knight's female agents helped convict Wolkoff for her role in the Tyler Kent affair. Upon her conviction on two charges under the Official Secrets Act and the passing of a ten-year prison sentence for attempting to send a letter in code to 'one Joyce in Berlin,' the betrayed Wolkoff was heard to threaten Miller's life. Interestingly enough, these women agents were not planted in the Right Club to elicit treacherous pillow-talk from men, (indeed, the middle-aged Mrs Amos reminded Miller of Miss Marple) but to befriend and entrap the women among potential British fascist saboteurs. Indeed, women had come to play a surprisingly prominent role in Captain Ramsay's Right Club by 1940, and while the Right Club had been organized as a predominantly male concern, the various patriotic societies of the extreme right were not willing to spurn female support under war-time conditions.[11]

After her cover was blown with the extreme Right, Miller moved on to counter-espionage work in the CPGB; to 'looking into the innumerable reports from people who dutifully communicated to the authorities their suspicion of some harmless character they took to be a Fifth Columnist;'[12] and in the summer of 1940 she worked in Holloway Prison interviewing suspect enemy aliens. This last task caused her some moral discomfort as she believed 'MI5, by overreacting, had caused unnecessary suffering to many blameless foreigners, and I couldn't help feeling guilty over my small part in the business.'[13] Miller was not alone in her criticism of MI5's methods, and Violet Markham, the first woman to sit on the Home Office Aliens Committee and the 18B Advisory Committee, expressed the apprehension that 'I have always thoroughly disliked everything I have heard of MI5 – I have bristled with Magna Carta and Habeas Corpus when their name is mentioned. Now I am mixed up with them.'[14] These initial personal reservations did not, however, prevent Markham from taking the anonymous denunciations and evidence supplied by MI5 at face value, from following her own agenda when she sat on the panel interrogating Sir Oswald Mosley, or from passing highly subjective judgements on 18B women.[15]

Women were also placed in less glamorous positions of authority over 18B internees as prison guards and camp commandants. Women police and the Women's Voluntary Service were on hand for the arrests of many BU members and supervised the transport of 18B women to the Isle of Man. In a turn of tragic irony, the feminine fascist utopian prophecy of women governing women was actualized in Holloway Prison and on the Isle of Man.

Dangerous Women: Sex, Sabotage and Segregation

From 1940 through to 1945, a grand total of 1,826 persons were interned under Defence Regulation 18B. Of a total of 747 BU members detained under Defence Regulation 18B 1(A), upwards of 96 were women.[16] The pattern of detentions and releases was as follows. The BU's summer of discontent began on 22 May 1940 when the Defence Regulations were passed, and in the course of the next two days 49 men and 10 women were arrested. Sir Oswald Mosley was arrested at his London flat at Dolphin Square and taken to Brixton Prison on 23 May 1940, while the authorities waited until 1 July 1940 to apprehend Diana Mosley at Savehay Farm, Denham. The BU was outlawed under DR18AA on 10 June 1940. There was a massive influx from 131 18B prisoners on 31 May 1940, to 1,428 by 31 August 1940, of whom some 600 were members of the BU or like organizations such as the Right Club, the Imperial Fascist League, The Link and the Nordic League. Olive Burdett (née Hawks), Norah Elam, Muriel Whinfield and Diana deLaessoe had already been detained when 37 more women were scheduled on the order of 30 May 1940, and by October 17 1940 another 30 women were added to the 18B prison population. The first contingent of 43 18B women was transported from Holloway to Port Erin, Isle of Man, on 20 June 1941. 'The leadership were not sent to the Isle of Man because the authorities felt it could strengthen the detainees' fascist attitudes.'[17] By mid-1941, over 500 of the remaining 671 18B detainees were interned on the Isle of Man, while 44 BU men remained in Brixton, and 25 women in Holloway. In September 1942, 17 18B women were under detention in Holloway, while by 2 February 1943, 25 18B women were detained in the same prison and a further 8 women were being held in Aylesbury and Edinburgh prisons. This small increase was not the consequence of fresh arrests but was because a few women had been permitted to return to Holloway from the Isle of Man for reasons of health or family concerns. By 2 March 1943 four more women had been released – Booth, Franklin, Swan and Marsten – and the 18B population in Holloway decreased to 23 women.[18] On 20 November 1943 the Mosleys were released from Holloway on the compassionate grounds that Sir Oswald

232

was suffering from phlebitis, and the married accommodation they had shared with four other couples since December 1941 was closed down. As it was explained to the War Cabinet in September 1944,

> of the persons originally detained as members of the BU some were found, on investigation, to be persons who had been attracted to the Union and had not realized the danger that the Union might be used for the purposes of hindering the war effort, and many of them were found to be persons with no political knowledge who had joined the Union because of personal grievances of various kinds. The policy of reviewing each of the cases periodically has been continued and, with the changes in the war situation, it has been possible, since April 1943, to release many more.[19]

Just over a dozen BU 18Bs had to wait until the end of the war to be released, and most restriction orders continued to be in effect until May 1945.

The total of ninety-six British Union women might well seem a small sample, and not representative of their numbers in the movement. Ann Page has argued that considering the size of the BU Women's Section, the number of women detained was quite small: 'Young women speakers on whose shoulders our Peace campaign had largely fallen because the men speakers were mostly in uniform, were a particular target, despite the Home Secretary's assurance to Parliament that national security was the reason for the clamp-down and not our propaganda activities for peace.'[20] However, it should also be kept in mind that the proportion of British fascist women to men interned roughly corresponded to the ratio of men to women detained under DR 12(5A), the Aliens Order. In the months of May and June 1940 the British Government interned 4,000 enemy alien women, as compared with 23,000 German and Austrian men, and after Italy entered the war on 10 June 1940, an additional 4,000 Italian men (and only 16 Italian women). That the internment of women was of a lesser priority is substantiated by the fact that the order to intern all German and Austrian men between the ages of 16 and 60 was issued on 12 May 1940, while the first order issued to arrest women only came on 27 May 1940. Furthermore, 'not only were considerably fewer women interned, but those women who were placed in camps were handled with more leniency (and no woman was ever sent overseas).'[21] Whether British fascist or enemy alien, the internment of women was considered in a different light from that of men. It is interesting to explore the reasons for this difference.

While the fact remains that far fewer women than men were interned either under DR 18B or as enemy aliens, the Fifth Columnist scare strongly evoked the ghost of Delilah and the *femme fatale* saboteur. In regard to British fascist women, Lord Harlech, Regional Commander of the North Eastern Region, feared that 'perhaps the most serious cause of disquiet is the continued activities of the wives of pro-Nazi and Fascist leaders after their husbands have been rounded up.'[22] When Sir Neville Bland, British Minister to the Dutch Government at the Hague, returned to Britain two days after Germany's invasion of Holland on 14 May 1940, he busied himself with drafting a report on the 'Fifth Column Menace.' In his report he claimed that 'the paltriest kitchen maid not only can be, but generally is, a menace to the safety of the country.'[23] Referring to the perceived urgency of interning alien women of this same untrustworthy type, Lord Elibank told the House of Lords on 23 May 1940: 'is it not well known that some of the greatest and most famous spies in the world were of the female sex? Is it not also well known that very often one female spy is better than ten men, or at least equal to ten men?'[24] Long after the invasion panic of 1940, on 30 June 1943 the Home Office's 'Suspect List in the Event of Anticipated Invasion' still included 710 British men and 310 British women. In July 1943 the Home Office 'Suspect List' included 550 British, enemy alien, and non-enemy alien women. Of this category of women J.L.S. Hale of MI5 minuted to the Home Office that 'it would be unwise to treat suspect women as if they would be less dangerous in invasion conditions than men. It may indeed be easier in some respects for an evilly-disposed woman to assist an invader than for her male counterpart.'[25] The perception of woman as a political animal distinct from the male was underlined by the different arrangements made for male and female 18B prisoners.

Months before the amendment of DR 18B, the authorities began considering what provision could be made for the internment of women. The sequestering of male and female political prisoners was taken for granted, and in January 1940 Norman Birkett, Chairman of the Home Office Advisory Committee, was informed that 'as regards women, we still have no establishment available other than the wing in Holloway Prison which has been set apart for that purpose. The Prison Commissioners have done their best to make the conditions in this special wing as little oppressive as possible, but we recognize the disadvantages of keeping women for long periods in this establishment.'[26] Whereas it was admitted that the existing facilities were in poor condition, it was anticipated that women should not be made to suffer under the same harsh conditions as their male counterparts. It was also never suggested that 18B women should be exiled to the colonies and Dominions, as many enemy alien men had been and as was being considered for 18B men. In July 1940, the Cabinet was informed that 'there are also a number of women who have been interned but I do not think it necessary that any of these should be removed from the country, nor do I contemplate that any of the men should be allowed to be accompanied by their wives and children.'[27] Similarly, when the War Office was asked to consider the internment under military custody of 18B detainees, assurances were asked for and given that 'the Secretary of State does not contemplate making any suggestion at a later date for the detention of any female in military custody.'[28] Traditional beliefs about the weaker sex informed the policy of internment, although the grounds for detaining BU women were not radically different from those for detaining the men.

'All Guilty in Varying Degrees': The Ideological Basis for Internment

As Ann Page has suggested, the majority of BU women were interned because of their vehement anti-war sentiments and the pro-active roles they played in the peace campaign.[29] In their defence, it can be said that the BU's anti-war policy and feminine fascist pacifism predated the outbreak of the Second World War by many years. Fighting their 'Mind Britain's Business' campaign during the Abyssinian Crisis of 1935, BUF speakers were instructed to answer any questions about the movement's intentions if war ensued in the following manner: 'We have the power, with public opinion behind us, by the force of that opinion to prevent an unjust war. If any country in the world ever attacked Great Britain, then Fascists would certainly fight for their country.'[30] As early as April 1936, BU women contributed articles to the press explaining the nature of their own anti-war beliefs.[31] Well before Mosley announced his 'Four Points for Peace,' the BU had been partly an anti-war movement.[32]

The outbreak of war saw the acceleration of the BU's women's peace campaign and the fortification of women's resolve to challenge and bait the powers that be. In an anti-war article published on 23 September 1939, one woman scoffed at the provision made for the Defence of the Realm.

> I suppose I'll have to be terribly careful what I write or else I shall be in for it – high-treason and what not ... . How we have worked for our country's peace only the Lord knows. When we think of the hours on the platform and street corner of the miles trudged giving out leaflets, of the bearing up under insult, our hearts sink and all seems so futile now. But think a while; without peace there can be no progress.[33]

Indeed, incidents of rhetorical treachery were not dealt with lightly as the following cases illustrate. In Bournemouth in the autumn of 1939, Miss Iris Ryder was fined £5 for comments made in a speech concerning BU women and peace, and she was also convicted for defacing an air raid shelter notice. She was later interned. On 23 October 1939 Anne Brock Griggs was in court charged with insulting words and disturbing the peace under the Public Order Act and Defence Regulations (1939) Section 39B after she told an audience in Limehouse: 'If Germans don't like Hitler they can get rid of him themselves. We do not need to send our sons to fight them. If ever a country wants a revolution now it is Great Britain.'[34] Even though she quit her BU post shortly thereafter, Brock-Griggs was among the first BU women interned. In April 1940 Miss Elsie Marjorie Steele was served with a fine of £5 and a fourteen-day sentence for telling an audience of about 300 in Bethnal Green: 'you don't see any of the rotten Government leaders in khaki. Remember it was Chamberlain, dictated by his Jewish masters, who declared war, not Hitler. As for the swine Churchill, we will remember Gallipoli and the Dardanelles, the rotten murderer.'[35] She was later interned.

The relationship between BU women and Britain's pacifist movement was indeed ambiguous.[36] There was disorder when BU women tried to sabotage a peace meeting organized by the Women's League Against War and Fascism at the Kingsway Hall on 31 January 1940,[37] but relations between the BU and the Peace Pledge Union were far more amiable. In February 1939 Florence Hayes, the BU's Women's Chief Organizer in Wessex, related that 'strangely enough, I've been offered a debate by the PPU when they can fix one up.'[38] Vera Brittain took on the PPU's detractors after some London newspapers had recognized close analogies between PPU and BU propaganda, and after Rose Macaulay had mentioned that 'occasionally when reading *Peace News*, I (and others) half think we have got hold of the *Blackshirt* by mistake.' In her single-minded dedication to the pacifist cause by 1939, Brittain 'resolved that if I was to be called a Fascist, I must prepare to endure even this ... . I am now aware that if it suits war-mongers to rechristen me a Fascist, not one of the names which I have been given as a feminist will rescue me from this totally incompatible accusation.'[39] The connection between the PPU and the extreme Right seemed to have gone beyond a mere tactical or ideological crossing of paths. In October 1939 the Home Office was in possession of the information that 'recently, nearly all the members of the Nordic League have joined the Peace Pledge Union. It is hardly necessary to point out that the Nordic League is no more pacifist than Hitler. The PPU is presumably regarded as a useful cover for activities calculated to embarrass the Government.'[40]

Significantly, members of the PPU were not targeted for internment under the Defence Regulations, while BU women who gave active expression to their anti-war views were the most likely to be interned. Writing to her sister in Holloway, Constance Pearson mused: 'I cannot understand why you with pacifist views are put in gaol while the Peace Pledge people were let off. They cannot have found anything on you about communication with the enemy as you don't like them and never did and don't know any either.'[41] Of course, BU women were not straightforward pacifists and it was the fascist – and thus potentially disloyal – filter through which they distilled their anti-war views which transformed them into public enemies.

The most disquieting aspects of the functioning of the Defence Regulations was that they represented retroactive justice and functioned according to a counter-factual futurology. A key element of the Government's case against Diana Mosley was that she had had privileged access to Hilter's pre-war inner circle. The Advisory Committee dwelt with great curiosity on her relationships with top Nazi officials, to the point that, in retrospect, Diana Mosley averred that 'if, between 1936 and 1939, I had been told that to have luncheon or dinner with Hitler would cost me three and a half years in prison and part me from my four children I should not have believed it, nor would anyone else.'[42] In dining with the dictators had some British women merely been breaking bread or breaking faith?

Mary Allen was denounced as a Fifth Columnist after an anonymous informant wrote to the Home Office of an incident in January 1938 when she told fellow guests at a Swiss hotel that Hitler was a friend,[43] and after Major Dupe, Head of Staff at Lympne airport, reported that Allen 'travelled to Germany frequently and always returned on German aircraft. She gave the Nazi salute to the pilot on alighting.'[44] Pre-war vacations to Germany were held highly suspect, and part of the evidence against the young Louise Fisher consisted of a postcard-size photograph of herself and her fiancée seated around a table on which were long-stemmed glasses and tall bottles of German wine. The origin of this piece of evidence, explained Louise, was that 'during the summer holidays of 1939 we had taken a fortnight's holiday in August visiting the Rhineland in Germany, and this photo was taken at the well-known Wein Dorf ... . My interrogator said that he presumed that this was a special banquet held in our honour by local National Socialist officials.'[45] The authorities also considered Nellie Driver a 'very dangerous woman.' As she recalled: ' I was accused of holding secret meetings in my home, and I explained in vain that the people seen visiting us one night were the Insurance Agent, the landlord, the Trade Union collector and my uncle.'[46] Admittedly, as in the cases of Louise Fisher and Nellie Driver, the Home Office could be over-diligent in the examination of evidence relating to BU women's contact with hostile powers.

In contrast, the actions of other BU women gave legitimate rise to suspicion. Muriel Whinfield's son, Peter, had gone to Germany and Italy after war broke out, and it was presumed he had attempted to emulate 'Lord Haw-Haw' by making contact with enemy broadcasting stations. Mrs Whinfield herself had travelled to Switzerland after war had been declared. She was still interned when in January 1942 she hoped Mosley would sign an affidavit on her behalf stating that she had been ignorant of the financial inner-workings of the BU. Mosley responded to this request by telling her lawyers how 'I don't want to start that sort of thing, I want to fight for the whole thing direct.' He believed that

> Mrs Whinfield of all people, she should be the last to expect to get out;
> I know, the Home Office knows and everybody knows why Mrs Whinfield
> is here. She is here because of her son, he is a nice boy and I dare say
> perfectly innocent, but he has done very foolish things, look at him in
> Germany, and again in Italy, goodness knows what he did, I don't know,
> but his mother no doubt encouraged him ... I do know that we have girls
> here who have only travelled to Bolton from Manchester, they cannot get
> out, much less Mrs Whinfield who has travelled allover[sic] the place.[47]

As Mosley suggested, some BU women were more 'guilty' than others. Nonetheless, given that the Defence Regulations were intended to be non-punitive, it was impossible to make the punishment fit the 'crime'. F.C. Watkins, Labour MP for Hackney Central, told the Commons on 21 July 1942, 'they are all guilty in varying degrees, and it rests with the Home Secretary to decide whether they are sufficiently guilty to be detained.'[48]

The Moral Conundrum: The Legality of 18B

In his a close study of the political and legal evolution of the Defence Regulations, A.W. Brian Simpson has argued convincingly that 'when war really came the official fears were found to be wholly misplaced, but by then it was too late to dismantle their legacy; hence the legal regime under which Britain fought the war was that of a totalitarian state.'[49] As it was never suggested that a person held under 18B had been guilty of any crime, the processes of arrest, interrogation, appeal and judgement were highly subjective and arbitrary.[50] Presumed guilty, and with no legal recourse to disprove charges, 18B prisoners were made to survive in a Kafkaesque world of accusations and denunciations. Diana Mosley's mother, Lady Redesdale, appealed to a number of her well-place acquaintances, and was consistently baffled by the suspension of habeas corpus and Magna Carta. She suggested to Lord Cranborne: 'why don't the Government give them a fair trial and shoot them if they are guilty of treason? Or let them out if they are innocent. What is there against it? And why should any who are innocent be branded for life with the odious suspicion never to be cleared up?'[51] Quite unashamedly, the Home Office explained why the administration of 18B functioned to no rhyme or reason, and why habeas corpus and rights under Magna Carta had been denied to British subjects:

> As a matter of fact, it is precisely because the potentialities for mischief of certain persons could not be brought within the scope of the criminal law that Parliament was persuaded that it was in the interests of national security to confer these exceptional powers of detention without trial. The policy is, of course, to bring to trial any person detained under 18B where there is sufficient evidence on which to base criminal proceedings.[52]

This policy as such was of limited success, and only two persons had been brought to trial after being detained: Mrs Christobel

Nicholson, who had been charged under the Official Secrets Act as part of the Tyler Kent case, acquitted, but immediately re-interned, and Anna Wolkoff.

In the first instance, arrests and captures were as erratic as life on the inside. Police did make an attempt to question Blanche Greaves, the active Woman District Leader for Kingston. Fortunately for her the police 'came once or twice and saw my mother, but I was working and never there. The weekend it all happened was the weekend we happened to be away on honeymoon.'[53] Similarly, Gladys Walsh, who had become D/L for Limehouse since the war, escaped capture. Walsh remembered: 'They did come for me, but I was in Surrey, we were bombed out ... . Although I am glad I never went inside, there were times when I wished I was among my own people during the war.'[54]

BU detainees certainly made much of the indiscriminate process of arrests as it was further proof of the illegality and anti-democratic basis of 18B. John Charnley could never understand why Mrs Toni Moran, a very active BU member and virulent anti-Semite, was never put in Holloway when so many non-active members were caught in the net.[55] R.R. Bellamy deemed it only partially auspicious that 'in the hit and miss operation of 18B, my wife was not one of those whose names appeared on the detention roll; she was left free to enjoy with the children the liberality of the local Public Assistance Board.'[55] In what might have been a monumental fumble, Elizabeth P. Goody was interned. Diana Mosley has described Goody as 'a nice little red-haired women, a member of the BU. She thought, as she'd never been very active, she had been arrested by mistake and it should have been Ann Good who was a wonderful person completely devoted to O.M. and to peace.'[57]

The experiences of those women who were arrested could be horrific. In the case of Miss L.M. Reeve, 'troops were sent to apprehend her; she was seized, put on a truck and driven off under armed guard.' When one of the non-commissioned officers in charge of the party began to admire her valuable gun dog, he told 'her that she was probably about to be shot [so] he asked if he could keep the dog.'[58] After the first flush of arrests, the War Cabinet admitted that 'the possibility that some mistakes have been made cannot be altogether excluded.'[59] Certainly it was not the intention that arrests should have been so anarchic, but the hit and miss operation did serve to keep the fascists guessing, and thus created a world of fear and psychological terror among members and former members of the BU.[60]

Judgment at the Berystede Hotel: Appeals, Tribunals and the Political-Psychologist's Couch

The Advisory Committee to Consider Appeals Against Orders of Internment was a body which was at liberty to pass its judgments based on almost wholly subjective criteria, aided by techniques of amateur psychoanalysis. During the one and only full-fledged, yet heated, parliamentary debate on 18B, F.C. Watkins explained: '[T]he purpose of the Advisory Committee is to try and look into their minds, to try to make out whether it would be safe for them to be allowed at large in the very critical and trying circumstances of to-day. That is not a legal question to be settled by lawyers. It is to be settled by decent, honest, intelligent people with an ability to weigh up human character and conduct.'[61] To further exacerbate matters, the Advisory Committee's decisions were not binding and were frequently set aside by either the Home Secretary or MI5. Louise Irvine remembered how 'hopes were always raised when one attended a tribunal, but the questions seemed so futile and puerile that I had no indication whether I would be released or not.'[62] Detainees also complained about the salaciously invasive nature of the Committee's questions, and the manner in which interrogators thought it appropriate to delve into the seemingly irrelevant particulars of private life.[63]

Very few full records of the appearance of women before the Advisory Committee are extant, but those that have not been weeded or destroyed give a picture of the Committee doubling as mental health board. (BU internee files were destroyed under the authority of Section 3(6) of the Public Records Act.) BU women were portrayed either as over-forceful personalities or as misguided eccentrics, and Mary Allen was pronounced to be 'a terribly conceited woman, a crank with a tremendous grievance.'[64] Their prosaic characterization of Ethel Annie Baggaley, a middle-aged spinster who served as W/D/L in Hulme, offers a vivid example of the Committee's socio-psychological techniques:

> There was nothing in Miss Baggaley's story to differentiate her from scores of women who support themselves in circumstances equally modest and equally self-respecting. She lived apparently a solitary life in lodgings apart from any relations she might possess. She is certainly, judging from her own account, not a woman of wide interests or experience in life, and it is not without pathos that National Socialism should have inspired this rather colourless existence with all the force of missionary fervour.[65]

The otherwise harmless Baggaley remained under detention until 1943 because she refused to perform war work if released; because her admiration for Mosley had continued unabated; and because she made no attempt to camouflage her approval of German methods and Nazi concentration camps. The persistence of her beliefs was perhaps not so surprising when it is considered that she was His Majesty's involuntary guest for three years.

In this capricious atmosphere of crime and punishment, detainees' legal advocates were at a similar loss at how to satisfy the authorities. For instance, in his appeal for Mrs Shelmerdine's release, the lawyer Oswald Hickson floated the sarcastic recommendation that 'it should be made a condition that as a punishment she should assist at Communist meetings and sell copies of the *Jewish Chronicle*.'[66] Not all the lawyers representing 18B cases exhibited such a high degree of creativity or sardonic sense of humour, and A.J. Adams sent the following didactic message to his client, Lucy Pearson:

> You must get this quite clear in your mind, that many of your fascist associates were definitely fifth columnists, that it was a political institution being manoeuvred for many purposes and that the perfectly good English who, like yourself were directed by its tenets were playing with fire and jeopardising thereby the whole of the democratic principles for which we are fighting.'[67]

From the perspective of 18B's themselves, however, a paradox emerges: in fighting to preserve democracy, the Government had refused British subjects their inalienable civil liberties.

Suffer Little Children: Politicizing Pathos

Unable to anticipate the authorities' political criteria for detention, detainee women resorted to appeals to their gaolers' humanity and demanded their freedom on the grounds of advanced age, motherhood, loss of employment or family responsibilities. The 18B Publicity Council published numerous stories of atrocities, and *Suffer Little Children* told the tale of one interned couple, where the wife, Mrs Birch, had been pregnant when arrested and also had no choice but to take her infant son to Holloway with her. The baby girl who was born in prison later died from whooping cough after the family was transported to the Isle of Man.[68] Similarly, the case of the Potter family cried out for empathy.

When Mrs Potter was arrested, her infant son 'whom she had weaned only recently, was taken from her arms and handed to the policeman's wife who had accompanied her, to take back to Norfolk for confinement to some institution.'[69] Diana Mosley herself had to leave behind her as yet unweaned 11-week-old infant when she was arrested. Her treatment upon reception at Holloway confirmed her belief in the superiority of conditions in Germany where 'supposing somebody had done the equivalent of what I have done ... I do not think they would be in prison. I absolutely know it. They have a respect for motherhood.'[70] Internment under 18B did little to convince British fascists that democratic government could offer women and children honour and sanctuary in their protected sphere.

Starting in October 1940 the Home Office permitted internees to write to MPs, and Sir Oswald Mosley took the first opportunity to petition Earl Winterton (Conservative MP for Horsham). He told Winterton how 'alone among British subjects, even in time of war, their children are deprived of both parents for a period which is already long, and is still indefinite. Meanwhile the relatively unfortunate aliens, ... are not only, I understand, detained as husbands and wives together, but have a seaside resort virtually handed over to them.'[71] Diana Mosley took it upon herself to make special appeals for the elderly women internees. When she was visited by Sir Walter Monckton on 26 April 1941, she brought forward the cases of Mrs Whinfield, who had an old husband who was very ill; Mrs Elam, whose elderly husband's illness had been exacerbated by his detention in Stafford Prison; and Miss Hayes who had an aged mother to care for.[72] These appeals on humanitarian grounds do not appear to have amounted to much, however. A Home Office communique of July 1941, headed 'The Suffering of Lady Mosley,' explained that 'Lady Mosley's representations on behalf of other 18Bs can hardly carry weight ... . There is little substance in any of this. The Mosleys and their followers are prone to recount alleged grievances in a somewhat misleading fashion whenever the opportunity offers.'[73]

18B women also hoped that women MPs might be especially willing to assist if they could be convinced that the incarceration of women and conditions in the prisons were women's issues. On her interned sister's behalf, Constance Pearson solicited three political women: Dr Edith Summerskill (Labour MP for Fulham West), Joan Lady Davidson (Unionist MP for Hemel Hempstead), and Mrs M.C. Tate (Conservative MP for Frome). She explained to

Dr Summerskill how 'after some thought I am writing to you because (1) you are a woman, (2) you are a doctor and (3) you are a member of Parliament ... . This is really a woman's business.'[74] Summerskill's response to Pearson's letter was perfunctory at best and she did little to pursue the matter of 18B women. Summerskill did, however, join forces with other political women, such as Eleanor Rathbone and Mrs Corbett-Ashby, who took a keen interest in the conditions of refugee women interned in the Isle of Man – a particular concern here was that Nazi and anti-Nazi women were being forced to live in the same close quarters.[75] Mrs Tate contested Pearson's allegation, while Lady Davidson, an old family friend, was appalled by the information related and made the effort to visit Holloway Prison early in 1941.[76] Just as it had been the case that BU women's commitments to fascist ideology transcended their feminist leanings during the 1930s, so during the war women MPs allowed their ideological loyalties to decide which issues should interest them as women.

The Sexual Politics of Incarceration: Women Living Under 18B

In prison, as a parallel to the tragically paradoxical realization of the BU's prophecy of women ruling women, BU detainees were also forced to live in a dystopian version of the classless society which fascist propagandists had advocated during the 1930s. The 18B population was made up of women of wide ranging social backgrounds, and, apparently, few concessions were made in favour of those women of higher social status. Diana Mosley remembered how 18B women were 'all ages from 18 to 65, from all classes, from every part of England; some intelligent, others less so, but they all had without exception one thing in common: love of country.'[77] Louise Irvine profited personally from this social and intellectual diversity and regarded her period of detention as an education: 'In Holloway there were so many talented women amongst our own BU members and each had her own characteristics to offer, which made Holloway such a rich experience.'[78] Even if some women attempted to glean all that was best out of living in confinement with like-minded political sinners, prison existence was universally acknowledged to be loathsome and hazardous.

During the early days of internment when the Prison Commissioners struggled to deal with the large influx of detainees, some 18B women were temporarily placed among remand prisoners, or occupied cells in the same wing with the enemy alien detainees. The latter situation caused BU women severe irritation and Lucy Pearson was appalled how upon reception at Holloway she had been 'locked up with a Russian refugee in a box about the size of a WC.'[79] 18B women had to contend with unsatisfactory hygiene, severe limitations on communication with family and friends, loss of privacy, only thirty minutes per day for exercise in the prison yard, inadequate food rations, long periods of lock-up and lights out, and the initial hostility of prison guards.[80] 18Bs also balked at the situation where the authorities 'insisted on all parcels being pooled and shared out by the prison officers among the women detained. Though these victims were willing and even eager to help each other, they naturally objected to this illegal and compulsory communism.'[81] Old ideological enmities died hard, and it was also considered surprising that Diana Mosley did not fulfil her husband's fascist leadership principle, and 'there was never a question of her becoming the women's leader in Holloway.'[82] Even in the all-female world of Holloway, Sir Oswald Mosley remained the women's uncontested Leader, and Lucy Pearson's pocket diary records that on 16 November 1940 internees held a 'tea dance for O.M.'s birthday. He is 44.'[83] It is not clear, however, if and how the women replicated the fascist para-military hierarchy on the inside. Perhaps the commotion caused by tribunals, unpredictable releases, threats of transport to the Isle of Man and so on prevented the establishment of stable self-government along fascist lines.

By far the most brutal conditions in Holloway related to the treatment of the women during air raids. In November 1940, Sir Oswald Mosley related: 'Holloway was hit by two bombs on Monday 14th last, and one wing was smashed, the neighbourhood is nightly subjected to intense bombardment. The women have no Anderson shelters. They are left in a locked building with additional risk of fire, in cells high above the ground, at just the right angle for bomb blast.' He was anxious to know: 'Why have they not been moved, in accord with our constant request, at least to a country prison for women?' Mosley came to the conclusion that 'to keep women prisoners locked up under bombardment is something new in the annals of a civilized power. For the men in this respect I make no complaint. Most of us ran much greater risks in the last war. But the case of the women and children in Holloway is an infamy.'[84] Other fascist beliefs died hard too as Mosley believed men could persevere while women's resolve would tend to break-down. Certainly it was natural that Mosley should have called upon his deep protectiveness for his women when they were faced with such dangers. Furthermore, it must also be noticed how both his status as Leader of his flocks, and his masculine fascism survived and even thrived during the internment.[85]

While the women were never evacuated to a prison in a rural area where they might have found sanctuary from the blitz, the majority of 18Bs were deported to the Isle of Man in 1941. The first plans were made in March 1941, when it was intended that after the Isle of Man (Detention) Bill became law, the Home Secretary desired 'to transfer to the women's internment camp about 90 women detained under DR 18B, 36 of whom are British Fascist and the remainder of various nationalities, and 30 women detained under Article 12(5A) of the Aliens Order.'[86] The plan to move 18B women met opposition on many levels. Dame Joanna Cruickshank, Commandant of the women's internment camp at Port Erin since its establishment in May 1940, and her officer Miss Looker, together resigned from their posts in May 1941 because they felt 'we neither of us have the right kind of training or experience, and I think I may add, temperament or inclination, to carry out a policy which may, I suppose, be increasingly repressive and where "security" and "intelligence" will be more and more important.'[87] Although the camp authorities on the Isle of Man had had many difficulties in quelling the tensions existing between Nazi and anti-Nazi women held behind the same barbed wire, the prospect of administering 18B with all its attendant covert aspects was a different matter.

Opposition to the impending arrival of 18Bs came from both islanders and alien inmates as well. It was reported how 'there is a very strong feeling on the Isle of Man against the 18B detainees, commonly referred to in the Island as "the traitors," and the arrival of Mosley in the Island would be likely to cause a sensation.'[88] For the alien women internees, the prospect of British fascist women joining them in their camp made the future look bleak. Livia Laurent (pseudonym), a German-Jewish internee, wrote about their fears: 'A number of boarding houses were to be cleared for the Fascists. They would live by themselves but mix with us in the street, come to the same classes and share camp life with us. Having learnt by experience, we wondered if going to a French lesson with a Fascist would make us Fascist as well.'[89] Islanders and inmates alike feared being branded disloyal if they fraternized with these public enemies, and in another turn of poetic justice

246

Britain's fascist anti-Semitic women were confronted with the kind of discrimination that they had espoused.

The first contingent of 43 18B women, including seven children, arrived on the Isle of Man on 21 June 1941.[90] The women made many complaints about their treatment in preparation for and during transport, but they seemed to be satisfied with the conditions they found once they settled in at Rushen Camp. Annie Lake, who was on the first transport, wrote to Labour MP Richard Stokes:

> I would like to say that we find here a completely different atmosphere – we are comfortably billeted in boarding houses, and the officials are all kind and helpful. A certain amount of prejudice has been spread before our arrival against 'the fascists' – of whom among the 50 odd souls only 14 can claim that distinction- – but already it has been realized that we are not as black as we are painted, and shopkeepers are not afraid to serve us.[91]

Nonetheless, Inspector Cuthbert, who took over command of the women's and married camps after Dame Cruickshank departed, testified to the fact that 'the 18Bs had a disturbing influence on the camps and things were never as smooth after their arrival.'[92]

Simultaneously with the move from mainland prisons to the Isle of Man came the escalation of 18B agitation for married couples to be allowed to be interned together. In June 1941, sixteen 18B men, and by July twenty-six 18B men, signed petitions to be admitted to the Married Camp on the Isle of Man.[93] Mosley too had made repeated requests to the effect that 18B married couples should be permitted to be detained together,[94] but it would not be until the end of 1941, proceeding some powerful intervention, that the request was granted. In November 1941 Winston Churchill wrote to the Home Secretary in support of the reunification of 18B couples.

> Is it true that when aliens are interned, husband and wife are interned in one place? If so, it seems invidious to discriminate against those of British nationality. Feeling against 18B is very strong, and I should not be prepared to support the Regulation indefinitely if it is administered in such a very onerous manner. Internment rather than imprisonment is what was contemplated. Sir Oswald Mosley's wife has been 18 months in prison without the slightest vestige of any charge against her, and separated from her husband.[95]

After the Prime Minister threatened to withdraw his support for the Defence Regulation, 18B husbands and wives were reunited in double-quick time. On 11 December 1941, thirteen 18B couples were admitted into the Married Aliens Internment Camp, Mereside, Douglas, and four couples were selected for Holloway Prison.

Class and the Myth of Preferential Treatment

Churchill's intervention to expedite matters in the case of 18B married couples was one of the few instances where detainees drew benefits from connections in high places. Some 18Bs suspected that upper-class fascists were being protected from the Defence Regulation, and the interned J.R. Smeaton-Stuart submitted a petition in which he cited Susannah Lady Pearson, Mrs Sherston and Basil Mill, as 'detainees of means and influence [who] received priority of interrogation and for release.'[96] In fact, Lady Pearson's Hollingbourne Manor was raided by Kent Police and she was arrested and taken to police headquarters in Maidstone on 4 June 1940. However, when her brother, Brigadier General Sir Henry Page-Croft, Conservative member for Bournemouth, learned of his sister's arrest 'his amazement was excelled only by his wrath.' After demanding an immediate interview with the Home Secretary, Sir John Anderson, 'there was an angry scene when he confronted the "Bengal Tiger," he stormed at him for his "outrageous act," for the stupidity and indecency of authorizing the arrest of a woman no longer young, who was completely devoted to her country, and wished only to serve it.'[97] Lady Pearson was released from police custody a few days after this showdown.

Viscountess Downe was also left at large, but her escape from internment may well have been as capricious as that of many other BU members who were overlooked. Although her house was searched by police, she confided to Lady Redesdale that 'I thought they meant to put me in too but that is passing now and it feels fairly safe again ... . I really feel so ashamed of being free!'[98] Lady Redesdale's notorious daughter, Unity Mitford, was spared internment not so much as a consequence of her aristocratic connections, but because she was too ill after her suicide attempt of 3 September 1939.[99]

The titled women who were interned in Holloway – Lady Howard of Effingham, Lady Domvile, and Diana, Lady Mosley among them – all had to adapt to the levelling experience of prison life. Lucy Pearson thought it scandalous how 'we were always addressed by our surnames, even the wife of Admiral Sir Barry Domvile being denied her title.'[100] Upper-class women did appear to find the adjustment to prison routine especially challenging. Diana Mosley allegedly told her mother 'that she and her class were tortured by continued close confinement, and that it was very different for the working-classes who were used to living in dirt and noise, always living on top of one another in the same small space, and are therefore used to it.'[101] The authorities had little sympathy for 'the sufferings of Diana Mosley' and she only received special treatment from fellow BU internees as 'there was nothing they would not do for me, they idolized M. and it was for his sake.'[102] Moreover, her close acquaintance with persons in high places actually militated against her – Diana's former father-in-law and her own sister, Nancy Mitford, were among those who had denounced her to the Home Office.

No matter what the realities of prison life, a myth of preferential treatment being conferred upon 18B women was spawned by both press and political opponents. 'A thoroughly British Woman' told the *Daily Express* that these traitors should be shut up in the Tower, but instead 'we drive them through the streets, give them nice food and smooth and stroke them ... when our husbands are labouring hard and we housewives are saving to buy War Bonds for Victory.'[103] The Rotherhite Co-op Women's Guild wrote to the Home Secretary protesting 'that Lady Mosley should be allowed preferdential[sic] treatment such has[sic] special apartments, mannequin parades and every comfort,'[104] while the husbands of working women were abroad fighting Nazism. The rather absurd episode of 18 March 1942, when 18B women held a fashion show in Holloway, led to questions being asked in the Commons on 26 March. Again the point was made, by Richard Sloan (Labour MP for Ayrshire), that the wives and daughters of British workers had far less freedom of choice in their own purchases. On 30 March 1942, the Home Office received an anonymous communication stating that the Holloway fashion show 'was a disgrace to this country. The mannequins are a gang of fifth columnists!'[105]

The Mosleys' release on 23 November 1943 also provoked a great public outcry, and communist women took it upon themselves to organize protests in place of their absent husbands. Speaking at a CPGB meeting on 2 December 1943, Mrs Lampert brought attention to the great gap between the living conditions of working class families and those of the Mosleys in Holloway before suggesting that 'in any case, there was no reason to release his wife; she should be made to suffer separation from her husband as the wives of the men in the forces were forced to suffer.'[106] The consistently hostile public reaction to 18B internees exemplified a certain brutalization of politics and scape-goating during the war; again, the would-be fascist persecutors became the victims and pariahs.

Fascist Philanthropy: The Activities of BU Women Outside Prison Walls

Struggling against both the authorities and public opinion, BU women worked diligently to maintain the comradeship and ceremony of BU days and help those less fortunate.[107] For the duration of the war BU activity as such ceased, while former members continued to group around the 18B Detainees (British) Aid Fund and the 18B Publicity Council. BU women had figured prominently in fund-raising activities before the war, and they continued to prove themselves to be formidable fascist philanthropists during the internment. While the Fund was presided over by two men, its Secretary was Mrs P.E. Jones, and Dr Margaret Vivian, Norah Elam, Viscountess Downe were all celebrated for their work on the Fund's behalf.

The 18B Detainees (British) Aid Fund was registered as a war charity with the LCC under the War Charities Act in 1940, and during the course of the war it gave sustained assistance to 140 families, temporary assistance in over 350 cases, paid for legal and medical services in 72 cases, offered after-release advice to over 200 cases, made personal representations to the Ministry of Labour in 143 cases, found employment for 34 persons and raised a total of 6,000 pounds.[108] Deeply moved by 'the suffering callously brought upon British wives and children by the removal from their homes of those whom no crime [was] alleged ... the 18B Fund also amounted [sic] an "adopt a family of a detainee" campaign.'[109]

The Fund hosted its own social events and concerts, but it would be the more clandestine activities of former BU members which drew the attention of the authorities. Close surveillance was made of BU men and women, and many of their meetings were quite evidently attended by agents or informants.[110] In the early days of 18B some sinister meetings were convened by extreme Right-wing elements to organize support for internees. At a get-together at Molly Stanford's flat on 12 November 1940 a plan was devised whereby 'money should be collected from those willing to help and be sent to various prisons on rotation. The sums were to be sent through Lady Mosley's sister so that it would appear as purely private gifts of money.'[111] On 16 November 1940, a party was held in London to celebrate Mosley's birthday, which was reportedly attended by 30 persons of both sexes. As if keeping vigil, 'at one end of the room was a large picture of Sir Oswald Mosley illuminated by lamps.'[112] Two years later on the same date, another party was held to commemorate Sir Oswald Mosley's birthday, at which former-detainee Agnes Booth 'made the most vindictive and fanatical speech. She dwelt at length on the hardships and injustices suffered by women fascists who had been interned and said that she would not rest until those responsible for 18B had paid dearly for this crime.'[113] Perhaps it may have been hoped that 18B would not only contain subversive fascist activity but cure BU members from their heretical beliefs, and the Advisory Committee certainly did frame its questions in such a way as to invite retractions and recantation. However, in most cases the oppressiveness of 18B functioned only to confirm fascist commitments and strengthen militant resolve – a not uncommon outcome of political imprisonment regardless of ideology.

The After-Effects of Internment and The Persistence of Belief

Prison conditions were held responsible for the physical and mental deterioration of many internees, and once at liberty Florence Hayes confided that 'my nerves have never recovered from Holloway you know, and even now, the least overstrain has its effects ... . All I am fit for now is to potter about the garden, feed the hens and dream of days gone by!'[114] While Hayes temporarily withdrew from political activities, she did attend the second concert hosted by the 18B Detainees (British) Aid Fund at the Kingsway Hall in 1944, after which occasion Robert Saunders wrote to one of their mutual friends: 'but whatever may have happened to her physically, her spirit is as fanatical as ever. I always feel that she will consider her life imperfect if she does not end her days being burnt at the stake for her ideals.'[115] Clearly, personal commitments to Mosley and to fascism triumphed over the thought-policing aspect of 18B, even as the vigilance of the Defence Regulations prevented their full expression.

Reactions among former BU members to Mosley's release exemplified at one and the same time the success of the Government's crack-down on fascist activity and the persistence of belief. While the CPGB was holding one 'Send Mosley Back to Jail' meeting after another,[116] the Leader's devoted followers agreed to remain silent so as not to give cause for his re-internment. Special Branch was in possession of information that BU members gathered in London to discuss the much-anticipated release, but agreed to circulate a letter advising all sympathizers not to breach the peace nor interfere with communist protesters.[117] When 18B was revoked in May 1945, former detainees wasted little time before regrouping under the Mosleyite banners. By examining the list of attendance for the 18B Social and Dance held at the Royal Hotel on 15 December 1945 and patronized by some 1,150 supporters, it was evident that the BU's much touted fraternity was reinforced and lent added vigour by internment under 18B.[118]

During the 1930s the BU had built a community of like-minded political dissenters who shared a vision of a Greater Britain. By the 1940s these individuals had been further united by political persecution and memories of shared suffering. In internment under 18B Britain's fascists finally found their martyrs. It was little wonder that the BU's anti-democratic doctrine was fortified by war-time political imprisonment, and when Diana Mosley was asked by the Advisory Committee, 'You have great contempt for democracy?', it was natural that she should respond as she did: 'Yes.'[119] However, what was more disturbing was the way in which 18Bs reinterpreted their experiences under the Defence Regulation; how they would make forced analogies between Britain's war-time policies and those of Nazi Germany; and how they became desensitized to the incomparably greater persecution suffered by European Jewry.

A common theme in the reminiscences of 18Bs was that Britain's war-time Government could claim no moral high-ground over Germany when British subjects had been interned in camps that were not substantially different from Nazi concentration camps. In 1941, Lucy Pearson was under the impression that 'even Hitler interns his women political prisoners in sanatoria and his men in camps whereas ours, both men and women, are given long terms of imprisonment in ordinary prisons where they are treated as convicts, except that they are denied a convicts right to a trial before a court of law.'[120] Robert Row, the post-war editor of *Action*, confounded sign with signifier when he claimed that 'these detention camps were in fact concentration camps. Thus the ludicrous position was reached of a Britain at war with the "Nazi concentration camp regime" while maintaining a concentration camp regime of its own.'[121] In the morally relativized universe of fascist revisionists, Diana Mosley wrote: 'as the years went by almost all the prisoners in Germany's camps were released; what happened during the war is another matter. By then we ourselves were imprisoned and silenced.'[122] More sensitive to memories of Nazi genocide – but still suggesting as illogical a proposition as Diana Mosley's oblique parallel between Hitler's crimes and the detention of fascists in Britain – was John Charnley's contention that 'if the British people had followed Mosley's lead we could have avoided war. Millions of lives would have been saved, and the subsequent horror of the Holocaust would have been averted.'[123] Through some exercises of intellectual contortion, former 18B detainees have consistently attempted to demonize Churchill's war-time administration by portraying themselves as innocent scapegoats on a par with the victims of Nazism.

After an examination of the human dimensions of 18B it is difficult not to feel some compassion for the women whose lives were interrupted because they had followed Mosley. Whenever human faces are grafted onto statistics even the most unsympathetic individuals cry out for pity or understanding. However, the attempt to understand cannot afford to ignore either the actions and intentions of Britain's fascist women towards lowering war-time morale, or the intolerance inherent in their feminine fascist mentality. A study of BU women under internment can neither afford to be an expedition in 'witchfinding'[124] nor a search to discover Britain's forgotten war-time martyrs.

Notes on Chapter 6

1   After the war, former Labour activist Hugh Ross Williamson confided to Mosley that 'it had been unofficially agreed, at the Labour Party Conference at Bournemouth in May 1940, that Mosley's arrest and imprisonment would be a condition of Labour's entering the government. While this could not be verified, Regulation 18B was passed the second day after Labour joined the government.' A.L. Goldman, 'Defence Regulation 18B: Emergency Internment of Aliens and Political Dissenters in Great Britain During World War II,' *Journal of British Studies*, 12, 2, (May 1973), 120–36.

2   ed. Stanley Olson, *Harold Nicolson: Diaries and Letter 1930–1964* (London, 1980), p.36. Entry for 6 January 1932.

3 'The Word': Special Investigation Report on 18B: It Might Have Happened to You!, (December 1943).

4 The Imperial War Museum's Sound Archive holds some 102 taped interviews with enemy alien internees. See Recordings Relating to Internment in Britain 2WW, 4/97.

5 HO45/25386/54–59. 'As a direct result of the increase in political surveillance this entailed, [Lord] Trenchard expanded Special Branch from 136 to 200 officers in 1934.' Richard Thurlow, 'State Management of the British Union of Fascists in the 1930s,' in ed. Mike Cronin, The Failure of British Fascism (London, 1996), p.40. 'By the outbreak of war, MI5 had 83 officers and 253 other ranks (almost all of them women).' F.H. Hinsley & C.A.G. Simkins, British Intelligence in the Second World War: Vol. 4: Security and Counter-Intelligence (London, 1990), p.10.

6 See HO144/21063/406–411.

7 Letter from Constance Pearson to Lucy Pearson, 12 October 1940, Essex County Record Office, D/DU/758/34.

8 Special Branch, 21 May 1940, HO45/25702.

9 'I also spent 5 years searching for the woman who was Mosley's secretary during the 1930s. I was sure she was working for the security services helping to provide information for those very comprehensive reports ... . Well, I located her and spoke to her several times on the phone ... I did pluck up the courage to ask her whether she was working for the security services. She denied it quite convincingly. But she would, wouldn't she.' Letter from Jeffrey Wallder to the author, 25 March 1997. What is more clear is that while Mosley was in Brixton prison preparing his defence, Maxwell-Knight, head of MI5's counter-subversion division, 'carefully monitored one of his secretaries.' Anthony Masters, The Man Who Was M (Oxford, 1984), p.140.

10 Joan Miller, One Girl's War (Dublin, 1986), p.23.

11 See Richard Griffiths, Patriotism Perverted (London, 1998).

12 Joan Miller, One Girl's War, p.61.

13 Joan Miller, One Girl's War, p.83.

14 Letter from Violet Markham to John Buchan, 23 October 1939, in ed. Helen Jones, Duty and Citizenship: The Correspondence and Political Papers of Violet Markham, 1896–1953 (London, 1994), p.155

15 Markham used the opportunity to question Mosley about those issues which interested her the most. She was the interrogator responsible for asking Mosley about his position on free speech, political control and liberties, and 'Q. What is the view you take? What about the position of women? ... Q. If women are going to be organized in trades, the numbers of industrial women workers is a small fraction of the whole ... Q. Are the poor spinsters left out? ... Q. They are not ruled out? You do not propose to deal with them as Hitler proposes to deal with them?' 3 July 1940, Advisory Committee, HO283/14/2–117. Markham

could also be among the most unforgiving on the Committee. In the case of Ethel Annie Baggaley, a middle-aged woman who had been W/D/L in Hulme and was interned on the General List of 30 May 1940, it was Violet Markham who still blocked her release in 1942. Baggaley 'appeared before the Committee again on 29th May [1942] (Mr John Morris, Miss Violet Markham and Mr Stuart Bunning), when Miss Markham and Mr Stuart Bunning recommended continued detention in view of the fact that she maintained her previous attitude unchanged and was explicit in her refusal to do war work.' Minutes, 25 June 1943, HO45/25710.

16 John Warburton & Jeffrey Wallder, 'The Regulation 18B British Union Detainees List,' British Union Collection, University of Sheffield, MS 201, 6/1. This thorough list reveals the names of 96 women who were presumed to be BU members. On further investigation, I have come across some women in the P.R.O files who are not on this list, such as Clara M. Sharland, who admitted in a letter to Lord Redesdale that she had joined the BU just before the war broke out.

17 Richard Thurlow, *The Secret State* (Oxford, 1994), p.253.

18 HO45/25752

19 PREM 4/39/4A/73

20 Ann Page – A Suburban Housewife, in ed. J. Christian, *Mosley's Blackshirts* (London, 1986), p.20.

21 Miriam Kochan, 'Women's Experience of Internment', in eds. D. Cesarani and T. Kushner, *The Internment of Aliens in 20th Century Britain* (London, 1993), p.148. There is also an interesting parallel with the treatment of women interned in Canada under Regulation 39 C of the Defence of Canada Regulations. While only 21 women were interned, most of them in Kingston Penitentiary, the conditions under which they were held were superior to those of their male counterparts. See Michelle McBride, 'The Curious Case of Female Internees,' in eds. Franca Iacovetta, Roberto Perin and Angela Principe, *Enemies Within: Italian and Other Internees in Canada and Abroad* (Toronto, forthcoming 1999), pp.196–227.

22 HO45/25726. The question of the urgency to detain the wives of British-born pro-Nazis was also raised in the House of Commons. See *Hansard*, HC, 11 July 1940, Vol. 362, Col. 1322–3.

23 Quoted in Peter and Leni Gillman, *'Collar the Lot!'* (London, 1980), p.102. After 1933, 50,000 refugees from Nazism arrived in Britain, 60% of whom were female. 'Of the 30,000 Jewish refugee women who came to Britain by the outbreak of war, up to 20,000 were allowed in on either domestic service or au pair permits.' Tony Kushner, 'Sex and Semitism,' in ed. Panikos Panayi, *Minorities in Wartime* (Oxford, 1993), p.130. At the start of the war 8,000 of these women were dismissed from their posts as a result of the dislocation of evacuation, anti-German feeling and some anti-Semitism.

24 *Hansard*, HL, 23 May 1940, Vol. 116, Col. 415.

25 Minutes, Home Office, J.L.S. Hale, 12 July 1943, HO213/2149. Certainly this demonizing of women during war-time was not the preserve of the British state. Addressing herself to a British readership, Katherine Thomas wished to point out how much more anti-woman was the Nazi state: 'the main principle underlying the Nazi attitude to women in one of extreme caution: a principle, one might almost say, of fear. To vary a British slogan, "keep it under your helmet: careless talk (to our women) may cost us our lives." Which is, significantly enough, as though women were dangerous potential enemies.' Katherine Thomas, *Women in the Nazi State* (London, 1943), p.97.

26 Letter from A. Maxwell to N. Birkett, 30 January 1940, HO45/25758.

27 Draft of Cabinet Memorandum Concerning the Removal of Detainees to the Colonies and Dominions, 19 July 1940, HO45/25767.

28 HO45/25752.

29 British fascist women were also under suspicion for their real or potential for acts of sabotage and national demoralization, and their articulated resistance to join the war effort. The following examples of the British fascist women's actions give some substance to these official fears. Mrs Violet Freeman was convicted on 6 July 1940 for printing and distributing sticky-backs advertising the New British Broadcasting Station. Olive Baker (Right Club) went on trial on 12 June 1940 for distributing pamphlets advertising the NBBS. Elsie Orrin was sentenced in June 1941 for inciting servicemen to disaffection by claiming that Hitler was a better leader than Churchill. Mrs Nora Briscoe (Right Club) and Miss Mollie Hiscox (founding member of the Link and BU) were convicted under the Treachery Act (1940) and Regulation 2A(1) of the Defence Regulations(1939) on 16 June 1941 after they were caught in a sting operation with official documents taken from the Ministry of Supply.

30 'Supplement to Speaker's Note – Emergency Issue, No. 2 [1935],' Robert Saunders Collection, University of Sheffield, File A.1.

31 See 'Women Don't Want War!: When Men Fight, Women Suffer: The Financier Reaps the Harvest,' *Blackshirt*, No. 155, 11 April 1936.

32 'Mosley's Four Points for Peace: (1) Disinterest in the East of Europe. (2) Disarmament in the West of Europe. (3) Return of the mandated colonies we do not need. (4) Development of that quarter of the whole globe which belongs to us – the glorious heritage of British Empire.' *British Union News*, No. 1 (262), June 1939.

33 'It was not in Vain, by a Woman Blackshirt,' *Action*, No. 186, 23 September 1939. The despair felt at the prospect of war by some BU women went beyond attacks on the Government. As one former Blackshirt relates, 'something else happened on 3 September, 1939. The father of our Branch Organizer in Leytonstone had been killed in the First World War. Our Branch Organizer's mother and grandmother could not face the ordeal of another war: they committed suicide.' Leonard Wise in ed. J. Christian, *Mosley's Blackshirts*, p.6.

34 Quoted in 'Chief Fascist Woman Officer Defied Police,' *Daily Herald*, 7 November 1939.
35 Quoted in 'Woman Fascist Fined 5 Pounds,' *Daily Herald*, 23 April 1940.
36 That women were Britain's natural pacifists was a common cultural assumption. 'If all men everywhere hated war as much as women do, there would be no wars. Why do women not go to war, except in eccentric twos and threes here and there? Because they really in the mass don't like it.' H.M. Swanwick, *Collective Insecurity* (London, 1937), p.284.
37 See *Action*, No. 205, 8 February 1940.
38 Letter from W/C/O/ Wessex, F.E. Hayes, to Robert Saunders, 22 February 1939, Robert Saunders Collection, University of Sheffield, File A.4.
39 Vera Brittain, 'Are We Fascists?' *Peace News*, May 1939. By the outbreak of war, PPU membership was 130,000, and *Peace News* circulation was 40,000 copies. 'In a handbook of May 1939 [the PPU] advised its members to co-operate with members of the Link and the Anglo-German Review, and urged them to make German pen friends and visit Germany, and it held meetings with the Link addressed by speakers from Germany.' F.H. Hinsley & C.A.G Simkins, *British Intelligence in the Second World War: Vol. 4: Security and Counter-Intelligence*, pp.20–1. As noted in Chapter Two, former suffragette and pacifist Dr Maude Royden, also became active in the British People's Party in 1940.
40 The Fascist Movement in the Country at the Present Time, 2 October 1939, HO144/22454/83–88. It should be mentioned that cases of real or suspected treachery chiefly emanated from extreme-Right organizations other than the BU. As Mosley stated, with some truth, 'there are in the little societies round about, they are mostly people we have chucked out, men and women who, exceedingly ineffective, whom I might suspect of being that [i.e. disloyal], they are mostly *non compos mentis* who would be no danger whatever, but I do not believe among my supporters there are any at all who would even sympathize with Germany in a struggle against that country.' HO283/13/2–125. Anna Wolkoff and Mrs Nicholson, also implicated in the Tyler Kent affair, were both Right Club. Nora Briscoe was a member of the Right Club and Mollie Hiscox a founding member of the Link. William Joyce and his wife Margaret had defected from the BUF in 1937 to form the National Socialist League. The broadcaster for German radio, Frances Eckersely, graduated from the BUF to the Imperial Fascist League when Mosley's policy was deemed not radical enough.
41 Letter from Constance Pearson to Lucy Pearson, 12 October 1940, Essex County Record Office, D/DU/758/34. The Lucy Pearson Papers are a unique source in that they offer some insight into the many dimensions of internment: personal diaries and correspondence, appeals to public figures and official documentation. What is most interesting about the correspondence between the sisters is that Constance seemed to be preparing Lucy's defence through the

letters she sent in to Holloway. Aware that all in-coming and out-going mail was censored, Constance's letters read like an appeal.

42 Diana Mosley, *Loved Ones* (London, 1985), p.217. At her hearing before the Advisory Committee to Consider Appeals Against Orders of Internment on 2 October 1940, Diana Mosley was asked: 'Q. Supposing [Hitler] came here – if I might put what I suggest is rather fanciful – would you welcome him? A. No. Q. What would you do? A. Personal friendship, private friendship, has nothing to do with one's feelings towards one's country.' HO144/21995/15–36.

43 14 June 1940, HO144/21933/326.

44 17 June 1940, Kent County Constabulary, HO144/21933/327–28.

45 Louise Irvine, 'Arrest and Imprisonment under Regulation 18b.: November 1940–November 1941: As Experienced by Miss C.L. Fisher (now Mrs Irvine).' Unpublished typescript.

46 Nellie Driver, *From the Shadows of Exile*, (unpublished autobiography) J.B. Priestley Library, University of Bradford, p.30.

47 H.M. Prison Holloway, Report of a Visit to the Mosleys by Mrs R. Roberts, Clerk to Mr O.Hickson, 29 January 1942, HO45/24891/445.

48 *Hansard*, HC, 21 July, 1942, Vol. 381., Col. 1458.

49 A.W. Brian Simpson, *In the Highest Degree Odious* (Oxford, 1992), p.46.

50 'Every fact and every circumstance in each individual case has been examined in the light of that supreme necessity [i.e. national security]. When all evidence has been heard and considered, and if any doubt remained that doubt was resolved in favour of the country and against the individual, whoever he or she may be, whether one of Hitler's entourage or a humble domestic worker ... . Persons interned under the provisions of Reg. 18B were furnished with a concise summary of the ground on which the Order was made ... . The examination of the appellants was conducted by the Committee on the material supplied by MI5, supplemented by the material contained in the Home Office files, and on further enquiry, as the occasion warranted, into the answers made to the questions as the examination proceeded. Where no such material existed information was obtained from the Police or the Local Tribunals, or similar sources.' Memorandum by the Advisory Committee, 10 January 1940, Norman Birkett K.C. to the Home Secretary, HO213/1733.

51 Letter from Lady Redesdale, Swinbrook, Oxford, to Lord Cranborne, Dominion Office, 13 December 1940, by kind permission of Brian Simpson. The unsympathetic Cranborne responded ... 'I understand very well the pain which they must have caused you. But I feel that they are not, truly viewed, an attack on liberty, but rather action which the community feels to be essential for the preservation of liberty.' Letter from Lord Cranborne to Lady Redesdale, 30 December 1940, by kind permission of Brian Simpson.

52 Note on the Question Why Prisoners Detained under Defence Regulation 18B Have Not Been Brought to Trial, HO45/24893/23.

53 Interview with Blanche Greaves, Archive of the Friends of O.M.

54 Interview with Gladys Walsh, Archive of the Friends of O.M.. In his study of local fascism in the East End of London and South West Essex, Linehan has looked into the issue of why the pattern of arrests was so arbitrary: 'The random and indiscriminate nature of the arrests, with relatively minor rank-and-file branch members detained, while some of those in more senior leadership positions were overlooked, suggests that the authorities may not have had an accurate picture of the BUF's membership structure in the region. We know that the Special Branch had to supplement its existing knowledge of BUF members with information supplied by the Board of Deputies at the outbreak of war ... . Apart from the approximately 246 detention orders that emanated from the Security Services and the Special Branch, there existed the list of names supplied by local Chief Constables. This comprised the remainder of the total number of 750 arrests made under DR 18b 1(A).' Thomas P. Linehan, *East London for Mosley* (London, 1996), p.180.

55 'In Hull we had two sisters in the movement, one of whom was particularly active and was excellent as a woman steward at noisy meetings, but she was not even questioned by the police, while the inoffensive and lapsed Leo Mortell was put in Walton Gaol with me.' John Charnley, *Blackshirts and Roses* (London, 1990), p.119.

56 R.R. Bellamy, *The Memories of a Fascist Beast*, p.111. Unpublished manuscript.

57 Letter from Diana Mosley to Brian Simpson [undated]. Her story continues: 'To make up, Ann Good (who was never arrested) came to the prison every week with food she could ill afford as presents for prisoners from the East End who were her friends.'

58 R.R. Bellamy, *Memories of a Fascist Beast*, pp.148–9.

59 War Cabinet, 20 July 1940, HO45/25767.

60 Even Eugenia Wright, who had attended a BUF meeting in Carlisle in the early 1930s as a girl of 14 and whose interest emanated from her attraction to a young Blackshirt in uniform, remembers: 'I eventually married and gave it no thought until the war began and my family teased me about the authorities looking for me as a fascist. That was a bit scary.' Letter from Eugenia Wright to the author, 6 May 1997.

61 *Hansard*, HC, 21 July 1942, Vol. 381, Col. 1455.

62 Louise Irvine, 'Arrest and Imprisonment under Regulation 18b: November 1940–November 1941: As Experienced by Miss C.L. Fisher (now Mrs Irvine).'

63 'This delving into quite irrelevant domestic matters was carried further than that, however, to an extent which can only be termed offensive. What was the purpose of cross-examining a man at length upon his having lived with a woman to whom he was not married; or pressing another for reasons why he should be "carrying on" with two women at the same time? If the purpose of the Committee was to examine public morality, that should have been made clear when they were appointed. If on the other hand it is believed by the

Home Secretary that deviations from the moral code go hand in hand with spying and treachery, then he can never have realized that the ideal spy or "agent" is the man who keeps clear of entanglements, rather than the one depicted, say, in the pages of Mr Bruce-Lockhart.' *"The Word": Special Investigation Report on 18B: It Might Have Happened to You* Then again, such voyeuristic interest in the sex lives of British fascist pre-dated 18B. Special Branch routinely reported with relish those incidents of deviant behaviour among BUF supporters throughout the 1930s.

64 Advisory Committee: Dissident Report by Mr G.H. Stuart Bunning, 30 November 1940, HO144/21933/294. To the Committee's credit, Stuart Bunning continued 'that, in trailing round in a ridiculous uniform she gives false impressions is also true, and I feel she is an unmitigated nuisance. These things, however, are not the business of the Committee and I cannot see enough in her short BU connection to justify even the mild restrictions impose upon her.' The Committee's assessment of Diana Mosley is another case in point. They reported, 'Lady Mosley appeared to the Committee to be an attractive and forceful personality, who stated her views with clearness and without ambiguity; and the Committee formed the opinion that the views she entertained were held quite sincerely. In these circumstances Lady Mosley could be extremely dangerous if she were at large.' Report of the Advisory Committee on the Case of Lady Diana Mosley, 4 October 1940, HO144/21995/39.

65 Supplementary Report on the Case of Ethel Annie Baggaley, Advisory Committee for Appeals Against Orders of Internment, 9 June 1943, HO45/25710.

66 October 1940, HO45/25758.

67 Letter from A.J. Adams and Adams Solicitors to Lucy Pearson, Essex County Record Office, D/DU/758/42/2.

68 *Suffer Little Children* (London, 18B Publicity Council [1943?]). The same Council also published the melodramatically titled *Persecuted Women in Britain To-Day* [1943?] which recounted its own atrocity stories: 'Young girls of 19 were torn from sheltered homes and thrust into the company of drunks and prostitutes; mothers were parted, without an hour's notice, from husbands and children; women of over seventy are still hobbling over the stone floors of Holloway Prison.'

69 R.R. Bellamy, *Memories of a Fascist Beast*, p.153.

70 Advisory Committee to Consider Appeals Against Orders of Internment, 2 October 1940: Diana Mosley, HO144/21995/15–36.

71 Oswald Mosley to Winterton MP, 25 November 1940, HO45/24891/251–55.

72 Holloway Prison: Visit by Sir Walter Monckton to Diana Mosley, 26 April 1941, HO144/21995/99. After refusing to sign the affidavit on Mrs Whinfield's behalf, Mosley suggested that her advocates should 'get her out through her husband's ill health if you like. She has money to buy herself out, others cannot.'

73 Minutes, 28 July 1941, HO45/25753.

74 Letter from Constance Pearson to Dr Summerskill MP, 20 October 1940, Essex County Record Office, D/DU/758/42/1.

75 Edith Summerskill MP wrote to Herbert Morrison on 24 January 1941: 'It has been brought to my attention that Friendly Enemy Aliens at the IOM who are strongly anti-Nazi are obliged to live and use the same rooms with pro-Nazi women. This leads to certain unpleasantness and consequently the anti-Nazi's are having a very unhappy life. Will you let me know if the women can be separated, as I believe the men were?' HO215/156. Mrs Dorothy Naftel, Secretary of the International Co-operative Women's Guild, visited the women's camp on the Isle of Man in January 1941. One of her main recommendations was that the de-nazification process should begin in the internment camps and the camps should be used as 'forcing houses for democracy.' HO215/55. In March 1941 Mrs Corbett-Ashby, in her capacity as Vice-Chairman of the Friendly Aliens Protection Committee, visited the women's internment camps on the IOM, and reported that 'rather inadequate division of Nazi and Fascist from anti-Nazi and anti-Fascist has been attempted, but the indifference and complacency in the women's camp is disturbing.' HO215/156. When the International Red Cross visited the women's camp as late as 16 February 1944, they still reported that 'this camp, which is set apart for women, even of different nationalities and political tendencies, presents by reason of the very fact problems different from those which are met elsewhere. In the long run, dissensions develop worse in female communities than among men.' HO215/74.

76 Lady Davidson visited Holloway with Miss Irene Ward in February or March 1941, HO45/25723.

77 Diana Mosley, *A Life of Contrasts*, (London, 1977) p.176.

78 Louise Irvine, 16 February 1991, on 'Mosley's Men,' Friends of Oswald Mosley Cassette Tape, British Union Collection, University of Sheffield.

79 Letter from Lucy Pearson to Lady Davidson, 31 December 1940, Essex County Record Office, D/DU/758/42/1.

80 Diana Mosley related: 'Some wardresses were rude but on the whole we gradually tamed them and they soon realized that there wasn't a traitor among the prisoners.' Letter from Diana Mosley to Brian Simpson, 7 December 1989.

81 *Persecuted Women in Britain Today*, p.9.

82 Louise Irvine, 'Recollections of Lady Mosley.' Unpublished typescript.

83 Lucy Pearson Papers, Essex County Record Office, D/DU/758/32.

84 Letter from Oswald Mosley to the 6th Earl (Edward) Winterton MP, 25 November 1940, HO45/24891/251–55. See also A.W. Brian Simpson, *In the Highest Degree Odious*, pp.232–3. It should be noted, however, that Lucy Pearson's entry in her pocket diary tells a somewhat different story: '25 June, 1940: An air raid alarm in Holloway, we were unlocked.' Essex County Record Office, D/DU/758/32.

85   Admiral Barry Domvile also revealed fascist masculinism when he remarked on the fortunate differences between the treatment of fascist men and women. On a visit to his wife in Holloway on the occasion of their Silver Wedding Anniversary in 1941, he was 'relieved to find that the conditions for all the poor women shut up by these political sadists were much less onerous than ours, but the whole thing was a very black blot on the escutcheon of the once chivalrous English ... . Shame on British manhood.' Admiral Sir Barry Domvile, *From Admiral to Cabin Boy* (London, 1947), pp.120–1.

86   Letter from J.F. Moylan to B.E. Sargeant, 28 March 1941, HO215/408.

87   Letter from Joanna Cruickshank to Sir John Moylan, 10 May 1941, HO215/405.

88   Memorandum re: Married Camp, 18 November 1941, HO215/1360. As one alien detainee explained: 'Shopkeepers went to great length explaining to us, their dear, dear aliens, that they would never serve a Fascist, never. If a Fascist came asking for as much as a pinch of salt, she would be shown the door in no uncertain manner. A dear old friend of ours who served teas in the garden when the weather was nice was emphatic in her exclamations that no Fascist would ever sit on her garden chairs. If we were unreliable, we could be blamed for it (murmurs of protest from our side) we weren't English. But English people should know better.' Livia Laurent, *A Tale of Internment* (London, 1942), p.118.

89   Livia Laurent, *A Tale of Internment*, p.118.

90   18B women also had to contend with intrusive press coverage, and the nascent paparazzi. Less than a decade after the *Daily Mail* had proclaimed 'Hurray for the Blackshirts,' the paper published exaggerated articles such as the following. '80 women's cabin trunks and travelling cases were stacked on the quay at a West Coast port last night. They were the "luggage in advance" of British Fascist women to be interned for the duration at Port Erin, Isle of Man... "It has a holiday air," a railway porter told men. "They must have contained hundreds of dresses."' '80 Luxury Trunks: Isle of Man Awaits Women Fascists,' *Daily Mail*, 12 June 1941. Transportees also complained how 'photographers were at the quayside and photographs of all of us carrying our belongings as we disembarked were taken.' Louise Irvine, 'Arrest and Imprisonment under Regulation 18b. November 1940–November 1941: As Experienced by Miss C.L. Fisher.' Annie Lake wrote to Richard Stokes MP that 'surely it is enough that women should be persecuted as we are, without being made into a puppet show for the press.' HO215/246. I think an important point to be made is that unlike the German concentration camps – which the 18Bs oft compared to their own camps – in Britain the internment was in the public domain, and visible to all.

91   Letter from Annie Lake to Mr Stokes MP, 23 June 1941, HO215/246.

92   Report by Inspector Cuthbert, 'The Internment of Women, Children and Married Couples, 1940–1945,' submitted 9 June 1947, HO213/1053.

93 Part of the objection to these two petitions of 9 June and 7 July 1941 was that 'over 75% of aliens now in [the married camp] are Jewish, and there is, therefore considerable risk that the introduction of 18B detainees, who are anti-Semitic, might have an unfortunate and disturbing result. As, however, the number of 18B married couples is so small, it ought to be possible to make satisfactory arrangements to accommodate the 18Bs in a separate house in the married camp by sanction that, if any trouble arises between them and aliens in the camp, or any other trouble, they would have to return to separate detention at Peel and Port Erin.' Memorandum: Re: Married Camp, 18 November 1941, HO215/1360.

94 On 27 August 1941, Mosley wrote to request that husbands and wives should be interned together: 'We have now been 16 months apart and have frequently made this request. For the sake of the women who have suffered enough in a London prison, I ask that this internment be outside London, but not so remote that the cost of solicitors travelling to see us would be prohibitive.' HO45/24891/169–70. The reply, which was dated 23 October 1941, denied his request.

95 Letter from Winston Churchill to the Home Secretary, 15 November 1941, HO215/360.

96 Report on the Functioning of Regulation 18B of the Defence Regulations(1939), HO45/25714. Ann Page claims that another category of women who were immune to 18B were BU women in the armed forces. None such woman was ever interned. See Ann Page in *Mosley's Blackshirts*, p.20.

97 R.R. Bellamy, *Memories of a Fascist Beast*, pp.132–3. See also *Hansard*, HC, 4 July 1940, Vol. 362, Col. 1011–12.

98 Letter from Dorothy Viscountess Downe, to Lady Redesdale, Sunday 21 [date?]. By kind permission of Brian Simpson.

99 Mosley felt he could speak freely about Unity: 'I can say with absolute safety anything I feel about my sister-in-law, because she is obviously, as any doctor would certify, much too ill to be interned or taken seriously. She is a very sick person, in fact she has a bullet through her head.' Advisory Committee to Hear Appeals Against Orders of Internment: Sir Oswald Mosley, 3 July 1940, HO283/14/2–117.

100 Letter from Lucy Pearson to Lady Davidson, Essex County Record Office, D/DU/758/42/1.

101 Visit of Lady Redesdale to Diana Mosley, Holloway Prison, 7 January 1941, HO144/21995/108. Diana Mosley also confided to Sir Walter Monckton how 'I miss my freedom. I never was in one place for more than one week. I was going about, and the noise is dreadful – these young ones are so very noisy they have the wireless so loud and sing, then some of them tap dance and have a gramophone. I like to be quiet.' Visit of Walter Monckton to Diana Mosley, Holloway, 26 April 1941, HO144/21995/99.

102 Diana Mosley, *A Life of Contrasts*, p.176.

103 *Daily Express*, 3 July 1940.

104 Letter from the Rotherhite Co-op Women's Guild to the Home Secretary, 7 May 1942, HO45/24892/9.

105 HO45/22495/97

106 Special Branch report of a meeting held at Chiswick Hall under the auspices of the Chiswick Branch of the CP, 2 December 1943, HO45/24893/23.

107 Volunteers claimed that the Fund was non-political, yet it was widely believed that the Fund was being used as a cover for the illegal BU. It was reported that 'the Fascist salute was given by some members of the audience at a meeting organized by a body calling itself the "18B Committee" in Holborn Hall yesterday. Mosley's name was shouted and there were cries of "Perish Judah" at the end of the meeting ... . Among the speakers were Mr Howard Crisp and Mrs Dudley-Elam, both ex-detainees.' *Daily Worker*, 7 December 1942. Similarly, it was reported that 'A branch of the notorious 18B Detainees (British) Aid Fund, recently described by the pro-Fascist *Right Review* as "the thinly disguised BUF" has just been established in the Manchester area.' '18b Friends Move North,' *Daily Worker*, 6 May 1943.

108 18B Detainees (British) Aid Fund, 'Notice of Winding Up of Accounts and Final Appeal,' August 1945, Robert Saunders Collection, University of Sheffield, File C.15.

109 G. Beckwell, 'Blackshirt Brotherhood in War,' *Comrade*, 9 (October/November, 1987).

110 Of his mother, Anne Beckett (née Cutmore), Francis Beckett writes: 'Certainly she was under surveillance. Why was she not arrested? I suspect she was more use at liberty, where she could be followed everywhere. She certainly believed she was constantly followed, and the files suggest that she was right. She was probably a way of keeping tabs on the Duke of Bedford, whom it was considered unwise to arrest and unsafe to leave at liberty, and of discovering information which could be presented to the Home Secretary as a reason for keeping my father in prison.' Letter from Francis Beckett to the author, 7 July 1997.

111 Special Branch report, 12 November 1940, HO45/25728/33.

112 HO45/25702

113 Special Branch report, 20 November 1942, HO45/25705.

114 Letter from F.E. Hayes to Robert Saunders, 1 August 1943, Robert Saunders Collection, University of Sheffield, File C.10.

115 Letter from Robert Saunders to Miss Griffin, 4 June 1944, Robert Saunders Collection, University of Sheffield, File C.15.

116 Special Branch reported that on 2 December 1943 the Chiswick CP and the Rails Group of the Paddington CP both held 'Jail Mosley' meetings; the North and South Branches of the CP held a similar meeting at the Civic Hall, Croydon on 12 December 1943; and also on 12 December, the London District

Committee of the CP held one in Hyde Park. HO45/24893/23, HO45/24893/ 25, HO45/24893/42, HO45/24893/44.

117 Special Branch report, 29 November 1943, HO45/24894/8. Miss Griffin admitted that 'it is very difficult to know what to do as if one expresses one's real feelings in the matter it might make matters worse not better. In fact Crawlay and Mrs Woods both turned up during the other week to ask whether they should write to the papers etc., but I advised them to keep quiet and do nothing as I feel however discreet they are it might not improve matters and after all the main thing is O.M. is out and as long as he is left out the best thing is to let things take there[sic] course.' Letter from Joan Griffin to Robert Saunders, 1 December 1943, Robert Saunders Collection, University of Sheffield. File C.10.

118 Special Branch listed the names of 125 of the more conspicuous patrons of this event, of whom 25 were women. HO45/24467.

119 Advisory Committee: Diana Mosley, 2 October 1940, HO144/21995/15–36. The administrators of the Defence Regulations were prepared for the hardening of anti-democratic sentiments among internees. On 21 May 1940, at a meeting to brief the Home Secretary for a War Cabinet meeting, Sir John Anderson expressed the reservation that 'he needed to be reasonably convinced that the BU might assist the enemy and that unless he could get such evidence it would be a mistake to imprison Mosley and his supporters who would be extremely bitter after the war when democracy would be going through its severest trials.' Quoted in F.H. Hinsley & C.A.G Simkins, *British Intelligence in the Second World War: Vol. 4: Security and Counter-Intelligence*, p.51.

120 Letter from Lucy Pearson to Rev. B.J. Coggle, 4 February 1941, Essex County Record Office, D/DU/758/42/1.

121 Robert Row, 'Detention Without Trial (Defence Regulation 18B) 1940/1943,' unpublished typescript.

122 Diana Mosley, *A Life of Contrasts*, p.135. She also says that 'when I knew Hitler the Russian crimes were actuality, the Chinese holocaust was in the future and so was the German.' p.128. Through her eyes, the Nazi extermination of six million Jews is deemed of limited significance by comparison with other crimes, and the very term 'holocaust' is denied its specific identification with Hitler's Final Solution. Some 18Bs were more honest about the survival of their anti-Semitism after the war, and Domvile held the 'Judmas' conspirators accountable for implementing the Defence Regulations. He wrote, 'we hear a great deal of the persecution of Jew by Gentile: in 18B we have the reverse process.' Admiral Sir Barry Domvile, *From Admiral to Cabin Boy*, p.86.

123 John Charnley, *Blackshirts and Roses*, p.62.

124 Churchill believed that the Fifth Columnist scare encouraged an atmosphere of 'witchfinding'. Quoted in Richard Thurlow, *The Secret State*, p.239.

Conclusion

Women, Fascism, and Fanaticism,

Past and Present

Part I

It is inevitable that the researcher or reader will bring to this contentious and emotionally-charged subject of women and fascism many preconceptions and expectations, especially about the anti-woman, anti-feminist and male-supremacist nature of fascism in ideology and in practice. Understandable anti-fascist prejudices may lead us to anticipate only the negation of tolerant political behaviour and the oppression of freedom of expression, and to presume that the membership of a fascist movement might consist of hapless, 'evilly-disposed,' and eccentric women, unwittingly manipulated by a male-chauvinist leadership and ideology. However, the history of women and fascism in Britain is many-faceted, and it has been by examining this problem through various methodological lenses – political structure, gender ideologies, biography, prosopography, personal memories, public records and popular perceptions – that we arrive at some unpredictable conclusions on the pro-active and non-coercive relationship between women and fascism in Britain.

The stereotypes of women under fascism have developed in the context of women's lived experience and political destiny under Fascist and Nazi regimes on the Continent. When the historical memory is directed back to the Fascist and Nazi states between the wars, the images of woman that are evoked are those of an inferior creature, again deprived of hard-won rights and her vote, relegated to the private sphere, denied employment in favour of her menfolk, frantically cheering for the charismatic leaders, and objectified as a breeder of race and nation. In women's history the fascist period was one of backlash, defeat, and both personal and collective tragedy.

The British Union of Fascists (BUF) self-consciously distanced itself from the patterns of continental fascism, and this was especially marked in the way that Sir Oswald Mosley differentiated the treatment of women in his own movement from the condition of womanhood in Nazi Germany. Mosley's generous tribute that 'my movement has been largely built up by the fanaticism of women,' and his claim that 'without the women I could not have got a quarter of the way,' illustrate both the BUF's integration and its exploitation of female enthusiasm. Certainly Mosley's sincerity in this regard can be questioned, and we could speculate whether progressive attitudes on the women question would have survived if British fascism had become more than a Utopian dream in the minds of a minority of 'fanatics.' Leagues away from parliamentary power, a movement on the periphery of political legitimacy, British fascism could well afford to offer a mixed bag of ideological options. It can also be presumed that, as a consequence of political marginality, the BUF was in no position to spurn the support of any section of society. Marching in Mosley's columns alongside distinguished war veterans, professional men, and former members of Conservative and Labour parties, were criminals, street hooligans, and, of course, women. Only by examining the phenomenon of *fringe* fascism do we see exposed in the boldest relief the intensity of women's agency.

It would be trivializing and patronizing to assume that these women were involuntary participants in the BUF's public displays of violence, in propagating anti-Semitism, and in aiding and abetting a British Fifth Column. This study seeks to give women their due as autonomous historical agents and avoid portraying them as manipulated victim figures, without applauding the results of their self-willed action. With the BUF's successful mobilization of female fanaticism, we are alerted to the fact that fascism's revolutionary challenge to democratic standards cannot simply be dismissed as a process of emancipating women from emancipation.

That British women were under no undue pressure to enlist in the BUF was partly due to the fact that to join was itself an act of rebellion, and demanded a disregard for public ridicule or official censure that can be called courageous. There was little that was subservient in the attitude of young Louise Irvine who believed that she was accepted into the BUF as an 'independent' and a 'free-thinking individual.' British Blackshirt women departed radically from mainstream politics, defied notions of respectable female political behaviour, and, through their willingness to engage in militant and illegal acts, demonstrated their profound commitment to revolutionary methods.

Part II

Women's involvement in Britain's fascist movement can be seen to have matured through a five-stage life cycle. In May 1923, the British Fascisti was founded by the ultra-patriotic ex-servicewoman, Rotha Lintorn-Orman. The BF appealed in equal measure to male and female members of Britain's armed forces as well as rearguard elements among the middle- and upper-middle-classes, and thus the precedent was set for the effortless collusion between the extreme-Right and female nationalist militancy. While the BF adopted the name of Mussolini's Italian creed, there was some truth in the charge that the movement merely represented 'Conservatism with knobs on', and we can term this first stage as the pre-natal or gestation period of British fascism.

In October 1932, Sir Oswald Mosley founded the British Union of Fascists, and from 1932 through to 1934 the BUF enjoyed the type of attention conferred upon a promising newborn. During this period of the first flush of youthful endeavour and high hopes the time was ripe for a plethora of ideological positions to be tested, and Lord Rothermere could proclaim 'Hurray for the Blackshirts' and his newspapers could relish the fact that 'Beauty Joins the Blackshirts.' Among the women who gathered around the youthful and youth-worshipping movement were Lady Cynthia Mosley, Maud, Lady Mosley, Lady Makgill, Mary Richardson, the late Earl Haig's two sisters, and Lady Houston. In response to the successful recruitment of women, the movement established its own Women's Section in 1933, launched *The Woman Fascist*, and opened the National Club for Women Fascists. Under the titular directorship of 'Ma' Mosley, the Women's Section enjoyed some independence from the male hierarchy, convened its own meetings and speakers' classes, and organized social and fund-raising events.

The BUF's graduation into the phase of its own adolescent rebellion was signalled by the actions of the Blackshirts at the

Olympia Rally of 7 June 1934. The innocence of childhood was lost, no longer could the BUF be given the benefit of the public's doubt, and thereafter the movement concentrated its propaganda efforts on London's East End and fortified its anti-Semitic campaign. From 1935 through to 1938 the BUF was hampered by rebellion within its own ranks; disillusionment and opposition to internal dictatorship was evident on the part of Maud, Lady Mosley, Mary Richardson, Sylvia Morris, and Mrs Carrington-Wood; and 1937 saw the creation of the National Socialist League, a more militant fascist gang, which eventually lured Mercedes Barrington and Anne Cutmore away from the BUF. In this atmosphere of internal discord, the Women's Section became progressively subservient to the male leadership and women were increasingly marginalized by the BUF's male-youth-gang mentality and reactive masculinism.

We can identify another shift in women's ideological and political positioning, starting in 1938 and lasting through to end of the 'Phoney War.' During this, the BUF's period of parenthood, greater emphasis was placed on women's maternal role and the fascist press increasingly became their forum to make pleas to protect their children against the threat of war. Within the movement this was also the time when women regained some control in the British fascist family by mounting their own Women's Peace Campaign, and by replacing men in leadership positions. Finally, with the passing of Defence Regulation 18B(1A) on 22 May 1940, the British Union was forced to enter its second childhood. The government crack-down on fascist activities led to a situation where BU members were to be seen but not heard in the constricted interior of their prison cells.

The influence of women at every stage of the movement's life cycle is demonstrated by the outstanding female personalities who jump out from the pages of the BUF's publications, by the visibility of certain women in the records compiled by the secret state, and by the vivid memories of gender co-operation and joint endeavour which have been diligently preserved by former members of the BUF. One purpose for providing a Who's Who as an appendix to this study is to challenge the conventional image of the fascist woman, particularly the impression that the BUF recruited mainly spirited middle-aged and eccentric middle-class women who had nothing better to do in their hours of idleness than bait the government, Jews, and communists. The socio-demographic and genealogical patterns of women joiners is striking for its diversity rather than for its neatness.

Generally speaking, all joiners were attracted by the BUF's offer of a political alternative. They warmed to Mosley's charismatic leadership and his glamorous celebrity status – after all, 'Every woman adores a Fascist'[1] – and to the Leader's ready solutions to British social, economic, and imperial decline. Whereas the authorities alleged that the majority of BU members were 'persons with no political knowledge who had joined the Union because of personal grievances of various kinds,' many fascist women, in fact, had previous political experience, and a shift in party allegiances from the Conservatives to the BUF was typical. On the personal level, the BUF also offered community and a social network – a rigorous regime of branch meetings, marches, paper selling, and dances. For Blanche Greaves, being W/D/L for Kingston 'was my life.' For the young East Ender, Gladys Walsh, 'going to the branch was like going to a second home.' Nellie Driver appreciated how the movement had 'plenty of romance in the form of drum corps, salutes, standards, emblems, uniforms and impressive demonstrations which made an appeal to me. From henceforth politics and social reform were to be my religion.' In the case of the middle-aged and unmarried Ethel Baggaley, National Socialism inspired a 'rather colourless existence with all the force of missionary fervour.'

Common to the family history of many of these women was the loss of either a father or partner during the Great War. Anne Cutmore, Marjorie Clare and Agnes Booth each lost their father in the war, and Lucy Pearson the man she intended to marry. Louise Fisher, Blanche Mann, Nellie Driver, and Yolande Mott were each fatherless when they joined the BUF. Many single young women joined the movement on their own initiative, and of this younger generation many met their future husbands in the BUF: Marjorie Aitken, Margaret Monk, Olive Hawks, Anne Cutmore, Blanche Mann, Heather Bond, Louise Fisher, Margaret Cairns, and Joan Thorpe. There was a very evident contingent of single women past the traditional age of marriage, and there can be little doubt that the BUF provided Lucy Pearson, Ethel Baggaley, Florence Hayes, Iris Ryder, Olga Shore, Muriel Currey, Dr Margaret Vivien, Mary Richardson and Mary Allen, with a surrogate family and sense of purpose. There were also many formidable husband-and-wife teams in the BUF, and in few cases does it seem that the women were any less committed than their husbands to fascist politics. First and foremost among the fascist couples were Oswald and Diana Mosley themselves, and their example was emulated

270

by Dudley and Norah Elam, Henry and Diana deLaessoe, Joe and Ruth Beckett, the Cottons in Exeter, Florence and Charles Elliott in Slough, William and Margaret Joyce, Tommy and Toni Moran, the Potters in Norfolk, and the Stephensons in Dorset West. Conversely, many married women were active in the BUF without the visible collaboration of their husbands: Muriel Whinfield, Anne Brock Griggs, Lady Pearson and Viscountess Downe each exemplified how wives could activate their radical political choices independent of their husbands. What is remarkable in all of these cases is that BUF women were free from the compulsion imposed by a patriarchal figure.

These patterns of female adherence surely imply a tension between the idealized structure of fascist organization along the lines of a *mannerbünd* and the actual mobilization of women's support. Admittedly, it was ironic, if not disingenuous, for male propagandists to invite women to build a more masculine Britain and to participate in the purge of the feminine from political behaviour; they advocated women's return to domestic roles once a fascist government was in place and the Corporate State had been implemented. However, we must not forget that BUF women offered little resistance to explicit male-supremacy and that they expressed few reservations about the BUF's rhetorical attacks on the contemporary feminist movement – indeed, the most virulent of these condemnations were launched by the ex-suffragettes themselves. It may be uncomfortable to acknowledge that part and parcel of their agency was the fact that BUF women purchased the whole ideological package, while simultaneously emulating the valiant suffragettes by preaching their fascist faith on street corners, and seeking to benefit from the Parliament Qualification of Powers Act (November 1918) by standing as British Union candidates.

Part III

In order to listen to the polyphony of voices and thus faithfully record the BUF's pronouncements on the woman question, this study has opted for an empirical approach. I have seen my role as that of a witness rather than a stern judge of the actions and intention of Britain's fascist women. Where appropriate, I have framed the questions that I have posed in the inter-war discourses on feminism and women's politicization. During the 1930s anti-fascists recognized that the position given to women 'is one of the surest measures of the level of a civilization,' and, on this count, 'Fascism is revealed in its most undisguised reactionary character.'[2] Thelma Cazalet-Keir told the Commons in 1941: 'I am sure that one of the tests of civilization of a country – and by civilization I mean democratic ways of life – is the position and status given to women.'[3] Grappling with the same question in reverse, is not one of the tests of a commitment to the equality of the sexes the acceptance of liberal democratic principles? With this as the premise, I have argued that regardless of the BUF's Promethean attempt to steal the fire of feminist militancy, no such doctrinal position as fascist feminism was, or is, possible.

While contemporary feminist methodologies explore some of the power dynamics essential to fascism, the problem is that they have seldom diagnosed the causes of the fascist pathology. We cannot, for instance, contextualize feminine fascism without at the same time examining the overriding masculine dimensions of British fascism and analysing how men gendered their political ideas and activities. Before rushing to judgement on feminist criteria, it is first necessary to explore the nuances of women's volition in spreading the virus of anti-democratic reaction and jingoistic intolerance.

Currently there appears to be a new direction in women's studies that might well accommodate and even applaud the strange history of the 'evil' fascist woman. Most prominently, Camille Paglia has spear-headed a movement of ideological dissent against the hegemony of the feminism of the contemporary academy. Paglia's *Sexual Personae* (1990), and her own charismatic personality, have ushered in a new tide of feminism, and refreshed and resurrected the notion that women are not victims, and that the *femme fatale* is as dominant, and indeed as domineering, a cultural type as the angel of the house. She has stressed 'the truth of sexual stereotypes and ... the biologic basis of sex differences,' in order to 'reaffirm and celebrate woman's ancient mystery and glamour.'[4] Her aspiration is no longer to re-empower women, because throughout history women had immense elemental power. Paglia's vision is a creative liberation, an affirmation of the beautiful and sublime, a celebration of cultural decadence and of art for art's sake. Not only does she seem to be claiming liberation from dogma for her literary subjects, but for herself as an author, and, by extension, for her reader and other aspiring authors. But what happens when we look at the topic of women and fascism in the light of this seemingly liberating conceptual framework? Here the situation becomes more ominous and menacing; the revision recommended may not lead us to higher planes of freedom, but to a new tyranny or a new extremism.

Paglia glorifies the wicked women of the past and celebrates both rhetorical and physical violence. The new goddesses are butch Amazon women; they are the vanguard of the Dionescian/Paglian reaction against dogmatic feminism. These cultural types are realized in Paglia's popular icons, in Elizabeth Taylor and Madonna, and in the 'Girl Power' pop of the Spice Girls.[5] They all exude a raw sexuality, appropriate traditionally masculine urges, and arm for the bloody battles of the never-ending sex war. In their provocation and insinuation, the Paglian women demonstrate the cant of the feminism of the academy, and replace the intellectual totalitarianism of orthodox post-structuralism with, what is in effect, boot-in-the-face fascism. The danger is not in recognizing and then reviving archetypes, but in the unquestioned glorification of the female gang, of pagan and amoral aggression, of identifying the next stage in women's emancipation from victim status in the recasting of woman as the victimizer. Is strangling the angel in the house best accomplished by substituting for the staid domestic ideal of femininity the 'Girl Power' of the female youth gang? Certainly, from the perspective of the majority in the mob, even palingenetic fascism can be liberating, and the essential fascist aesthetic of the banalization of aggression strives towards new heights of sublimity. But what is really accomplished for the advancement of civilization, civility, and inclusive citizenship by casting the new woman as the sexual animal gone wild? Is female demagogy really the alternative to patriarchy and male domination?

I have argued that the BUF's model for organization was the male youth gang. Through their own participation in the British fascist movement, and in their enthusiasm for Mosley, BUF women sanctioned the male youth-gang-model, and agitated for their own admission to this para-military horde. It can be seen how the pro-active and provocative fascist female of the inter-war period could be resurrected in accordance with the resuscitated matriarchal model of the sexy female youth gang. BUF women could be re-evaluated as mislaid heroines, as misrepresented feminine essentialists, and as prefigurative dissenters from the atrophied intellectualism of the contemporary academy. In their recourse to violence, in their ratification of the union between sex and aggression, and in their rhetoric of condescension and negation directed towards the feminism espoused by the all-female pressure groups working

273

within the democratic system, BUF women foreshadow much of what Paglia is offering as the alternative to orthodox feminism in our own time.

However, as I have also argued, Mosley's women were fascists first and foremost, and it is as important to evaluate the content of their fascist beliefs as it is to contemplate the ways in which they reconciled their womanly natures with their political ideals. Certainly the history of women is not one and the same as the history of feminism, nor is the history of fascism one and the same as the history of man. Within fascist constructs we can identify the power struggles of sexual politics and the attempt to achieve sexual mastery over all opponents. But fascism is not principally a response to the intrigues of sexual politics, as the Channel Four series *Mosley* (broadcast in February and March 1998) might have us believe. Fascism and National Socialism are about world domination, racial persecution, the quashing of individualism and human creativity, the repression of freedom of expression and action, and the cult of the personality of a leader who is not first among equals but dictator. BUF women prioritized their national, regional, imperial, racial and political identities above their sense of being members of a women's community. It is therefore more important to analyse their actions and intentions within the frameworks of political ideologies and political culture, than to fit them into feminist paradigms and into feminist critiques of patriarchy.

While it would be negligent not to refer to the contemporary debates within feminism when studying this one aspect of women's history, it would at the same time be ahistorical to impose the theories of these warring intellectual factions onto women's experiences during the 1930s. With the exception of the Edwardian women's suffrage movement, in any period prior to 1945 there is a high probability that our historical subjects were not personally preoccupied by gender issues. Consequently, applying the rarefied categories of feminist criticism to the culture of feminine fascism may not get to the heart of the matter. BUF women were going against the tide of the (gender-neutral) ideologies of liberalism, parliamentary conservatism, socialism, and communism, rather than defining their rebellion as an anti-feminist reaction. Feminism was not their enemy – political ideologies of the Left and the liberal-democratic system were. We must seek a middle road of analysis which does not lose sight of the ethical dimension of women's political behaviour and belief. Whether as a female researcher examining a topic of women in history, or as a political historian looking at this one aspect of the British fascist phenomenon, the guiding principle I have tried to follow is to allow these historical agents to damn themselves, where appropriate, by recording and placing in context their intolerant utterances, their anti-humanist reaction against all those outside a narrowly defined British race, and their praise for Nazi methods. Just as it has to be recognized that fascist women were not simply manipulated victims but often participants in their own right, so it needs to be recognized what sort of political movement it was in which they participated.

Notes

1   'Every woman adores a Fascist,/ The boot in the face, the brute/ Brute heart of a brute like you.' Sylvia Plath, 'Daddy,' in *Ariel* (London, 1963).
2   R. Palme Dutt, *Fascism and Social Revolution* (New York, 1934) p.218
3   *Hansard*, HC, 20 March 1941, Vol. 370, col. 347.
4   Camille Paglia, *Sexual Personae* (New York, 1991), p.xiii.
5   Paglia could as easily have chosen the BUF's own Unity Mitford, Diana Mosley, Audrey Hepburn's mother Ella deHeemstra as emblematic of glamorous women behaving badly.

Appendix

Who's Who in the History of

Women and Fascism in Britain

Although fascism tends to adhere rather slavishly to the leadership principle and foster its reputation based on the actions and intentions of its most prominent leaders, leaders are not worth their mettle without followers. Any inroads that Britain's fascist movement might have made between 1923 and 1945 were the result of the committed activism of the rank-and-file as well as of their leaders. In order to come to terms with the content and tone of women's fascist propaganda, and place in context the political choices and public behaviour typical of fascist activists, it is helpful to examine the patterns of participation, personal histories, and biographies of joiners. Furthermore, by tracing women's fascist activities and locating the areas where women's participation was most prevalent, it is possible to highlight the degree and intensity of women's agency in Britain's fascist movement.

This final section is meant to provide an anecdotal complement to the examination of party structure and ideology, as well as standing as a running data base. As such, this *Who's Who* is inevitably incomplete, and I would hope that it may bring forth even more information through the release of public records and the memories of those who knew certain individuals among the figures in the history of women and fascism in Britain.

The persons identified in this section are those who were members of Lintorn-Orman's British Fascisti, Sir Oswald Mosley's British Union of Fascists, or who were active participants in other extreme right organizations such as the Right Club, the Link, the Imperial Fascist League, the Anglo-German Fellowship, and the Nordic League. The focus is on the women who surface through public records, in the memories and memoirs of their comrades, and in primary sources related to British fascism. However, I have also included certain men whose stories intersect most closely with women in the movement, either because they were married to or connected by family relations to women activists, or because they played significant roles in the implementation of the movement's women's policy and the ideology of feminine fascism. The inclusion of men

276

illuminates issues of gender relations and fascist sexuality, and underlines the claim that the story of women's activism cannot be properly told in isolation from the development of male and masculine identities within the movement.

Persons are identified by the symbols appearing after their name: (^) member of the British Fascisti, (*) member of the British Union of Fascists, (+) member of another fascist or Anti-Semitic organization, and (| | |) interned under DR 18B. Many entries are followed by more than one symbol, as it was not unusual that an individual would hold joint membership in more than one fascist organization, and it also follows that being a member of the BU was the most common prerequisite for internment under the DR 18B. Also included in this section are entries for other women whose lives converged with Britain's fascist movement. These include fellow travellers of the Right, sympathizers, and some women who were suspected of pro-Nazi activities during the Second World War, or, conversely, women recruited to monitor fascist activity and administer the Defence regulations.

The information contained in this section is gleaned from a combination of sources, including the BF's and BUF's newspapers, reports from the local and national press, public records, and my correspondence with former members of the BUF. I am particularly grateful to Robert Row, John Warburton and Jeffrey Wallder for their help in identifying rank-and-file members of the BUF, for sharing with me their recollections and their stories about fellow BUF members, and for giving me access to interview material which forms part of the archive of the Friends of O.M.

Legend
^   Member of the British Fascists
*   Member of the British Union of Fascists
+   Member of another Fascist or Anti-Semitic Organization
| | | Interned under the Defence Regulations 18B

Adair, Mrs ^
Wife of Commander of the Men's Units, Belfast. She ran the Belfast FCC for the British Fascists in 1927.

Ailesbury, Marchioness of ^
Member of the British Fascisti. In September 1927 she accepted the appointment of Honorary Vice-President of the British Fascist Organization and was thus elected to the Grand Council.

Aitken, Miss Margery*
Aitken received four years of training as a nurse in Melbourne Hospital in Australia. In 1934 she was Commandant of the BUF's Women's Defence Force (or the

S.P.S., a very athletic all-women formation of the BUF). In December 1934, after violent scenes at a meeting in Manchester, Aitken appeared in court as a witness against six anti-fascist protesters. In 1935, she sat on the BUF Production Directory at NHQ. In March 1935 she worked for the Women's Section as leader of the Special Propaganda Squad, earning a salary of £200 per annum. She was a skilled fencer. She married Dr A.M. Moore, who was the BUF Medical Adviser and a consultant at the London Hospital. She was from a military family which played a large part in the early BUF. Her father was Commander Aitken, Royal Navy. One of her brothers served in the RAF and was killed in a flying accident near Pulborough, Sussex, in 1934 or 1935. Another brother, Lionel, was very active in the movement from its inception, joined the RAF in 1939, reached the rank of Squadron Leader, and died on active service. (In May 1934 Special Branch reported that Deputy Administrative Officer Aitken was in charge of the Western area for the BUF. In July 1935 it was reported that Commander Aitken was of the Recruiting Department, and that Mary Richardson was a close friend of the Aitken family).

Alderidge, Mrs E.G.*
Women's District Leader in Shipley (Yorkshire) in 1940.

Allen, Commandant Mary Sophia *
(Born 12 March 1878, and died 16 December 1964). Daughter of Thomas Isaac Allen, Manager of the Great Western Railway and Margaret Carlyle. Allen was educated at Princess Helena College, Ealing. She was an active member of the WSPU and had great admiration for the Pankhursts. As a militant suffragette act, in July 1909, with 13 other women, she broke the windows of the Home Office and was fined £5 plus 2/6d costs, or a month in the Second Division. She chose prison and after a sixty-hour hunger strike she was released. She accompanied Keir Hardie and the Home Secretary, Herbert Gladstone, on a tour of inspection of conditions in Holloway on 13 August 1909. As a result of her second prison term she became ill, and Mrs Pankhurst forbade her to risk imprisonment again; she then became an organizer for the WSPU in Edinburgh. Her association with Margaret Damer Dawson began in August 1914, and Allen was one of the early recruits to the Women's Police Force. In 1915, with Miss Harburn, she was chosen to go to Grantham as a representative of the Women's Police, where a military camp had been set up. In May 1915 she was transferred to Hull. Awarded the OBE in 1917. In July 1919, with a number of her officers, she attended a Royal Garden Party at Buckingham Palace, held especially for representatives of the women's war services. After the war she founded the Women's Police Reserve, an unofficial body whose object it was to train women for entry into the Police Force. In May 1921 Mary Allen and her 'Unofficial Women Police' were fined 10/- and ordered to pay 10 guineas

278

costs for the unauthorized wearing of a uniform similar to that of the Metropolitan Police. In 1922, she stood as a Liberal candidate for the St George Division of Westminster and came at the bottom of the poll with 1,303 votes (6.5%). In March 1923 her renamed Women's Auxiliary Service was invited by the War Office to send six members to Cologne to help German police combat venereal disease. She went to Germany to make the necessary arrangements in June 1923. The Women's Police were withdrawn from Germany in August 1925. She visited the United States in 1924 on behalf of the Women's Police. In 1926 she attended the International Police Congress and Exhibition in Berlin, where she met General O'Duffy, representing the Irish Free State Police, by whom she was much impressed. During the General Strike of May 1926 she appealed to women to join her Service, and was proud to accept an offer of assistance from Emmeline Pankhurst. In 1927 she attended a League of Nations conference on the traffic in women. She launched *The Policewoman's Review* in May 1927. Attended *Le Congrès International Feministe* in Berlin in May 1929, where it was mistakenly presumed that she was a Commandant in the Metropolitan Policewomen division and wore their uniform. She attended a gathering in Sao Paulo, Brazil, to speak on her London branch of the police in July 1931. In 1933 she and her Women's Auxiliary Service visited the BF Ltd. In November 1933 she formed the Women's Reserve to enrol women to serve in times of emergency (this had no official backing). She visited Germany in January 1934 and met Hitler and Goering. Addressed a meeting of the January Club in March, and again in April 1934. In March 1935 she wrote a series of three articles for the *Sunday Dispatch* on her experiences as a suffragette and as a police woman. In May 1935 she visited Warsaw, and in February 1936 she went to Cairo (on holiday). In 1936 she visited Spain at the invitation of General Franco, and it was reported that she advocated a Fascist International. She was also a member of the Friends of National Spain. By February 1939 it was reported that she was an adherent of the BU, although her connection was being kept secret because she was thought to be in a position to obtain valuable information through her contacts. Robert Row claims that she was very useful in speaking up for the BU with the top men at Scotland Yard, as she knew them all. In July 1939 she attended private meetings at the home of Margaret Bothamley – while she claimed these were only tea parties, Special Branch assumed subversive activities were discussed on these occasions. She claimed that she joined the BU in December 1939. Like her fellow ex-suffragette friend, Norah Elam, Allen was involved in the cause of animal defence and she was a member of the council of the Anti-Vivisection Society. In November and December 1939 she attended meetings to organize collaboration between The Link, the BU, and the Right Club, and on 11 December she was present at a lunch held at the Ladies' Carlton for BU women. She attended the London Administration luncheon on 1 March 1940, and was given a seat of honour. She spoke at a BU Women's Peace meeting at Friend's House on 13 April 1940. In March, April and May 1940 she was alleged to have attended secret meetings convened by various pro-Nazi and anti-Semitic organizations at 48 Ladbroke Grove W11. An Order under DR 18B was made against her and served on 16 June 1940. She came before the Advisory Committee on 6 November 1940 but was never interned. She joined Mosley's Union Movement after the war and lived in Cornwall with a woman 'friend'.

Allen, William E.D.*

The Chairman of the Directors of David Allen & Sons Limited, a private company of printers and lithographers. Served as Conservative MP for West Belfast. Member of the New Party. Author of *BUF: Oswald Mosley and British Fascism* (1934). He was involved in Mosley's Museum Investments Ltd and radio advertising project in the mid-1930s. It was through his bank account that foreign funds from Mussolini were channelled into the BUF. With J.F.C. Fuller, he visited Germany in 1935 as a representative of the BUF. He was an MI5 agent and reported to Maxwell-Knight on the activities of the BUF.

Amos, Miss Marjory (a.k.a Amor)+

Her real name was Marjory Mackie. She was an MI5 agent planted in the Right Club by Maxwell-Knight. Her name appears on the Right Club ledger of *ca.*May 1939. Miss Mary Stanford admitted to attending a house-warming party given by Miss Amos at 24 Marson Mews in April or early May of 1940.

Andrews, Mrs*

BU member in Islington. Attended a meeting of BU elements on 23 November 1943.

Annsley, (Lady) Clare*

In 1928 and again in 1929 she contested Bristol West for Labour, and on both occasions lost to the Conservative candidate. In 1931 she stood as the Labour candidate in Bedford, and lost to the Conservative candidate. She was a member of the BUF. David Pryce-Jones records that during the 1930s she also worked for the Peace Pledge Union. She was present at a dinner at Claridge's hosted by the Anglo-German Fellowship to welcome Gertrud Sholtz-Klink, who visited London in March 1938. Present at the 18B Social and Dance held at the Royal Hotel on 15 December, 1945. Active in the British People's Party after the war.

Atkinson, Mrs Katherine^

Member of the BF's Grand Council and a close friend of Nesta Webster, with whom she had collaborated in writing the pamphlet, *The Communist Menace*. Her son was John Baker White, Assistant Director and then Director of the Economic League between 1926 and 1939. In 1923 White was recruited to run 'Section

D', a secretive private intelligence gathering agency operated by the British Empire Union. In his capacity with the BEU he visited the BF headquarters in 1923.

Baggaley, Miss Ethel Annie* | | |

(Born *ca.*1888). She worked as a secretary for 11 years in a Manchester firm, Humphries Jackson & Ambler, metal window manufacturers. She joined the BU in 1935, when she was 47 years old, and became an active party worker. She became Women's Canvass Officer, and in 1937 was promoted to the position of W/D/L of the small Hulme Branch. She took part in the Middleton by-election in 1940, canvassing and distributing BU pamphlets. Her address was given as 43 Sloane Street, Moss Side, Manchester, on the Home Office Schedule for detention. She was interned as a member of the BU on the General List of 30 May 1940, and detained in Holloway on 3 June 1940. She came before the Advisory Committee on 15 October 1940 and her release was denied. Her case was reviewed by the Home Office in January 1942 and it was decided that the Order should be maintained. She appeared before the Advisory Committee again on 29 April 1942, and Violet Markham recommended that her detention should continue as Baggaley still maintained her fascist views and refused to engage in war work. She was released from detention in July 1943.

Baker, Mrs Olive* +

A school teacher in Germany. She returned to England in 1939 and was in contact with Admiral Barry Domvile of the Link. Alternately, she has been described as a thirty-nine-year-old nurse who had joined the BUF in 1939. On 12 June 1940 she was committed for trial for distributing postcards advertising the New British Broadcasting Station. While awaiting trial she cut her wrist and wrote 'Hail Mosley' and 'Heil Hitler' in blood in her cell. She was convicted at Bristol Assizes on 5 July 1940, and sentenced to five years imprisonment. She was presumed to have been Domvile's mistress.

Barker, Colonel (a.k.a Valerie Arkell-Smith)+

(1895–1960) She was born in Jersey, the daughter of Thomas William Barker (d.1918). She attended a convent school in Belgium from 1913 to 1914. During the Great War she first lived in Surrey with her parents, then joined the Scout movement, later became a VAD nurse, and also served with the Women's Auxiliary Air Force in France. Married an Australian officer, Second-Lieut. Harold Arkell-Smith, in Milford in 1918. They had two children, and then divorced in 1923. From 1919 to 1922 she lived near Paris as Mrs Pearce Crouch, with Capt. Pearce Crouch, believed to be an Australian officer. From 1922 to 1923, under the name of Mrs Pearce Crouch, she occupied a farm in Clymping. On 14 November 1923, as 'Colonel' Barker, s/he married Elfreda

Haward in a Brighton Church. Haward was later to claim that she never discovered that 'my husband was anything but the man he claimed to be.' In 1927 the 'Colonel' rented a flat in Mayfair, joined the National Fascisti, opened a restaurant in the West End, and then secured a post as a hotel clerk. S/he was described as head of the National Fascisti in London, and in 1927 was charged at West London for possessing a revolver without a license. Sent for trial and acquitted. Barker was photographed placing a wreath on the Cenotaph at the head of his NF men in 1927, and at that time posing as Colonel Leslie Ivor Gauntlett Bligh Barker, claimed to have won the DSO, Croix-de-Guerre, and Legion of Honour. In 1927 Barker was arrested after a brawl between two fascist groups, and appeared in court with a bandage around the head claiming that s/he suffered from nervous problems after sustaining injuries in the First World War. On 5 March 1929 s/he was arrested for contempt of court when s/he failed to attend a bankruptcy hearing, and was taken to Brighton Prison where the gender 'masquerade' was discovered. On 7 March 1929 she was admitted to Holloway Prison. On 25 April 1929 she pleaded guilty to making a false statement on a marriage register and was sentenced to nine months imprisonment. She was released from Holloway on 15 December 1929. On 4 September 1934 s/he was in the news again, accused of stealing a woman's handbag from a telephone kiosk. Now calling herself John Hill, s/he denied the charge and was found not guilty at West Sussex Quarter Sessions. In 1937, going by the name James Hunt and employed as a man-servant, s/he pleaded guilty to the charge of the theft of £5 from her employer, Adrian Scott of George St., Hanover Square. In 1937, Barker was the main attraction in a peep show in Blackpool. Died in Suffolk in 1960.

Barraclough, Mrs M.*

Member of the BUF. In December 1935 she became acting Women District Officer for Chelmsford.

Barrington, Miss Mercedes* +

Often mentioned that she was a suffragette. Performed war work and later did welfare work in East London slum areas during the Great War. Assisted the Conservative Party at elections from 1918. Became a prominent member of the BUF early in 1935. In January 1937 she became BU prospective parliamentary candidate for Fulham West. She was a speaker in the BUF campaign for the LCC elections in 1937. In May 1937 the National Directors of the National Socialist League appointed her to the post of County Women's Officer (London).

Beaumont, Mrs* | | |

A BUF member in Freckenham. Detained under DR 18B. According to Lucy Pearson's pocket diary, she was released from Holloway on 1 August 1940.

Beaumont, Miss+

Member of the Imperial Fascist League and the Britons.

Beckett, John* + | | |

(1894–1964). An officer in the First Middlesex Territorial Cadet Battalion from the age of twelve to fourteen. Grammar School education. During the Great War he enlisted in the First King's Shropshire Light Infantry. He was twice wounded and discharged as unfit for further service with an excellent army character in March 1917. Honorary Secretary of the Labour Party Advisory Committee on Fighting Services for four years. A member of the first executive of the 'Comrades of the Great War' when it was formed in 1914. Contested Newcastle-upon-Tyne (North) in 1923 as a Labour candidate and came at the bottom of the poll. Elected Labour MP for Gateshead in 1924. Elected Labour MP for the Camberwell, Peckham Division, in 1929. In 1930 he ran away with the mace. Failed to win the Camberwell, Peckham, seat in 1931, at which time he was a leading member of the ILP. Became a member of the BUF in March 1934. He was appointed editor of *Action* in March 1936. With William Joyce, he formed the National Socialist League in April 1937, but later resigned due to the virulence of Joyce's anti-Semitic propaganda. Became Secretary of the British Council against European Commitments (founded by Lord Lymington) and Secretary of the British People's Party (President Lord Tavistock, 12th Duke of Bedford) which grew out of it. He was involved in the Peace Pledge Union. He was interned on 22 May 1940 and detained until 1943. Beckett was half Jewish; his mother's maiden name was Solomans. This was known in the BU at the time when he held the post of Director of Policy.

Beckett, Ruth* + | | |

Member of the BU. She and her husband, Joe Beckett, were members of the Southampton branch. (Joe Beckett was a boxer and gained his first important boxing victories in 1914. On 27 February 1919 he defeated Bombardier Billy Wells and thus became English heavyweight champion. After being defeated twice by George Carpentier, Joe retired from the ring.) Her name appears on the Right Club ledger of *ca.* May 1939. She was interned under DR 18B, when she had a three-week-old baby. On the Home Office Schedule for detention her address is given as 223, Winchester Road, Southampton. Joe Beckett was also interned. According to Lucy Pearson's pocket diary, she was released from Holloway on 2 December 1940. They became members of the Union Movement after the war. She died on 12 December 1952.

Bell, Miss Doreen*

She had socialist sympathies before she was converted to Mosley's fascism upon reading *The Greater Britain* in 1934. Began her work for the BUF in

Bognor, Sussex. She was the director of the camp at Selsey, organized for BUF women in August 1936. On 4 October 1936 she addressed a meeting proceeding the BU women's march in Manchester. In November 1936 she was conducting propaganda work outside the Women's Exchanges in Manchester. In January 1937 she became BU prospective parliamentary candidate for Accrington. In March 1937 she spoke and canvassed in East London in support of the BU's candidates in the LCC elections. Addressed a BU meeting at Duckett St Stepney on 28 July 1937, and spoke on the recent LCC elections, her work in the North of England, Spain and trade unionism. In June 1938 she married A.G. Findlay, Director of Public Relation for the BU. Shortly after the war, Findlay left her with two small children.

Berger, Elizabeth+ | | |
Member of the Imperial Fascist League. Interned under DR 18B. Her name was found in 'Jock' Houston's address book. She was still listed among those under detention in Holloway in May 1943. Present at the 18B social and dance held at the Royal Hotel on 1 December 1945.

Betts, Mrs*
In May 1934 she was Women's Officer for the Battersea Branch of the BUF, located at 243 Battersea Park Rd., SW.

Bidie, Mrs E. Kathleen* | | |
She was a BU activist in Haslemere. Detained under DR 18B, and, according to Lucy Pearson's pocket diary, she was released from Holloway on 22 November 1940.

Birch, Mrs Josephine* | | |
She was married to Walter E. Birch. (He had been a BUF member in Norfolk, joined the movement in 1934 during the *Daily Mail* campaign, but resigned in 1936. He was also alternately described as a builder in Norwich and a schoolmaster). They were the subject of the 18B Publicity Council's pamphlet *Suffer Little Children*. She was German by birth but British by nationality after marriage. They were arrested on 31 May 1940: he for 'hostile associations' and taken to Brixton, she for 'hostile origins' and taken to Holloway. When arrested she had an infant son and was in the advanced stage of pregnancy. After a fortnight, the 15-month-old boy was taken from his mother and placed in a Public Institution and returned to his parents one year later in May 1941. Her second child, a girl christened Evelyn Josephine, was born on 27 January 1941. Mother and two children were transported to the Isle of Man in June 1941. The infant girl contracted whooping cough and died on 15 November 1941.

284

Black, Miss*

A follower of Mosley since the days of the New Party when she had been in charge of the party's financial affairs. From the movement's formation, she held a paid position in the BUF's Accounts Department, acting as Cashier at NHQ. By 1937 she was opposed to Neil Francis-Hawkins and his coterie, and in January made complaints of the administration of the movement's finances. By the end of September 1939 she relinquished her post on the BUF staff.

Blake, Miss^

Member of the British Fascists. Area Commander for Edinburgh. Conceived the idea for the Fascist Children's Clubs in June 1925.

Blakeney, Brigadier-General Robert Byron Drury^ * +

(1872–1952). He managed the Egyptian State Railway (1919–23). He was the second president of the British Fascisti, taking over from Lord Garvagh who resigned in January 1924. Editor-in-Chief of the *Fascist Bulletin*. In 1924 he organized the movement into a private company, limited by guarantee with a capital of one hundred £1 shares. On 26 November 1924 he was the main speaker at a BF meeting for the London area at Holborn Town Hall. In February 1925 he was the main speaker at a British Fascisti dinner at the Lyceum Club. One of five members who resigned from the BF Grand Council in April 1926, and established a new league, the Loyalists. Member of the Imperial Fascist League, the Britons, and the BUF. Associated with the Nordic League. Attended the BUF's London Administration luncheon on 28 February 1939. During World War Two he served in the Home Guard, the ARP service and the National Fire Service.

Blucher, Princess+

Born Evelyn Stapleton-Bretherton into a prominent English Catholic family, and in 1907 she married the fourth Prince Blucher von Wahlstatt (d.1931), a Silesian land owner who had been educated in England at Stonyhurst. They spent the First World War in Germany, and returned to England shortly after with a mission to 'reunite the broken ties of friendship between the two countries.' She was a member of the Anglo-German Fellowship, the Nordic League and her name also appears on the Right Club ledger.

Bonora, Mrs Blanche Olga*

Member of the BUF. British born widow of an Italian. She sent a letter to the *Fascist Quarterly* (Vol. 1 No. 3, July 1935) commenting on the possible adverse publicity to be expected after the publication of Irene Clephane's *Towards Sex Freedom*. Ceased her BU activities before the war and became an Air Raid Warden in the Royal Borough of Kensington. Reported to Special Branch that on a visit to the BU's Westminster (St George) branch on 12 October 1939, she had seen a number of steel helmets and white metal ARP badges. Charles Watts, the D/L, informed her that the intention was for BU members to wear these and pose as Air Raid Wardens in the East End and proceed to 'beat up' all the Jews. Disgusted with these plans of wartime demoralization, she decided to become a passive member of BU.

Booth, Mrs Agnes* | | |

BUF speaker and member in Lancashire. As she related in *Action*, her mother lost both her husband and her son in the Great War. Contributor to BUF publications (1938). Interned under DR 18B, along with her daughter, Nancy Booth. She attended and gave a speech at a gathering to celebrate Sir Oswald Mosley's birthday on 16 November 1942. She spoke about the injustices and hardships suffered by 18B women and said she would not rest until those responsible for the Defence Regulation had paid for their 'crime.' Her husband was also present. Attended a meeting of BU elements on 23 November 1943. Present at the 18B social and dance held at the Royal Hotel on 1 December 1945.

Bosc, Miss B.*

An active member of the BUF. In November 1937 she became Women's Canvass Organizer for the 1st London Area.

Bothamley, Miss Margaret Frances+

The daughter of a colonel. She has been described as 'the scourge of the Jews.' Bothamley was founding member of the Imperial Fascist League, an activist in the Anglo-German Fellowship, a speaker for the Acton and Ealing branch of The Link, and secretary of the Central London Branch of the Link (founded January 1939). She also contributed to *The Patriot*. In 1939 she held private meetings at her flat at 67 Cromwell Rd., Kensington, attended by Mary Allen and others. Her tea and cocktail parties usually preceded meetings of the Nordic League or The Link. Her name appears on the Right Club ledger of *ca*.May, 1939 ('NSL' also appears beside her name, indicating a possible connection with the National Socialist League). On 30 July 1939 she flew from Croydon to Salzburg as part of The Link's expedition to form a German branch, and returned with Domvile on 6 August. A few days later, she went to Germany again, and, during the course of the war, worked for the Germans in broadcasting in English. She was brought to trial in March 1946 for her wartime activities, and given a very light sentence of only one year in the First Division.

Bowie, Mrs*

Speaker in the BUF's campaign for the LCC election in 1937.

Box, F.M.*

Officer at NHQ. Involved in a controversy over Mary Richardson's appointment to take charge of part of the Lancashire area. Threatened to resign in January 1935. He was opposed by Beckett, Chesterton, Leaper and Raven Thomson. Reported that he resigned from the BUF in December 1935.

Boyle, Miss Nina^

She was an ardent suffragist before the war. She and Damer Dawson organized the Women Police Volunteers in 1914, and Boyle served as second-in-command. In February 1915, due to personality clashes, Damer Dawson resigned from the WPVs, formed the Women Police Service, and took virtually all members with her. Boyle was left as head of the much diminished WPV. She had visited Russia during the great famine on behalf of the Save the Children Fund. In January 1926 she addressed a meeting of the British Fascists Women's Units on 'Conditions in Soviet Russia' at Caxton Hall.

Bramely, Mrs^

Wife of Lieutenant-Colonel Bramley. Both were present at a British Fascisti dinner at the Lyceum Club in February 1925.

Brigg, Miss W.E.^

Officer-in-Charge of the British Fascists' London Special Patrol. On 26 September 1928 she was awarded the 2nd class Order of the Fasces, taken to her by Lintorn-Orman. She died on 28 September 1928 and her funeral was conducted with full fascist honours. On 4 October 1931 the BF held a memorial service for Area-Commander Brigg at St Margaret's Church in Putney.

Briscoe, Mrs Nora Constance Lavinia+ |||

(Born *ca*.1900) Member of the Right Club. She was widowed in 1932, and she sent her son to Germany in 1936 to be brought up as a German. Worked as a temporary short-hand typist at the Ministry of Supply since 20 January 1941, and suspended from duty on 16 March 1941 due to her arrest. With Miss Hiscox, she was caught with copies of official documents taken from the Ministry of Supply and charged at Rochester Row Police Station on 15 March 1941. Appeared before the magistrate on 17 March 1941 on charges under the Treachery Act (1940) and Regulation 2A(1) of the Defence (General) Regulations, 1939. Convicted and sentenced to five years penal servitude at the Central Criminal Court on 16 June 1941.

Brock-Griggs, Mrs Anne* |||

Wife of an architect, H. Thomas Brock-Griggs, and mother of two children. She first achieved notoriety in the BUF as a speaker, holding outdoor meetings in London and the Home Counties. Early in 1935 she joined the staff of the BUF as Woman Propaganda Officer. Sat on the BUF's Research Directory and on the Production Directory in 1935. The author of *Women and Fascism: 10 Important Points* (1936). In February 1936 she began editing the 'Woman's Page' in *Action*. Appointed Women Administrative Officer (Southern) in 1936, at the salary of £260 per annum. In May 1936 she visited Germany, where she attended May Day celebrations. On 20 June 1936 she addressed a meeting at the Women's Institute in Dorset; this meeting clashed with a 'Great Peace Rally' held in Dorchester and addressed by Vera Brittain, Dick Sheppard, Donald O. Soper, George Lansbury and Lawrence Houseman. In September 1936 her role was defined as concentrating her propaganda work on women in the East End of London. On 14 November she was in Dorchester to address women members in the district. By January 1937, after the BUF's reorganization following the Public Order Act, she was made one of two Chief Women's Organizers. Addressed a meeting at Piggott St, Limehouse, on 12 February 1937, and spoke on housing conditions and the untarnished reputation of Mosley. BU candidate for Limehouse in the LCC elections of March 1937, polling 2,086 votes. Became the BU prospective parliamentary candidate for South Poplar in March 1937. On 25 March 1938 she spoke at the South Dorset Branch of the National Council of Women at Weymouth. In May 1939 she was given one month's notice from her post at NHQ, but it was reported that she intended to stay on as a volunteer worker. In October 1939 she was arrested while addressing a meeting in Limehouse and charged under the Public Order Act and Defence Regulations, 1939, Section 39 B. She appeared at Thames Public Court on 23 October 1939 and was remanded for a fortnight, bail being fixed at £20. Her case was heard on 6 November, and the prosecution dropped the more serious charges under Section 39B. She was bound over for one year in a sum of £50. One of the two principal speakers at the launch of the Women's Peace Campaign on 28 February 1940 at Holborn Hall. By February 1940 it was reported that she was slackening in her enthusiasm for the BU and planned to resign. Mosley claimed that she had been dismissed from her appointment since the war on grounds of inefficiency. She and her husband were interned under DR 18B. Her health suffered badly from prison conditions while she was detained. She came back to the Union Movement after the war to play an inactive part and she attended reunion dinners. She eventually had a nervous breakdown, and died of cancer in the 1960s.

Bullivant, Millicent^ *

During the 1930s she resided at 94 Chestnut Avenue in the Forest Gate Ward. Her parents were middle-class conservatives with a family lineage in Norfolk. She was a member of the British Fascists in West Ham. Assistant to A. Richardson who was District Organizer of the West Ham Branch of the BUF in 1934. She was employed as a secretary for the Sales Manager of Yardley of London Ltd.

Butler, Lady^

She was a patron of the British Fascists 'Mi Careme' Ball at the Hotel Cecil in London on 5 March 1926.

Camfield, Miss M.E.* | | |

She was a member of the BU in Tunbridge Wells and Newcastle. On the Home Office Schedule for detention her address was given as 36 Red Hall Drive, Heaton, Newcastle. She was detained under 18B, and according to Lucy Pearson's diary, she was released from Holloway on 2 December 1940.

Carrington-Wood, Mrs H.*

North West London Organizer for the BUF. In 1935 *The Star* reported her resignation. She wrote a letter to Mosley declaring that 'the promises made on Fascist platforms and in Fascist literature are inadequate to appease the anxiety of the womenfolk, who naturally do not want to risk going back to where they were before the Suffragettes.' Mosley's reply simply acknowledged her letter. In March 1935 she wrote to the *Hampstead and Highgate Express* and explained how after the BUF's scheme for re-organization was presented in January 1935 'several women met at the house of one of the members to discuss proposals which would ensure the advancement under Fascism of the position of women in this country. It was then decided that four of the participants would go to Sir Oswald Mosley ... with a petition. The holding of this meeting became known at Fascist Headquarters, and was ruled as being out of order; it was democratic.'

Carruthers, Mrs M.*

A speaker for the BUF in the East London campaign in 1936. Speaker in the BUF's campaign for the LCC elections in 1937. In November 1937 she became Women's Canvass Organizer for the 3rd London Area. In August 1938 she spoke at a women's meeting in Streatham, advocating non-intervention in European quarrels.

Chadwick, Lady^

Wife of Sir Burton Chadwick. They were both present at a British Fascisti dinner at the Lyceum Club in February 1925.

Charnley, John* | | |

Born in Leeds in December 1909. Joined the BUF in Southport in 1933. His three brothers, Sydney, Alf, and Peter, were also members, as he discovered to his surprise when attending a Leader's meeting at Leeds Town Hall in 1934. Acted as a steward at the Olympia Rally of 7 June 1934. BU prospective parliamentary candidate for Hull East. Interned under DR 18B on 3 June 1940, and held at the Ascot Camp. He made an appeal before the Advisory Committee in the late summer of 1940. Released in November 1943. His wife was not a member of the BU. Author of *Blackshirts and Roses: An Autobiography* (1990).

Chesterton, Arthur Kenneth*

Born in South Africa on 1 May 1899 and died in 1973. His second cousins were G.K. and Cecil Chesterton. He was educated at Berkhamstead School. An officer during the Great War: first a private in East Africa, then a commissioned officer on the Western Front, winning the Military Cross. He returned to South Africa in 1919 and became a journalist for the *Johannesburg Star*. In 1922 he fought in the so-called Red Revolt in the Witwaterstrand in South Africa. He returned to Britain and worked in English provincial journalism, becoming managing editor of a group of Devon newspapers when he was 29 years old. He was a drama critic and a close friend of Shakespeare-scholar Professor G. Wilson Knight. He was involved with the Citizen's Defence League in Devon in 1931–32 and in 1931 stood unsuccessfully as a CDL candidate for the Babbacombe ward in the local council elections of 1931. On 5 August 1933 he married a Fabian Socialist teacher, Doris Terry. He joined the BUF in 1933. In May 1934 he was Officer-in-Charge for the Midland Area of the BUF. By 1938 he edited all the BUF's journals, wrote Mosley's biography, *Portrait of a Leader*, and became Director of Publicity and Propaganda. He resigned from the BUF in 1938. His name appears on the Right Club ledger of *ca.* May 1939. He joined the British Army in the Second World War, and he was invalided out on general health grounds in 1944. Appointed first leader of the National Front in 1967.

Clare, Constance*| | |

BU official in Hove. Sister of Marjorie. She and her sister resided at 56 Golstone Villas, Hove. Detained under DR 18B. Released well before her sister, some time before December 1940.

Clare, Marjorie* | | |

Her father died as a result of wounds sustained during the Great War. BU official in Hove and District Treasurer in Brighton. She was also Women's District leader in Brighton. She resided at 56 Goldstone Villas, Hove. Detained under DR 18B on 3 June 1940 with Lucy Pearson. Lucy Pearson made attempts to expedite her release after she herself had been freed.

Clarke, Mrs* | | |

A schoolteacher in Worcester. According to *It Might Have Happened to You!*, she was arrested in Liverpool just after the police had arrested her eldest son and taken him to Walton Gaol. Her youngest son, who was 10 years old, was subjected to interrogation before he was placed in an institution.

Clarke, Miss Peggy*
In July 1936 Robert Saunders, D/L West Dorset, was informed that Miss Clarke, a resident of 1 Livingstone, Southern Rhodesia was interested in joining the BUF.

Collins, Margaret*
A contributor to the weekly publication *Truth*. In April 1937 she was employed at the Press-Propaganda Section of the Research Department at BUF NHQ. Married to Bowie, the *Blackshirt* and *Action* cartoonist.

Collins, Winifred Grace*
BUF supporter. She was assaulted by one Nellie Tuck (age 17, of Shepherds Bush, arrested 7 June, 1934) during the Olympia Rally.

Cordery, Mrs Ursula E.*
In the summer of 1935 she was the Manchester Women's Organizer and launched an experiment where women speakers opened ordinary Blackshirt meetings. In November 1937 she became Women's Canvass Organizer for the 2nd London Area. Contributor to BUF publications (1938).

Cornes, Miss Gladys E.M.* |||
BU Women's District Leader and District Treasurer in Leeds West. Interned under DR 18B. According to Lucy Pearson's pocket diary, she was released from Holloway on 22 November 1940.

Cossar, Miss Jean*
She left Newcastle in 1923 to become the Women's Organizer for the Conservative Association in the Wansbeck division and was later transferred to the South Hackney Conservative and Unionist Association. Joined the Newcastle Branch of the BUF in 1934; she had been attracted to the BUF by the slogan 'Britain buys from those who buy from Britain.'

Cotton, Mrs L.T.* |||
Member of the BU in Exeter. On 30 October 1938 her husband addressed a meeting in Market Square. After an unfriendly reception from the crowd, Mrs Cotton struck a member of the audience in the face. Her address was given as Fruit and Flower Farm, Branscombe, and her name appears on the Home Office Schedule for detention.

291

Cruickshank, Dame Joanna

(Born *ca.*1875). Previous experience in the nursing profession. Matron-in-Chief of the RAF Nursing Service from 1918–30. She was honoured with the DBE in 1930. She also held the position of Matron-in-Chief of the Order of St John of Jerusalem and the British Red Cross. Commandant of the Women's Internment Camp in the Isle of Man. Resigned in May 1941, before the transfer of 18B women to the Isle of Man.

Cunard, (Lady) Emerald

(1872–1948) Prominent London hostess who expressed Nazi sympathies during the 1930s. Born Maud Burke in San Francisco. She married Sir Bache Cunard (d.1925), grandson of the founder of the shipping line, on 17 April 1895, after which they lived at Nevill Holt, Leicestershire. Her only child, Nancy, was born on 10 March 1896. She had intimate friendships with the author George Moore, with whom she shared a love for Wagnerian opera, and Sir Thomas Beecham, the musical director. She moved to Carlton House Terrace in 1920, the most fashionable and expensive address in London, and the Prince of Wales became one of her regular guests. In 1926 she changed her Christian name to Emerald. In the same year she moved to 7 Grosvenor Square. Her relationship with her daughter collapsed by 1931, and the two differed markedly in their political sympathies. (Nancy was a vehement anti-fascist, worked as a correspondent during the Spanish Civil War, had a very public affair with the black jazz musician Henry Crowder, and organized a protest upon the release of Diana and Oswald Mosley in 1943). Lady Cunard knew Diana Guinness well in the early 1930s, nick-named her 'Golden Corn,' and hoped she would take over the leadership of London Society in due course. Fascinated by the new Germany and the Nazis, she planned a trip to Germany in 1933. By the early 1930s her social set changed from one consisting mainly of artists to one consisting of the Prince of Wales and Prince George, as well Mrs Wallis Simpson. In 1935 she was seen at the Opera with Herr Joachim von Ribbentrop. In June 1935 the Prince of Wales suggested at the Annual Conference of the British Legion that its members should 'stretch forth the hand of friendship' to Germany; in high society it was rumoured that he had been influenced by pro-Nazism via Mrs Simpson and Lady Cunard. On 10 March 1938 von Ribbentrop gave a farewell tea party at the German Embassy in Carlton House Terrace – Lady Cunard was present. During the Second World War she occupied a suite at the Dorchester Hotel.

Currey, Miss Muriel (OBE)*

From the 1920s she was part of a set of Britons, including Major James S. Barnes, Harold E. Goad, and Francis Yeats-Brown, who admired Fascist Italy. She contributed to *The English Review.* Contributed articles to the *Blackshirt*

(1934) on women under Italian Fascism. In March 1934 she addressed a dinner meeting of the January Club at the Hotel Splendid, Piccadilly, speaking on 'The Corporate State.' With Harold E. Goad, Director of the British Institute in Florence, she co-authored *The Working of the Corporate State* (1934). Honorary Secretary for the London Group for the Study of the Corporate State. Author of *A Woman at the Abyssinian War* (1936), which recounted her experiences in Abyssinia in 1935.

Cutmore, Miss Anne* +

Born 19 January 1909 in Clapham, South London. She was the second of three daughters of James and Florence Cutmore. Her father was employed as a law writer by the Solicitors Law Stationery Society. James Cutmore joined the army in 1916 and he died at the front in France in March 1918, when he was 40 years old. After his death the family went to New Zealand, where Anne's mother had relatives, but they came back to England a few years later. Anne wanted to be an actress and she learned shorthand and typing at Pitmans, and found temporary work while she studied at RADA. Pitmans sent her to the BUF Headquarters to work as Dr Forgan's secretary. She was briefly engaged to Selwyn Watson, who had composed the movement's song and who was part of a group of artistic young men who were attracted to fascism. In 1934 she was secretary to the Deputy Leader, Dr Forgan. Contributor to BUF publications, and was the drama critic for *Action* (1935–36). She met John Beckett through Forgan, when the latter was trying to attract Beckett away from the Labour Party. In September 1936 it was reported that she was John Beckett's mistress and lived with him. Present at a 'bottle party' held at the flat of Miss Walters for dissenting elements of the BUF on 17 March 1937. She left the BUF with Beckett in 1937 when he and Joyce formed the National Socialist League. The name 'Mrs A.E. Beckett' appears on the Right Club ledger of *ca.*May, 1939. She was also part of the British People's Party, and researched and wrote the BPP pamphlet 'The Truth About This War,' which MI5 presumed John Beckett had written. Throughout the war Anne worked for the Duke of Bedford, President of the BPP, visited John Beckett regularly in his various places of detention, and campaigned for his release. She married John Beckett, and they had a son, Francis Beckett (a journalist) in 1945.

Dalton, Lady

On 30 November 1934 she put her house at the disposal of the BUF for an 'At Home' at which Lady Mosley was present.

Dewis, Eileen*

Frequent contributor to the *Blackshirt* (1936), with a concentration on women workers.

Dillon, (Hon.) Pamela*

The Mitfords were her cousins through the Stanleys. A contemporary of Unity Mitford at St Margaret's School. After she left school, her mother put her to work in the offices of the Women's Section of the BUF. She worked as an office telephonist under Lady Makgill, who was also one of her cousins. She arranged meetings, stewarded some of them, but left the post after three months because she was 'completely a-political'. When she married, she became Lady Onslow.

Diment, Mrs Alieen*

Born in Kennington, London. She joined the BUF in West Dorset as a Division II member on 25 January 1937. She described her profession as housewife. She resided at The Crest, Owermoigne, Dorset, and concentrated her efforts on distributing BUF literature in the village.

Domvile, Lady+ | | |

Wife of Sir Barry Domvile, founder of the Link. On 16 July 1939 she and her husband attended Mosley's Earl's Court rally, where they were seated next to Lady Redesdale, and the Fullers. On 26 July 1939 she and her husband attended a dinner party hosted by the Mosleys, patronized by the leading figures of Britain's pro-Nazi, anti-Semitic societies. Lady Domvile and her daughter attended the inaugural meeting of the British Council for Christian Settlement in Europe in Red Lion Square on 14 October 1939, as well as Mosley's meeting at the Stoll Theatre on 15 October. On 22 November Admiral and Lady Domvile and their daughter took part in a meeting that marked the beginning of collaboration between Mosley, Ramsay and Domvile. Attended the BU London Administration luncheon on 1 March 1940. Friends with Mary Allen. Interned under DR 18B on 7 July 1940. With her husband, she first went before the Advisory Committee in September 1940, and on 5 November for a second time when it was decided their detention should continue. She was released in November 1941. Her son, Compton Domvile, was also interned as he had been a member of the Sheffield Park Branch of the BU, and another son was killed on active service during the war.

Domvile, Admiral Sir Barry+ | | |

He was Director of Naval Intelligence (1927–30), and President of the Royal Naval College (1932–34). First visited Germany in 1935 where he was 'struck by the gross discrepancy between the facts of daily life in Germany, and their warped representation to the British public by their Daily Press.' Upon his retirement he wrote *By and Large* (1936) in which he praised Hitler's Germany. Member of the Council of the Anglo-German Fellowship, which closed down in September 1939. Founded the Link in July 1937, and membership grew to a level of 4,300 by June 1939, and also spawned branches in the provinces. Domvile was also associated with the Council for Christian Settlement in Europe. Believer in the existence of a Judao-Masonic plot, which he termed 'Judmas'. He attended secret meetings convened for the purpose of organizing collaboration between the BU, The Link and the Right Club in 1939 and 1940. On 7 July 1940 the Domvile's home in Roehampton was searched by police, and the same evening he and his wife were served with warrants for their detention under DR 18B. He was first held in 'F' Wing of Brixton Prison, and moved to 'C' Wing after his first appearance before the Advisory Committee in September 1940, occupying a cell next to Sir Oswald Mosley. Called before the Advisory Committee again on 5 November 1940, when it was decided he and his wife should remain under detention. On 9 February 1941 he was allowed to visit his wife in Holloway, on the occasion of their Silver Wedding Anniversary – Oswald Mosley accompanied him to Holloway to see Diana. He was released from Brixton on 29 July 1943. In 1943 he wrote his memoir, *From Admiral to Cabin Boy*, which could only be published in 1947, by Boswell Ltd.

Donovan, Bryan David Errington* | | |
(Born 1898 in Cork–1985) Joined the Army in August 1914 when he was 16-years-old and served in France from January to July 1915, and then in India and Palestine. Received a commission in 1917. He had been a Labour Party election agent for many years before he joined the BUF. He became a member of the BUF in 1933 and was on the BUF staff for five years. From 1936 to 1940 he acted as Assistant Director General. Interned on 25 May 1940 and appeared before the Advisory Committee on 8 July 1940. One of six BU leaders whose releases were considered last among 18Bs. Suspension Order issued on 2 October 1944.

Donovan, Mrs Yvonne Heather Fitzgerald (née Bond)* | | |
(*ca*.1915–82) She joined the BUF in 1934, when she was 19 years old. Women's District Leader for Westminster Abbey District. Before her marriage she lived in a flat at Dolphin Court with another BU member, Cynthia Martin. She married David Errington Donovan in January 1940, and Oswald and Diana Mosley and Neil Francis Hawkins were present at their wedding. Found on the search of the couple's flat at 5 Pembridge Crescent W11 was a loose leaf book containing reports of BU women's meetings held, and from this it was ascertained that Mrs Donovan held an executive post in the BU. Also found on this search was a file of correspondence dealing with the Women's Drum Corps, of which she was drum major. She was interned under DR 18B on 30 May 1940, and released under a suspension order made in pursuance of DR 18B(2) in November 1940 on condition that she reside with her parents, report weekly to police, and not engage in any BU activities. According to Lucy Pearson's pocket diary, she was released on 13 November 1940. Her father,

Manager RAC Club Epsom, was also interned. In January 1941 she asked that
the first two restrictions be lifted, and on 9 February she said she wanted to
live with Mrs Stuckey, whose husband was also interned, and work on the
latter's farm in Berkshire.

Downe, (Viscountess) Dorothy^ *
Former lady-in-waiting to Queen Mary, wife of George V. During the Great
War she ran the RFC Auxiliary Hospital. She managed her Hillington estate
in Norfolk herself, without the services of a land agent. She was County
Commander of North Riding, Yorkshire County Command, for the British
Fascists. The Viscount and Viscountess Downe were patrons of the British
Fascist 'Mi Careme' Ball, held at the Hotel Cecil in London on 5 March 1926.
In October 1926 she took the chair, while Lintorn-Orman gave a short speech,
at a meeting of BF Women's Units in Harrogate. On 2 November 1927 she
chaired and addressed a BF meeting in the West Riding, Harrogate Area at
the Hydro Spa, and on 3 November 1927 she chaired a BF meeting at the
Crescent Cafe, York. She was President of the Conservative Women's
Association of Scarborough for eight years, after which she became chairman
of the Conservative Women's Association of King's Lynn, and member of
the Central Office Committee for Philip Stott College. She was a magistrate
for Yorkshire and later for Norfolk. R.R. Bellamy remembered that she joined
the BUF in mid-1933 after hearing Mosley speak at a meeting at the Corn
Hall, King's Lynn. Following a visit to Germany, she gave a lecture on conditions
in Germany at the King's Lynn Branch of the BUF in December 1934. She
resigned from the presidency of the Scarborough and King's Lynn Conservative
Women's Association and from the Conservative party at the beginning of
1937. Became BU prospective parliamentary candidate for North Norfolk in
June 1937. One story is that Lady Downe was to have afternoon tea with
the Queen, when she informed her 'I've joined the Blackshirts, Ma'am.' 'Is
that wise, Dorothy, is that wise?' asked Queen Mary. Attended the London
Administration luncheon on 28 February 1939. Attended the London
Administration luncheon on 1 March 1940. She visited Diana Mosley two
days before the latter was interned. Her house in Hillington was searched,
but she was not arrested. It was suspected that she was never interned under
DR 18B because of her social position and connections in high places. During
the course of the war she corresponded with Lady Redesdale, Diana Mosley's
mother, and worked on behalf of internees by sending care packages. She
rejoined the Union Movement after the war, and died in 1958.

Downes, Miss O.P.^
In June 1926 she was the Officer in Charge of the Fascist Children's Clubs.
She was Assistant Director of Women's Units for the British Fascists, and

for a short time temporary County Commander, London Women's Units, before June 1926.

Driver, Nellie * | | |

(1914-1981) She was born in Nelson, and her father served with the Royal Field Artillery for four years during the Great War. When she was five years old, the family moved to Middlesborough, where her father worked in the ship-yards. They returned to Nelson some years later, where her parents opened a shop, which soon failed. Educated at a Council school. When she was 14 years old her father became ill; he could no longer work in the mill, and he was denied a disability pension, 'the period since his war service terminated being too long.' Her father died at age thirty-nine, when she was fifteen, and her mother returned to work in the mill as a chain-weaver. Nellie worked in a sweet factory between the ages of fourteen and sixteen. Upon turning sixteen she was dismissed by the sweet factory, and remained unemployed for many years. In 1935 a former school friend wrote to Nellie to tell her that she had joined the BUF, and both Nellie and her mother were instantly attracted to Sir Oswald Mosley's policies. Mother and daughter joined the BUF together. With no branch yet in Nelson, Driver organized one in 1936: she was appointed Women's District Leader, while a young man from Barrowford was appointed D/L. The Nelson branch attracted nearly one hundred members. Although only a man could serve as District Leader, Driver remembered that she was 'running the place at the finish.' Driver organized many branch events, including a meeting at the Palace Theater addressed by Mosley. She organized paper selling drives, she opened a small BUF bookshop near the centre of town, and she was the *Blackshirt* correspondent for Lancashire, contributing articles on the cotton trade and the plight of mill workers. She was invited to the BUF headquarters in Great Smith Street for a training course in leadership, on which occasion she was given a tour of the London branches, and also addressed the women of the Limehouse branch. Driver was not remunerated by the BUF, but she did receive the bronze award for merit, which allowed her to add 'H.S.' (honoured for service) after her name on all official documents. She was also graded a public speaker. Mosley recognized Driver's contribution to his movement, and whenever he came North, he made a special request to meet her. She attended several speaker's schools in Manchester, went on the Bermondsey March (1938), and attended the Earl's Court rally (1939). As a result of her BUF activities, she appeared in court on two different occasions. The first time, in 1937, she was fined 5/- for defacing a railway poster by affixing a small sticky propaganda label to it on the railway platform, and later, in 1940, she was summoned to appear in Colne Police Court to answer to the charge of receiving a shilling subscription after the receipt of such a subscription was declared illegal, for which she was bound over for twelve months. Driver was arrested in October 1940 under DR 18B, and a policeman and his wife took her down to London by train, where she was detained in Holloway Prison. She first came before the Advisory Committee in December 1940, at the hotel at Ascot, but was not released. She wrote to her MP, Mr S.S. Silverman, and was pleasantly surprised when he arranged an interview with her in Holloway, although he was unable to secure her release. During Driver's internment in Holloway she became again attracted to religion, and it was during this period of her life that she converted to Catholicism– her mother was a Baptist and her father had been Church of England. In Holloway, Driver formed the Society for the Elimination of Unnecessary Noise, as a reaction against the din caused by the banging of tin pots and kettles. Her name was on the first list for transport to the Isle of Man, and she departed on 16 June 1941. In June 1942, only one of the six Englishwomen still in the camp at Port Erin, Driver received a letter from the Home Office that her case was to be re-opened, and she was sent back to Holloway. She left the Isle of Man for Holloway on 6 July 1942, attended an Advisory Committee hearing at Burlington House in August, and was released in September. At first she experienced difficulty in obtaining employment, as 'such a stigma remained on those who had been innocent victims of "spy mania,"' but finally she was taken on by an electrical engineering company in Nelson, where she was still employed some twenty years later at the time when she was writing her autobiography. At Christmas 1943 she and her mother were received into the Catholic Church, and the zeal with which she had once served the BUF was transfused into her work for the Church. Driver did not rejoin the Union Movement after the war. Author of *From the Shadows of Exile*, an autobiography, *The Mill: A Novel*, a fictionalized account of social conditions and local fascist activism in a Northern town, and poetry, some of it written in local Lancashire dialect, all unpublished.

Drummond, Mrs Flora

Leading suffragette in the WSPU. A firm presented her with accessories of military uniform especially designed for her as field marshal and she wore a peaked cap in the WSPU colours, an epaulette and a sash lettered 'General.' During the suffragette movement she was nicknamed 'Bluebell' and 'the Precious Piglet.' In 1917 Emmeline and Christabel Pankhurst and their two lieutenants, Annie Kenney and Flora Drummond, turned the WSPU into the Women's Party. Spoke at the Albert Hall on 17 April 1926: 'The men who think today that there is no weapon but the strike will get used to hearing from us that there are other weapons.' Founder of the Women's Guild of Empire in 1928, an organization dedicated to opposing strikes and communism. Her Women's Guild of Empire opposed fascist activities in the East End in 1936, and in 1937 went among women voters to urge them to vote against the BUF candidates in the LCC elections. She held a meeting at the Bethnal Green Library in October 1937 which was disrupted by BUF women. In August 1937 she spoke on the early days of the Women's Suffrage Movement on the BBC broadcast 'I Saw the Start' (commented on in *Action*, 28 August 1937).

Dudley Ward, Mrs+

Attended a meeting of the January Club in 1934. Member of the Nordic League. Richard Griffiths has identified her as Maidie Florence, divorced wife of Major Charles Dudley Ward. She was also involved with the RSPCA and the Animal Defence Society, and her anti-Semitism was closely connected with her abhorrence for kosher methods of animal slaughter. She published *Jewish Kosher* (1944).

Duff, Mrs Douglas* | | |

Widow of an officer of the 9th Lancers – whom she had left due to his drunken habits. She had explored in Tibet, where she travelled without the permission of the Government of India, acquired a pilot's licence and was said to have qualified as Able Seaman in one of Gustave Erikson's sailing barques. Mrs Douglas Duff of Folkstone had joined the BU after the war began. In November and December 1939 she was recorded to have attended meetings to organize the collaboration of Mosley, Ramsay and Domvile. See *The Mirror*, 6 June 1940. She was interned under 18B.

Duff-Miller, Mrs* | | |

Women's organizer of the Paddington branch of the BUF in 1935. Interned under DR 18B in 1940. Her case was heard by the Advisory Committee.

Dundas, Ian Hope* | | |

Born 13 June 1908 in Yokenham. Son of the 26th Chief of Dundas, Admiral Sir Charles Dundas and Mrs Monroe. He served three years in the navy (1926–29) and left with the rank of acting sub-lieutenant. He worked as an MP's secretary before joining the BUF in 1933. Chief of Staff of the BUF. He married Pamela Ernestine Dorman in December 1933, the niece of Ernest Shackleton, the polar explorer. Mosley acted as best man at the wedding, and the bride wore a dress trimmed with golden fasces. The marriage ended in divorce five years later. In January 1936, with the reorganization of the movement, he assumed charge of the Leader's department. He was responsible for opening negotiations with the BBC in an attempt to get the BUF included in the BBC's roster of political parties that were allowed to broadcast on radio, a bid that was unsuccessful. He himself broadcast from Italy on numerous occasions before the war. Earned an annual salary of £416 (the highest paid official). In March 1937 he was struck off the pay roll and resigned from the movement. In September 1939 Special Branch reported that he 'sailed to India on 19 August: he gave out before he left that he had secured a good post with an Indian potentate and had severed all connections with the movement.' He was interned under DR 18B.

Dunn, Lady+

She was a member of The Link, and had joined on an expedition to Salzburg in August 1939 whose mission it was to found a German branch of The Link. She attended meetings in November and December 1939 to organize collaboration between The Link, the BUF and the Right Club.

Durrant, Ella* +

Member of the BU. On 1 March 1940 she attended the London Administration luncheon at the Criterion restaurant. In 1940 she attended secret meetings convened by fascist groups in Britain to co-ordinate their activities after war broke out. Cohabited with Aubrey Lees in 1940. In 1940 she was employed as a governess by Lees' sister. On 10 November 1940 she attended a meeting at the flat of Molly Stanford where the means of organizing aid for 18Bs was discussed. Married Lees in 1942.

Durrell, Miss Emily Dorothea V.* | | |

BUF member. Interned under DR 18B in 1940. Sister of the master of Winchester.

Eckersley, Mrs Frances Dorothy+

(18 December 1893, in Aldershot–1971). She was related to the literary Stephen family. A well-known pro-German fascist, a close friend of both William Joyce and Unity Mitford, and a fanatical admirer of Hitler. First married Edward Clark on 10 August 1921, and they had a son, James Royston Clark (b.1923). Clark had studied music composition with Schönberg and Busoni in Berlin, and at the time of their marriage he was employed by the BBC music department. They later divorced. In October 1930 married to Captain Peter Eckersley (1892–1963: he was the BBC's first Chief Engineer and worked for Mosley and the Museum's Investments radio scheme, after being dismissed from the BBC because he had been cited in a divorce case). She was a member of the Independent Labour Party up until 1935. In 1935 she went to visit Germany with her husband and was very impressed by the social benefits of the Nazi regime. With her husband, she visited Germany on every summer holiday up to 1939. In 1937 she went with Unity Mitford to the Osteria Bavaria restaurant where they saw Hitler. She joined the Chelsea branch of The Link in 1937. In 1938 became a member of the Imperial Fascist League. She was also a member of the Anglo-German Fellowship. In July 1939 she left England for Germany and attended

300

the Salzburg Festival and the Nuremberg Rally (had also attended in 1937 and 1938). Her name appeared on the Right Club ledger of *ca.*May 1939 (the 'IFL' beside her name also indicated her association with the Imperial Fascist League). She was responsible for recruiting William and Margaret Joyce for the German radio, both of whom she knew through her involvement in extreme-right organizations in Britain. From December 1939 to January 1943 she broadcast for the Nazis on German radio. From December 1939 to October 1941 she was a daily announcer on the German radio. From October 1941 to February 1942 she was employed in correcting translations of German news and bulletins into English. From February 1942 to January 1943 she had to read English newspapers and reports of BBC transmissions and mark items which the German radio could contradict. Until May 1943 she broadcast twice a month as 'Jeannett' in the play 'Women to Women.' In 1943, owing to an accident, she ceased to work for the German radio. She was imprisoned by the Gestapo in December 1944. Her son, James Royston Clarke (b. London, 24 March 1923) also assisted the enemy. She was detained by the British authorities in an internment camp in Recklinghausen in October 1945.

Edwards, Joan E.*

Born in Jersey. Contributor to the *Blackshirt*. Author of 'How Fascism Came to Jersey' describing a debate between a Deputy of the Jersey Parliament and a Blackshirt.

Eglington and Winter, (Countess)^

Member of the British Fascists. County Commander for Ayrshire and Wigtonshire.

Elam, Mrs Norah (a.k.a Dacre-Fox)* | | |

Born *ca.*1878. Imprisoned three times as a suffragette and given a medal with three bars. During the Great War she was a member of several Government commissions, she recruited in South Wales, and worked in a munitions factory. She stood unsuccessfully as an Independent candidate for Richmond Surrey in 1918, polling 3,615 votes (20.5%), and was for a short time a member of the Conservative Party. She joined the BUF in 1934 with her husband. Dudley Elam (d. December 1948) had been Chairman of Chichester Conservatives until 1934, which he left to join the BUF. She became BU County Women's Officer for West Sussex. In November 1936 she became the BU prospective parliamentary candidate for Northampton. Contributor to BUF publications (1935–40). Before and after the declaration of war she took charge of part of the BU funds. In November and December 1939 she and her husband attended meetings of the Mosley-Ramsay-Domvile group, gathered together to make plans for collaboration, and on 11 December she was present at a lunch held at the Ladies Carlton at which event all 'drank a silent toast to the Leader.' Her flat was raided by Police on 18 December 1939. She attended the London Administration luncheon on 1 March 1940. When her offices of the London and Provincial Anti-Vivisectionist Society were raided in August 1940, found in her possession was a letter listing eight names together with a note from Mosley stating that she had his full confidence. Interned under DR 18B and never made an appeal in front of the Advisory Committee. Her husband, Regional Inspector for Surrey, was also interned, and he was released before she was. With Unity Mitford, Mr and Mrs Elam visited the Mosleys in Holloway on 24 December 1941. She was one of two speakers at a meeting organized by the 18B (British) Aid Committee in December 1942. Present at the 18B Social and dance held at the Royal Hotel on 1 December 1945.

Elliott, Florence (née Simmons)*
BU Women's District Leader in Slough. She was present as a heckler at a meeting addressed by Neville Laski at the Kingston Guildhall in 1939. She married Charles Elliott, pre-war District Leader for Slough, and they became very active after the war in Bournemouth, where he became branch leader. Her husband was detained under DR 18B. She and her husband were founding members of the Union Movement in Bournemouth. Died in September 1982.

Ellis, Molly Blanche* | | |
Non-active BUF member in Leeds. Wife of John Ellis (b. 1900), director of Motor Distributors, Leeds, and he held Army contracts for transport and laundry. They had two children, aged 7 and 10 in 1940. She and her husband entertained Mosley on several occasions when he was visiting Leeds. She and her husband were interned under DR 18B in June 1940, and her detention order was revoked in September 1940.

Forgan, Doctor Robert*
Born 5 December 1886 in Edinburgh. Received the MC, and was the specialist medical officer to Lanarkshire County Council (1921–29), member of the Glasgow City Council (1929–31), and Labour MP for West Renfrew (1929–31). Part of the Mosley Secession from the Labour Party in 1931. Leading member of the January Club. Deputy Leader of the BUF (1932–34). Anne Cutmore served as his secretary. Resigned from the BUF in August 1935.

Francis-Hawkins, Neil^ * | | |
Born ca.1907 in Reading; his father was a doctor. Active in the British Fascisti since 1923. He was Master of Ceremonies at the BF's Frivolity Ball on 4 April 1930, held at the Nothumberland Rooms, Trafalgar Square.

Became a member of the BUF upon its formation in 1932. Occupied a salaried post in the BUF from March 1933 in charge of the London Command and Director of Blackshirt Organization. In the summer of 1933 he was deprived of the Order of the Fasces, once bestowed on him by the BF Executive Committee. In July 1935 he temporarily assumed charge of the Women's Section of the BU, along with his other duties as Director of Propaganda. He became Director General of the BU in 1936. He was leader of a contingent in the BU which advocated the propagation of the Blackshirt, semi-military psychology and wished to see bands, uniforms, and marches as central to the development of the movement. As of 15 March 1937 he was in complete control of the administration of the movement. Lived in a flat at 32 Grosvenor Gardens Mews North SW1 with his sister. As Mosley's lieutenant , he attended secret meetings for co-ordinating fascist groups in Britain after the outbreak of war. Detained under DR 18B on 23 May 1940. Appealed before the Advisory Committee on 4 July 1940. Released in October 1944. Nicholas Mosley claims that he was a homosexual.

Franzel, Mrs*
In May 1934 she was Women's Officer for the Islington Branch of the BUF.

Fredricks, Mr Kay*
A paid official at the BUF's Chelsea HDQ. He was assaulted by three men in Shaftesbury Ave. W. in May 1933, while selling fascist literature. He was a witness in the Brighton Trunk Murder trial. He had been living on the earnings of the murdered prostitute, Violet Kaye.

Freeman, Mrs Violet L.
In 1940 she was 52 years old, and described as a housewife. On 6 July 1940 it was reported that Rex (or Wilfred) Freeman, a railway porter who lived with his parents at 90 Keyneston Rd., and his mother had been convicted for printing and distributing sticky-backs advertising the New British Broadcasting Station. He had joined the BUF in 1938 and was a member and propaganda officer for the BU in Stoke Newington; he received a sentence of five years and his mother one in 1940.

Fuller, General John Frederick Charles*
(1878–1966). Educated at Malvern. Military historian and an expert on tank warfare. In 1931 he was elected Conservative MP for Manchester, Ardwick. In the 1930s he contributed to *The English Review*. He was responsible for the reorganization of the BUF in 1935. In 1935, with W.E.D. Allen, he visited Germany as a representative of the BUF. He attended the 50th birthday

celebration for Hitler in Berlin on 20 April 1939. On 26 July he attended a dinner party hosted by the Mosleys, bringing together the leading figures in Britain's pro-Nazi 'patriotic societies.' Both his name and that of Miss E. Fuller appeared on the Right Club ledger of *ca.*May, 1939. In November and December 1940 Fuller and his wife attended meetings to organize the collaboration between Mosley's, Ramsay's and Domvile's organizations. On 1 March 1940, with his wife, he attended the London Administration luncheon at the Criterion restaurant. Reported to be prominently connected with the Nordic League in 1939, and on 27 March addressed a meeting of the NL patronized by 'expensively dressed society ladies', speaking on 'The Hebrew Mysteries.' Reported to be willing to help organize aid for 18B internees in November 1940.

Gallagher, Mrs | | |
Interned in December 1939 after MI5 reported her to be an enemy agent. Austrian by birth and married to a British subject.

Gill, Elizabeth*
Born *ca.*1902. Grew up in Norfolk and from a family of agricultural workers. Contributor to BUF publications (1934).

Girling, Mrs OBE, J.P.
Successful Labour candidate in the LCC elections of March 1937, victorious over William Joyce. Condemned the BU candidates in the election for waging a dirty fight. On 23 February 1943 the *Daily Worker* reported that she had received four anonymous threatening letters from fascists declaring that 'the time will come when she will regret certain statements made about William Joyce.'

Glasgow, Countess of^
On 5 March 1926 the Earl and Countess of Glasgow were patrons of a Grand 'Mi Careme' Ball organized by the British Fascists, held at the Hotel Cecil, London. The Earl of Glasgow, privy Councillor, owner of Kelburn Castle, Ayrshire, also attended meetings of the BUF's January Club.

Godden, Gertrude M.
Author of *Mussolini: The Birth of the New Democracy* (1923). In May 1925 she wrote a description and a history of the Kibbo Kift Kindred. In June 1925 she submitted a report on the Federation of British Youth. Both were submitted to the Special Branch for their perusal.

Good, Miss Ann* | | |
In June 1936 she opened a BUF women's meeting in Balham. Speaker for the BUF during the East London campaign. In November 1937 she became Women's Canvass Organizer for the 7th London Area. On the Home Office Schedule for

detention her address was given as 3 Kersley Road, Stoke Newington. Interned under DR 18B in Holloway, (but Diana Mosley claims she was never arrested). Diana Mosley remembers that it was possible that Elizabeth Goody, a relatively inactive member, was interned by mistaken identity, and Good, who was a very active supporter of Mosley and peace, tried to compensate by visiting Holloway regularly and bringing food parcels for the women she had worked with in the East End. She worked on behalf of the 18B (British) Detainees Fund, and in December 1941 received a donation from Lady Redesdale, half of which she sent to the London Committee and the other half she kept to help women who might be destitute upon release. Attended a meeting of BU elements on 23 November 1943. Present at the 18B Social and Dance held at the Royal Hotel on 15 December 1945. She became Mosley's secretary after the war and was a speaker for the Union Movement. She died in 1979.

Goody, Mrs Elizabeth Phyllis* | | |

Member of the BUF. Interned in Holloway prison under DR 18B. Probably arrested due to a mix-up in names; Ann Good being a more active member of the BU. While she was still in detention, her husband attended a gathering in London to celebrate Oswald Mosley's birthday on 16 November 1942. Present at the 18B Social and Dance held at the Royal Hotel on 15 December 1945.

Grace, Miss Alice^

In January 1925 she chaired a BF meeting at Dulce Domun, High Street, Leek, with the object of organizing a Women's Unit of the BF in Leek.

Graham, Mrs Bertha Colin*

An active fascist. Wife of a rector. Fined for bell-ringing in 1940.

Greaves, Blanche (née Mann)*

(Born *ca.*1915) Her father died when she was seven: he was born in Poplar, the East End; he did not serve in the Army due to a blood complaint, but was a Special Constable during the First World War, and he had been an electrical engineer. Her mother, born in Kent, joined the BUF before her daughter, having been a strong Conservative all her life. She had two brothers and a sister. She was educated at Putney High School (1926–31), on a Masonic grant, and then went to clerks' college for a year to study typing and short-hand. During the 1930s she worked as a secretary for the Lloyds brokers in the City and for the London Press Exchange. She joined the BUF's Kingston branch in 1934. She became Woman District Leader in Kingston. She played the base drum in the BU's Women's Drum Corps. She marched in the BUF rally on Cable Street in 1936, and she performed with the Women's Drum Corps at the Earl's Court rally in 1939. She met her husband in the movement (he was a non-active member of the branch), and they were on their honeymoon in 1940 when members were being arrested under 18B.

Greenfield, Mrs Winifred* | | |
BU activist. Wife of the Headmaster of Poole Grammar School, and her address was given as Chalmore, Orchard Avenue, Poole, on the Home Office Schedule for detention. Interned under DR 18B. According to Lucy Pearson's pocket diary, she was released from Holloway on 27 August 1940.(She may have been a member of the Peace Pledge Union as Pearson wrote 'PPU' next to her name.)

Greenlaw, Miss^
District officer for the British Fascists in East London. She was one of the original members of the London Special Patrol. She chaired BF meetings in East London at East Ham, Forest Gate, and Walthanstow in December 1927. Officer in Charge of the Fascist Children's Clubs in Silvertown. Awarded the 3rd class Order of the Fasces. She died on 5 November 1928 at her home in Silvertown. Her funeral was carried out with full fascist honours on 10 November 1928.

Griffin, Miss Elizabeth Joan W.* | | |
BU official in Bournemouth, where she served as District Treasurer. She was one of the 'unholy trinity' at the Bournemouth branch where she, Flo Hayes and Iris Ryder ran the show, and the male District Leader was consigned to oblivion. In 1938 she belonged to Team 2 of the 'Southern Raiding Teams' whose objective it was to ride through villages and stop where a crowd formed to give speeches. When Iris Ryder was arrested for making a speech during the BU peace campaign, Griffin organized an appeal to pay her fine. Interned under DR 18B, and on the Home Office Schedule for detention, her address is given as 16 Braidley Road, Bournemouth. She became housekeeper to Major and Mrs de Laessoe, after their release in 1943.

Griffiths, Mrs*
In May 1934 she was Women's Officer for the Clapham Branch of the BUF, located at 23 South Side, Clapham Common.

Grundy, Mrs Edna*
Born in Whitney Bay. Both she and her husband, Sydney, were members of the BUF and the Union Movement. She was 29 years old when she joined the BUF, after attending a Mosley meeting in Brighton. Sydney Grundy was interned on the Isle of Man under 18B. With her two young children, she moved from Brighton to London in 1942 – her husband was released in September 1944. She committed suicide in 1970, and twenty years after

her death, her husband revealed to their son, the writer Trevor Grundy (b.1940), that his mother was, in fact, Jewish. During the 1950s, his parents' support for Mosley was as fanatical as ever, Trevor became a leader of the youth wing of the Union Movement. See Trevor Gundy, *Memoir of a Fascist Childhood* (1998).

Gueroult, Mrs Una*

WOC London, Streatham Branch, for the BUF in 1934. She was also a member of the BUF's Women's HDQ. In June 1934, with Francis-Hawkins, she was in charge of a 25,000 shilling fund in aid of the launch of the London's Command's extensive propaganda campaign. Accompanied Lady Mosley on a visit to the new headquarters at Linden House, Chiswick, in October 1934. Contributor to the *Blackshirt* (1934). She left the BUF by April 1938.

Haig, Miss C.A.W.*

In June 1934 the *Sunday Dispatch* reported that she and her sister, Mrs Haig-Thomas, had joined the BUF. Their brother was the late Earl Haig.

Hamilton, Lady Douglas+

Member of the Nordic League in May 1939.

Hamlin, Mrs Eleanor (née Sizer)^

On 27 July 1929 she married Mr W. Hamlin, son of Councillor Hamlin, at Christ Church, Woburn Place. Their wedding was attended by a BF Guard of Honour. Both were active members of the BF in the Holborn Area.

Hansell, Mrs Florence*

Member of the BUF in Bethnal Green. During the war she collected for the 18B Detainees Fund, and she joined the Union Movement in Bethnal Green after the war. Died in December 1950.

Hardinge, Lady Alexandra+

A god-daughter of Queen Alexandra. Her husband, Sir Arthur Hardinge, former Ambassador to Spain, was a member of the BF Grand Council in the late 1920s. By the late 1930s, she was widowed and in 1939 she toured the country speaking on the subject of Germany, expressing pro-Nazi opinion, and claiming that she knew Hitler personally. She was also a member of the Anglo-German Fellowship, and might have been a member of the Nordic League.

Harris, Mrs*

Women's Section leader for Westminster St George's, in charge of Mitcham. She also became Senior Women's Canvass Organizer for London in 1937.

Hawks, Miss Olive* | | |

(1917–92). Educated at Eltham Hill Secondary School. She was employed first by the Amalgamated Press in the editorial department and subsequently by the Wellington Press as a reader. Joined the BUF in 1933 and was a frequent contributor to BUF publications (1934–40). In 1937 she was employed in the Research Department of the BU. Speaker for the BUF's campaign for the LCC elections in March 1937. In June 1937 she became BU prospective parliamentary candidate for Camberwell (Peckham). In November 1937 she became Women's Canvass Organizer for the 11th London Area. In May 1938 the BUF press claimed that by writing letters of protest to the local press, she was instrumental in preventing the Jewish MP for Peckham, Lewis Silkin, from opening a new Odeon cinema in Peckham High Street. In May 1939 she was given one month's notice from her position on the BUF staff, along with her future husband, F.E. Burdett (commercial traveller, District Leader in Peckham). Married F.E. Burdett in September 1939, but the marriage did not survive the war. She was a prominent speaker in the Women's Peace Campaign of 1940, and author of the campaign's pamphlet. She succeeded Anne Brock-Griggs as Chief Women's Organizer in 1940. Interned under DR 18B on 23 May 1940. Moved to the Isle of Man on 11 August 1941, and returned to Holloway on 4 April 1942 after petitioning to return to London so that her parents could visit her regularly. She was released in 1944. Author of *What Hope for Green Street?* (1945), which she wrote while interned. With Dr Eustace Chesser (the medical writer and sexologist), Hawks co-wrote *Life Lies Ahead: A Practical Guide to Home-Making and the Development of Personality* (1951). It was rumoured that Hawks and Chesser had an affair. After a 15-year-long search Jeffrey Wallder, a researcher into the pre and post-war lives of BUF members, has traced Hawks' movements after the war. He has discovered that she left Britain for Greece in 1948, where she met and married a Greek soldier younger than herself, and became Olive Katsamangos. Together the couple returned to London, where they had two sons, and in 1964 emigrated to Australia. She died of heart failure, alone in her a flat in Perth, and her body was not found until a few days later.

Hay, Michael* +

Expelled from the BUF for sodomy. By 1935 he was Chief assistant to A.S. Leese in the Imperial Fascist League. Friendly with J.F.C. Fuller.

Hayes, Miss Florence Emily* | | |

(Born *ca.* 1896) BU member, speaker and organizer. Women's District Leader in Bournemouth and Women's County Officer for West Hants. She was also asked by Anne Brock-Griggs to be in charge of women's organization for Dorset – her correspondence with Robert Saunders date back to July 1937, through to after the war. She was part of the 'unholy trinity' at the branch where she, Elizabeth Griffin and Iris Ryder ran the show, and the male D/L was consigned to oblivion. In 1938 she belonged to Team 2 of the 'Southern Raiding Teams' whose objective it was to ride through selected villages and stop to speak where there was a crowd. In February 1940 she was offered a debate by the Peace Pledge Union. Together with Hugh Ross Williamson, she addressed a BU peace meeting on 11 February 1940 at the Centenary Hall, Poole. She was a school mistress in Exeter, and lost her job after being interned. On the Home Office Schedule for detention, her address is given as 13, Winston Road, Moordown, Bournemouth. She was released some time after April 1941, as Lady Mosley made an appeal for her release on 26 April 1941. On 18 July 1941 Diana Mosley requested that Lady Redesdale should send Miss Hayes £5, as she had been very good to her when they were together in Holloway, and expressed surprise that she had been released as she was an ardent follower, speaker and organizer for the BU. To Robert Saunders, Hayes expressed that 'my nerves never recovered from Holloway you know, and even now, the least overstrain has its effect.' Present at the 18B Social and Dance held at the Royal Hotel on 1 December, 1945. After the war she turned to Spiritualism.

Heemstra, Baroness Ella de*
Born in Austria in 1889, into a Dutch aristocratic family. Married Joseph V.A. Hepburn-Ruston (b.1889) in September 1926 in Jakarta, and mother of the actress Audrey Hepburn (b.1929). She visited Germany with Unity Mitford in 1935. She separated from her husband in 1935, and they divorced three years later. She contributed to the *Blackshirt*: 'The Call of Fascism' (*Blackshirt*, No.105, April 26, 1935.) Diana Mosley recalled having met her in Germany in 1937 or 1938. Captain Hepburn-Ruston was interned under DR 18B.

Hill, Miss Edith Mary Bowers*
On 26 March 1934, Bowers Hill, of Montreal, married Richard Charles O'Hagan of Chelsea and son of a barrister, at the Chelsea Register Office in a 'fascist wedding.' Both were members of the BUF: the bride, 25 years old, wore the short grey flannel skirt and regulation blackshirt and the groom, 22 years old, wore the blackshirt uniform. A bodyguard from HDQ attended the wedding and gave the fascist salute as the couple left the register office, and a reception was held at BUF HDQ, King's Rd. They spent their honeymoon in Rome, where they hoped to pay their respects to Mussolini.

Hilton, Mrs*
Active member of the BUF. In November 1937 became Women's Canvass Organizer for the 8th London Area.

Hiscox, Miss Gertrud Blount (a.k.a. Mollie)* + | | |

(Born *ca.*1911)Visited Germany regularly since 1935 and claimed to have been in Munich at the time of the Munich Crisis. As a tourist agent for German holidays, she visited Germany for part of each summer. A founding member of The Link in 1937. In possession of BU membership cards for 1937, 1938 and 1940. Wrote a letter to Hitler on 31 August 1939 pledging her support, which was returned by the censor. Attended a social gathering of the Right Club in April 1940. Occupied a flat at 60 Stanhope Gardens SW7 in 1941. In 1941 she was caught with copies of official documents from the Ministry of Supply and charged at Rochester Row Police station on 15 March 1941. Appeared before the magistrate on 17 March 1941 on charges under the Treachery Act, 1940, and Regulation 2A(1) of the Defence(General) Regulations, 1939. Convicted and sentenced to five years penal servitude at the Central Criminal Court on 16 June 1941. By 1944 she was engaged to Richard 'Jock' Houston.

Hook, Mrs Phyliss* | | |

BU member in Guilford. Her sister, Miss Durrell, was also interned. Their brother was the master of Winchester. Her case was heard by the Advisory Committee in *ca.* October 1940.

Horne, Lady^

She was a patron of the British Fascists' 'Mi Careme Ball,' held at the Hotel Cecil in London on March 5 1926.

Houghton, Hon. Mrs^

In 1926 she was appointed County Commander, London Women's Units, in place of the temporary Commander, Miss O.P. Downes, Assistant Director of the Women's Units. She spoke at a meeting of Women's Units at Trafalgar Square in October 1926, expounding the importance of Empire Preference.

Houston, (Lady) Lucy D.B.E.

(1858 to 29 December 1936) Born Fanny Lucy Radmall, daughter of a box maker. Married Fred Gretton, and then married Theodore Brinckmann in 1883, the heir to a baronetcy. She divorced Brinckmann in 1895. In 1901 she married the 9th Lord Byron (d.1917). Supported the suffragette campaign, spoke for 'Votes for Women' at meetings on Hampstead Heath, and financed the Pankhursts. Set up and financed a rest home for nurses in Hampstead during the Great War. When King George V instituted the Order of the British Empire, she was the fifth woman in the realm to receive the honour of DBE. She married Sir Robert Paterson Houston (1853–1926), owner of the Houston line of steamships, in 1922. She was the proprietor of the

Saturday Review, which from 1931 to 1936 expressed a general tone of pro-Mussolini opinion. In November 1933 the *Blackshirt* reprinted her article from the *Saturday Review*, 'The Day of Remembrance' (*Blackshirt*, No.31, 25 November–1 December 1, 1933). She had a Belgian griffon dog whom she called Benito, after Mussolini. In November 1936, along with Lord Queensborough, Lord Camrose and Lord Bearstead, she backed Lt. Col. Seton Hutchinson in his attempt to form the National Worker's Party, a new movement devoted to combating communism. In November 1936 it was reported that she was again toying with the idea of contributing to the BUF. Her death in December 1936 was seen as a blow to the BUF in its bid to fight a General Election, as without her donation this would be financially impossible.

Houston, Richard 'Jock'* + | | |
Born 2 August 1903 in Macclesfield, Cheshire. A painter by trade and a trade unionist before joining the BUF. Became a member of the BUF in 1934 first at the Islington Branch and then at Shoreditch. Became a paid speaker for the BUF in November 1935. Left the BUF in October 1936. It was alleged that he was expelled from the BUF in 1937, and he went on to form the Nationalist Association. Involved in the Nordic League, and a close friend of Captain Ramsay. Worked as a street book-maker starting in 1938. Married since *ca*.1927 with three children, but separated from his wife by 1940 and living with Miss Hiscox. He was with Miss Hiscox during the six months he evaded arrest under 18B, between May and December 1940. Arrested on 13 December 1940 when he was living with Hiscox at 71 Chiswick High Road under the assumed names of Mr and Mrs Hudson.

Howard of Effingham, Lady* | | |
Hungarian by birth, and married to the 6th Earl of Effingham. Her maiden name was (Manci) Malvina Gertler. Member of the BUF. In 1940 she was accused of 'acts prejudicial' for making contact with persons in the services and embassies with intention to transmit information to the enemy. She was detained on 10 February 1941. On 16 July 1941, the 28 year old Lady Howard of Effingham was released from Holloway Prison, where she had been detained for five months under DR 18B. The marriage was dissolved in 1946.

Hudson, Mrs Alma V.* | | |
BU prospective parliamentary candidate. Wife of Commander Charles E. Hudson, the District Leader at Bognor Regis. She acted as Women's District Leader for Bognor. Her address was given as Arnen, Limmer Lane, Felpham, on the Home Office Schedule for detention. She had three teenage children at the time of her internment under DR 18B.

Huntington, Lady^

Present at a British Fascisti dinner at the Lyceum Club in February 1925.

Inglis, Miss*

In January 1934 she organized the Women's Section of the Edinburgh branch of the BUF.

Ingram, Mrs Marie Louise Augusta*

(Born *ca*.1898) German by birth. She came to Britain in 1922 and married an RAF sergeant – it was a marriage of convenience. She later married William Swift, an employee in the naval dockyards at Portsmouth. At the time of her arrest, she was employed as a maid in the home of a prominent naval officer. Swift and Mrs Ingram, both active members of the BU, were convicted on 2 July 1940 of conspiracy to assist the enemy. It was alleged against them that they had set up an underground organization to be used by the enemy to carry out harbour espionage and that they attempted to seduce sailors from their duty. Ingram was sentenced to 10 years and Swift to 14 years imprisonment.

Irvine, Mrs Louise (née Fisher)* | | |

Born in 1915 in Chester. Religion: Church of England. Her father was an ardent Labourite who died when she was 15 years old. Her mother died one year later. A student at Cheshire County Training College, Crewe, from 1933–35, studying English and History. Attended her first BUF meeting in Crewe during her second year at college. In 1936, after leaving college and obtaining her first teaching post, she joined the BUF at the headquarters in Stafford St. in Birmingham. She became Women's District Leader in Birmingham, and she ran the BU headquarters' bookshop. She met her future husband when she joined, and he had just become District Leader for Birmingham. In the summer of 1939 she and her fiancé visited the German Rhineland. Her fiancé was interned under DR 18B in June 1940, and held at Walton Gaol, Stafford Prison, and Peel Camp on the Isle of Man – after 18 months imprisonment he was called up and served in the army for four-and-a-half years. She was interned under DR 18B in November 1940. For the first weeks she was put in C Wing, Holloway prison, which was used for 18Bs, alien detainees and convicted prisoners, and she later transferred to F Wing, which was used for 18B and BU detainees. In F Wing she met Lady Mosley for the first time. She met Norah Elam when they were both in F Wing in Holloway Prison. Early in 1941 she came before the Advisory Committee at the Berystede Hotel, Ascot. She was sent to Port Erin, the Isle of Man, in May 1941. On 7 July 1941 her then fiancé, S.L. Irvine, signed a petition requesting that they should be admitted to the Married Camp on the Isle of Man. In October 1941 she was returned to Holloway to attend a tribunal at Burlington House, and was then returned to the Isle of Man. On 10 November 1941 she was notified that her detention was terminated with the conditions that she state the address to which she was going, and within 24 hours of arrival there report to the local police station. She returned to Birmingham and was reinstated as a teacher. In 1944 she applied for a teaching post in Halifax and was accepted. In January 1992 she spoke at a dinner hosted by the Friends of O.M. in commemoration of women Blackshirts.

Ives, Miss V.* | | |
Member of the BU Women's Drum Corps. She won the BU bronze distinction. Interned under DR 18B.

Jackson, Miss E.+
In May 1937 the National Directors of the National Socialist League appointed her to the post officer i/c London Women's Canvass Corps.

Jackson, Mrs Annabel Huth+
On 11 December 1939 she attended a lunch at the Ladies' Carlton where all guests 'drank a silent toast to the Leader,' Sir Oswald Mosley. The collaborative meetings between Mosley's, Domvile's and Ramsay's inner circles in the months of February, March and April 1940 were all held at her house in Ladbroke Grove. The meeting of 17 April was attended by Mosley, the Elams, Lady Pearson, Mrs Whinefield, Miss Laurie (daughter of Professor A.P. Laurie), Mrs Duff and Lady Dunn.

Johannesen, Mrs Caroline May* | | |
She was a BU member in Cobham, Surrey. Detained under DR 18B, and, according to Lucy Pearson's pocket diary, released from Holloway on 13 August 1940.

Johnston, Margaret Mathilda Elizabeth*
Wife of Jack Johnston, a high profile BU member in the East End of London (interned under DR 18B in 1940). She stood as BU candidate for Bethnal Green West Ward in the Municipal elections of 1 November 1937, polling 354 votes.

Jones, Mrs Phyllis Evelyn*
Honourable Secretary of the 18B Detainees (British) Aid Fund. She resided at 5 Mersham Road, Tornton Heath, Surrey. Attended a meeting of BU elements on 23 November 1943. Present at the 18B Social and Dance held at the Royal Hotel on 1 December, 1945.

Joyce, Mrs*

She married William Joyce on 30 April 1927. Involved in an intimate affair with E.H. Piercey of NHQ in 1934, and it was alleged that he was the father of the child she was expecting.

Joyce, Mrs Margaret Cairns* +

(1911–72) Born in Trafford Park, Manchester on 14 July 1911, the daughter of Mr and Mrs Robert White (father employed at a chemical works). An active member of the BU in Carlisle. Married William Joyce in February 1937. Joined the National Socialist League and became assistant treasurer in November 1938. Left for Germany with her husband on 25 August 1939. She began broadcasting to England in November 1940 until May 1942, giving weekly talks to women, dealing mainly with women's economic problems and contrasting the British system unfavourably with the German. She took a lover, Nicky von Besack, a Wehrmact Intelligence officer, and in August 1941 William Joyce sued her for divorce on the grounds of her infidelity. She counter-sued, alleging cruelty. Their divorce was granted, but in February 1942 they remarried in a discreet ceremony in Berlin. Detained in military custody in June 1945. In January 1946 it was decided on compassionate grounds that she would not be prosecuted. She later moved to Ireland.

Joyce, William^ * +

Became a member of the BF in 1923 when he was 17 years old. He first came to the notice of Special Branch when he acted as chairman of a meeting held in Hyde Park by the British Fascisti on 24 March 1924. He had a first-class honours degree in English from Birkbeck. In October 1924 he received a razor cut on the right cheek during an affray between fascists and communists at Lambeth when defending a Tory candidate for the General election, the Jewish Jack Lazarus. Left the British Fascisti in 1925 and became an active member of the Conservative Party. Married his first wife on 30 April 1927. Joined the BUF in March 1933, becoming a member of the HDQ staff and Area Administrative Officer for the Home Counties. On 26 March 1934 he spoke at a meeting at the Town Hall Chelsea on the exploitation of women in the labour market. In August 1934 he was appointed Director of Propaganda. Stood for the BU in Shoreditch for the LCC elections of 4 March 1937, polling 2,564 votes (15%). Leader of a contingent within the BU that wished to see the development of the Policy-Propaganda dimension of the movement, the securing of recruits in factories and workshops, and the building of an efficient election machinery. Resigned from the BUF on 2 April 1937. Joyce and Beckett inaugurated the National Socialist League. His name appears on the Right Club ledger of *ca.* May 1939. His name was on the original 18B list for immediate detention, and in August 1939 he was warned that he would be detained under the Emergency Powers Act – he and Margaret Joyce left for Berlin. On 18 September

1939 he entered the service of the German radio. In June 1942 Joyce was appointed chief commentator on the European Station's English-language service. Joyce came up for trial on 17 September 1945 on three counts of High Treason; he was convicted and hanged.

Kell, Mrs (a.k.a Pfeffer) | | |

Interned in December 1939. Contracted a marriage of convenience to a British subject. Acquainted with members of the Nazi Party.

King, Miss Louise Ann* | | |

Born in London and educated at St George's Catholic School, Walthanstow. In the 1930s she was controller of the *Daily Mail's* Women's Canvass Staff. In January 1937 she became BU prospective parliamentary candidate for Ilford. In November 1937 she became joint Women's Canvass Officer with Mrs T.A. Ruffer of the 9th London Area. Interned under DR 18B, and on the Home Office Schedule for detention, her address was given as 1 Pine Avenue, Ipswich. According to Lucy Pearson's pocket diary, she was released from Holloway on 13 September 1940.

Kirby, Miss C.A.^

One of the original members of the BF's London Special Patrol. Contributor to the *British Lion*. In 1928 wrote an article 'The Case for Emigration' (No.27) calling for the end of alien immigration to Britain. In the summer of 1933 she was deprived of the Order of the Fasces, once bestowed on her by the BF Executive Committee.

Knight, Mrs R.*

In November 1937 she became BU Women's Canvass Organizer for the 5th London Area.

Knights-Smith, Miss^

In January 1925 she presided over a British Fascist meeting held at Elkes Cafe, to consider the desirability of forming a Women's Branch of the BF in Uttoxeter.

de Laessoe, Mrs Diana* | | |

(born *ca.* 1882) According to Diana Mosley, she was of German origin but had driven an ambulance in England during the Great War while her husband was at the front. She and her husband, Henry H. A. De Laessoe, were interned under DR 18B. She was arrested on 23 May 1940. The couple was allowed to be detained together in Holloway prison in 1941, and released the same day as the Mosleys. Iris Ryder took the elderly and destitute couple into her home after their release.

Lake, Annie | | |
Interned first in Holloway, and in June 1941 she was transferred to the Isle of Man, along with 43 other women, of whom only approximately 14 were fascists. Wrote to Richard Stokes of the Home Office in June 1941 complaining of the treatment of women internees during the transfer.

Lane, Lieutenant-Colonel A.H.+
He had served with Kitchener in Egypt, then with Milner in South Africa. A member of the Britons and the Imperial Fascist League. Author of *The Alien Menace*, with a foreword by Lord Sydenham of Combe. In 1929 he presented 100 copies of his book to the BF's Fascist Children's Clubs Department.

Leather, Miss V.*
BUF member in Dorset West. In May 1939 she took the Election Agent's Correspondence Course of Instruction in order to obtain an Agent's Certificate. She was still a member of the BU in November 1939, and appeared on Saunders' membership list, her address recorded as Wyards, Studland, Swanage.

Lemmy, Mrs*
She held British Union garden parties in Tulworth.

Lees, Aubrey T.O.* + | | |
Brought back to England from Palestine by the Foreign Office in 1939 because he had been engaging in pro-Arab and anti-Semitic activities. Joined the BU, the British People's Party and Ramsay's Right Club upon his return. His name appears on the Right Club ledger of *ca.*May 1939. Attended secret meetings convened by the BU after the outbreak of war. In 1940 he resided at 10 Courtfield Gardens SW5 and cohabited with Ella Durant, also a member of the BU. Order of Detention dated 19 June 1940. Order of Detention revoked on 27 September 1940. Attended a meeting at the flat of Molly Stanford on 10 November 1940 where the means of organizing aid for 18Bs was discussed. He remained under Restriction Order until 1944.

Leon, Mrs*
In May 1934 she was Women's Officer for the Kensington Branch of the BUF, located at 16A Penywern Rd. Earl's Court Road, SW.

Lindsay, Mrs Denise Terisa Marguerita Mary*
In August 1939 she was arrested during a BUF demonstration in Parliament Square, taken to Bow Street and bound over for three months for obstructing a police constable. She claimed that she was trying to cross the Square to meet her husband who was distributing BU leaflets. Her age was given as 27,

her address in Earl's Court, and her occupation as assistant to a veterinary surgeon.

Link, Lydia (a.k.a. Lewinska) | | |
Interned in December 1939, with her sister, Maria Lewinska. Naturalized British subject of Polish origin and member of the NSDAP. Immigrated to Australia after the war.

Linton, Jenny*
Contributor to the *Blackshirt* (1934–35). Author of 'Fascist Women do not want Equal Rights with Men: They Desire only the True Women's Place in the Community' (*Blackshirt*, No. 80, 2 November 1934). In November 1934 she interviewed five fascist women and asked why they joined the Blackshirts (*Blackshirt*, No. 82, 16 November 1934). Jeffrey Wallder is certain that the name was a *nom de plume*, but does not know whose.

Lintorn-Orman, Miss Rotha Beryl^
(1895 to March 1935) Grand-daughter of a field marshal, Sir John Lintorn Simmons (1812–1902). Daughter of Major Charles Orman of the Essex Regiment. In 1909 she commanded the First and Second Bournemouth troop of Girl Guides. During the war she served with the Women's Reserve Ambulance, and then with the Scottish Women's Hospital Corps. She was sent to Serbia in 1916 and was twice awarded the Croix de Charité for gallantry in action. Ill with malaria in 1917, she returned to London and joined the British Red Cross and served as Commandant of the Motor School at Devonshire House. On 6 May 1923 she formed the British Fascisti. In February 1924 New Scotland Yard presumed she was an ex-suffragette, assisted in running the Fascisti by some 'very harmful lunatics' – there is no evidence, however, that she was involved with the struggle for votes for women. She was one of the original members of the BF's London Special Patrol. Together with members of her Women's Unit, she was attacked by men and children in the East End in May 1927. On 5 May 1927 her letter to the editor of the *Morning Post* was published, in which she negated the allegations made by the *Daily Worker* that the BF was arming for the next general strike. Also in May, a 'woman correspondent' for the *Morning Post* reported on her visit to the FCC in Kensington, and her interview with Lintorn-Orman, when Lintorn-Orman claimed that 'we have clubs now in practically all the industrial towns of the country and all over London.' (*Morning Post*, 9 May, 1927). In September 1927 she appeared as a witness at Westminster Police Court when two BF officials, Captain Robert Smith and Miss Norah Granton Ray were charged with assaulting Fred Edwin Firminger, an undergraduate of Lincoln College, Oxford. (It was alleged that Firminger had gone to BF headquarters in Fulham Road to pick up some papers

on behalf of Mr Judge, recently discharged editor of the *British Lion*, and was assaulted by the two BF officers and taken to Chelsea police station). After Lintorn-Orman's testimony the judge ruled that there was no case to answer. On 28 October 1927 she visited the Irish Commands of the BF and attended meetings in Ulster organized by Mrs Warring. In July 1932 it was reported in *British Fascism* that she was at last recovering from an illness, a heart attack and a serious fall. In November 1932 it came to the notice of the authorities that she and her colleagues were implying in letters sent to other bodies that the BF had special relations with the Police; as a result she was interviewed and warned by the Police to cease making such insinuations. Also in November, in a letter to the *Daily Telegraph*, Lintorn-Orman explained how the BF offered to assist the authorities as the hunger marchers were converging on London, and together with several senior BF officers, Lintorn-Orman called at BUF headquarters asking Mosley if he would permit his members to join in the establishment of an anti-riot squad – Mosley refused. In May 1934 she was presented with a clock engraved with the date 6th May 1934 and bearing the Fascist badge in celebration of the BF's 11th anniversary. In June 1934 it was reported that she had not taken an active part in the BF for some time, and was in the country suffering from an illness caused by excessive drinking. On 17 July she met with BUF officials at St Stephen's House SW and turned down plans for a merger between the two organizations. After her death, the finances of the BF were found to be in dilapidated condition. In June and July 1935 statutory meetings of the creditors and shareholders of the British Fascists Ltd. were held at the Board of Trade offices, and the limited company went into receivership.

Lister, Mrs Madge* | | |
She was a member of the Castleford or Lincoln Branch of the BUF. Sister of D/L for Normanton (Yorkshire), Leonard Jarvis. When he joined the Army on 2 December 1939 she took over as temporary D/L. Her address was given as Miners Arms, Castleford on the Home Office Schedule for detention. Interned under DR 18B. According to Lucy Pearson's pocket diary, she was released from Holloway on 8 November 1940.

Lucas, Lady
Attended the BUF's London Administration luncheon on 28 February 1939.

Lucas, Mrs Doris (née Harding)^
Member of the London Special Patrol. In October 1931 she married R.C. Lucas of the 1st London Area of the British Fascists at Paddington Registry Office. In the summer of 1933 she was deprived of the Order of the Fasces, once bestowed upon her by the Executive Committee of the BF.

Ludovici, Captain Anthony Mario+

(1882–1971). He had at one time been private secretary to August Rodin, and had served in the First World War. Expounder of Nietzsche's philosophy, virulent anti-Semite and anti-Feminist. In 1936 Lord Lymington (Gerard Wallop) broke away from the back-to-the land English Mistery movement, and formed the the pro-Nazi English Array. Ludovici was also a member of the English Array. He contributed to *The New Pioneer*, started by Lord Lymington and John Beckett in 1939, and under the pseudonym 'Cobbett' authored *Jews, and the Jews in England* (1938). He belonged to the Right Club, and his name appears on the Right Club ledger (of *ca.* May 1939). In 1945 his address was 'The Hampstead,' Rishangles, Suffolk. Associations with known persons of anti-Semitic and pro-German views during the war, including A.T.O Lees. His name was found in 'Jock' Houston's address book.

Lyons, Miss Eileen*

In June 1934 the *Sunday Dispatch* reported that she was organizing a special flying club for women members of the BUF in Gloucestershire. Contributor to BUF publications (1936–37).

Mahon, Mrs*

In May 1934 she was Women's Officer for the Paddington Branch of the BUF.

Makgill, Sir Donald*

Sir Donald was Baronet of Kemblack and formerly a lieutenant in the Coldsteam Guards. One of the BUF Contact Officers – with duties to attract members and gain support from other organizations – and one of the founders of the January Club. Suspended with his wife from the BUF in April 1934 and not permitted to take part in any BUF activities. He resigned from the BUF in May 1934.

Makgill, (Lady) Esther*

She had been Esther Bromley before she married Sir Donald Makgill. She was O.C. Women's Department of the BUF(1933–34). In December 1933 she attended the wedding of Ian Hope Dundas to Pamela Ernestine Dorman. Present at the opening of a bazaar at Women's Headquarters in December 1933. Suspended from the BUF in April 1934 due to revelations of serious deficiencies in the funds of the Women's Section. Resigned from the BUF in April 1934. In July 1937 she was sentenced to six months for seven charges of using worthless cheques to obtain goods on false pretences. She later remarried and became Mrs Esther Murray.

Markham, Mrs Violet

(1872–1957)An anti-suffragist during the Edwardian period. She addressed the inaugural meeting of the London branch of the National Anti-Suffragist League on 5 November 1908 at the Queen's Gate Hotel, Kensington. She spoke on the Anti-Suffrage platform at an Albert Hall rally on 29 February 1912. During the war she was converted to the cause of votes for women. Worked for the National Service Department during the Great War. In 1917 she was appointed a Companion of Honour. After the First World War she sat on numerous Government Committees: she chaired the Central Committee on Women's Training and Employment; from 1934 she was the statutory woman member of the Unemployment Assistance Board, and after 1937 its Deputy Chair; she was periodically consulted by the armed forces and the Foreign Office for her expertise on educational programmes. She was first asked to sit on the 18B Committee by Sir Samuel Hoare in October 1939 – the first woman to sit on the Committee. From 1940 she sat on the Home Office 18B Advisory Committee hearing appeals against orders of internment, working alongside Mr Norman Birkett (other members of the Tribunal were: John Morris, Mr O'Sullivan, Archibald and Jacqueline Cockburn, Sir Arthur Hazelrigg). She sat on the Aliens Appeal Court from November 1939. Later in the war she was appointed Chairman of the Committee set up by Parliament to investigate conditions in the Women's Services. Author of *Return Passage: The Autobiography of Violet Markham* (1953). After the Second World War she went to Germany for a brief period to talk to German women about the importance of becoming active citizens.

Marsden, Miss*

In September 1938 it was reported that she was in charge of the organization of meetings at BU NHQ, but intended to resign because of Francis-Hawkins' 'high-handedness.' She obtained visits with Oswald Mosley when he was interned in 1940; her visits were not allowed as of 6 July 1940.

Marston, Miss Kathleen* | | |

An employee of the BU in 1940, McKecknie's secretary. On 1 March 1940 she attended the London Administration luncheon at the Criterion restaurant. Interned in Holloway under DR 18B. Attended a meeting of BU elements on 23 November 1943.

Marten, Miss Angela^

Organized the Fascist Children's Club in the North West District of London. Killed in a sailing accident on 30 July 1927. After her death the FCC in the North West was named after her in memory. Her mother, Mrs Marten, was presented with a silver frame, engraved with the BF badge and inscription.

Martin, Miss Cecilia*

In November 1937 she became Women's Canvass Organizer for the 6th London Area. A Special Branch report of the surveillance of Heather and B.D.E. Donovan's flat on 23 May 1940 records that two fellow members of the BUF called in the evening and stayed the night: these were George Sutherland Mackay of 18 Horbury Crescent, Kensington Park Rd W1, and his wife Joan Cecilia Mackay (née Martin).

Maxwell-Knight, Charles^

(1900–68) He was born in Mitcham, Surrey, and his father, Hugh Knight, was a bankrupted solicitor (d.1914). He was educated at Worcester, the Incorporated Thames Nautical Training College. He left Worcester in September 1917 and spent the last year of the Great War as a mid-shipman in the Royal Naval Reserve. Towards the end of 1923 he joined the BF, either as an anti-fascist mole, through conviction, or to obtain information on communist activities. Recruited to MI5 by Vernon Kell in April 1925. In 1925 he married Gladys Poole, the BF's Director of Women's Units (she committed suicide in 1935). He served both as the BF's Publicity Officer, Deputy Chief of Staff and as its Director of Intelligence. In September 1926 he became a member of the BF Grand Council. In 1927 he relinquished his position as BF Deputy Chief of Staff, but continued to be an active member and served as its Director of Intelligence for some years after that date. In 1930 he was put on MI5's payroll as a case officer, and following his success in the Woolwich Arsenal spy case in 1938, was appointed head of B5b, a newly created section established to supervise the placing of agents in 'subversive' organizations. Maxwell-Knight and his agents uncovered the Nazi espionage activities of Tyler Kent and Anna Wolkoff, both of whom had close links with Captain Ramsay's Right Club and Mosley's BUF.

Mayne, Mrs Barbara (née McRae)^

Officer-in-Charge of the 2nd London Special Patrol. Daughter of Lieutenant-Colonel and Mrs McRae-Gilstrap. She married Captain Henry Laharde Mayne (formerly of the King's Own Scottish Borderers) at Ballimore Otter Ferry, Argyll, on 12 June 1929. Upon her marriage she resigned from the L.S.P. Founder of the Fascist Dogs' Club in 1929.

McShane, Yolande (née Mott)*

Her father was a captain on the Cunard line. In 1935, when she was 18 years old, she joined the BUF with her mother. She became Women's Branch Leader for Wirral's Hoylake/West Kirby Branch. She was later made Women's District Inspector for all Merseyside. Left the BUF in 1937 when she and her mother moved to Chester. She joined the Red Cross in 1937–38 and became a nurse.

When war was declared she was called to report to duty at the Chester County Mental Hospital. Did war work on a farm in Shropshire, then worked for the Women's Police Force in Liverpool (driving ambulances and replacing male drivers). Author of *Daughter of Evil* (1980).

Menzies of Menzies, Lady^

Member of the British Fascisti.

Mereweather, Miss I.G.*

Member of the BUF. In December 1935 she became acting Women District Officer for Bristol Central.

Metcalfe, Alexandra (a.k.a. Baba)

Youngest daughter of Lord Curzon and Mary Leiter. Married Major 'Fruity' Metcalfe on 21 July 1925. Major Metcalfe, MVO, MC, had been Aide-de-Camp to the Prince of Wales, and the Commander-in-Chief in India. She and her husband attended meetings of the January Club. She went to the Nuremberg rally in 1934. Nicholas Mosley has confirmed that Baba and Sir Oswald had a very close and intimate relationship throughout the 1930s. During Mosley's internment, she sought the help of many of her friends and acquaintances, including Winston Churchill.

Meyer, Mrs P.*

In November 1937 she became Women's Canvass Organizer for the 10th London Area.

Meyerhof, Mrs Eva (a.k.a. Livia Laurent) | | |

Interned in Holloway Prison and then in the Isle of Man under the category of 'hostile origins.' Published her poetry in the *Poetry Review* in May–June 1941. She was not allowed to send any of her work from the internment camp and took on a legal adviser to settle the issue in June 1941. Permission for internees to write for publication while in internment was denied by the Secretary of State in August 1941. An application for her release was made by the Jewish Refugee Committee, Bloomsbury House, in 1941. Under the *nom de plume* of Livia Laurent, she published *A Tale of Internment* (1942).

Miller, Joan+

(died 1984 in Malta). MI5 agent under Maxwell-Knight ('M'). She infiltrated Captain Ramsay's Right Club in 1940, in which organization MI5 had already planted two agents, one of whom was Mrs Amos. Posing as a War Office employee, Miller was accepted into the Right Club and befriended Anna Wolkoff, and later gave evidence at the Wolkoff trial. After her cover was blown with the extreme-Right, she spied on the CPGB for a short time. During the summer of 1940 she worked at Holloway prison, interviewing women enemy alien internees. She had an unconsummated affair with Maxwell-Knight, whom she came to suspect was homosexual.

Mitford, Miss Unity Valkyrie*

(1914–48) Fourth daughter of Lord and Lady Redesdale. She made her debut in 1932 and attended many dances, escorted by her pet grass-snake, Enid, slung around her neck. On 7 July 1932 Diana Guinness gave a ball in her honour at 96 Cheyne Walk. In August 1933 she left for Germany where she was entertained by Ernst Hanfstaengl, and, with her sister Diana, attended the first Nuremberg Rally which began on 31 August 1933. On 9 February 1935 Hitler invited Unity to join him at his table at the Osteria Bavaria. In April 1935 Hitler and Oswald Mosley met in Munich and the Fuhrer gave a lunch party in Sir Oswald's honour at which Unity was present, along with the English-born Frau Winifred Wagner and the Duchess of Brunswick, the ex-Kaiser's only daughter. In the summer of 1935 she attended the summer festival at Hesselberg, and on June 23, in front of an audience of approximately 200,000, she made a short speech in which she expressed her solidarity with the German people and pledged her support to Julius Streicher. In London, on 13 July 1935, it was noted by the press that Unity dined with Duff Cooper, Secretary of State for War. Unity was in Germany for the Olympic Games in the summer of 1936. When the message from the King announcing his abdication was read to both Houses of Parliament on 10 December 1936 she was in the gallery of the House of Lords. On 5 March 1938 Unity wrote to her cousin, Winston Churchill, about the situation in Austria and the misrepresentation of Hitler's Anschluss in the British press. When Hitler marched into Austria on 14 March 1938 Unity was there to met him. Unity returned from Vienna in April, and on 10 April 1938 she attended a Labour Party rally at Hyde Park when angry crowds suddenly turned on her and tore off her swastika badge. On 15 December 1938, with her parents, she attended a party of the Anglo-German Fellowship in Bloomsbury. (Founded in late 1935 by merchant banker Ernest Tennant, the Anglo-German Fellowship was also supported by Unity's father, Lord Redesdale, and other peers ranging from Lord Mount Temple to Lord Londonderry and the Duke of Wellington, Conservative MPs Lieutenant-Colonel Sir Thomas Moore MP and Sir Asheton Pownall MP, as well as prominent business men). On 18 March 1939 Unity published an article in the *Daily Mirror* in which she argued in favour of Anglo-German friendship. In March 1939 she returned to Germany, and established herself in a flat in Munich from which, it was rumoured, a Jewish family had recently been evicted. On 6 May 1939 she arrived to spend the weekend at Hitler's mountain retreat, Berchtesgaden. On 3 September 1939 she entered the English

Gardens in Munich and shot herself with a small pistol. In January 1940, with a bullet in her brain and half paralysed, she was permitted to leave Germany for England. On 3 January 1940 she arrived at Folkestone. On 20 February 1940 a debate erupted in the House of Commons over a plan to move her to Inchkenneth, her family's recently acquired Scottish island, and Oliver Stanley, Secretary of War, announced that the move should not be made. Accompanied by Norah Elam, with whom she was then staying at 5 Logan Place SW, she visited the Mosleys in Holloway on 25 March 1943. On 29 July 2 1944 the Home Secretary, Herbert Morrison, granted permission for Unity Mitford to live on Inchkenneth.

Monk, Miss Margaret*

Employed at National Headquarters of the BUF as assistant to the Leader since April 1934. In March 1935 she was earning 200 pounds per annum. Engaged to John Garnett, Organizer of National Transport for the BUF, and in September 1938 they left for a holiday in South Germany. She visited Diana Mosley in Holloway on 2 July 1940. She visited Oswald Mosley once he was interned in 1940; her visits where not permitted as of 6 July 1940. In September 1940 Mosley requested that she act for him in his absence and file current newspapers for his personal use. Jeffrey Wallder suspects that she was working with the security services, helping to provide information for Special Branch reports. When interviewed by Wallder, she denied it.

Moran, Toni (a.k.a. Mrs Sharpe)*

BU speaker in Manchester, known to be notoriously anti-Semitic. She frequently visited her husband, Tommy Moran, at the Ascot camp when he was interned, but she was never interned.

More-Nesbitt, Mrs Hamilton^

During the Great War she was an Inspector in the Women's Police in Edinburgh. Member of the British Fascists. Vice-President of the BF's Scottish Women's Units. In January 1925 she was elected a member of the General Headquarters Council of the BF.

Morris, Miss Sylvia* +

Born ca.1914 and daughter of Dr E. Morris of Donington. Started her career working in greyhound kennels, and by the time she was a member of the BUF, she worked as a freelance journalist. Began to work for the BUF in Lincolnshire. In November 1936 she became BU prospective parliamentary candidate for Holland with Boston. On 12 April 1937 the *Daily Telegraph* reported that she had been expelled from the BUF. To the reporter she said that her immediate expulsion had followed an interview with Mosley at NHQ in London, when differences of opinion arose between them. Joined the National Socialist League and became Acting League Leader for Holland with Boston in April 1937. On 31 October 1940 she wrote to the Home Secretary, Herbert Morrison, on behalf of British men and women interned under 18B and 'appealed to [him] as a Socialist.'

Mosley, (Lady) Cynthia (née Curzon)*

(23 August 1898–16 May 1933) Second daughter of Earl Curzon of Kedleston (d.1925) and Mary Leiter (d.1906). Educated at Eastbourne in 1916. In the winter of 1916–17 she worked as a clerk in the War Office, and in 1918 she was on a farm as a land girl. Took a short welfare course at the London School of Economics, including social work in the East End. She met Oswald Mosley when both were in Plymouth to help Nancy Astor in her by-election campaign of 1919. Married Oswald Mosley on 11 May 1920. In 1924 she joined the Labour Party with her husband. On 21 September 1925 she was adopted as Labour candidate for Stoke-on-Trent. In the General Election of May 1929 she won the seat for Stoke-on-Trent, with a majority of 7,850 over her opponent Colonel Ward, winning 26,548 votes (58.7%) She took her seat on 27 June 1929 and made her maiden speech on Widow's Pensions in October. Joined the New Party in 1931 and resigned from the Labour Party. In April 1933 she travelled to Rome with her husband to meet Mussolini and they took the fascist salute. In April 1933 the *Daily Herald* reported that the Women's Section of the BUF was being organized and was under the guidance of Lady Cynthia Mosley and Lady Makgill. In July 1935 the Archbishop of Canterbury, Dr Cosmo Lang, opened the Cynthia Mosley Day Nursery in London.

Mosley, (Lady) Diana (née Mitford)* | | |

Born in June 1910, fourth child of Lord and Lady Redesdale. Married Bryan Guinness, son of the Minister of Agriculture, on 28 January 1929 and they had two sons. In January 1932 the artist Dora Carrington borrowed a gun from the estate of Mr and Mrs Bryan Guinness which she used to commit suicide. Diana met Oswald Mosley early in 1932 at a party. Diana gave a ball at 96 Cheyne Walk in honour of her sister Unity Mitford on 7 July 1932 – Sir Oswald Mosley attended. On 11 April 1933 it was revealed in the Press that Diana was suing Bryan Guinness for divorce. In the summer of 1933 she accompanied Unity Mitford to Germany, a trip that changed the latter's life. Invited to the first Nuremberg Parteitag starting on 31 August 1933 by Putzi Hanfstaengl. Went again to the Nuremberg Parteitag in 1934. She became friends with Hitler early in 1935. She had a motor accident on 19 July 1935 after which she required sixteen stitches. On 27 October 1935 she attended a demonstration in Hyde Park hosted by the British Non-Sectarian Anti-Nazi Council where the speakers

were Attlee and Mrs Despard, and where she was the only one to vote against
their resolution, and gave the fascist salute. With Unity, she attended the Olympic
Games in Berlin in 1936. Married Sir Oswald Mosley on 6 October 1936 in
Berlin. In November 1938 the news broke that she and Sir Oswald had been
married in Berlin two years earlier. On 26 July 1939 she and Sir Oswald hosted
a dinner party at their London home at 129 Grosvenor Road, gathering together
the leading figures in Britain's pro-Nazi 'patriotic societies.' In August 1939,
with Unity, she went to Bayreuth for the Festival and there had an interview
with Hitler who told them that war between Germany and Britain was inevitable.
In May-June 1940 she took charge of paying BU salaries once her husband was
interned. On 25 June 1940 her former father-in-law, Walter Guinness, sent a
letter to the Home Office concerning her activities in Germany, her pro-Nazism,
and recommended her immediate internment. She was arrested at Savehay Farm
on 29 June 1940 when she was still nursing her 11 week-old baby. Her case
was heard by the Advisory Committee on 2 and 4 October 1940. In April 1941
she brought an action against the Home Secretary for damages for breach of
statutory duty. In December 1941 it was decided that certain married couples
could live in a separate block in Holloway and the Mosleys were reunited. Released
from Holloway on 20 December 1943. Present at the 18B Social and Dance
held at the Royal Hotel on 1 December 1945.

Mosley, (Lady) Katherine Maud*

(1874 to 20 June 1948) Daughter of Captain J.H.E. Heathcote. Born in Shropshire,
the second child in a family of three sisters and two brothers. She married the
heir of Rolleston, Oswald Mosley, in 1895 and they had three sons. She left
her husband soon after their children were born. Chairman of the Central
Committee of Women's Branches of the BUF from March 1933, she had
her offices at the Women's Headquarters at 12 Lower Grosvenor Place. In
December 1933 she attended the wedding of Ian Hope Dundas to Pamela
Ernestine Dorman. Present at the opening of a bazaar at Women's Headquarters
in December 1933. On 30 January 1934, at a meeting organized by BUF women
at the Guildhouse, Eccleston Square, she made an appeal for British women
to join the BUF and explained how 'only my great belief in this movement has
attracted me from my grandmotherly armchair to a stool in the office of a
youth movement.' On 7 May 1934 she opened the headquarters of the new St
Pancras branch of the BUF in Arlington Rd., Camden Town, and the ceremony
consisted of her unveiling a photograph of her son, Sir Oswald Mosley. She
visited the Edinburgh and Dumfries branch in June 1934, and was threatened
by posters reading 'Give Maud Some Bouquets.' Visited the Brixton and Richmond
branches in August 1934. In September 1934 she led the women's contingent
into Hyde Park at a BUF rally, amid a storm of abuse from the massed opposition.
In January 1935 she opposed the appointment of Mary Richardson to take charge

of part of the Lancashire area, and threatened to resign. Attended the Blackshirt Jubilee Ball at the Greyhound Hotel, Croydon, in May 1935. Attended the London Administration luncheon on 28 February 1939. On 26 July 1939 she was a guest at a dinner party hosted by the Mosleys, attended by the leading figures of Britain's pro-Nazi 'patriotic societies.' Attended the London Administration luncheon on 1 March 1940.

Mosley, Vivien

Born 25 February 1921. First child of Sir Oswald and Lady Cynthia Mosley. In December 1933 it was reported by the *Fascist Week* that she opened a bazaar at the Women's Headquarters of the BUF. Escorted by her aunt the Baroness Ravensdale, in the summer of 1937 she visited Munich and the Degenerate Art Exhibition. Subject of an article 'Beaverbrook Press and Miss Vivien Mosley' (*Action*, No. 172, 10 June 1939).

Newitt, Mrs Margaret Elizabeth | | |

Born 14 April 1891, her maiden name was Winter. She came to Britain in 1921 from Germany to marry Mr Newitt (d.1931), an insurance agent. In 1935 she opened her own domestic agency, alleged to be a cover for the German authorities to place German women who might be agents in situations in Britain. Detained for hostile origins and associations on 6 November 1940. Interned in the Women's Internment Camp, Port Erin. Her case was heard by the Advisory Committee in April 1941, and reviewed in October 1942. Released in May 1945.

Newnham, Mrs* | | |

Member of the BU. Wife of Henry Newnham, who was the editor of *Truth* in 1940. She was detained in July 1940 under DR 18B.

Nicolle, Edmee Lucienne | | |

One of the first presidents of the French Red Cross. In September 1940 she was sent to London as Director of the French Red Cross and four days later interned in Holloway Prison. In June 1941 she was released on the request of Marshal Pétain and with the help of the American Ambassador in Vichy. When she returned to Vichy, she declared to the correspondent of *Transocean*, Karl Ludwig Schmidt, that 1,200 women suspected of being fifth columnists were in Holloway, and suffering under harsh conditions.

Nicholson, Mrs Christobel Sybil+ | | |

(*ca.*1889–1974) Born in Surrey where her father was a doctor of divinity. She was first educated in Scarborough. She studied and qualified as a medical doctor at Charing Cross during the Great War, and later practised in the East End of

London. When she was 16 years old she had an illegitimate daughter, and mothered another illegitimate child in 1930. In 1934 she married Admiral Wilmot Nicholson – he too was a member of the Right Club, also somehow involved in the Tyler Kent affair, but never interned. Both were involved in the Anglo-German Fellowship and were also close friends of Captain Ramsay and of Admiral Domvile. They lived at Ashburn Gardens, close to both Ramsay's London home in Onslow Square and to the Russian Tea Room. Her name appears on the Right Club ledger of *ca*.May, 1939. Interned under DR 18B in the summer of 1940. She was involved in the Tyler Kent affair: she had acquired some of the Roosevelt-Churchill correspondence of the Tyler Kent collection, copied them out, and hid them in the lavatory of her flat. Her daily woman found them and took them to the police. Charged under the Official Secrets Act and acquitted, but on leaving the court she was rearrested and re-detained under 18B. Released on 2 September 1943.

Norbury, Mrs M.L.* | | |
Women's District Leader in Ripon, Yorkshire, in 1940. She and her husband, Captain Norbury (D/L Harrogate), were both interned under DR 18B.

O'Grady, Mrs Dorothy P.
She lived in Sandown, where she ran a boarding house, which was rumoured to welcome Nazi tourists. At the outbreak of war Mr O'Grady volunteered as a reserve fireman, and left for the mainland, while his wife remained in Sandown. She was found with documents related to the First Canadian Division which was stationed in the area. Her trial on charges of coastal espionage began at the Hampshire Assizes, in the Great Hall of Winchester Castle, on 17 December 1940. In December 1940 she was sentenced to death under the Treachery Act for making plans to assist the enemy and cutting telephone cables on the Isle of Wight. On appeal her sentence was reduced to 14 years imprisonment. See *The Times*, 18 December 1940.

Orrin, Elsie Sara Constance*
(*ca*.1892 to 4 September 1962) Member of the BU and a private language teacher. Resident of Woodville Rd, Leytonstone. In June 1939 the 47-year-old Orrin was arrested for selling BUF newspapers and shouting anti-Semitic slogans outside a Jewish-owned grocery store at 202 High Road, Leytonstone. In June 1941 she was sentenced to five years imprisonment by Mr Justice Humphreys for inciting servicemen to disaffection. To two soldiers in a public house at Little Eaton in Hertfordshire, she had said that Hitler was a good ruler, and a better man than Churchill. See *Manchester Guardian* 26 June 1941. She became organizer for the Union Movement's St Marylebone branch.

Owen, Mr B.A.*

Born in London in 1890 and married to a German woman. Proprietor of the English Language Institute in Berlin. Announced the formation of a BUF branch in Berlin 28 January 1934.

Paarman, Miss F.^

Member of the British Fascists. Area Commander for Bournemouth. She organized the Holiday and Training Camp for women fascists in New Forest in the summer of 1925.

Page, Anne*

She joined the Women's Section of the BUF in 1933. She wrote her recollections of women in the movement in *Mosley's Blackshirts* (1986).

Parkinson, Dinah*

From an old Conservative family, and before her conversion to the BUF a supporter of the Conservative Party. Contributor to BUF publications (1936–38).

Parkinson, Mrs Florence* | | |

A BU member in Manchester. Detained under DR 18B, and her address was given as 22 Edilon Road, Crumpsall, Manchester, on the Home Office Schedule for detention. According to Lucy Pearson's pocket diary, she was released from Holloway on 11 December 1940.

Parkyn, Dorothy*

Contributor to BUF publications (1938), related her experiences in canvassing for the BUF in 'Canvassing Tonight?' (*Action* No. 105, 19 February 1938).

Parry, Mrs M.* | | |

She was a BU member in Eastbourne. Detained under DR 18B, and according to Lucy Pearson's diary, released from Holloway on 1 November 1940.

Passy, Mrs^

In 1928 she was County Commander, London Women's Units. She organized a Fascist Fête in 1928 on the grounds of Garrick's Villa, Hampton Court, lent to the BF by Mr and Mrs Hugh McConnell. In September 1929 she represented the GHQ Council at the funeral of Miss W.E. Brigg. In the summer of 1933 she was deprived of the Order of the Fasces, once bestowed on her by the BF Executive Committee.

Pastorelli, Miss Lena* | | |

A prominent speaker and propagandist for the BU's Women's Peace Campaign in 1940. Interned under DR 18B.

Pearson, Miss Lucy Marion Heath* | | |

(Born ca.1880) Employed as a Home Office Factory Inspector. She was a deeply religious High Church Anglican. Her mother, who died on 13 June 1935, had once been Chairman of the local Conservatives at Boxmoor. Active BU member in Hove, Suffolk. Her pocket diaries for 1937, 1938, and 1939 show how her life was structured around BU activities: she attended speakers classes, branch meetings, study circles and made note of many marches and rallies. On 20 January 1940 she attended the Donovan-Bond wedding at St Marlius, Epsom. On March 1 1940 she attended the London Administration Luncheon at the Criterion Restaurant. She was arrested on 3 June 1940 and taken to Holloway. Her address on the Home Office Schedule for detention was given as 50 Norton Road, Hove. On 12 June 1940 the Home Office wrote to inform her that she had been suspended from duty from her post in the Home Office and that she would no longer be paid a salary, due to her arrest. On 18 June 1940 her sister, Miss Constance Pearson, visited her in prison (her sister also petitioned three woman politicians – Dr Summerskill MP, Lady Davidson MP, and Mrs Tate – on her sister's behalf in order to bring to their attention the treatment of British women under 18B). She went before the Advisory Committee on 9 October 1940. On 16 November 1940 she attended a Tea Dance in Holloway in honour of O.M.'s birthday. On 29 November 1940 the Bishop of Chichester came to visit her in prison. On 15 December 1940 a tea party was held in her honour in Holloway and she was released on 16 December. After her release she expressed the desire to work within a religious organization towards establishing a 'Christian Society.' She wrote to the Archbishop of Canterbury about conditions under 18B on 4 January 1941. She visited the Mosleys in Holloway on 10 April 1942. Her private papers are held in the Essex County Record Office.

Pearson, Mrs Norah* | | |

BU official in Bournemouth. On 1 March 1940 she attended the London Administration luncheon at the Criterion restaurant. Interned under DR 18B, and on the Home Office Schedule for detention her address is given as Cotlands Road, Bournemouth. Member of the Union Movement in Bournemouth. Died in October 1949. Her married name was Falls.

Pearson, (Lady) Susannah Grace* +

(d. 10 April 1959) Commandant of the Hertfordshire VAD Hospital during the Great War. Wife of Sir Edward Pearson (d.1925), a contractor. Sister of Henry Page-Croft and she was a relation of Major Cleghorn LHQ, Contract Officer for the BUF at NHQ. She organized and ran the Sandwich branch of the BUF from 1934. She became BU prospective parliamentary candidate for Canterbury in December 1936. Before the war, R.R. Bellamy moved to

Canterbury to help organize that Parliamentary division for Lady Pearson, who was to contest the seat for the BU in the General Election due to take place in the autumn of 1939. She was also a member of The Link, and involved with the British People's Party: in July 1939 she went down to speak in support of the BPP's candidate in the Hythe by-election, H. St John Philby. In November and December 1939 she took part in meetings to organize collaboration between Mosley's, Ramsay's and Domvile's groups. Attended the London Administration luncheon on 1 March 1940. In 1940 her Hollingbourne Manor was raided by Kent police and she was taken to police headquarters at Maidstone where she was kept in a cell for several days. Her brother, Under-Secretary for War (1940–45), intervened with the Home Secretary on her behalf. She came under Restriction Order 18A. She was the subject of Mr Davidson MP's questions to the Home Secretary in the House of Commons on 4 July 1940, and again on 11 July when he asked for assurances that 'no modification of those restrictions will take place because of the fact that the lady is related to a member of the Government.' It was alleged that she, along with Mrs Sherston and Basil Mill, were given preferential treatment in connection with the Defence Regulations because they were persons of means and influence. Visited the Mosleys in Holloway on 4 October 1941. Present at the 18B Social and Dance held at the Royal Hotel on 1 December 1945.

Pennoyer, (Lady) Winifred^

She was a patron of the British Fascists 'Mi Careme' Ball, held at Hotel Cecil in London on 5 March 1926.

Perriman, Miss L.*

In November 1937 she became Women's Canvass Organizer for the 4th London Area.

Perry, Mrs*

In May 1934 she was women's officer for the South East Regional Headquarters of the BUF.

Perry, Anne-Marie Louise Frida|||

Born in 1903 in Germany to German parents. Married a British subject in February 1933 for the purposes of acquiring British nationality. Admitted to being a prostitute, a 'freelance dance hostess and partner,' and was thus alleged to be in the position of obtaining valuable information for the enemy. In September 1938 she offered her services to British Intelligence for purposes of espionage. After the outbreak of war she approached a German official and actually considered the possibility of accepting a post as a German agent. Interned under the Defence Regulations and the Aliens Order on 9 September

1939. She came before the Advisory Committee on 21 February 1941. She requested to be moved from the Isle of Man to Holloway in June 1942, but her request was denied. Released on 13 January 1944.

Pfister, Mrs*
Conductor of the BUF Women's Choir in 1934.

Piercey, Eric Hamilton* | | |
Born 6 September 1901. Leader of the National Defence Force, which was amalgamated with the BUF. BUF member at NHQ. Involved an intimate affair with Mrs Joyce in 1934, and in December of that year reappointed as Chief Inspector of Branches. In March 1937 he was struck off the pay-roll and resigned from the movement.

Pitt-Rivers, Captain George Henry Lane F.+ | | |
Grandson of General Pitt-Rivers, the founder of the Pitt-Rivers Museum in Oxford. After a career in the Army (Captain, Royal Dragoons) and the colonial service, he became active in anthropological circles during the 1920s. A Dorset landowner. Author of *The Clash of Cultures and the Conflict of Races*. A life member of the Eugenics Society and Secretary-General and Honorary Treasurer of the International Union for Scientific Investigation of Population Problems (1928–37). Supporter of Nazi Germany, he taught in Germany during the 1930s. He joined Lord Lymington's British Council Against European Commitments. He attended meetings in 1940 to co-ordinate the efforts of extreme-Right wing organizations to establish a fascist government in Britain. He was a close friend of Barry Domvile, and Domvile was a guest at his house when he was arrested and interned under DR 18B in 1940. Pitt-Rivers was also interned until 1942.

Potter, Mrs 'Gillie'* | | |
She was many years younger than her husband and had been a secretary in London when she met Albert Potter, a Boer War and World War I veteran. They moved to Norfolk and opened a transport café, the walls of which were adorned with photographs of Mosley and fascist posters, and they became active Norfolk members of the BU. She was interned in Holloway under DR 18B in 1940 and detained for over six months. Her infant son was taken away from her by a policewoman and returned to Norfolk to be placed in an institution. Albert Potter lost his business due to his arrest, and he died immediately after release.

Primo de Rivera, Senorita Pilar
Leader of the Women's Section of the Falangists in Spain. Contributor to BUF publications and author of 'Women Falangists: From Sacrifice to Victory' (*Action*, No. 87, October 16, 1937).

Pye, Miss Margaret *

Active BUF member. She was born in Ardwick, daughter of an Indian Mutiny veteran and niece of a Crimean war veteran. In November 1938 she contested the Manchester municipal elections for the BU in All Saints, winning only 23 votes (0.81%).

Raby, Rosalind*

Active member of the BUF. Visited Nazi Germany in 1934 to examine the condition of women under the new regime. She sat on the Production Directory at NHQ in 1935. Contributor to BUF publications (1934–35).

Radford, Miss D.E.*

BUF member in Dorset. She resided at 7 High West Street, Dorchester.

Ramsay, Captain Archibald Henry Maule+ | | |

(d.1955) Educated at Eaton and Sandhurst, and ex-Army. Lived in Kellie Castle in Arbroath. Conservative MP for Peebles and South Midlothian from 1931 to 1945. Closely associated with Admiral Domvile, whom he met first at a party at the German Embassy in 1938. Member of the Nordic League, addressed their meetings, and in late 1938 became a member of the NL's council. He also had links with the Militant Christian Patriots. Founded the pro-Nazi, anti-Semitic Right Club in May 1939, a secret society whose principle aim was to inform Conservatives of the Jewish Menace. Present at a dinner party hosted by the Mosleys on 26 July 1939, marking the beginning of collaboration between the Right Club, the Nordic League, The Link and the BU. The Right Club membership list (also known as the 'Red Book') contained the names of many members of 'high society', including 100 'ladies', as well as less respectable figures who were already active in other extremist organizations. The Red Book was seized my MI5 in 1940, among the documents found when Tyler Kent's flat was raided by agents in May. He was interned under 18B and kept in Brixton prison with Mosley and Domvile. He appeared before the Advisory Committee in July 1940, but was not released until 1944.

Ramsay, Mrs Ismay+

Eldest daughter of the 14th Viscount Gormanston, and widow of Lord Ninian Crichton-Stuart who died in the First World War. Married Captain Ramsay, founder of the Right Club. Her name appears on the Right Club ledger of *ca.*May 1939. She was reported to be willing to organize aid for 18B internees in November 1940.

Raven-Thomson, Mrs*

German by birth, wife of Alexander Raven-Thomson. Conducted a business in Haymarket, W., the Anglo-German Agency for Domestic Servants which had both 'Aryan' and Jewish employees on its books. In October 1939 the business was being used for selling Air Raid Precautions requisites.

Raven-Thomson, Alexander* | | |

In May 1934 he was Chief of the Research Department for the BUF. In July 1934 he was reported to be Director of Policy at NHQ. On 21 September 1936 he was charged with provocative language, using insulting words and behaviour at a meeting in Bethnal Green, and remanded for a week on his own recognisance of £10. In 1937 he became the BU prospective parliamentary candidate for South Hackney. In March 1937 he was struck off the pay-roll, but opted to remain as a voluntary worker. He was among five leaders of the BU who were the last to be released from internment under DR 18B. He had an intimate relationship with Olive Burdett (nee Hawks) while both were interned, and his step-daughter pleaded with the authorities to prevent the two from communicating.

Ravensdale, (Baroness) Irene

Born in January 1896. Eldest daughter of Lord Curzon and Mary Leiter. She was sent to Germany for two years before she made her debut in 1914. During the Great War she worked for the Charity Organization Society for three years. In 1917 she started her work in the Highway Clubs of East London. Made a world tour in 1927, and in 1934 travelled around the world again. Attended the BUF's Albert Hall meeting and the Olympia Rally of 7 June 1934. On 27 June 1934 she acted as hostess for the Blackshirt Cabaret Ball at the Princess Galleries, Piccadilly. Travelled to Soviet Russia, and to Abyssinia for the coronation of Emperor Haile Selassie. She visited Italy for the birthday of Rome in 1935. An official guest of the German Government at the Nazi Parteitag at Nuremberg in 1936, along with Lord Mount Temple, Sir Harry Brittain, Sir Frank and Lady Newnes and Admiral Barry Domvile. She took her niece, Vivien Mosley, to Munich in the summer of 1937. In May 1940 the Home Secretary, Sir John Anderson, approached her to ask if she had any evidence that Oswald Mosley would betray his country as a fifth columnist. She said she had no evidence of this, but she felt that if Mosley felt a British form of National Socialism in conjunction with Hitler desirable for England, then he might do anything. Treasurer of Sir Francis Younghusband's World Congress of Faiths. Author of *In Many Rhythms: An Autobiography* (1953).

Ray, Miss I.N.G.^

Assistant Chief-of-Staff, Women's Units. She was employed at BF headquarters in charge of the Fascist Children's Clubs. In August 1926 she and Captain

Robert Smith were charged with the alleged assault on an Oxford undergraduate at the BF's headquarters at Fulham Road. They were acquitted. On 28 October 1927, accompanying Lintorn-Orman, she visited the Irish Command. In 1928 she accompanied Lintorn-Orman to the Fascist Fête at Hampton Court, where the members of the London Special Patrol, Women's Units, and members of the London Women's Units formed a guard of honour on their arrival. She was a pall-bearer at the funeral for Miss Brigg O/C London Special Patrol in September 1928. In the summer of 1933 she was deprived of the Order of the Fasces, once bestowed on her by the BF Executive Committee.

Rayner, Mrs Hugh, OBE*

During the Great War she drove an ambulance. Before joining the BUF, she was chairman of the Women's Branch of the Conservative Party in Whitechapel and a member of the Metropolitan Area Council of the party. She was also assistant commissioner of the Boy Scouts. In June 1934 the *Sunday Dispatch* announced that she had joined the BUF.

Reeve, Miss L.M.* | | |

Worked in domestic service in London before she saved enough money to secure business training. She became assistant to an estate agent, and in 1927 took over the agency in Norfolk and managed an estate of 1,110 acres, becoming the only woman in Britain directing an agricultural property of that size. She became a Rural District Councillor in 1928. She was a good shot and a leading member of the Norfolk Shooting Syndicate. She performed yeoman work for the BUF in Norfolk. She became the BU prospective parliamentary candidate for Norfolk S.W. in November 1936. Contributor to BUF publications and author of a series in *Action* 'Politics at the Pig and Whistle' (1937–38). In 1940 she was denounced as a German agent by her neighbours, and troops were sent to apprehend her, under armed guard. Interned for a short time under DR 18B. According to Lucy Pearson's pocket diary, she was released from Holloway on 6 December 1940. During the war Lord Walsingham's estate, where she lived and worked, was requisitioned as a military training ground. After being twice evicted from her farm on the estate, she hanged herself from a beam in one of the out-buildings.

Richardson, Miss Mary*

(1883–1961) She was raised in Belleville, Ontario, where her grandfather was a bank manager. Came to Britain when she was sixteen years old. Became a dedicated suffragette after hearing a Pankhurst speech at the Albert Hall. During suffrage days she went by the pseudonym of 'Polly Dick.' In 1913 the Home Secretary reintroduced forcible feeding in the cases of Mary Richardson and Rachel Peace, both on remand for arson. Committed acts of arson, and in March

1914 slashed Valesquez's *Rokeby Venus* in the National Gallery. She was released from Holloway on 30 July 1914 for an appendix operation. The story went that when she was breaking shop windows in the West End before the outbreak of war in 1914 she knew Mussolini well, when he was a prominent Italian Socialist and the editor of *Avanti*. Thus when the Italian Fascists marched on Rome in 1922 she sent him a stinging letter accusing him of betraying all his principles. In reply he despatched a telegram with just five words: 'Some day you will understand.' She adopted a son, Roger, after the war. After her suffragette activities, she settled in Cambridgeshire to raise ducks with a woman friend. She had joined the Labour Party in 1916. She contested Middlesex, Acton, in 1922 as a Labour candidate, winning 6,069 (26.2%), and again in 1924 for Independent Labour, winning 1,775 votes (7.6%). Contested Hampshire, Aldershot, as a Labour candidate in 1931, winning 4,091 votes (15.6%). A member of the New Party. In December 1933 it was announced that she had joined the BUF. Assistant d.o. of the BUF Women's Section in January 1934. By May 1934 she was the chief organizer of the Women's Section. On 24 April she opened a National Club for Fascist Women at 12 Lower Grosvenor Place. She organized the Blackshirt Cabaret Ball at the Princes Galleries, Piccadilly, on 27 June 1934. Speaker at meetings at the BUF branches at Dulwich and Brentwood in September 1934. On 16 October 1934 she represented the BUF in a debate organized by the Hampstead Garden Liberal Women's Association. In October 1934 she was injured in a motor accident on her way back to London after addressing a meeting in Bedford. Appointed to take charge of part of the Lancashire area in January 1935, spawning vehement opposition from Lady Mosley and F.M. Box. Her appointment was alleged to be at the insistence of Risden, organizer in Lancashire. John Warburton, President of the 'Friends of O.M.', recalled that Richardson was still with the BUF in 1936, while the official documents imply that she left the movement in 1935. In his research, Durham has uncovered that in November 1935 Richardson was living in Welwyn Garden City, and that during the general election of that year she addressed a meeting of the Welwyn War Resisters (she was also identified as the new honorary secretary of the group). She stated that she had been expelled from the BUF in February 1935. Author of *Laugh A Defiance* (1953), a recollection of her experiences in the WSPU.

Riddell, Miss Enid+ | | |

Member of the Nordic League. Her name appeared on the Right Club ledger of *ca.* May 1939, and she became very active in Right Club activities in 1940, and was implicated in the Tyler Kent Affair. She lived in a flat in Chesham St., Belgravia, near the Wolkoff's Russian Tea Room. Griffiths has described her as 'upper-middle-class and fairly well heeled, being used to dining at the very best restaurants.' She was also closely acquainted with Del Monte from the Italian Embassy. She was interned under DR 18B.

Rinder, Olive
Contributor to the New Party's *Action* and editor of the 'Women's Page'.

Risden, Wilfred*
Born 28 January 1896 in Lower Merton, Somerset. In May 1934 he was Director of Propaganda for the BUF. In March 1934 Risden and R.A. Plathen, both of National Headquarters, were sent out to the Norfolk and Suffolk areas to counter the propaganda tour of A.W.F. Whitmore on behalf of the British Fascists. In 1937 he acted as chief agent for the BU in the LCC elections. In May 1939 he was given one months notice from his position as Electoral Adviser and Propaganda Administrator.

Robb, Rhonagh Maureen (a.k.a. Sperni)
A British subject born in Brighton, Sussex, in 1914. Since 1937 she passed as the wife of John C.A. Sperni. She went to Italy with Sperni, where he obtained employment with the Ministry of Popular Culture and was a broadcaster for Rome Radio. Robb was also employed by the Ministry and broadcast from Rome Radio a series of fifteen talks entitled 'From Me to You,' which addressed listeners in Britain.

Row, Robert* | | |
Member of the BU in Lancaster. Detained under DR 18B. Post-war editor of *Action*.

Ryder, Miss Iris* | | |
Member of the Bournemouth branch of the BU where she, Flo Hayes and Elizabeth Griffin ran the show and consigned the male D/L to oblivion. She was a first cousin of the Duke of Hamilton. Active in the BU's Peace Campaign. In 1939 she was convicted for defacing an air raid shelter notice. See *Daily Herald*, 24 October 1939. In 1939 she was fined £5 for her part in the peace campaign and an appeal was made to all members to help her pay the fine. Interned under DR 18B, and her address is given as Sun House, Links Road, Parkstone, on the Home Office Schedule for detention. She had an eight-acre market garden near Norwich, and after their release ex-18Bs Nommensen and Major de Laessoe worked on it with her.

Sanford, Mrs Mabel Helen *
In November 1936 she wrote to Robert Saunders, D/L West Dorset, to request that she and her daughter become members of the BUF. She complained about the 'painted gezebels of women in these days of so-called emancipation' and the 'powerful mischief' perpetrated by the Jews in England.

Sangster, Mrs E.*

Member of the BUF. In December 1935 she was appointed Women District officer for Acton and Ealing.

Scrimgeour, Miss Ethel+

Her brother, Alex Scrimgeour, a wealthy stock-broker, generously funded Joyce and Beckett's National Socialist League until his death in 1937. He left instructions for his sister, Ethel, to continue payments to the NSL, which she did, and she also became close friends with William Joyce. She visited Joyce in his cell before he was hanged in 1946.

Sharman-Crawford, Miss I.*

BUF Member of the Chelsea Branch. Contributor to the *Blackshirt* (1934–35).

Sharland, Clara M.* | | |

She was an Australian who had been living in Germany. She joined the BU on coming to England, just two months before war broke out. Interned under DR 18 in Holloway (her prisoner number was 5152). On 15 January 1942 she wrote to Lord Redesdale from Holloway thanking him for her share of an anonymous gift of £5.5 which he had forwarded.

Sharpe, Mrs*

Wife of Lt. Col. Charles Sutton Sharpe, a prominent member of the BUF. It was reported that she attended private meetings at the flat of Margaret Bothamley in 1939.

Shaw, Miss*

At one time attached to the BUF NHQ, but by January 1937 in charge of all women's work in the Northern Administration. Made complaints against the administration of the Northern branches, and the work of J.J. Hone, Controller of the Northern Administration.

Shelmerdine, Mrs Rita K.* | | |

She joined the BU in Manchester in August 1938. As a member she had helped at meetings and sold copies of *Action*. Interned on 11 July 1940. Her husband was Philip Shelmerdine, a BU official, also detained, and both were interrogated at the notorious Latchmere House. They had two small children in 1940, aged five and two. She began habeas corpus proceedings against the Home Secretary in October 1940. In his letter to the Private Secretary on 21 October 1940, Mr Hickson suggested that her release should be conditional on her willingness to assist at communist meetings and sell copies of the *Jewish Chronicle*. The Advisory Committee recommended her release in October 1940, contrary to the views of MI5. According to Lucy Pearson's pocket diary, she was released on 13 November 1940.

Sherston, Mrs | | |

Wife of 2nd Lt. W.E. Sherston, an Old Etonian who farmed from Otley Hall, Ipswich. He was a BU member and Regional Inspector for Suffolk. He was interned under 18B and he remained in custody until 1943. She was interned under DR 18B and released on 8 August 1940. Both she and her husband brought habeas corpus proceedings in 1940. J.R. Smeaton-Stuart alleged that she was released after only six weeks detention because she was a detainee of means and influence.

Shore, Miss Olga*

A business-woman employed in shipping and marketing. Contributor to BUF publications (1934–36). On 21 November 1934 she spoke for fascism in a debate on 'Democracy v. Fascism,' held at the National Women's Citizens' Association, Purley. She was very active in Lancashire in 1933–34. Appointed Women's Organizer (Northern) in 1936, at a salary of £260 per annum. She led a BU women's march in Manchester on 4 October 1936. Resigned from the BUF by April 1938.

Shores, A.G.^

Acting O.C. Women's Units and Transport Officer of the BF in 1934.

Smith, Miss N.E.^

One of the original members of the BF's LSP, Pall-bearer at the funeral of Miss Brigg O/C London Special Patrol, in September 1929. Before Brigg's death she was Duty Officer London Special Patrol, and after she was promoted to Officer Commanding London Special Patrol.

Stanford, Mary (a.k.a Molly)* + | | |

(Born *ca.*1895) Member of the Right Club, and her name appears on the Right Club ledger of *ca.*May, 1939. Attended a social gathering of the Right Club in April 1940. She lived at Queen's Gate Terrace, Kensington – close to Anna Wolkoff and Captain Ramsay. Already under suspicion, her flat was raided by police in March or April 1940. Throughout the 'phoney war' she was able to correspond with Margaret Bothamley, through an intermediary, Colonel F.W.R. Macdonald, a leading member of the IFL and a resident in Brussels. Interned under DR 18B and released on 23 September 1940. On 10 November 1940 she hosted a meeting at her flat at 45 Queen's Gate Gardens to discuss means of organizing aid for 18Bs. She was re-detained in Holloway on 19 February 1943. Present at the 18B Social and Dance held at the Royal Hotel on 1 December 1945.

Stansfield, Nellie*
She was a BUF steward at Mosley's meeting in the Free Trade Hall, Manchester, in November 1934. She was injured at the meeting and treated for a sprained elbow. She was reported to be 22 years old and resident of 38 Bucklow Drive, Northenden.

Steele, Majorie* | | |
One of two principal speakers at the launch of the BU's Women's Peace Campaign on 28 February 1940. An employee of the BU in 1940. On 23 April 1940 the *Daily Herald* reported that Mrs Elsie Marjorie Steele, aged 22, of Elm Park Avenue, Stamford Hill, was fined £5, sentenced to 14 days imprisonment, and bound over in £5 to keep the peace for six months. She was accused of using insulting words at a meeting in Bethnal Green likely to cause a breach of the peace by calling Chamberlain a 'rotten peace monger' and Churchill a 'rotten murderer.' Interned in Holloway under DR 18B.

Stephenson, Mrs Gladys* +
With her husband, Dr Stephenson, she was a member of the West Dorset branch of the BUF. She joined in November 1934. In April 1936 Saunders described her as 'very keen' and explained how she 'does much good work among Conservative women.' In May 1938 she consented to becoming temporary Women's District Leader, while Robert Saunders was D/L. She was requested to attend the Leader's Conference at the Royal Hotel, Bristol, on 26 June 1938. She and her husband appeared on Saunders' (hidden) membership list of the District compiled in November 1939. She attended meetings of The Link in Wells in 1940.

Stevens, Mrs*
BU member in Southampton. Attended a meeting of BU elements on 23 November 1940.

Stockfish, Kathleen*
She was Women's District Leader in Richmond. She later married William Trump, also a member of the BUF.

Stout, Miss Almaz^
Present at the British Fascisti dinner at the Lyceum Club in February 1925. At this event the toast to 'the ideals of Italy' was proposed by Cavalier Sambucetti and she submitted the toast of the guests.

Stuckey, Derek Richard* | | |
Born 5 October 1916, in London. Joined the BUF in February 1934. In October 1936 he became the vice-President of the Oxford University National Socialist Club. In May 1938 he became the Assistant Secretary, and in September 1938

Secretary to the Federation of British Universities Fascist Associations. In January 1939 he became D/L of the Combined English Universities. In June 1939 he became District Inspector for university districts. From August 1939 he was in charge of BU activities in teacher training colleges, among school teachers and school boys. Registered as a conscientious objector. Married in November 1939. His wife, Gladys M. Stuckey, a veterinary surgeon, was also a member of the BU. He was interned and detained in Brixton Prison on 2 June, 1940. Released under suspension order on 19 September 1941.

Surtees, Mrs*

With her husband, the District Treasurer, she was an active BU member in West Dorset. Both she and her husband appear on Saunders' (hidden) membership list of 30 November, 1939. Their address was 26 Victoria Park Road, Bournemouth.

Sutherland, Mme. Anita^

Member of the British Fascists. A 'well-known singer.' In autumn 1925 she offered to train a class of fascist speakers.

Sutherland, Mrs M.A.*

She owned a cafe in Stepney and was the friend and confidant of many East London Blackshirts. She retired to Norfolk. Died in January 1975.

Swann, Marta & Arthur* | | |

He was born 1909 in Lowestoft, Suffolk to a long line of fishermen. With George Surtees, he started the Lowestoft branch of the BUF in 1935. He acted as District Treasurer, while Surtees was the D/L. In 1935 he was appointed as an agent for the Prudential Assurance Co. and remained there until 3 June 1940. He attended the march on the day of the Battle of Cable Street, the May Day rally from Westminster to Bermondsey in 1938, and, in 1939, Mosley's May Day rally from Victoria Embankment to Ridley Road, and the Earl's Court rally. Arrested and interrogated under DR 18B on 3 June 1940, and taken to Ascot Internment Camp. He and his wife, Marta, were allowed to be interned together in married quarters in Holloway prison where they were the Mosleys' neighbours.

Swift, Ruth M.^

Member of the British Fascists. Propaganda officer for the Camberley Area in 1926. Contributor to *The Fascist Bulletin*.

Sydenham of Combe, Lady^

Wife of Lord Sydenham of Combe, one of two English board members on CINEF. Both husband a wife were members of a variety of radical-right pressure groups. Close friends and associates of the Duke of Northumberland. Member of the British Fascists. She directed the Fascist Children's Clubs. She was head of the British Women's Patriotic League.

Tagart, Miss Helen Bourn*
Assistant, secretary and companion to Commandant Mary Allen. She accompanied Allen to Spain, as Franco's guests. Her BU membership card was found in a police search of the house she shared with Allen at Danehill, Lympne, Kent in June 1940.

Taylor, Mrs E.*
Member of the BUF. In December 1935 she was appointed Women District Organizer for Sheffield.

Taylour, Miss Fay* + | | |
Racing car driver of Irish origin. She won the Ladies' Race at Brooklands at 98 m.p.h in 1931. She became a member of the BU in 1939, after the outbreak of war. Before joining BU, she was a member of the Right Club, and her name appears on the Right Club ledger of *ca*.May, 1939. Interned under DR 18B. Died 2 August 1983.

Temple of Stowe, (Countess)^
The Earl and Countess Temple of Stowe were patrons of the British Fascists Grand 'Mi Careme' Ball, held at Hotel Cecil, London on 5 March 1926.

Temple Cotton, Mrs L.* | | |
(born ca. 1880) Active BUF member in Devon. A market gardener, she and her son Rafe were attracted by Mosley's agricultural policy, and the BU's campaign for a large British Air Force. Widow of Lieutenant-Colonel Temple Cotton D.S.O. who was killed in action at Thiepval in 1917 commanding the South Lancashire Regiment. Two sons: Rafe Temple Cotton (born ca. 1909, joined the O.T.C. both at Reading University and Wellington College, and BU District Inspector for Devon, prospective parliamentary candidate for Exeter, one of the eight men to whom Mosley intended to delegate responsibility of the movement in the event of his own incapacity, and also interned), and Paul Temple Cotton (born ca.1912, joined the O.T.C. at Cambridge University, then in the Colonial Service, and joined up in 1940 and became an airman and squadron leader). In May and June 1939 she and her son Rafe visited Germany, wearing BU badges and allegedly expressing pro-Nazi opinions, but she claimed they were only on vacation. She was awarded the bronze distinction by the BU in January 1940, but never received it. Interned under Dr 18B because she assisted her son in his efforts in favour of a negotiated peace with Germany. She first appeared before the Advisory Committee on 23 July 1940, and released in November.

After internment, she was engaged in assisting her son in the work of his market garden at Branscombe. She appeared before the Advisory Committee on 12 April 1943 to object to restrictions placed upon her by the Suspension Order of 8 November 1940. However, MI5 was still under the impression that Mrs Temple Cotton was dangerous and that she continued to express fascist views, that Rafe 'was completely under the domination of his mother,' and that she was 'a very eccentric person of a hysterical nature.' As a consequence, the Home Office refused to relax the conditions of her release. The authorities were in possession of information that after her release Mrs Temple Cotton was still in contact with Mrs Whinfield, and that she had tried also to arrange meetings with Mrs Domvile. See HO45/23673.

Thomas, Mrs*
Speaker for the BUF's campaign for the LCC elections in 1937.

Tilley, Miss Alma Doris*
Member of the BUF in 1934. Involved in a case in which she made allegations that she was dismissed from her employment by reason of her political convictions. Her case went before the Court of Referees on 25 July 1934 at Shepherds Bush and she was represented by Mr F. Canning, case officer of the BUF. Her claim was allowed.

Tisler, Mrs Catherine*
Stood as a BU candidate for St Pancras Ward No.1 in the Municipal elections of 1 November 1937. She polled 113 votes.

Vernon, Miss*
In 1934 she was clerk under the Chief of Staff at National Headquarters. In March 1935 she was earning £200 per annum in her post as an officer of the Chief of Staff.

Vivian, Dr Margaret*
A leading expert on drugs and the drug trade during the 1920s and 1930s. She treated addicts in her own clinic, and sat on the Home Office panel for dealing with the problem. She was a member of the BU living in Bournemouth where she ran her nursing home, and was also active in the British Union Against Vivisection. In May 1938 she donated £20 towards the purchase of a propaganda van for the Dorset district. During and after the war she corresponded with Robert Saunders, and was active in aiding BU 18B detainees by sending packages to prison.

Wallace, Miss*
In June 1934 she was reported to be an active member of the Roman branch of the BUF. She was head of a typewriting agency in Rome.

Wallace, Miss A.*

In June 1934 it was reported that she had been appointed as head of the Girl's Section of the Fascist Youth Movement and that girls were forming sections in many well-known public schools.

Walsh, Gladys (née Libiter)*

(Died 31 December 1990) Her parents originally came from Surrey, and she was born in Stepney. Her father was an engineer. She reached a turning point in her life at age sixteen when she attended a concert organized by the Communist Party in East London. She joined the BU's Limehouse Branch in May or June 1936, shortly after its birth, as a non-active member, and became an active member after the Battle of Cable Street of 4 October 1936. Her mother was also a member, and they joined together (mother died at the age of 101 in 1973). She attended the Selsey camp for a day and she attended the Earl's Court rally in 1939. After the outbreak of war she was appointed Limehouse District Leader, upon the request of Mick Clarke (former Bethnal Green D/L and a NHQ official), after the men were called up. Because of her appointment she was sought by Special Branch, but evaded detention under 18B. During the Blitz they were bombed out and she went to stay with family in Surrey. She attended the 18B Detainees Fund dinner at the Royal Hotel in 1945. She was involved with the post-war movement until her son was born in 1949. She lived in Ireland from 1973, and then in Clacton, Essex. She contributed letters and poems to *Comrade* (1987–90).

Walters, Miss*

She had been employed in the mailing department at the BUF NHQ. On 17 March 1937 she held a 'bottle party' for dissenting elements of the BUF, including the Joyces, Goulding, F. Green, E.B. Hart, D. Auton, G. Whish and Miss Ann Cutmore.

Warburton, Joan (née Thorpe)*

(14 February 1914 to 8 March 1997) Religion: Church of England. Her father was a poorly-paid civil engineer, and her mother was from Devon and a former school teacher. Her mother voted Liberal and her father Conservative. She came from a family of two sisters and two brothers. She had an invalid younger sister who she used to push in a wheel-chair around the locality, and they sometimes stayed to listen to public meetings. Miss Thorpe worked as a junior clerk. She joined the New Party when she was 17 years old, following her brother, six years her senior, into the Party. She joined the BUF at its birth in 1932. She belonged to the Great St. George Street Branch of the NP(1931); 'Black House,' Chelsea (1932) and the

Battersea Branch (1932–40). She was very active for the first four years, and attended the Albert Hall meetings (1934), Olympia (1934), and Earl's Court (1939). Her fiancé, John Warburton, was in the Army from the outbreak of the war, and she was in an essential industry and thus not directed. Never interned but interrogated by Special Branch in 1940. She married on 21 March 1942 after her fiancé had been invalided out of the Army. The names of Mrs and Mr Edmund Warburton appeared on a report of a meeting hosted by C.F. Watts on 20 November 1942. With her husband, they established the 'Friends of Oswald Mosley' in the 1980s.

Warring, Mrs Dorothy Grace (a.k.a Harnett)^ +
Member of the British Fascists. An author. She was appointed Area Commander Ulster Women's Units on 11 July 1927. On 28 October 1927 she organized meetings in Ulster when Lintorn-Orman and Miss Ray made a visit to the Irish Command. On 28 January 1928, at a meeting at Kensington Town Hall, she spoke on the situation in Ulster and in Ireland. In September 1931 she was raised to the Second Degree of the Order of the Fasces. Joint Editor of *British Fascism* in 1934. In May 1934 she was Propaganda Officer for the BF. In June 1934 she visited the Women's Section of the BUF and lectured on welfare work in Italy. As a British subject in Italy, with ties to the BUF, in 1936 she was conducting pro-Italian and anti-sanctionist propaganda. Member of The Link.

Warnett, Mrs Margaret*
Member of the Shoreditch Branch of the BUF. Stood as a BU candidate for Kingsland Ward in the Municipal elections of 1 November, 1937. Polled 110 votes. Died in June 1938.

Waters, Mrs Florence^
Born *ca*.1890. Member of the BF and House Officer of BF headquarters. She was struck on the head and treated in hospital when the BUF raided BF headquarters at 22 Stanhope Gardens in July 1934. In 1934 she was presented with the Order of the Fasces for loyal service and presence of mind on the evening of 20 July 1934. In 1934 she was Chief Clerk of the Women's Section of the BF.

Watts, Charles Frederick* | | |
Born 17 January 1903 in Surrey. He joined the RAF in January 1924, served with Lawrence of Arabia, and was discharged in 1930. Married Ethel May Jiltman on 18 June 1933. In January 1937 he was appointed officer-in-charge of the Pimlico BU's Branch and on 30 September 1937 Mosley awarded him the 'Gold Distinction' order for valuable work. He was also appointed

officer-in-charge of the Taxi drivers' branch. He became D/L of the Westminster St George Branch. When his house was searched by police in May 1940 it was noted by the officers that his three young children gave the fascist salute and said 'P.J.' (Perish Judah). Watts was interned on 23 May 1940. He came before the Advisory Committee on 9 July 1940 and again on 19 September 1941. The detention order was suspended on 17 November 1941. He organized a gathering to celebrate Oswald Mosley's birthday on 16 November 1942.

Webster, Mrs Nesta^

Born last of fourteen children near Barnet in Hertfordshire. Her father, Robert Cooper Lee Bevan, was educated at Trinity College, Oxford, and became a director of Barclay's Bank. Her mother, Frances Shuttleworth, was from a Whig family in Lancashire. Educated at Brownhill, and Westfield College, Hampstead. During the Great War she worked at War Supplies Depots. A close friend of the Duke of Nothumberland's and frequent contributor to the *Morning Post*. She published many books which charted the world conspiracy of Jews, Freemasons, and high financiers; *World Revolution: The Plot Against Civilization* (1921) was her first in this genre. She was a member of the Anti-Socialist Union and author of the ASU's anti-socialist handbooks and one of their leading researchers. She was present at the major meeting for the Arab Delegation organized by the right-wing National Political League at the Hyde Park Hotel in March 1922. She wrote a series of articles for the BF's *The Fascist Bulletin* from May 1926 to January 1927. She spoke at a meeting organized by the Fascist Children's Clubs at Kensington Town Hall on 17 December 1926. She became a member of the BF as County Commander Staff G.H.Q Women's Units on 17 December 1926 and sat on the Grand Council in 1927. She gave a series of four lectures on the history of socialism, pacifism, internationalism and subversive movements at the Chelsea Town Hall, Lower Hall in February 1927. She served as Hon. Director of the Patriot's Inquiry Centre, opened in November 1927 at 51 Tothill St. Westminster. Still well respected in the world of anti-Semitic 'patriotic societies,' and in October 1938 Sir Barry Domvile enlisted her to help The Link. She contributed to the Duke of Northumberland's *The Patriot* right up to the Second World War.

Wedgewood, Miss OBE^

Member of the British Fascists. In 1925 she was County Commander of Women's Units for Staffordshire and Cheshire. Co-chair of BF meeting in Leek in January 1925 and speaker at a BF meeting at Elkes' Café in January 1925 to consider the desirability of forming a Women's Branch in Uttoxeter.

Welsh, Mrs Foster^

Allegedly a Southampton member of the British Fascists. In January 1927 she was elected councillor and Sheriff of the Borough of Southampton, the first woman to hold this position in all of England.

Westcott, Mrs Erna Marie (née Umlauf) | | |

Born in Breslau on 24 March 1907 of German parents. From 1935 to May 1938 she was in Brussels on behalf of the *Rheinische Westfalische Zeitung* with the object of maintaining liaison between Germany and the Rexist movement in Brussels. In 1936 she met Mr Gerald Hulme Westcott, a British member of the Antwerp firm Wescott & Co., and they married in May 1938. Interned under the Defence Regulations for hostile origins and associations. Came before the Advisory Committee on 10 December 1942. She suffered from active pulmonary tuberculosis in 1943 and was admitted to Brompton Hospital for treatment. She was released from Holloway on 5 January 1944.

Whinfield, Mrs Muriel* | | |

Born *ca.*1879. Wife of a Lieutenant-Colonel H.G. Whinfield who commanded the Queen's Royal Regiment. She was chairman of the Alton branch Women's Conservative Association for five years before resigning to join the BUF in 1936. She became BU prospective parliamentary candidate for Petersfield (Hants) in December 1936. Contributor to BUF publications: 'Women and Politics' (*Action*, No. 115, 30 April 1938). She was Chairman of the District Nursing Association in Hampshire. She lived on a farm called Shaldon, just north of Alton in Hampshire. She went to Germany and/or Switzerland after war broke out. Her son Peter was detained by January 1940. She attended the London Administration luncheon on 1 March 1940. She was interned under DR 18B on 24 May 1940. Lady Mosley appealed for her release on several occasions, placing emphasis on her advanced age and her need to attend to her husband, who suffered from a heart condition. Released on an order of suspension on 1 August 1942. With her son, Peter, she emigrated to South Africa after the war.

Williams, Miss D.*

Member of the BUF. In December 1935 she was appointed Women District Officer for Winchester.

Wilson, Colonel Henry Christopher Bruce^ *

Responsible for the attempted bail-out of the BF in 1934 when he contributed £500 pounds with which pressing debts could be liquidated. He had a private meeting with Mosley on 13 July 1934, agreeing that the BUF should absorb the BF. After a meeting at St Stephen's House in London on 17 July 1934, Wilson was met by opposition from Miss Lintorn-Orman on the merger of

the BF and BUF. Consequently, he proceeded to take steps to liquidate the
BF Ltd. and turn out the organization from the Headquarters at St. Stephen
House, which were rented in his name, and join the BUF regardless of the
decision reached by Lintorn-Orman and her supporters.

Wilson, Mrs Lillian*
Stood as BU candidate for Bethnal Green North Ward in the Municipal elections
of 1 November, 1937. She polled 665 votes. Attended a meeting of BU
elements on 23 November 1943.

Winch, Elizabeth*
Editor of the *Woman Fascist*, the paper published by BUF Women's Headquarters
from March to October 1934. BUF journalist (1933–34).

Wolkoff, (a.k.a. Volkoff), Miss Anna+ | | |
(1903–69) Her father, Admiral Nicholas Wolkoff, had been aide-de-camp to
the Czar and the last naval attaché at the Imperial Russian Embassy in London.
The family remained in London after the Bolshevik Revolution. With her father,
she ran the Russian Tea Rooms in Harrington Gardens, South Kensington.
She was a high-class dressmaker, her clients including Wallis Simpson and Pamela
Jackson (née Mitford). She was naturalized in 1935. In July 1939 she visited
Czechoslovakia, as a guest of the Princess of Litchtenstein, and there met
Mr. Frank, a close associate of Sudeten German leader Henlein, who alerted
her to the imminent German-Soviet Pact. By 1940 she was a leading member
of the Right Club and her name appears on the Right Club ledger of *ca.* May
1939. Attended the BU London Administration luncheon on 1 March 1940.
Attended a social gathering of the Right Club in April 1940. Interned under
DR 18B. Her father was also interned and not released until 1944. She was
brought to trial at the Old Bailey on 23 October 1940, and convicted in
November 1940 on a charge of attempting to send a letter in code 'to one
Joyce in Berlin'. She was sentenced to ten years penal servitude. She obtained
documents that Tyler Kent stole from the American Embassy, and through
the Romanian Embassy, she sent them to 'Lord Haw-Haw' as material for his
broadcasts from Berlin. She was released in June 1946 after serving only five
of her ten year sentence. She died in a car accident in 1969.

Wroughton, Mrs A.M.^
She ran the Women's Section of the BF for a time around 1924 to 1926.

Zouche of Harygworth, Baroness^
Member of the British Fascists. Among a group of the more obscure notables
who displayed signs of paranoia and disenchantment.

Bibliography

Archives and Collections

Essex County Council Archive, Chelmsford:
 Diaries of Lucy Heath Pearson, D/DU 758/9/1–42

J.B. Priestly Library, University of Bradford:
 Nellie Driver, *From the Shadows of Exile* (unpublished autobiography)
 Nellie Driver, *The Mill: A Novel* (unpublished)
 Tyepscripts of interviews conducted by Stuart Rawnsley with former Lancashire members of the British Union of Fascists between 1976–1978.

McMaster University, Hamilton, Ontario:
 Vera Brittain Papers
 George Catlin Papers
 Winifred Holtby Material
 Frank Waters Papers

National Museum of Labour History, Manchester:
 Pamphlets, 322–339.9
 Press Cuttings, FAS/1–7
 Replies to Fascist Questionnaire, LP/FAS/34/1–522

Public Record Office, Kew:
 Cabinet: CAB 66, CAB 67
 Home Office: HO 45, HO 144, HO 213, HO 214, HO 215, HO 283, HO 382
 Foreign Office: FO369, FO371
 Metropolitan Police: MEPO 2, MEPO 3, MEPO 4, MEPO 546, MEPO 548, MEPO 572
 Premier: PREM 4
 Prison Commission: PCOM 2, PCOM 9
 Ramsay MacDonald Papers: PRO 30

Special Collections and Archives, University Library,
University of Sheffield:
 British Union Collection
 Cooper Collection
 Fascism in Great Britain Collection
 Fascism in Europe Collection
 Joyce Papers
 Saunders Papers

Winston Churchill Archive, Churchill Archive Centre,
University of Cambridge:
 CHAR 20/1–163

Audio-taped Material, Interviews and Correspondence

'Mosley's Men,' Audio-tape issued by Friends of O.M., 1996

Interview with Blanche Greaves by Jeffrey Wallder. Audio-tape, property of the Friends of O.M., 1991. Transcribed by the author.

Interview with Gladys Walsh. Audio-Tape, property of the Friends of O.M. Transcribed by the author.

Interview with Nicholas Mosley, Lord Ravensdale, by the author. Audio-tape and transcript, 1996.

Correspondence in the author's possession with: Francis Beckett, Louise Irvine, Diana Mosley, Nicholas Mosley (Lord Ravensdale), Robert Row, Jeffrey Wallder, John Warburton, and Eugenia Wright.

Newspaper Files Consulted

Action, 1931
Action: Britain First, 1936–40
The Blackshirt, 1933–40
British Fascism, 1930–34
The British Lion, 1926–30
British Union Quarterly, 1937–40
Comrade: Newsletter of the Friends of O.M., 1986–97
Daily Mail, 1933–34

The Fascist Bulletin, 1925–26
Fascist Quarterly, 1935–36
The Fascist Week, 1933–34
Labour Woman, 1930–39
Manchester Guardian, 1934–36
The Times, 1924–36

Other Newspapers Cited

The Abolitionist
Bulletin and Scots Pictorial
Daily Herald
Daily Telegraph
Daily Worker
Evening News
Everyman
Hampstead and Highgate Express
Isle of Man Weekly Times
London News
Morning Post
New Leader
News Chronicle
The Patriot
Peace News
Yorkshire Post
Sunday Dispatch
Time and Tide

Unpublished Manuscripts and Typescripts

Bellamy, R.R., *The Memoirs of a Fascist Beast.* Copy with A.W. Brian Simpson
Irvine, L., 'Arrest and Imprisonment under Regulation 18b: November 1940–November 1941: As Experienced by Miss C.L. Fisher (now Mrs Irvine).' Copy sent to the author by Louise Irvine
Irvine, L., 'A Woman's Viewpoint of the 30's.' Unpublished article. Copy sent to the author by Louise Irvine
Row, R., 'Detention Without Trial (Defence Regulation 18B) 1940/1943.' Copy with A.W. Brian Simpson
Wallder, J. & Warburton, J., 'The Regulation 18B British Union Detainees List.' British Union Collection, University of Sheffield

Warburton, Joan C. (neé Thorpe), 'Myself and the New Party.' Unpublished type-script. Archive of the Friends of O.M.

Warburton, Joan C. (neé Thorpe), 'Yourself and British Union.' Unpublished re-sponses to a questionnaire. Archive of the Friends of O.M.

Unpublished Dissertations

Cullen, S.M., *The British Union of Fascists, 1932–1940: Ideology, Membership and Meet-ings*. M.Litt., Oxford (1987)

Hendley, M., *Patriotic Leagues the Evolution of Popular Patriotism and Imperialism in Great Britain 1914–1932*. PhD, University of Toronto (1998)

Rawnsley, Stuart J., *Fascism and Fascists in Britain in the 1930s: A case study of Fascism in the North of England in a period of economic and political change*. PhD, University of Bradford (1981)

Ritschel, D., *The Political Economy of British Fascism: The Genesis of Sir Oswald Mosley's 'Modern Alternative'*. MA., McGill (1981)

Printed Sources: (a) Books

Allen, M.S., *The Pioneer Policewoman*, London, 1925

Allen, M.S., *Lady in Blue*, London, 1936

Allen, M.S. & Hayneman, J.H., *Woman at the Cross Roads*, London, 1934

Barnes, J.S., *The Universal Aspects of Fascism*, London, 1928

Bell, A.O. (ed.), *The Diary of Virginia Woolf*, London, vol. IV, 1982

Berry, P. & Bishop, A. (eds), *Testament of a Generation: The Journalism of Vera Brittain and Winifred Holtby*, London, 1985

Bishop, A. (ed.), *Vera Brittain, Diary of the Thirties 1932–1939: Chronicle of Friend-ship*, London, 1986

Bottome, P., *The Mortal Storm*, Boston, 1938

Brittain, V., *Testament of Youth*, 9th edn, London, 1935

Brittain, V., *Testament of Experience: An Autobiographical Story of the Years 1925–1950*, London, 1957

Broad, L., & L. Russell, *The Way of the Dictators*, London, 1935

Bryant, A.(ed.), *The Man and the Hour: Six Studies of Six Great Men of Our Time*, London, 1934

'Cato', *Guilty Men*, London, 1940

Charnley, J., *Blackshirts and Roses: An Autobiography*, London, 1990

Chesser E., & Hawks, O., *Life Lies Ahead: A Practical Guide to Home-Making and the Development of Personality*, London, 1951

Chesterton, A.K., *Oswald Mosley: Portrait of a Leader*, London, 1937

Christian, J. (ed.), *Mosley's Blackshirts: The Inside Story of the British Union of Fascists 1932–1940*, London, 1986

Clephane, I., *Towards Sex Freedom*, London, 1935

Constantine, M., (pseud.) *Swastika Night*, London, 1937

Cresswell, C.M., *Keystone of Fascism: A Study in the Ascendancy of Discipline*, London, 1929

Currey, M., *A Woman at the Abyssinian War*, London, 1936

Dangerfield, G., *The Strange Death of Liberal England*, London, 1935

Drennan, J., *BUF: Oswald Mosley and British Fascism*, London, 1934

Domvile, B., *From Admiral to Cabin Boy*, London, 1947

Dutt, R.P., *Fascism and Social Revolution*, New York, 1934

Forbes, R. (ed.), *Women of all Lands: Their Charm Culture and Characteristics*, London, 1938–39

Goad, H.E. & Currey, M., *The Working of a Corporate State*, London, 1934

Godden, G., *Mussolini: The Birth of a New Democracy*, London, 1923

Greene, G., *The Ministry of Fear*, London, 1943

Greenwood, W., *Love on the Dole*, London, 1933

Grundy, T., *Memoir of a Fascist Childhood: A Boy in Mosley's Britain*, London, 1998

Gunther, J., *Inside Europe*, London, 1936

Haider, C., *Do We Want Fascism*, New York, 1934

Hamilton, M.A., *Remembering My Good Friends*, London, 1944

Hamilton, C., *Life Errant*, London, 1935

Hamilton, C., *Modern Italy: As Seen by an English Woman*, London, 1932

Hamilton, C., *Modern England as Seen by an Englishwoman*, London, 1938

Hawks, O., *What Hope for Green Street?*, London, 1945

Hitler, A., *Mein Kampf*, trans. Manheim, R.. Boston, 1971

Holtby, W., *Women and a Changing Civilization*, London, 1934

Holtby, W., *South Riding: An English Landscape*, London, 1936

Holtby, W. & Ginsbury, N., *Take Back Your Freedom*, London, 1939

Isherwood, C., *Goodbye to Berlin*, London, 1939

Ishiguro, K., *The Remains of the Day*, London, 1989

Jones, H. (ed.), *Duty and Citizenship: The Correspondence and Political Papers of Violet Markham, 1896–1953*, London, 1994

Kirkpartick, C., *Women in Nazi Germany*, London, 1939

Lafitte, F., *The Internment of Aliens*, Harmondsworth, 1940

Landau, R., *Love for a Country: Contemplations and Conversations*, London, 1939

Laurent, L., *A Tale of Internment*, London, 1942

Leese, A.S., *Out of Step: Events in the Two Lives of an Anti-Jewish Camel Doctor*, Privately published, 1951

Lewis, S., *It's Can't Happen Here*, New York, 1935

Lorimer, E.O., *What the German Needs*, London, 1942

Ludovici, A.M., *Woman: A Vindication*, London, 1923

Ludovici, A.M., *The Future of Woman*, London, 1936
Marchand, L. (ed.), *Selected Poetry of Lord Byron*. New York, 1951
Marriot, A.R., *Dictatorship and Democracy*, Oxford, 1935
Martindale, H., *Women Servants of the State 1870–1938: A History of Women in the Civil Service*, London, 1938
McCutcheon Raleigh, J., *Behind the Nazi Front*, London, 1941
Mitchison, N., *The Home and a Changing Civilization*, London, 1934
Mitford, J., *Hons and Rebels*. London,1960
Mitford, J. *A Fine Old Conflict*. London, 1977
Mitford, N., *Wigs on the Green*, London, 1935
Mitford, N., *Pigeon Pie*. London, 1940
Mitford, N., *The Pursuit of Love*, London, 1945
Mitford, N., *Love in a Cold Climate*, London, 1949
Mosley, C. (ed.), *Love from Nancy: The Letters of Nancy Mitford*, London, 1993
Mosley, D., *A Life of Contrasts: The Autobiography of Diana Mosley*, London, 1977
Mosley, D., *The Duchess of Windsor*, London, 1980
Mosley, D., *Loved Ones: Pen Portraits*, London, 1985
Mosley, O., *The Greater Britain*, London, 1932
Mosley, O., *Fascism: 100 Questions Asked and Answered*, London, 1936
Mosley, O., *Tomorrow We Live: British Union Policy*, London, 1938
Mosley, O., *My Answer*, London, 1946
Mosley, O., *The Alternative*, Ramsbury, 1947
Mosley, O., *Mosley: The Facts*, London, 1957
Mosley, O., *My Life*, London, 1968
Muggeridge, M., *The Thirties: 1930–1940 in Great Britain*, London, 1940
Muggeridge, M., *Chronicle of Wasted Time, Part 2: The Infernal Grove*, London, 1973
Mussolini, B., *The Corporate State: Speeches on the Corporate State*, 2nd edn, Florence, 1938
Mussolini, R., *My Life with Mussolini*, with Chinigo, M., London, 1959
Mussolini, B., *Fascism: Doctrines and Institutions*, New York, 1968. (First pub. in English: 1935)
Newitt, H., *Women Must Choose: The Position of Women in Europe Today*, London, 1937
Nichols, B., *News from England/ or A Country Without a Hero*, London, 1938
Nicolson, H., *The English Sense of Humour and other Essays*, London, 1956
Nicholson, N., *Portrait of a Marriage*, London, 1973
Olson, S. (ed.), *Harold Nicolson: Diaries and Letters 1930–1964*, London, 1980
Orwell, G., *Keep the Aspidistra Flying*, London, 1936
Orwell, G., *The Road to Wigan Pier*, London, 1937
Orwell, S. & Angus, I. (eds), *The Collected Essays, Journalism and Letter of George Orwell*, 4 Vols, Harmondsworth, 1980
Osborn, R., *The Psychology of Reaction*, London, 1938
Pankhurst, C., *Unshackled: The Story of How We Won the Vote*, London, 1959

Pethick-Lawrence, E., *My Part in a Changing World*, London, 1938

Pope, E.R., *Munich Playground*, London, 1943

Pound, E., *Jefferson and/or Mussolini*, London, 1935

Priestly, J.B., *Black-out in Gretley: A Story of – and for – Wartime*, London, 1942

Rathbone, E.R., *War can be Averted: The Achievability of Collective Security*, London, 1938

Ravensdale, Baroness, *In Many Rhythms: An Autobiography*, London, 1953

Reich, W., *The Mass Psychology of Fascism*, trans. Carfagno, V.R.. Harmondsworth, 1970

Richardson, M., *Laugh a Defiance*, London, 1953

Rudlin, W.A., *The Growth of Fascism in Great Britain*, London, 1935

Russell, B., *A History of Philosophy and its Connection with the Political and Social Circumstances from the Earliest to the Present Day*, New York, 1946

Russell, D., *The Tamarisk Tree: My Quest for Liberty and Love*, London, 1975

Sarfatti, M.G., *The Life of Benito Mussolini*, trans. Whyte, F., London, 1925

Spark, M., *The Prime of Miss Jean Brodie*, London, 1961

Spengler, O., *The Decline of the West*, London, 1961 (First pub. in English: 1932)

Storm Jameson, M., *In the Second Year*, London, 1936

Strachey, R., *The Cause: A Short History of the Women's Movement in Great Britain*, London, 1928

Strachey, J., *The Menace of Fascism*, London, 1933

Strachey, R. (ed.), *Our Freedom and its Results by Five Women*, London, 1936

Swanwick, H.M., *Collective Insecurity*, London, 1937

Thomas, K., *Women in Nazi Germany*, London, 1943

Wagner, S., *Germany in my Time*, London, 1935

Waugh, E., *Waugh in Abyssinia*, London, 1936

Webster, N., *World Revolution: The Plot Against Civilization*, London, 1921

Webster, N., *Spacious Days: An Autobiography*, London, 1949

Weininger, O., *Sex and Character*, London, 1906

Wells, H.G., *Experiment in Autobiography: Discoveries and Conclusions of a Very Ordinary Brain (Since 1866)*, New York, 1934

Wells, H.G., *The Holy Terror*, New York, 1939

Wilkinson, E. & E. Conze, *Why Fascism*, London, 1934

Wilson, A., *Walks and Talks Abroad: Diary of a Member of Parliament in 1934–36*, London, 1936

Wodehouse, P.G., *The Code of the Woosters*, London, 1937

Woolf, V., *Three Guineas*, London, 1938

Printed Sources: (b) Articles and Pamphlets:

Allen, E., *It Shall Not Happen Here*. London, [1940?]

Allen, W.E.D., *Fascism in Relation to British History and Character*, London, 1933

Birch, L., *Why They Join the Fascists*, London, 1937

Blakeney, R.B.D., 'British Fascism', *Nineteenth Century and After*, 97 (1925), 132–42

Brock Griggs, A., *Women and Fascism: 10 Important Points*, London, 1936

Browning, H., *Women Under Fascism and Communism*, London, 1935

Catlin, G.E.G., 'Fascist Stirring in Britain,' *Current History*, 9 (1934), 542–7

Chesterton, A.K., *Why I Left Mosley*, London, 1938

Communist Bookshop, *Fascism: Its History and Significance*, London, 1924

Communist Party of Great Britain, *Put Mosley Back in Prison*, London, 1943

Douglas, J.L., *Spotlight on Fascism: Facts about Fascism, Men Behind Mosley, Culture Killers, Landlord, Leader and Captain Kidd*, London, [1935?]

Driberg, T., *Mosley? No!*, London, [1946?]

Fascism: the Enemy of the People, London, 1934

Fascist War on Women: Facts from Italian Gaols, London, 1934

Free German League of Culture in Great Britain, *Women Under the Swastika*, London, 1942

Hawks, O., *Women Fight for Britain and for Britain Alone*, London, 1940

Independent Labour Party, *They Did Not Pass: 300,000 Workers Say No to Mosley: A Souvenir of the East London Workers' Victory Over Fascism*, London, 1936

'Investigator', 'The Fascist Movement in Great Britain', *Socialist Review*, 1 (1926), 22–9

Joad, C.E.M., 'Prolegomena to Fascism,' *Political Quarterly*, 2 (1931), 82–99

Joyce, W., *Fascist Education Policy*, London, 1936

Joyce, W., *National Socialism Now*, London, 1937

Labour Research Department, *Who Backs Mosley?: Fascist Promise and Fascist Performance*, London, 1934

Liberty Restoration League, *The Defence Regulations: Was Parliament Misled?*, London, 1940

Melville, C.F., *The Truth About the New Party*, London, 1931

Milner, L.B., 'Fighting Fascism by Law', *The Nation*, 136, 3 (1938), 65–7

Mosley, O., *Fascism in Britain*, London, 1933

Mosley, O., *Blackshirt Policy*, London, 1936

Mosley, O., *The British Peace and how to get it*, London, 1940

Soviet War News, *Women Against Hitler: Report of Mass Meeting of Women held in Moscow, September 7th, 1941*, London, 1941

St George, H., *18B: In Search of Justice*, London, [n.d]

'Vindicator', *Fascists at Olympia: A Record of Eye-Witnesses and Victims*, London, 1934

Webster, N., *Germany and England*, London, 1939

Wynn, J., 'It Might Have Happened to You', *The Word*, Special Investigation Report on 18B. Birmingham, 1943

Young Communist League, *10 Points Against Fascism*, London, [1934?]

18B Publicity Council, *Shall Justice Prevail?: Defence Regulation 18b and the Constitution*, London, 1941

18B Publicity Council, *Runnymede Reversed: Tyranny Today and Tomorrow?*, London, [1942?]

18B Publicity Council, *Persecuted Women in Britain Today*, London, [1943?]

18B Publicity Council, *Suffer Little Children*, Surrey, [1944?]

Secondary Works: (a) Books

Adams, R., *A Woman's Place 1910–1975*, London, 1975

Andrews, G., Fishman, N., & Morgan, K. (eds), *Opening the Books: Essays on the Social and Cultural History of the British Communist Party*, London, 1995

Annan, N., *Our Age: Portrait of a Generation*, London, 1990

Arendt, H., *The Origins of Totalitarianism*, London, 1958

Baker, D., *Ideology of Obsession: A.K. Chesterton and British Fascism*, London, 1996

Ballaster, R. *et al.*, *Women's Worlds: Ideology, Femininity and the Woman's Magazine*, London, 1991

Barkan, E., *The Retreat of Scientific Racism: Changing Concepts of Race in Britain and the United States between the World Wars*, Cambridge, 1992

Barrow, A., *Gossip: A History of High Society from 1920 to 1970*, London, 1978

Beckman, M., *The 43 Group*, 2nd edn, London, 1993

Beddoe, D., *Back to Home and Duty: Women between the Wars, 1918–1939*, London, 1989

Benewick, R., *The Fascist Movement in Britain*, London, 1972

Bergmeier, J.P. & Lotz, R.E., *Hitler's Airwaves: The Inside Story of Nazi Radio Broadcasting and Propaganda Swing*, New Haven, 1997

Blee, K.M., *Women of the Klan: Racism and Gender in the 1920s*, Berkeley, 1991

Blee, K.M. (ed.), *No Middle Ground: Women and Radical Protest*, New York, 1998

Bleuel, H.P., *Sex and Society in Nazi Germany*, trans. Brownjohn, M.J. Philadelphia, 1973

Blythe, R., *The Age of Illusion: Some Glimpses of Britain between the Wars, 1919–1940*, Oxford, 1983

Brewer, J.D., *Mosley's Men: The British Union of Fascists in the West Midlands*, Hampshire, 1984

Bridenthal, R. *et al.*, *When Biology Became Destiny: Women in Weimar and Nazi Germany*, New York, 1984

Brittain, V., *Lady into Woman: A History of Women from Victoria to Elizabeth II*, London, 1953

Brookes, P., *Women at Westminster: An Account of Women in the British Parliament 1918–1966*, London, 1967

Bullock, A., *Hitler: A Study in Tyranny*, Long Acre, revised edn, 1964

Bullock, I. & R. Pankhurst (eds), *Sylvia Pankhurst: From Artist to Anti-Fascist*, London, 1992

Burke, B., *Rebels with a Cause: The History of Hackney Trade Council 1900–1975*, London, 1975

Campbell, B., *The Iron Ladies: Why Do Women Vote Tory?*, London, 1987

Cannadine, D., *Aspects of Aristocracy: Grandeur and Decline in Modern Britain*, New Haven, 1994

Cannadine, D., *The Decline and Fall of the British Aristocracy*, New Haven, 1990

Cannadine, D., *History in Our Time*, New Haven, 1998

Carey, J., *Intellectuals and the Masses: Pride and Prejudice among the Literary Intelligentsia 1880–1939*, London, 1992

Cesarani, D. & Kushner, T., *The Internment of Aliens in Twentieth Century Britain*, London, 1993

Cheles, L., Ferguson, R., & Vaughan, M. (eds), *The Far Right in Western and Eastern Europe*, 2nd edn, London, 1995

Chisholm, A., *Nancy Cunard*, London, 1979

Clarke, P., *Hope and Glory*, London, 1996

Coleman, V., *Adela Pankhurst: The Wayward Suffragette*, Melbourne, 1996

Collis, M., *Nancy Astor*, London, 1960

Cowling, M., *The Impact of Hitler: British Politics and British Policy 1933–1940*, Cambridge, 1975

Cresswell, Y.M., *Living with the Wire: Civilian Internment in the Isle of Man during the Two World Wars*, Douglas, Isle of Man, 1994

Crew, D.F. (ed.), *Nazism and German Society, 1933–1945*, London, 1994

Cronin, M. (ed.), *The Failure of British Fascism: The Far Right and the Fight for Political Recognition*, London, 1996

Cross, C., *The Fascists in Britain*, London, 1961

Currell, M., *Political Woman*, London, 1974

Durham, M., *Women and Fascism*, London, 1998

DeGrand, A., *Italian Fascism: Its Origins and Development*, Lincoln, 1982

DeGrazia, V., *How Fascism Ruled Women*, Berkeley, 1992

Eatwell, R., *Fascism: A History*, London, 1995

Eysenck, H.J., *Uses and Abuses of Psychology*, Harmondsworth, 1953

Fielding, D., *Emerald and Nancy*, London, 1968

Foot, M., *Loyalists and Loners*, London, 1986

Friedlander, *Reflections of Nazism: An Essay on Kitsch and Death*, trans. Weyr, T. New York, 1984

Fussell, P., *The Great War and Modern Memory*, London, 1975

Fussell, P., *Abroad: British Literary Travelling between the Wars*, Oxford, 1982

Gannon, F.R., *The British Press and Germany 1936–1939*, Oxford, 1971

Garrison, D., *Who's Who in Wodehouse*, New York, 1987

Gattens, M.-L., (ed.) *Women Writers and Fascism: Reconstructing History*, Gainesville, 1995

Gilbert, M. & Gott, R., *The Appeasers*, London, 1963

Gillman, P. & Gillman, L., *'Collar the Lot!: How Britain Interned and Expelled its Wartime Refugees*, London, 1980

Goldman, W., *Women, the State and Revolution: Soviet Family Policy and Soviet Life 1917–1936*, Cambridge, 1993

Grainger, J.H., *Patriotisms: Britain 1900–1939*, London, 1986

Graves, P.M, *Labour Women: Women in British Working-class Politics 1918–1939*, Cambridge, 1994

Green, M., *Children of the Sun: A Narrative of 'Decadence' in England after 1918*, New York, 1976

Griffin, R., *The Nature of Fascism*, London, 1991

Griffin, R., (ed.), *Fascism*, Oxford, 1995

Griffiths, R., *Fellow Travellers of the Right: British Enthusiasts for Nazi Germany 1933–9*, London, 1980

Griffiths, R., *Patriotism Perverted: Captain Ramsay, the Right Club and British Anti-Semitism 1939–40*, London, 1998

Guinness, J. & Guinness, C., *The House of Mitford: Portrait of a Family*, Harmondsworth, 1984

Hamilton, A., *The Appeal of Fascism: A Study of the Intellectual and Fascism 1919–45*, London, 1971

Harrison, B., *Separate Spheres: The Opposition to Women's Suffrage in Britain*, London, 1978

Harrison, B., *Prudent Revolutionaries: Portraits of British Feminist between the Wars*, Oxford, 1987

Harrison, J.R., *The Reactionaries*, London, 1966

Higginbottom, M.D., *Intellectuals and British Fascism: A Study of Henry Williamson*, London, 1992

Hinsley, F.H. & Simkins, C.A.G., *British Intelligence in the Second World War: Vol. 4, Security and Counter-Intelligence*, London, 1990

Holmes, C., *Anti-Semitism in British Society 1876–1939*, London, 1979

Holton, S.S., *Feminism and Democracy: Women's Suffrage and Reform Politics in Britain 1900–1918*, Cambridge, 1986

Holton, S.S., *Suffrage Days: Stories from the Women's Suffrage Movement*, London, 1996

Hynes, S. *The Auden Generation*, London, 1976

Infield, G.B., *Eva and Adolf*, New York, 1974

Irving, D., *The War Path: Hitler's Germany 1933–9*, London, 1978

Izzard, M., *A Heroine in Her Time: A Life of Dame Helen Gwynne-Vaughan 1879–1967*, London, 1969

Jeansonne, G., *Women of the Far Right: The Mothers' Movement and World War II*, Chicago, 1996

Joannou, M., *'Ladies Please Don't Smash These Windows': Women's Writing, Feminist Consciousness and Social Change 1918–38*, Oxford, 1995

Kennedy, P. & Nicholls, A. (eds), *Nationalist and Racialist Movements in Britain and Germany before 1914*, Oxford, 1981

Kent, S.K., *Making Peace: The Reconstruction of Gender in Interwar Britain*, Princeton, New Jersey, 1993

Koch, E., *Deemed Suspect: A Wartime Blunder*, Toronto, 1980

Koonz, C., *Mothers in the Fatherland: Women, the Family and Nazi Politics*, London, 1987

Kushner, T., *The Persistence of Prejudice*, Manchester, 1989

Kushner, T. & Lunn, K. (eds), *The Politics of Marginality: Race, the Radical Right and Minorities in Twentieth Century Britain*, London, 1990

Kushner, T. & Lunn, K. (eds), *Traditions of Intolerance: Historical Perspectives on Fascism and Race Discourse in Britain*, Manchester, 1989

Larsen, S.U. *et al.*, *Who Were the Fascists: Social Roots of European Fascism*, Bergen, 1980

Lassner, P., *British Women Writers of World War II: Battlegrounds of their Own*, London, 1998

Law, C., *Suffrage and Power: The Women's Movement 1918–1928*, London, 1997

Lebzelter, G.C., *Political Anti-Semitism in England 1918–1939*, Oxford, 1978

Lewis, D.S., *Illusions of Grandeur: Mosley, Fascism and British Society 1931–81*, Manchester, 1987

Lewis, J., *Women in England 1870–1950: Sexual Divisions and Social Change*, Sussex, 1984

Lunn, K. & Thurlow, R.C. (eds), *British Fascism: Essays on the Radical Right in Inter-war Britain*, London, 1980

Linehan, T.P., *East London for Mosley: The British Union of Fascists in East London and South-West Essex 1933–40*, London, 1996

Lock, J., *The British Policewoman: Her Story*, London, 1979

Mandel, W. F., *Anti-Semitism and the British Union of Fascists*, London, 1968

Masters, A., *The Man Who Was M: The Life of Maxwell Knight*, Oxford, 1984

McShane, Y., *Daughter of Evil: The True Story*, London, 1980

Melman, B., *Women in the Popular Imagination in the Twenties: Flappers and Nymphs*, London, 1988

Milfull, J. (ed.), *The Attractions of Fascism: Social Psychology and Aesthetics of the 'Triumph of the Right'*, New York, 1990

Miller, J., *One Girl's War: Personal Exploits in MI5's Most Secret Station*, Dublin, 1986

Millett, K., *Sexual Politics*, London, 1970

Mizejewski, L., *Divine Decadence: Fascism, Female Spectacle and the Making of Sally Bowles*, Princeton, 1992

Mosley, N., *Rules of the Game: Sir Oswald and Lady Cynthia Mosley 1896–1933*, London, 1982

Mosley, N., *Beyond the Pale: Sir Oswald Mosley and Family, 1993–1980*, London, 1983

Mosley, N., *Efforts at Truth: An Autobiography*, London, 1994

Mosse, G.L., *Nazi Culture: Intellectual, Cultural and Social Life in the Third Reich*, trans. Attanasio, S., New York, 1968

Mosse, G.L., *Nationalism and Sexuality: Respectability and Abnormal Sexuality in Modern Europe*, New York, 1985

Mosse, G.L., *Fallen Soldiers: Reshaping the Memory of the World Wars*, Oxford, 1990

Mosse, G.L., *The Image of Man: The Creation of Modern Masculinity*, Oxford, 1996

Mulally, F., *Fascism Inside England*, London, 1946

Nugent, N. & King, R. (eds), *The British Right: Conservative and Right-wing Politics in Britain*, Westmead, 1977

Oldfield, S. (ed.), *This Working-Day World: Women's Lives and Culture(s) in Britain 1914–1945*, London, 1994

Owings, A., *Frauen: German Women Recall the Third Reich*, New Brunswick, 1994

Panayi, P., *Minorities in Wartime: National and Racial Groupings in Europe, North America and Australia during the Two World Wars*, Oxford, 1993

Paglia, C., *Sexual Personae: Art and Decadence from Nefertiti to Emily Dickinson*, New York, 1991

Passerini, L., *Fascism in Popular Memory: The Cultural Experience of the Turin Working Class*, trans. Lumley, R. & Bloomfield J., Cambridge, 1987

Patai, D., *The Orwell Mystique: A Study in Male Ideology*, Amherst, 1984

Pedersen, S., *Family, Dependence and the Origins of the Welfare State: Britain and France, 1914–1945*, Cambridge, 1993

Pickering-Iazzi, R. (ed.), *Mothers of Invention: Women, Italian Fascism and Culture*, Minneapolis, 1995

Power, M., *Our History: The Struggle Against Fascism and War in Britain 1931–1939*, London, 1978

Pryce-Jones, D., *Unity Mitford: A Quest*, London, 1976

Pugh, M., *The Making of Modern British Politics*, Oxford, 1982

Pugh, M., *The Tories and the People 1880–1935*, Oxford, 1985

Pugh, M., *Women and the Women's Movement in Britain 1914–1959*, London, 1992

Pugh, M., *State and Society: British Political and Social History 1870–1992*, London, 1994

Purvis, J. (ed.), *Women's History: Britain, 1850–1945: An Introduction*, London, 1995

Raeburn, A., *The Militant Suffragettes*, London, 1973

Rees, P., *Fascism in Britain*, Sussex, 1979

Ridley, J., *Mussolini*, London, 1997

Rogger, H. & Weber, E. (eds), *The European Right: A Historical Profile*, London, 1965

Romero, P., *E. Sylvia Pankhurst: Portrait of a Radical*, New Haven, 1987

Rosen, A., *Rise Up, Women!: The Militant Campaign of the Women's Social and Political Union 1903–1914*, London, 1974

Rubinstein, W.D., *A History of the Jews in the English-speaking World: Great Britain*, Houndmills, 1996

Rupp, L.J., *Mobilizing Women for War: German and American Propaganda 1939–1945*, Princeton, 1978

Sage, L. (ed.), *The Cambridge Guide to Women's Writing in English*, Cambridge, 1999

Sayers, J., *Biological Politics: Feminist and Anti-feminist Perspectives*, London, 1982

Segrave, K., *Policewomen: A History*, Jefferson, 1994

Sheridan, D. (ed.), *Wartime Women: An Anthology of Women's Wartime Writing for Mass-Observation*, London, 1990

Shoemaker, R. & Vincent, M. (eds), *Gender and History in Western Europe*, London, 1998

Simpson, A.W.B., *In the Highest Degree Odious: Detention Without Trial in Wartime Britain*, Oxford, 1992

Singer, K., *The World's Greatest Women Spies*, London, 1951

Skidelsky, R., *Oswald Mosley*, London, 1975

Skidelsky, R., *Interests and Obsessions: Selected Essays*, London, 1993

Smith, H.L. (ed.), *British Feminism in the Twentieth Century*, Aldershot, 1990

Spackman, B., *Fascist Virilities: Rhetoric, Ideology and Social Fantasy in Italy*, Minneapolis, 1996

Sontag, S., *Under the Sign of Saturn*, New York, 1980

Stephenson, J., *Women in Nazi Society*, London, 1975

Stevenson, J. & Cook, C. (eds), *Britain in the Depression: Society and Politics 1929–1939*, 2nd edn, London, 1994

Sternhell, Z., *The Birth of Fascist Ideology: From Cultural Rebellion to Political Revolution*, trans. Maisel, D., New Jersey, 1994

Storm Farr, B., *The Development and Impact of Right-wing Politics in Britain 1903–1932*, New York, 1987

Symons, J., *The Thirties: A Dream Revolved*, London, 1960

Tangye Lean, E., *The Napoleonists: A Study in Political Disaffection, 1790–1960*, London, 1970

Thalman, R. (ed.), *Femmes et Fascismes*, Paris, 1987

Thébaud, F. (ed.), *A History of Women in the West: Vol. V, Toward a Cultural Identity in the Twentieth Century*, London, 1994

Theweleit, K., *Male Fantasies: Women, Floods, Bodies, History*, trans., Conway, S., Cambridge, 1977

Thurlow, R., *Fascism in Britain: A History 1918–1985*, Oxford, 1987

Thurlow, R., *The Secret State: British Internal Security in the Twentieth Century*, Oxford, 1994

Todd, N., *In Excited Times: The People Against the Blackshirts*, Whitely Bay, 1995

Wagar, W., *H.G. Wells and the World State*, New Haven, 1961

Wallach Scott, J. (ed.), *Feminism and History: Oxford Readings in Feminism*, Oxford, 1996

Webber, G.C., *The Ideology of the British Right 1918–1939*, London, 1986

Wentworth-Day, J., *Lady Houston D.B.E: The Woman who Won the War*, London, 1958

West, R., *The Meaning of Treason*, London, 1949

West, W.J., *Truth Betrayed*, London, 1987

Wheelwright, J., *Amazons and Military Maids: Women who Dressed as Men in Pursuit of Life, Liberty and Happiness*, London, 1989

Whitelaw, L., *The Life and Rebellious Times of Cicely Hamilton: Actress, Writer, Suffragist*, London, 1990

Winter, J., *Sites of Memory, Sites of Mourning: The Great War in European Cultural History*, Cambridge, 1995

Wohl, R., *The Generation of 1914*, London, 1980

Woolf, S.J. (ed.), *Fascism in Europe*, London, 1981

Secondary Works: (b) Articles, Pamphlets, and Chapters in Edited Volumes

Alberti, J., 'British Feminists and Anti-Fascism in the 1930s,' in Oldfield, S. (ed.), *This Working- Day World*, London, 1994, 111–22

Baker, D., 'The Extreme Right in the 1920s: Fascism in a Cold Climate, or "Conservatism with Knobs On"?,' in Cronin, M. (ed.), *The Failure of British Fascism*, London, 1996, 12–28

Beckett, F., 'The Rebel Who Lost His Cause,' *History Today*, 44, 5 (May 1994), 36–42

Bock, G., 'Antinatalism, Maternity and Paternity in National Socialist Racism,' in Crew, D.F. (ed.), *Nazism and German Society, 1933–1945*, London, 1994, 110–40

Bock, G., 'Nazi Gender Policies and Women's History,' in Thébaud, F. (ed.), *A History of Women in the West*, London, 1994, 149–76

Bock, G., 'Equality and Difference in National Socialist Racism,' in Wallach Scott, J. (ed.), *Feminism and History*, Oxford, 1996, 267–90

Bock, G., 'Women's History and Gender History: Aspects of an International Debate,' in Shoemaker, R. & Vincent, M. (eds), *Gender and History in Western Europe*, London, 1998, 25–42

Breeders of Race and Nation: Women and Fascism in Britain Today. Birmingham, 1989

Brewer, J.D., 'The British Union of Fascists: Some Tentative Conclusions on its Membership,' in Larsen, S.U. *et al.* (eds), *Who Were the Fascists*, Bergen, 1980, 542–56

Bruley, S., 'Women and Communism: A Case Study of the Lancashire Weavers in the Depression,' in Andrews, G., Fishman, N., & Morgan, K. (eds), *Opening the Books*, London, 1995, 65–82

Caplan, J., 'Introduction to Female Sexuality in Fascist Ideology', *Feminist Review*, 1 (1979), 59–66

Cesarani, D., 'Joynson-Hicks and the Radical Right in England After the First World War,' in Kushner T. & Lunn K. (eds), *Traditions of Intolerance*. Manchester, 1989, 118–39

Cohen, P., 'The Police, the Home Office and Surveillance of the British Union of Fascists,' *Intelligence and National Security*, 1, 3 (1986), 416–34

Cohen, S. 'In Step with Arnold Leese: The Case of Lady Birdwood,' *Patterns of Prejudice*, 28, 2 (1994), 61–76

Cronin, M., '"Tomorrow We Live" – The Failure of British Fascism?,' in Cronin, M. (ed.), *The Failure of British Fascism*, London, 1996, 1–11

Cullen, S., 'Leader and Martyrs: Codreanu, Mosley and Jose Antonio,' *History*, 71, 233 (1986), 408–30

Cullen, S., 'The Development of the Ideas and Policy of the British Union of Fascists,' *Journal of Contemporary History*, 22, 1 (1987), 115–36

Cullen, S.M., 'Political Violence: The Case of the British Union of Fascists,' *Journal of Contemporary History*, 28 (1993), 245–67

Cullen, S., 'Four Women for Mosley: Women in the British Union of Fascists, 1932–1940,' *Oral History*, 24, 1 (1996), 49–58

Davin, A., 'Imperialism and Motherhood', *History Workshop*, 5 (1976), 9–65

DeGrand, A., 'Women Under Italian Fascism', *Historical Journal*, 19 (1976), 947–68

DeGrazia, V., 'How Mussolini Ruled Women,' in Thebaud, F. (ed.), *A History of Women in the West*, London, 1994, 120–48

Durham, M., 'Suffrage and After: Feminism in the Early Twentieth Century,' in Langan, M. & Schwarz, B. (eds), *Crises in the British State 1880–1930*, London, 1985, 179–91

Durham, M., 'Women and Fascism,' in Kushner, T. & Lunn, K.(eds), *The Politics of Marginality*, London, 1990, 3–18

Durham, M., 'Gender and the British Union of Fascists,' *Journal of Contemporary History*, 3 (1992), 513–27

Durham, M., 'Women in the British Union of Fascists,' in Oldfield, S. (ed.), *This Working-Day World*, London, 1994, 101–8

Eck, H., 'French Women Under Vichy,' in Thébaud, F. (ed.), *A History of Women in the West*, London, 1994, 194–225

Forbes, A., 'Lady in the Dark,' *Times Literary Supplement*, 3898 (26 November 1976), 1482

Fraddosio, M., 'The Fallen Hero: The Myth of Mussolini and Fascist Women in the Italian Social Republic (1943-5),' *Journal of Contemporary History*, 31 (1996), 99–124

Genevois, D.B., 'The Women of Spain from the Republic to Franco,' in Thébaud, F. (ed.), *A History of Women in the West*, London, 1994, 177–93

Goldman, A.L., 'Defence Regulation 18B: Emergency Internment of Aliens and Political Dissenters in Great Britain During World War II,' *Journal of British Studies*, 12, 2 (May 1973), 120–36

Gordon, L., 'Review Essay: Nazi Feminists?' *Feminist Review*, 27 (1987), 97–106

Gorham, D., '"Have We Really Rounded Seraglio Point?"': Vera Brittain and Inter-war Feminism,' in Smith, H. (ed.), *British Feminism in the Twentieth Century*. Aldershot, 1990, 84–103

Gottlieb, J., 'Suffragette Experience Through the Filter of Fascism,' in Eustance, C. (ed.), *A Suffrage Reader*, London, 2000, 105–25

Gottlieb, J., 'Women and Fascism in the East End,' *Jewish Culture and History*, 2 (1999), 31–47

Griffin, R., 'British Fascism: The Ugly Duckling,' in Cronin, M. (ed.), *The Failure of British Fascism*, London, 1996, 141–65

Grossmann, A., 'Feminist Debates About Women and National Socialism,' *Gender and History*, 3, 3 (1991), 350–8

Hannam, J., 'Women and Politics,' in Purvis, J. (ed.), *Women's History*, London, 1995, 217–45

Hendley, M., '"Help us to Secure a Strong, Healthy, Prosperous and Peaceful Britain": The Social Arguments of the Campaign for Compulsory Military Service in Britain, 1899–1914,' *Canadian Journal of History*, 30 (1995), 261–88

Hendley, M., 'Constructing the Citizen: The Primrose League and the Definition of Citizenship in the Age of Mass Democracy in Britain, 1918–1928,' *Journal of the CHA*, 7 (1996), 125–51

Hermand, J., 'All Power to the Women: Nazi Concepts of Matriarchy,' *Journal of Contemporary History*, 19 (1984), 649–67

Hesse, S., 'Fascism and the Hypertrophy of Male Adolescence,' in Milfull, J. (ed.), *The Attractions of Fascism*, New York, 1990, 158–75

Holmes, C., 'Government Files and Privileged Access,' *Social History*, 6, 3 (1981), 333–50

Holmes, C., '"British Justice at Work": Internment in the Second World War,' in Panyai, P. (ed.), *Minorities in Wartime*, Oxford, 1993, 150–65

Holton, S.S., 'In Sorrowful Wrath: Suffrage Militancy and the Romantic Feminism of Emmeline Pankhurst,' in Smith, H. (ed.), *British Feminism in the Twentieth Century*, Aldershot, 1990, 7–24

Hope, J.G., 'British Fascism and the State 1917–1927: A Re-Examination of the Documentary Evidence,' *Labour History Review*, 57, 3 (1992), 77–83

Hope, J.G., 'Surveillance or Collusion? Maxwell Knight, MI5 and the British Fascisti,' *Intelligence and National Security*, 9, 4 (1994), 651–75

Jarvis, D., 'Mrs Maggs and Betty: The Conservative Appeal to Women Voters in the 1920s', *20th Century British History*, 5, 2 (1994), 129–52

Jeffreys, S., 'Women and Sexuality,' in Purvis J. (ed.), *Women's History*, London, 1995, 193–216

Jones, J.R., 'England,' in Rogger, H. & Weber, E., *The European Right*, London, 1965, 29–70

Kean, H., 'Searching for the Past in Present Defeat: the Construction of Historical and Political Identity in British Feminism in the 1920s and 1930s', *Women's History Review*, 3, 1 (1994), 57–80

Kean, H., 'The "Smooth Cool Men of Science": The Feminist and Socialist Response to Vivisection,' *History Workshop Journal*, 40 (1995) 16–38

Kennedy, P., 'The Pre-war Right in Britain and Germany,' in Kennedy, P. & Nicholls, A. (eds), *Nationalist and Racialist Movements in Britain and Germany before 1914*, Oxford, 1981, 1–20

Kent, S.K., 'Gender Reconstruction After the First World War,' in Smith, H. (ed.), *British Feminism in the Twentieth Century*, Aldershot, 1990, 66–83

Kochan, M., 'Women's Experience of Internment,' in Cesarani, D. & Kushner, T. (eds), *The Internment of Aliens in Twentieth Century Britain*, London, 1993, 147–66

Koonz, C., 'The Competition for a Women's Lebensraum,' in Bridenthal *et al.* (eds), *When Biology Became Destiny*, New York, 1984, 199–236

Kushner, T., 'Politics and Race, Gender and Class: Refugees, Fascists and Domestic Service in Britain, 1933–1940,' in Kushner T. & Lunn, K.(eds), *The Politics of Marginality*, London, 1990, 49–58

Kushner, T., 'Sex and Semitism: Jewish Women in Britain in War and Peace,' in Panayi, P. (ed.), *Minorities in Wartime*, Oxford, 1993, 118–49

Kushner, T., 'The Fascist as "Other"?: Racism and Neo-Nazism in Contemporary Britain', *Patterns of Prejudice*, 28, 2 (1994), 27–46

Kushner, T. & Lunn, K., 'Memory, Forgetting and Absence: The Politics of Naming on the English South Coast,' *Patterns of Prejudice*, 31, 2 (1997), 31–50

Land, H., 'Eleanor Rathbone and the Economy of the Family,' in Smith, H. (ed.), *British Feminism in the Twentieth Century*, Aldershot, 1990, 104–23

Laqueur, ' Orgasm, Generation, and the Politics of Reproductive Biology,' in Shoemaker, R. & Vincent, M. (eds), *Gender and History in Western Europe*, London, 1998, 111–48

Lebzelter, G.C., 'Anti-Semitism: A Focal Point for the British Radical Right,' in Kennedy, P. & Nicholls, A. (eds), *Nationalist and Racialist Movements in Britain and Germany before 1914*, Oxford, 1981, 88–105

Levine, P., '"Walking the Streets in a Way No Decent Woman Should": Women Police in World War I,' *Journal of Modern History*, 66, March (1994), 34–78

Lunn, K., 'The Ideology and Impact of the British Fascists in the 1920s,' in Kushner, T. & Lunn, K. (eds), *Traditions of Intolerance*, Manchester, 1989, 140–54

Lunn, K., 'British Fascism Revisited: A Failure of Imagination?,' in Cronin, M. (ed.), *The Failure of British Fascism*, London, 1996, 166–80

Macciocchi, M., 'Female Sexuality in Fascist Ideology', *Feminist Review*, 1 (1979), 67–82

Mandel, W.F., 'The Leadership of the British Union of Fascists,' *Australian Journal of Politics and History*, 12 (1966), 360–77

Manning, M., 'The Irish Experience: The Blueshirts,' in Larsen, S.U. *et al.* (eds), *Who Were the Fascists*, Bergen, 1980, 557–67

Mason, T., 'Women in Germany, 1925–1940: Family, Welfare and Work. Part I,' in *History Workshop*, 1 (1976), 74–113

Matthews, J.J., 'They had Such a Lot of Fun: The Women's League of Health and Beauty Between the War,' *History Workshop*, 30 (1990), 22–54

Mayall, D., 'Rescued from the Shadows of Exile: Nellie Driver, Autobiography and the British Union of Fascists,' in Kushner T. & Lunn, K. (eds), *The Politics of Marginality*, London, 1990, 19–39

McBride, M., 'The Curious Case of Female Internees,' in Iacovetta, F. *et al.* (eds), in *Enemies Within: Italian and Other Internees in Canada and Abroad*. Toronto, forthcoming, 196–227

Midgley, C., 'Ethnicity, "Race" and Empire,' in Purvis, J. (ed.), *Women's History*, London, 1995, 247–76

Miller, C., 'Geneva – The Key to Equality: Inter-war Feminists and the League of Nations', *Women's History Review*, 3, 2 (1994), 219–45

Mitchell, M., 'The Effects of Unemployment on the Social Condition of Women and Children in the 1930s,' *History Workshop Journal*, 19 (1985), 105–27

Mock, W., 'The Function of "Race" in Imperialist Ideology: The Example of Joseph Chamberlain, ' in Kennedy, P. & Nicholls, A. (eds), *Nationalist and Racialist Movements in Britain and Germany before 1914*, Oxford, 1981, 190–203

Mosse, G.L., 'Fascist Aesthetics and Society: Some Considerations,' *Journal of Contemporary History*, 31 (1996), 245–52

Niethammer, L., 'Male Fantasies: An Argument for and with an Important New Study in History and Psychoanalysis,' *History Workshop*, 7 (1979), 176–86

Oosterhuis, H., 'Medicine, Male Bonding and Homosexuality in Nazi Germany,' *Journal of Contemporary History*, 32, 2 (1997), 187–205

Oram, A., 'Repressed and Thwarted, or Bearers of the New World? The Spinster in Inter-war Discourse', *Women's History Review*, 1, 3 (1992), 413–34

Payne, S.G., 'The Concept of Fascism,' in Larsen, S.U. *et al.* (eds), *Who Were the Fascists*. Bergen, 1980, 14–25

Poole, A., 'Oswald Mosley and the Union Movement: Success or Failure?,' in Cronin, M. (ed.), *The Failure of British Fascism*, London, 1996, 53–80

Pryce-Jones, D., 'Mothers for the Reich,' *Times Literary Supplement*, 3877 (2 July 1976), 827

Purvis, J., 'From "Women Worthies" to Poststructuralism? Debate and Controversy in Women's History in Britain,' in Purvis, J. (ed.), *Women's History*, London, 1995, 1–22

Rich, P., 'Imperial Decline and the Resurgence of English National Identity,' in Kushner, T. & Lunn, K. (eds), *Traditions of Intolerance*, Manchester, 1989, 33–52

Rose, S.O., ' Sex, Citizenship and the Nation in World War II Britain,' *American Historical Review*, 103, 4 (1998), 1147–76

Schwarz, A., 'British Visitors to National Socialist Germany: In a Familiar or in a Foreign Country?,' *Journal of Contemporary History*, 28 (1993), 487–509

Searle, G., 'The "Revolt of the Right" in Edwardian Britain,' in Kennedy, P. & Nicholls, A. (eds), *Nationalist and Racialist Movements in Britain and Germany before 1914*, Oxford, 1981, 21–39

Smith, E.R., 'Jewish Responses to Political Anti-Semitism and Fascism in the East End of London, 1920–1939,' in Kushner, T. & Lunn, K. (eds), *Traditions of Intolerance*, Manchester, 1989, 53–71

Smith, H., 'British Feminism in the 1920s,' in Smith, H. (ed.), *British Feminism in the Twentieth Century*, Aldershot, 1990, 47–63

Sohn, A.-M., 'Between the Wars in France and England,' in Thébaud, F. (ed.), *A History of Women in the West*, London, 1994, 92–119

Sponza, L., 'The Internment of Italians in Britain,' in Iacovetta, F. *et al.* (eds), *Enemies Within: Italian and Other Internees in Canada and Abroad.* Toronto, forthcoming, 360–95

Stibbe, M., 'Women in the Nazi State,' *History Today*, 43 (November 1993), 35–40

Summers, A., 'The Character of Edwardian Nationalism: Three Popular Leagues,' in Kennedy, P. & Nicholls, A. (eds), *Nationalist and Racialist Movements in Britain and Germany before 1914*, Oxford, 1981, 68–87

Thane, P., 'The Women of the British Labour Party and Feminism, 1906-1945,' in Smith, H. (ed.), *British Feminism in the Twentieth Century*, Aldershot, 1990, 124–43

Thébaud, F., 'The Great War and the Triumph of Sexual Division,' in Thébaud, F. (ed.), *A History of Women in the West*, London, 1994, 21–75

Thurlow, R., 'State Management of the British Union of Fascists in the 1930s,' in Cronin, M. (ed.), *The Failure of British Fascism*, London, 1996, 29–52

Tosh, J., 'What Should Historians do with Masculinity: Reflections on Nineteenth Century Britain,' in Shoemaker, R. & Vincent, M. (eds), *Gender and History in Western Europe*, London, 1998, 65–85

von Saldern, A., 'Victims or Perpetrators?: Controversies about the Role of Women in the Nazi State,' in Crew, D.F. (ed.), *Nazism and German Society*, London, 1994, 141–65

Ware, V., *Women and the National Front*, Birmingham, 1978

Webber, G.C., 'Patterns of Membership and Support for the British Union of Fascists,' *Journal of Contemporary History*, 19 (1984), 575–606

Wheelwright, J., '"Colonel" Barker: A Case Study in the Contradictions of Fascism,' in Kushner T. & Lunn, K. (eds), *The Politics of Marginality*, London, 1990, 40–8

For Reference

Bellamy, J.M. & Saville, J. (eds), *Dictionary of Labour Biography*, London, 1979

Cosner, S. & Cosner, V., *Women under the Third Reich: A Biographical Dictionary*, West Port, Connecticut, 1998

Craig, F.W.S. (ed.), *British Parliamentary Election Results 1918–1949*, Glasgow, 1969

Craig, F.W.S. (ed.), *Minor Parties at British Parliamentary Elections 1885–1974*, London, 1975

Dictionary of National Biography

Europa Biographical Dictionary of British Women

Hansard

Who's Who

Index

Made in United States
Troutdale, OR
12/17/2023

16040345R00219